W9-BZO-867

WOW!
The Wonders Of Wetlands

Produced through a partnership between

Environmental Concern Inc. and The Watercourse

Principal Authors

Background Material for Teachers: Alan S. Kesselheim

Original Version of WOW!: Britt Eckhardt Slattery

Illustrations (unless otherwise noted): Britt Eckhardt Slattery

Activity Section: Edited and Reformatted by Susan H. Higgins and Mark R. Schilling

Environmental Concern Inc.

The Watercourse

Funding for this edition was provided by the Environmental Protection Agency, Region VIII, and by the U.S. Department of the Interior, Bureau of Reclamation.

First Printing, 1995
Second Printing, 1996
Third Printing, 1997
Fourth Printing, 1998
Fifth Printing, 2000

Environmental Concern Inc.
P.O. Box P
St. Michaels, MD 21663-0480

The Watercourse
201 Culbertson Hall
Montana State University
Bozeman, MT 59717-0057

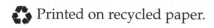 Printed on recycled paper.

ISBN 1-888631-00-7

About Environmental Concern Inc. and The Watercourse

Both Environmental Concern Inc. (EC) and The Watercourse are recognized leaders in the fields of water education and wetland awareness. Their partnership in producing *WOW!: The Wonders Of Wetlands* is a union of proven talents and experience in the areas of education, networking, publishing, and field work.

Environmental Concern Inc.

201 Boundary Lane, P.O. Box P, St. Michaels, MD 21663 (Phone) 410-745-9620 (Fax) 410-745-3517

Since its inception in 1972, EC has been a leader in the field of wetland restoration and construction; has operated the nation's premier wholesale wetland nursery; and, more recently, has become active in the field of wetland education. EC's Education Department has been training professionals in the fields of wetland science and education and conducting research in wetland horticulture since 1986. EC provides a broad range of professional services and publications focused on wetlands.

Environmental Concern Inc. staff involved with producing this edition of WOW!
Edgar Garbisch, President
Mark L. Kraus, Director of Education
Mark Schilling, Assistant Director of Education

The Watercourse

201 Culbertson Hall, Montana State University, Bozeman, MT 59717-0057 (Phone) 406-994-5392 (Fax) 406-994-1919

The goal of The Watercourse is to promote and facilitate public understanding of atmospheric, surface, and ground water resources and related management issues through publications, instruction, and networking. Currently, The Watercourse has two programs: The Watercourse Public Education Program for all water users, and Project WET (Water Education for Teachers) for young people and educators. The Watercourse has numerous publications in addition to outreach programs and instructional exhibits.

The Watercourse staff, 1995
Dennis Nelson, Director
Sandra Robinson, Assistant Director
Linda Hveem, Business Manager
Susan Higgins, Project Manager
Jennie Lane, Curriculum Writer
Alan Kesselheim, Writer/Project Leader
George Robinson, Technical Assistant to the Director
Nancy Carrasco, Administrative Support

New Educational Resources from Environmental Concern Inc. and The Watercourse

Contact Environmental Concern Inc. (EC) for information about POW!: *The Planning of Wetlands*, a guide for educators wishing to create, restore, enhance, and/or monitor wetlands with students in or near schoolyards. For details about this and other wetland publications visit our website at www.wetland.org. Current wetland resources and a Wetland Kids page are also available through our Education Department web pages.

EC's *Wetland Journal* is a quarterly publication that focuses on current wetland news and information for people active or interested in wetland issues. It is available through EC for a $30 membership fee .

Contact Project WET, through The Watercourse, for information on the *Project WET Curriculum and Activity Guide* for formal and nonformal educators. The guide contains a comprehensive selection of hands-on activities covering a wide array of water-related issues. The *Project WET Curriculum and Activity Guide* is ideal for educators who want to broaden their water study units beyond wetlands.

View other water resource publications and materials on The Watercourse website www.projectwet.org.

Acknowledgements

This edition of *WOW!: The Wonders Of Wetlands* is the product of years of effort by several organizations and a number of dedicated individuals. The original document, published by Environmental Concern Inc. in 1991, was written and illustrated by Britt Eckhardt Slattery, and it remains the soul of this new edition. Britt has also contributed new illustrations for this publication. Special recognition is also due to Environmental Concern staff members Mark Schilling and Mark Kraus for their valuable input throughout the long process of writing, editing, and producing this edition.

The Watercourse wetlands advisory board played a substantive role in conceptualizing and outlining this new edition, as well as offering its editorial and professional advice throughout. Thanks to:

Eleanor Abrams, doctoral candidate in science education, Louisiana State University
Dave Chapman, environmental science teacher, Okemos, Michigan
Tom DeVries, marine science teacher, Vashon, Washington
Kathy Gallagher, consulting geohydrologist, Bozeman, Montana
Kristen Gottschalk, education specialist, Lower Platte Natural Resource District, Wahoo, Nebraska
Jack Greene, earth sciences teacher, Logan, Utah
Susan Higgins, project manager, The Watercourse, Bozeman, Montana
Tom Hruby, senior ecologist, Department of Ecology, Olympia, Washington
Lucretia Krantz, wetland ecologist, Wildfowl Trust of North America, Grasonville, Maryland
Mark Kraus, wetlands ecologist and director of education, Environmental Concern Inc., St. Michaels, Maryland
Jon A. Kusler, attorney and executive director, Association of State Wetland Managers, New York
Nancy LaPosta-Frazier, science teacher, North Kingstown, Rhode Island
Terry Mesmer, wildlife professor, Department of Fisheries and Wildlife, Utah State University
Dennis Nelson, director of The Watercourse and Project WET, Bozeman, Montana
Lori Painter, science teacher, Enid, Oklahoma
Anne Riley, hydrologist and executive director, California Natural Resources Foundation
Julie M. Ritchie, chemistry teacher, Cynthiana, Kentucky
Sandra Robinson, assistant director of The Watercourse, Bozeman, Montana
Jim Stutzman, wildlife biologist, U.S. Fish and Wildlife Service, Black Eagle, Montana

The entire Watercourse staff was involved in the development of this book. An effort like this takes years and requires a broad array of expertise. Many of the small but critical steps taken along the way aren't obvious in the final product. Everything from making sure that budget categories matched purchases to proofreading early drafts was handled by staff members whose contributions are gratefully acknowledged.

Specific recognition is due to several Watercourse staff members. Alan Kesselheim researched and wrote the Background Material for Teachers section of this edition of *WOW!* and helped edit the activities. Susan Higgins coordinated all aspects of the project's implementation and development and spearheaded the reworked activity section. Jennie Lane was a consultant on activity revisions, and Chris McCrae handled much of the necessary library research. Dennis Nelson, Sandra Robinson, Susan Higgins, and Linda Hveem provided essential editorial feedback. Thanks, as well, to the Project WET network of crew members, state coordinators, and advisory council members.

The individuals and organizations who contributed photographs deserve credit for making the book an attractive and multidimensional document. The staff at SkyHouse Publishers, and especially Julie Schroeder, Susan Ferber, Beth Judy, and Cheryl Carroll, worked their magic to create a book with style, grace, and functional beauty.

Thanks to the staff of the Tennessee Valley Authority (TVA) for their permission to use portions of their publications, *Homemade Sampling Equipment, Water Quality Series, Booklets 1 and 2*. TVA Illustrations in Chapter 6 of *WOW!* were originally drawn by Claudia Denton.

This edition of *WOW!: The Wonders Of Wetlands*, along with support for printing, distribution, and promotion, is made possible by funding from the Environmental Protection Agency, Region VIII, and from the United States Department of the Interior, Bureau of Reclamation.

The original version of *WOW!: The Wonders Of Wetlands* was developed with funding from Chesapeake Bay Trust of Annapolis, Maryland, and Asea, Brown, Boveri, Inc. of Stamford, Connecticut. Technical assistance was provided by Edgar Garbisch, Mark Kraus, Gwen Thunhorst, Don MacLean, Sue McIninch, and Michael Slattery. Technical and educational review was provided by Bill Sipple, Anne Galli, Irvine Wilson, Gary Heath, JoAnn Roberts, George Newberry, and Mark Schilling. Field testing was provided by Dennis Kirkwood and the staff of the Harford Glen Environmental Education Center; Otter Point Project teachers Gordie Thorpe, Chris Eyer, Joan Johnson; and many other teachers who participated in workshops in several states. Funding for those workshops was provided by Asea, Brown, Boveri, Inc.; Baltimore Gas & Electric; Chesapeake Bay Trust; Chevron Companies; Clark Lead Charitable Trust; Exxon USA; National Environmental Education and Training Foundation; National Fish & Wildlife Foundation; Shell Oil Company Foundation; Times Mirror Magazines; Weyerhaeuser Company Foundation; and private contributors.

Contents

Part II: The Activities

An Orientation to
WOW!: The Wonders Of Wetlands

WOW!: The Wonders Of Wetlands *is for educators. Classroom teachers, refuge managers, nature center interpreters, park service educators, and others will find useful background material and stimulating activities to fit their programs.*

The first part of *WOW!* is filled with background material for teachers preparing wetland study units. It is divided into six chapters, each starting with a short list of themes and recommended activities to address those themes. Information throughout the background chapters is cross-referenced to specific activities. Sidebars (see "Index to Sidebars," p. xii) and subheadings help orient the reader to important topics.

Chapter 6, ("Action for Wetlands," p. 53) is particularly useful to educators. It contains material on organizing field trips, making inexpensive sampling equipment, and getting involved in wetland enhancement and stewardship.

The rest of the guide is brimming with proven wetland activities, separated into five logical groupings (see Contents). Each activity includes curriculum planning information in easy-to-access shaded areas and under boldface headings (see "Activity Format" p. xvi). Suggestions for wetland study units for various age groups and logical activity sequences are found in "Activities by Grade Level" (p. xvii) and "Planning Guide: Suggested Wetland Study Units" (p. xiv). All activities are correlated with the National Science Education Standards developed by the National Academy of Sciences (p. 331). The resource list at the back of the guide (p. 326) will lead you to more sources of wetland information and activities, and the appendix (p. 317) discusses creating a wetland in your schoolyard. Technical terms not explained in the text are listed in the glossary, (p. 320).

The content of your wetland study unit will depend on available time, student ages, and many other factors. Ideally, a comprehensive unit should include at least one introductory activity, followed by one or more activities from each of the other four activity sections (e.g. water, soil, etc.).

Whether you are new to wetland study and nervous about getting your educational feet wet or an expert wetland science teacher ready to wade right in, *WOW!* will be both useful and provocative.

Planning Guide

Suggested Wetland Study Units

As an educator, only you know the abilities and limitations of your students. The activities in *WOW!: The Wonders Of Wetlands* are labeled with grade level ranges to be used as guidelines. Any activity can be adapted or used in part to suit the needs of students of any age or level. *WOW!: The Wonders Of Wetlands* has been designed so that lessons may be used individually or as an entire unit. You are strongly encouraged to incorporate these lessons into disciplines other than science! It is important to tie environmental studies to social studies, language, mathematics, and other skills.

If you choose to dedicate a block of time in your program to the study of wetlands, use the suggested units on the following page to help in your planning. It would be wonderful if every educator could use all of the activities in this manual, but this, of course, is unrealistic. If you are like most educators, the time to spend on one topic is sadly limited, so make the most of it! Try to use at least one general wetland introductory activity plus one each from the plants and animals, water, soil, and culture/issue sections. If you have more time, look through *WOW!* for extra activities to add even more fun to the unit.

All units on wetlands should culminate in an action project of some kind—even a small one (see pp. 288-316).

Grades K-2: Three-Day Unit

- Introducing Wetlands (at least one of the ideas)
- Let the Cattail Out of the Bag!
- Wetlands in the Classroom! (the display only)
- Wetland Metaphors (as appropriate)

Field Day:
- Springo! (Introducing Wetlands)
- Do You Dig Wetland Soil?

Grades K-2: Five-Day Unit or Longer

All activities for three-day unit, plus:
- Salt Marsh Players
- Nutrients: Nutrition or Nuisance? (Part I, or Parts II and III)
- What a Boat!

Field Days:
- Water We Have Here?
- Combine Wet 'n' Wild and Whose Clues?
- Nature's Recyclers

Grades 3-6: Three-Day Unit

*Choose from the following. Several are short enough to combine with others. Start with those marked with * and add the others as time permits.*
- * Introducing Wetlands (at least one of the ideas)
- * Wetland Metaphors
- * Hear Ye! Hear Ye! or Hydropoly! (advanced students)
- Marsh Market and Marsh Mystery (advanced students)
- Treatment Plants
- Soak It Up!

Field Day:
- * Combine Wet 'n' Wild and Whose Clues?
- * Water We Have Here?
- * Wetland in a Pan or Runoff Race
- * Do You Dig Wetland Soil?
- * How Thirsty Is the Ground?
- Wetland Weirdos
- This Plant Key Is All Wet! (as appropriate) and Wetland Wheel

Grades 3-6: Five-Day Unit or Longer

Activities from three-day unit, plus selections from the following, as appropriate to grade level:
- Wetlands in the Classroom!
- Water Under Foot or Recipe for Trouble
- A Rottin' Experiment
- Nature's Filter
- Nutrients: Nutrition or Nuisance? (Part III) or Marsh Munchies

Field Days:
- Tracking Plants and Keeping Track
- Run for the Border
- Helping Wetland Habitats
- Over Hill and Dale
- Life in the Fast Lane

Grades 7-12: Three-Day Unit

*Choose from the activities for grades 3-6, as appropriate to grade level. Then add those marked with * below, and add the others as time permits. Also:*
- * Wetland Habitats
- * Hear Ye! Hear Ye! or Hydropoly!
- * A Drop in the Bucket
- Water Purifiers
- Wetland Address

Field Day:
Choose from the activities for grades 3-6, but set up stations at the field site and have students conduct the activities independently. Be sure to tap into:
- Water We Have Here?
- Get Involved!
- Helping Wetland Habitats

Grades 7-12: Five-Day Unit or Longer

Activities from three-day unit, plus selections from the following, as appropriate to your students:
- Chrysti the Wordsmith on Wetlands
- People of the Bog
- Regulation Rummy
- Water Under Foot
- Recipe for Trouble
- A Rottin' Experiment

Field Days:
- Tracking Plants and Keeping Track
- Run for the Border
- Over Hill and Dale
- Water We Have Here?
- Get Involved!

Activity Format

Grade Level
Suggests appropriate learning levels, organized as K-12. Most activities can easily be adapted for higher and lower grades.

Subject Areas
Lists disciplines to which the activity applies.

Duration
Approximate time needed to complete the activity.

Setting
Indicates appropriate location to conduct the activity.

Skills
Identifies skills to be applied in the activity.

Charting the Course
Suggests concepts associated with other *WOW!* activities that could be addressed prior to, in conjunction with, and as a follow-up to the activity.

Vocabulary
A list of significant terms found within the activity.

Each activity in Part II is presented in a special format, as follows:

Summary
Supplies a brief description of the concepts, skills applied, and affective dimensions.

Objectives
Describes the qualities or skills students should possess after participating in the activity. To measure accomplishment of these objectives, see Assessment.

Materials
Lists supplies needed to conduct the activity and describes how to prepare materials prior to engaging in the activity.

Making Connections
Describes the relevance of the activity to students' lives and presents the rationale for conducting the activity.

Background
Provides relevant information about activity concepts or teaching strategies.

Procedure
Warm Up
Gets everyone ready for the activity and acquaints learners with concepts to be addressed. Provides the instructor with preactivity assessment strategies.

The Activity
Consists of a step-by-step procedure and is the main part of the lesson. The main component of each step is presented in boldface type. Some activities are organized into Parts, or sub-activities.

Wrap Up and Action
Brings closure to the lesson and includes questions and activities to assess student learning.

Action moves learners beyond the classroom and involves friends, family, and community, state, national, and international audiences.

Assessment
Identifies and presents diverse assessment strategies that relate to the activity objectives.

Extensions
Provides additional activities for further investigation into concepts addressed in the activity.

Resources
Lists, in some activities, of selected references that provide additional background information. For activities that do not list references, see Resources, p. 326, for additional information.

Activities by Grade Level

The grade levels suggested below are intended as general guidelines. Many of the activities may be easily adapted for higher or lower grade levels or for other sorts of groups.

Page		K	1	2	3	4	5	6	7	8	9	10	11	12
70	*Section 1: So This Is a Wetland!*													
71	Introducing Wetlands	✓	✓	✓	✓	✓	✓	✓	✓	✓	✓	✓	✓	✓
78	Let the Cattail Out of the Bag!	✓	✓	✓	✓	✓	✓	✓						
80	Wetlands in the Classroom!	✓	✓	✓	✓	✓	✓	✓	✓	✓				
85	Wetland Metaphors		✓	✓	✓	✓	✓	✓	✓	✓	✓	✓	✓	✓
87	Wetland Habitats							✓	✓	✓	✓	✓	✓	✓
93	*Section 2: The Wetland Community (plants and animals)*													
94	Wetland Weirdos						✓	✓	✓	✓	✓	✓	✓	✓
99	Wet 'n' Wild	✓	✓	✓	✓	✓	✓	✓	✓	✓	✓	✓	✓	✓
104	Whose Clues?	✓	✓	✓	✓	✓	✓	✓	✓	✓	✓	✓		
109	Marsh Market			✓	✓	✓	✓	✓	✓	✓				
112	The Wetland Gourmet	✓	✓	✓	✓	✓	✓	✓	✓	✓	✓	✓	✓	✓
116	Marsh Mystery							✓	✓	✓	✓	✓	✓	✓
120	Treatment Plants				✓	✓	✓	✓	✓	✓	✓	✓	✓	✓
123	This Plant Key Is All Wet!					✓	✓	✓	✓	✓	✓	✓	✓	✓
129	Wetland Wheel					✓	✓	✓	✓	✓	✓	✓	✓	✓
138	Tracking Plants and Keeping Track							✓	✓	✓	✓	✓	✓	✓
143	Run for the Border							✓	✓	✓	✓	✓	✓	✓
147	Wetland Address							✓	✓	✓	✓	✓		
152	Life in the Fast Lane					✓	✓	✓	✓	✓	✓			
157	*Section 3: Drip, Drop, Dribble, and Splash! (water)*													
158	A Drop in the Bucket							✓	✓	✓				
162	Soak It Up!					✓	✓	✓	✓	✓	✓			
165	Salt Marsh Players					✓	✓	✓	✓					
174	Water We Have Here?				✓	✓	✓	✓	✓	✓	✓	✓	✓	✓
188	Nutrients: Nutrition or Nuisance?	✓	✓	✓	✓	✓	✓	✓	✓	✓				
192	Marsh Munchies							✓	✓	✓				
199	Recipe for Trouble						✓	✓	✓	✓	✓	✓	✓	✓
204	Water Under Foot							✓	✓	✓	✓	✓	✓	✓
210	Runoff Race				✓	✓	✓	✓	✓	✓	✓	✓	✓	✓
212	Wetland in a Pan					✓	✓	✓	✓	✓	✓	✓	✓	✓
215	Water Purifiers							✓	✓	✓	✓	✓	✓	✓
220	Over Hill and Dale					✓	✓	✓	✓	✓	✓	✓	✓	✓

An Invitation

It is just after dawn. Mist steams off the still water, luminous with early sunlight, evaporating as the air warms. The canoe skims across the water. Your paddle splashes gently with each stroke.

Ducks fly quickly past you, their muffled wingbeats audible before you can see them through the mist. A swan extends its graceful neck and stirs nervously as you paddle by its nest. A red fox melts into a thicket of alders. The animal is utterly silent, a red blush of fur full of sunrise, gone so suddenly that you question whether you saw it at all. A kingfisher gives its startling, rattly call as it flies from a branch overhanging shallow water.

Town, full of busy traffic and industry, is barely out of sight. A heavily used highway skirts the slough less than a kilometer away. But the wetland swallows you up so completely, occupies each of your senses so profoundly, that the nearby urban scene slips from your thoughts.

With almost a twinge of guilt, you relish this respite from routine. Usually you work on lesson plans in your office or at the library, but this morning is different. As the day warms and you continue to explore, your mind churns with ideas for a wetland field trip.

You imagine a team of students mapping the vegeta-

Alan S. Kesselheim

tion. Another group gathers soil samples. Perhaps someone in the class will glimpse the same red fox you just saw. Mentally you begin to assemble your supplies—dip nets, rubber boots, bird books, jars for water samples, binoculars. Why haven't you done this before? . . .

Wetlands are powerful places in which to learn. They are environments of intense, dynamic activity, humming with life. Because wetlands are often the last places to be settled by humans, they often comprise a region's last wild and pristine land. Not uncommonly, they are nestled within urban and suburban settings and are surprisingly accessible to large numbers of people. Plants and animals take advantage of wetland bounties by developing fascinating behavioral strategies and

remarkable adaptations. Compact areas illustrate major ecological concepts such as food webs, habitat niches, and the hydrologic cycle.

Wetlands have been referred to as "nature's kidneys" because of their filtering and nutrient-processing functions. They are also called "nature's supermarkets" because of their astounding productivity. Both of these descriptions are accurate, but limited.

In order to more completely understand the importance of wetlands, we must see them in the larger context, as crucial links in a watershed, as essential contributors to the health and stability of entire ecosystems. Taken as a whole, wetland environments are an important factor in maintaining global health. Slowly, we are beginning to recognize the value of these long unappreciated environments as havens for beleaguered species, buffers against storms and floods, cleansing agents in the nutrient cycle, spots of aesthetic refreshment. Places to learn.

By midmorning you have finished your reconnaissance of the small swamp. The sun is well overhead and the early morning flurry of wildlife has long since settled down. Even so, there is a subdued hum, a charge in the air, as if the insects and birds and mammals, even the lush plant life, emanate a nearly palpable energy.

Your mind hums along with ideas as well. As part of your study unit, you hope to meet with community members who have a variety of perspectives on wetland management. You know a farmer who has dealt with wetlands on his land for decades. Perhaps the mayor will agree to meet with the class, along with a contrac- tor, a game warden, an environmental lobbyist, and a real estate developer. You can imagine students researching the human history in this wetland.

As you beach the canoe and prepare to return to town, you realize that you feel unaccountably refreshed, as if awakening from a much needed nap or returning from a pleasant vacation.

Ken DeYonge

Part I

Background Material for Teachers

Wetlands & People:
Through Time and Across Borders

Try to imagine yourself in the Wyrie Swamp in arid South Australia, 10,000 years ago. You are in a small camp at the edge of the swamp. The people—your people—are primitive and scantily clothed by twentieth-century standards, but skilled in the strategies of survival in a difficult land. Everyday tools like stone grinders, wooden boomerangs, and the digging sticks that you use to unearth nutritious plant roots lie about here and there. The setting is an oasis of life and water in the midst of a desert, a focal point in your life and the lives of your neighbors. It is not simply a source of water and shade, but an environment full of plants and animals for food, reeds for woven baskets, and sticks and thatching material for simple shelters. Your ancestors have used this swamp-side camp for generations. It will, you assume, remain an integral aspect of your people's world forever.

We can imagine this scene because we have found the preserved bits and pieces of that culture sealed under wetland soil layers that were deposited when the water levels rose and buried the campsite ("A Rottin' Experiment," p. 245). Since that prehistoric moment, which we can vaguely reconstruct through the artifacts preserved in the earth, much has changed, but much remains the same.

Ancient peoples, not unlike modern societies, found themselves lured by the wetland bounty and, at the same time, confronted by wetland challenges. They used wetland materials to weave baskets, to make boats, and to build shelters to protect them from the elements. They harvested wild rice from canoes; killed ducks, geese, and other animals for their meat; and hunted wetland mammals for their pelts ("The Wetland Gourmet," p. 112). At the same time, they had to build structures to escape ever-present water, find vehicles that could travel through the maze of channels ("What a Boat!" p. 278), protect themselves from periodic flooding, and ward off insect pests.

Wetlands & the Big Picture

Nothing stands alone. The more we understand about nature's balance, the clearer it becomes that the earth is an interconnected and dynamic whole.

Our awareness of the large-scale environment and our ability to have an impact on broad ecosystems is relatively new. It is only recently that the human population has reached levels that strain the environment's capacity to sustain them. And it is only in the last 200 years that our technology and industry have grown powerful enough to significantly disrupt environmental equilibrium on a global scale.

This "big picture" point of view is gaining credence and acceptance in theory, but it is still difficult to implement on local and individual levels. To a farmer in need of more crop acreage, a city-planning board desperate for housing sites, or a construction firm building a highway interchange, the loss of a wetland or two in exchange for the benefits of their project seems like a reasonable tradeoff.

However, when these decisions are multiplied thousands of times and thousands of wetlands are altered or lost, one at a time, the cumulative impact becomes globally significant ("A Drop in the Bucket," p. 158). Humans, like all living things, struggle to find a balance with our environment, and we need to be aware of our place in that picture.

We juggle immediate needs such as food, income, and building materials against less tangible rewards like wildlife diversity, a beautiful lakeshore, peaceful backcountry, and a sense of harmony with the environment. Balancing this equation is a true dilemma, and perhaps our biggest environmental challenge.

Changes in one corner of an environment begin a chain of events with the power to affect everything from microscopic organisms to the earth's atmosphere. Few environments illustrate this point more powerfully than wetlands.

Eliminate a species and it affects the food web, changes the dynamics of habitat selection, and disrupts the rhythm of an ecosystem. Create wetlands by

(continued)

A stark reminder of past cultures. This human skull was photographed at a remote tundra peatland in northern Canada. Layers of permafrost prevented the traditional Inuit (Eskimo) from performing underground burials, so they buried their dead under mounds of rock. Over the years some of these rock piles have broken apart, exposing the bones from members of a culture that maintained essentially a Stone Age existence well into the twentieth century.

The Nebraska farmers whose tractors get stuck in muck every spring are bound to feel a little adversarial about wetlands at the same time that they may enjoy having ducks and other wildlife on their land. Avid bird-watchers will be enthusiastic supporters of the wetlands they visit to observe wood ducks and soras, herons and rails, while the roads they commute to work on may have been built across swamps. A real-estate developer might imagine subdivisions and shopping malls where wetlands stand in the way. That very same damp acreage might house alligators and egrets and lure thousands of tourists every year.

Laws and attitudes reflect the shifts in viewpoints that occur over time, as circumstances change. Not long ago in America, both law and policy strongly encouraged wetland draining and dredging. Farmers found assistance for turning wetlands into croplands. Growing cities dredged and filled wetlands at a staggering pace to accommodate new roads, factories, and housing developments. At present, however, a political commitment has been made to strive for no net loss of wetlands. This policy requires that all wetlands lost to development or resource extraction be replaced with wetlands of equivalent stature. Although wetlands remain threatened, the pendulum of public opinion and awareness has swung toward preservation and stewardship.

The written record documents the persistent cultural ambiguity toward wetlands. An anonymous fifteenth-century individual wrote that the peatlands he lived in represented "the fatness of the earth gathered together at the time of Noah's flood." Another anonymous source from the same region referred to the environs as "an atmosphere pregnant with pestilence and death."

Sir Arthur Conan Doyle's *The Hound of the Baskervilles* describes the Great Grimpen Mire. "Slimy water plants sent an odour of decay and a heavy miasmatic vapor into our faces, while a false step plunged us more than once thigh-deep into the dark, quivering mire."

Shakespeare used the following wetland curse in *The Tempest*:

As wicked dew as e'er my mother brushed
With raven's feather from unwholesome fen,
Drop on you both!

· · · · · · · · · · · · · · · ·

All the infections that the sun sucks up
From bogs, fens, flats, on Prosper fall, and make him
By inch-meal a disease.

Lewis and Clark's journals repeatedly record the mixed blessings of their wetland surroundings. On the 12th of June, 1804, Clark penned his impressions in awkward prose. "The bank of the river and and [sic] continus back, well watered and abounds in Deer Elk and Bear The Ticks & Musquiters are very troublesome."

Not all the literary imagery is negative. Henry David Thoreau wrote, "I enter the swamp as a sacred place—a sanctum sanctorum. There is the strength, the marrow of Nature."

Walden Pond is a far different place today than it was when Thoreau found inspiration along its shores. Even so, it remains something of a sanctuary for residents of the Boston area.

And Gerard Manley Hopkins composed the following plea for wet and wild places:

What would the world be, once bereft
Of wet and of wildness? Let them be left,
O let them be left, wildness and wet;
Long live the weeds and the wilderness yet.

building a dam and it changes everything from water temperature to the economics of tourism.

Wetlands, because of the intensity of their chemical and biological activity, are important to global vitality. They accept, break down, and make available nutrient matter. They absorb heavy metals, filter out toxins, produce a massive food base, process nitrates, and release oxygen into the atmosphere while removing carbon dioxide and other greenhouse gases. Wetlands are a significant element in the water cycle ("Water Under Foot," p. 204). They store vast quantities of water, and wetland vegetation contributes to the earth's water cycle through the process of evapotranspiration.

Wetlands themselves are not simply a distinct unit within an environment. The entire interconnected watershed—streams and rivers, lakes and ponds, underlying ground water, seeps and springs that lie in the catchment basin between ridgetops—depends on wetland functions. Wetlands in every watershed contribute to flood control, bank stabilization, pollution control, the recharge and discharge of ground water, and habitat for myriad plants and animals, including humans.

The big water picture encompasses the entire hydrologic cycle, and, among other things, balances precipitation, runoff, evaporation, transpiration, and groundwater recharge through percolation and infiltration. Wetlands are an integral part of this liquid system.

The Sweet Track and the Muskeg Express

If you have ever tried to walk straight through a swamp or bog, you have some idea of the difficulties faced by wetlanders who need to travel overland.

In 1732 Carl Linnaeus crossed the European peatlands inhabited by Laplanders. He made the following despairing report.

"Shortly afterwards began the muskegs, which mostly stood under water; these we had to cross for miles; think with what misery, every step up to our knees. The whole of this land of the Lapps was mostly muskeg. . . Never can the priest so describe hell, because it is no worse. Never have poets been able to picture Styx so foul, since that is no fouler."

Northwestern Europe is covered, in large measure, by peatlands. As Linnaeus attested, travel through that country can be difficult, sometimes almost impossible. But without the ability to travel, residents are stranded from the rest of the world.

For 6,000 years or more, Europeans have constructed roadways and walkways across the peat. The more than 1,000 ancient roads of log, plank, or stone that have been identified are a small fraction of the total. Some are several meters wide and extend many kilometers, while others are little more than narrow pathways across a short section of wet country.

One of the better-studied European road sites is in Somerset, England, and is known as the Sweet Track. It is only 2 kilometers (1.2 miles) long and a mere 20 to 30 centimeters (8 to 12 inches) wide. It connects a rock ridge with an island of bedrock across a reedy swamp. It was constructed some 6,000 years ago in what is thought to have been a short, concentrated burst of effort. Study has revealed that all the trees used to construct the track were felled in the same year. Evidence of repairs to the track covers only about a decade, so it is likely that the track was built quickly and abandoned after only a few years.

Given the antiquated tools the Somerset people would have used, the road-building project must have required a tremendous effort. Cutting trees,

(continued)

Modern speech is also full of wetland phrases, most of which bear negative connotations ("Chrysti the Wordsmith on Wetlands," p. 280). We get "bogged down," "swamped with work," "mired in details," "caught in a quagmire." Our popular culture reinforces the negative imagery by using wetland settings and imaginary wetland creatures in productions like *Swamp Thing* and *Creature from the Black Lagoon.*

Wetlands have often, through the centuries, been seen as wasted lands—difficult, unhealthy places. A great deal of human toil has been spent in draining, dredging, filling, and otherwise transforming wetlands into "useful" property.

Historically, wetlands have been perceived as obstacles to progress and development, from high-rises to airports, farm fields to railroad tracks. Much of the valuable real estate in Florida is set on drained and filled portions of the Everglades. Mexico City covers what used to be a large lake and its associated wetland. Major American urban centers like Chicago and Boston were built, at least in part, on former wetlands. However, undeveloped and open landscapes grow more and more valuable. Increasingly, wetlands are seen as assets, especially within urban ecosystems.

Miami, Florida, a city built partly on wetlands.

But that is not the whole story. Throughout history and around the globe, various peoples benefitted from wetland settings and made use of the resources there, rather than trying to get rid of them. The world's "wetlanders" thrive in proximity to wetlands, and their cultures are linked to these lands. In addition to furnishing homes and supporting subsistence economies, wetlands produce such marketable products as timber, cranberries, peat, animal furs, tannin, fish and shellfish, and wild rice—no small bounty.

The Caribou Inuit (Eskimo) of northeastern Canada lived in har-

Caribou of the Porcupine Herd graze across the Alaskan tundra in the shadow of the Brooks Range.

mony with their peatland environment for centuries. The caribou that fed on the mosses and lichens covering the tundra sustained Inuit culture. The Inuit made their summer tents out of caribou hides, wore hide garments, ate well or starved depending on the success of their caribou hunts, and burned caribou fat in their soapstone lamps through the long arctic winters. Without the peatland, the caribou couldn't have survived, and without the caribou, the Inuit culture would never have developed.

Wetland resources are culturally important in many parts of the world. Wetland reeds provide thatch for housing and material for fencing in Romania, Iraq, and Japan. Manicured wetlands that have been turned into rice paddies produce food for half the world's population. European salt marshes have been used over millennia for grazing, field hay, and thatching.

A rice paddy in Thailand.

making planks, fashioning pegs—all would have been slow and painstaking labor. It has been estimated that the short road required 600 planks, 3,600 pegs, and 350 poles.

Wetlands confront modern engineers with similar problems. In Canada, one of the most arduous railroad projects in history connected the prairies of southern Manitoba to the Hudson Bay port of Churchill. To do so, the rails had to cross hundreds of kilometers of swamp, muskeg, and quaking bog.

Discussion about, and fitful starts at, this daunting endeavor spanned some 30 years before the arctic port of Churchill was finally opened to shipping in 1931. In the winter of 1924, 3,000 workers developed a strange track-building technique peculiar to the peatlands of the subarctic.

Crew working on the "Muskeg Express" railroad line during the winter of 1929-30

They laid a rough corduroy road of brush and log in the snow and set the tracks on top. Come spring, when the snows melted, some of the track was left as much as three meters (ten feet) off the ground. Work trains carrying gravel crept gingerly along these treacherous tracks, dropping thousands of tons of fill along the way. The gravel sifted through the thawing snow and the upper layers of wet peat until it rested on the firm foundation of permafrost. In some places the crews dumped 20 to 30 cubic meters (26 to 39 cubic yards) of fill for every surface meter of forward progress!

That train, known colloquially as the "Muskeg Express," still operates today. "Express" is said tongue-in-cheek, because for long sections of track the engineers only dare charge along at 50 to 70 kilometers (30 to 40 miles) per hour. The grain terminal the train was built to serve has never amounted to much, but Churchill has become a tourist attraction and wildlife-viewing destination.

Great river systems and their deltas are home to many wetlanders. The Mississippi, the Amazon, the Nile, the Tigris and Euphrates, and the Rhone, all laid claim to their resident cultures, and continue to do so today, generation after generation.

The Cajuns of Louisiana migrated south from Acadia (Nova Scotia) in the 1700s and have flourished ever since in the huge wetlands associated with the Mississippi River. They have successfully adapted their living quarters, vehicles, diets, and economy to the conditions imposed by the inescapable presence of water. Simple dugout boats (and modern motorboats) take them through the intricate web of waterways. Their homes float on waterlogged foundations or are raised up on stilts. Fish, waterfowl, shellfish, and wetland mammals make up much of their diet. Timber, animal fur, shrimp, and crayfish harvests maintain the Cajun economy.

Halfway around the globe from Louisiana, people known colloquially as "Marsh Arabs" live where the waters of the Tigris and Euphrates Rivers converge and flow into the Persian Gulf. Technically they are residents of Iraq and Iran, but their link to this wetland area makes the informal name more relevant. They have built islands in the delta to support their houses, they travel largely by boat, and they harvest the reeds, fish, and other resources of their water-dominated surroundings. Theirs is a culture inextricably bound to a wetland, a culture which has evolved, over centuries, a harmonious relationship with a challenging environment.

Laplanders of northern Europe, Camarguais along the Rhone River in southern France, Amazonian Indians of Brazil, and rice farmers in Thailand are all examples of peoples wedded to wetlands, whose cultures and fortunes rise and fall in tandem with the health of their wetland surroundings.

Several Native American peoples (including the Seminole and Miccosukee) have lived in Florida's wetland settings for centuries. Even their modern villages reflect the importance of wetland resources, such as roof-thatching material.

courtesy of South Florica Water Management District

Wetlanders' part in the prehistoric human saga has been exposed through rich and copious archaeological findings ("People of the Bog," p. 266). Perhaps the most famous archaeological site of all time, Olduvai Gorge in central Africa was a lake margin one million years ago, when the hominid ancestors and scattered artifacts we study today were part of a living wetland culture.

Nine thousand years ago, at a time when the great ice sheets had just retreated, wetlanders lived in the Kuk Swamp in Papua New Guinea. This valley-floor swamp produced fertile soils that were systematically farmed by long-term residents. Scientists have found evidence of plant domestication, elaborate agricultural practices, and early attempts at wetland drainage.

Remarkably preserved artifacts have also been uncovered in the delta of the Abe River in Japan. Roughly 2,000 years ago, catastrophic flooding buried bowls and ladles, log boats, pieces of clothing, bamboo fish traps, and other articles attesting to a thriving wetlander culture. These pieces of evidence prove the importance of wetland resources for clothing, transportation, shelter, and food.

The people who drained wetlands in New Guinea 9,000 and 10,000 years ago and those who built roads and tracks across the peatlands of northern Europe 6,000 years ago may have pondered the same dilemma we face today. How can cultures take advantage of the rich storehouse of resources and benefits associated with wetlands without destroying that very wealth for future generations? At present the challenge is greater than ever before because there are more of us—billions more. Wetlands, like all undeveloped ecosystems, are in danger of being overwhelmed by our sheer numbers and appetite for space.

How can cultures take advantage of the rich storehouse of resources and benefits associated with wetlands without destroying that very wealth for future generations?

Wetlander Cultures and Sites: A Sampler

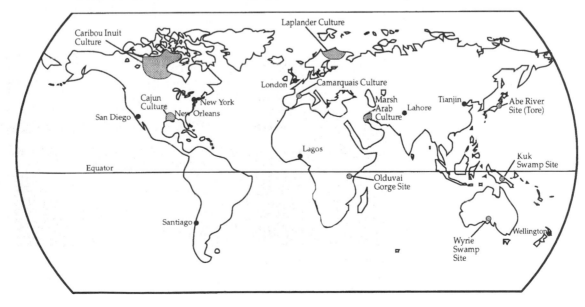

2 Defining Wetlands

Wetlands. The word sparks a barrage of sensory images: Places where it is prudent to wear rubber boots. Shallows teeming with migratory water birds. A desert oasis loud with the chorus of spring peepers. The damp, pungent smell of a salt marsh.

We know, from informal experience, much of what defines a wetland—an appearance of vegetation, places where we expect to see specific birds and mammals, environments marked by the dominant presence of water ("Introducing Wetlands," p. 71). But wetlands are more subtle, varied, and full of surprises than these superficial observations suggest.

The term wetland describes an incredible array of landscapes. It is equally correct when applied to mangrove swamps in brackish water along Florida's coastline and to peaty tundra in Siberia, to a prairie pothole in a cultivated North Dakota field and to marshes along the Rhone River delta in southern France.

It doesn't help that wetlands have been called by many (sometimes exotic) names, or that in separate locations identical wetland environments sport different labels. Depending on where you live you might know wetlands as fens, sloughs, pocosins, muskeg, playas, mires, moors, carrs, glades, or flats, to name a few ("Chrysti the Wordsmith on Wetlands," p. 280).

To confuse matters further, a wetland may not even appear obviously wet! A desert spring might run only one season out of four, but that periodic presence of water defines its status. The mosses and peat beds characteristic of a tundra or alpine wetland may be only faintly spongy most of the time, but the poorly drained soil, high water table, and cool climate undeniably create a wetland environment.

It can be helpful to visualize many wetlands as transition zones between land and water—the shallow margins of freshwater lakes, crowded with cattails, frogs, and sunning turtles;

tidal marshes redolent with salt and mud, exposed at low tide to opportunistic explorers or predators; or swamps along the banks of rivers, periodically inundated by floodwaters.

By definition, transition zones blend into the bordering environments. When does a salt marsh become an ocean? At what point is the edge of a lake a swamp, and at what point is a lake a deepwater environment? How do we mark boundaries in a world that resists neat cubbyholes?

Wetland Delineation

The process of deciding where a wetland starts and ends is known as delineation. Soil, plants, and water characteristics are the defining wetland indicators (see below), but actual delineation is difficult because of the many environments that qualify as wetlands and the changeable nature of wetland conditions.

Over the years, various federal manuals have been developed and millions of dollars spent in the quest for a straightforward and universal delineation strategy. The Natural Resources Conservation Service, U.S. Army Corps of Engineers, U.S. Fish and Wildlife Service, Environmental Protection Agency, and National Academy of Sciences have all had a voice in the delineation debate, with considerable input from other groups.

The struggle over proper delineation continues to foment political wrangling and differing scientific opinion. Meanwhile, the need for a sensible, easy-to-apply strategy becomes increasingly urgent.

In all cases, delineation concentrates on the three tip-offs to wetland environments ("Run for the Border," p. 143):

1. *hydric (saturated) soils;*

2. *hydrophytic (water tolerant) plants; and*

3. *a specific hydrologic regime.*

Delineation concentrates on the three tip-offs to wetland environments:

**1. hydric soils;
2. hydrophytic plants; and
3. hydrologic regime.**

Hydric Soils

Hydric soils are saturated long enough during the growing season to create an anaerobic (low oxygen) state in the soil horizon. This lack of available oxygen limits the number of plant species that can survive there ("Wetland Weirdos," p. 94; "How Thirsty Is the Ground," p. 239).

Some wetland soils are dominated by organic material (partially decomposed plants) and are categorized as peats or mucks. In these soils, plant decomposition is slower than accumulation, so soil layers grow thicker each year. Organic wetland soils tend to develop in environments that are saturated for a significant portion of the year and are dominated by mosses or herbaceous emergent vegetation (cattails, manna grass, cordgrass).

Soils with a high mineral content (sand, silt, clay), on the other hand, tend to form in warm, wooded wetlands and other locations that are water-saturated for only a portion of the growing season. Here, organic decomposition keeps pace with accumulation. Soils exposed to fast currents are usually mineral as well, since organic material is flushed away.

Climate, which affects the length of the growing season, has a profound impact on both the rate of organic production and the rate of decomposition ("A Rottin' Experiment," p. 245; "Nature's Recyclers," p. 226). Cool, northern latitudes or high altitudes, for instance, tend to produce peats, since low temperatures inhibit decomposition.

Anaerobic conditions create some distinguishing soil characteristics. The best way to study soil is to dig a hole 30 to 45 centimeters (12 to 18 inches) deep and use your senses to search for the following indicators:

1. sulfurous (rotten egg) smell

2. color: green, dark gray, brown, or black are good indications of wetland soil

3. water collecting in the hole, or soil that has a wet feel (sticks together in ball or oozes between fingers)

4. mottled coloring (red or black concentrations that result from mineral staining)

5. "gleyed" soils (gray, blue-gray, green-gray colors, typical of hydric mineral soils)

6. oxidized rhizospheres (mottling along plant rootlets in mineral soils resulting from excess oxygen escap-

Sample soil layers in a wetland

TOPSOIL
ORGANIC LAYER (HYDRIC)
GRAY LAYER
GRAY WITH MOTTLES
GLEYED SOIL

> Climate, which affects the length of the growing season, has a profound impact on both the rate of organic production and the rate of decomposition.

ing from plant roots, interacting with bacteria, and staining the surrounding soil with oxidized iron).

Hydrophytic Plants

Hydrophytic plants have adapted to thrive in wetlands despite the stresses of an anaerobic and flooded environment. Most upland plants take in oxygen through root systems and distribute it through their stems and leaves. To succeed in their waterlogged environment, wetland plants must employ other strategies such as long, oxygen-transporting tubes (emergent reeds), the ability to float on shallow water (lilies), or buttressed trunks (cypress trees). Plants are often the most obvious indicators of a wetland ("Tracking Plants and Keeping Track," p. 138; "Wetland Wheel," p. 129). Common wetland plants include cattail, wild rice, bulrush, jewelweed, duckweed, and water hyacinth.

courtesy of South Florida Water Management District

Cypress knees along the Loxahatchee River in Florida protrude above the river's normal high water level.

Most of the obvious wetland plant adaptations have to do with capturing and transporting oxygen. Look for clues like:

1. "knees" in a tree's root system that jut out of the ground and extend above the high water mark, where they may take in oxygen (cypress)

2. shallow or exposed roots that pick up oxygen from surface, aerobic soil layers

3. plants with hollow tubes or sacs that transport oxygen to the roots (reeds, grasses, sedges)

4. buoyant, floating plants with root systems that dangle in the water

5. swollen (buttressed) tree trunks that are usually thickened to the height of deepest water inundation.

The sources and levels of wetlands' water are far from constant.

The Hydrologic Regime

The hydrologic regime, or the dynamic and dominant presence of water, is the defining circumstance of a wetland. The water level is typically at, just below, or just above the ground's surface, creating the saturated conditions that lead to the development of hydric soils and the presence of hydrophytic plants.

The sources and levels of wetlands' water are far from constant. Tides ebb and flow, periodic storms dump exceptional rainfall, wet and dry seasons alternate, flood and drought raise and lower the water level. Water in a wetland may come from many sources including salty ocean tides, ground water seeps, a rainy climate, periodic river flooding, and pooled water resting on top of a poorly drained soil layer.

The pattern of water's fluctuation (called a hydroperiod) can take place daily, yearly, or over a longer span of time. In some cases the pattern is very regular (tides), but in other situations it is quite unpredictable (periodic flooding). In either scenario, the hydroperiod is critical to the type of wetland that evolves and to the adaptive strategies developed by resident species. If we consider wetlands organisms, the changing rhythms of water can be seen as their all-important breathing. Even minor shifts in water levels or the timing of wet and dry periods have profound effects on the very functionality of wetland habitats ("Soak It Up!" p. 162).

Although water is the defining circumstance of a wetland, it isn't always easy to find. Some wetlands are only damp, and some are saturated just below the surface. Others are intermittently flooded. And some flooded conditions are so sporadic that the area never becomes a true wetland at all. When water is sporadic or hidden, it is easy to conclude that an area doesn't qualify as a wetland even though, in fact, it does.

Still, if you look closely, wetland sites will usually show signs of water:

1. spongy or mushy ground (if you kneel, do your knees get wet?)

2. mud or dried mud cracks in low spots

3. water staining on tree trunks or other vegetation

4. mottled or darkly stained vegetation (from previous flooding)

5. depressions where water might collect

6. topographic evidence of water (gullies or stream channels).

Global Distribution and Factors Influencing Wetland Formation

Six percent of the earth's land surface (8.6 million square kilometers, or nearly 3.5 million square miles) is classified as wetland. To put this in perspective, that is an area just slightly smaller than the entire United States, including Alaska and Hawaii. More than half of that total lies within tropical or subtropical latitudes in rain forests, river deltas, and coastal swamps. The vast majority of the remainder is locked up in boreal (northern) peatlands. Canada alone has fully 15 percent of the world's wetland acreage. Salt pans in arid climates may qualify as wetlands, as do wet river bottom forests, cranberry bogs, river estuaries, salt tidal flats, and moist alpine tundra.

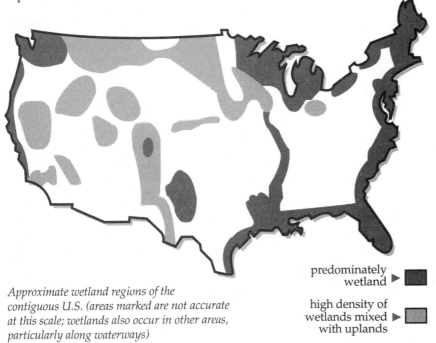

Approximate wetland regions of the contiguous U.S. (areas marked are not accurate at this scale; wetlands also occur in other areas, particularly along waterways)

predominately wetland ►

high density of wetlands mixed ► with uplands

Many factors influence the distribution and extent of wetlands:

1. seasonal fluctuations in rainfall and snowmelt that contribute to yearly flooding

2. low-lying topography that collects surface water

3. drainage properties of soil that either allow water to quickly seep away or trap it in place ("Soak It Up!" p. 162)

4. glacial history that translates into an environment pocked with depressions

5. mean temperatures during the growing season that affect evaporation and plant growth.

The interaction of these parameters determines the potential for wetlands, as well as their specific nature. Any one of them can encourage or curtail the possibility of wetland formation ("Wetlands in the Classroom!" p. 80).

Five important wetland environments are described below ("Wetland Habitats," p. 87).

Although much of the prairie pothole region lies in semi-arid country, it is an area marked by a density of small ponds and wetlands, as in this view of northern Montana.

Jim Stutzman

When the vast ice sheet retreated northward, gouging the earth with boulders and abandoning hunks of underground ice to melt, it left behind a topography rife with small, water-filled depressions.

The prairie pothole region of North America, an area of 780,000 square kilometers (300,000 square miles), is full of thousands of tiny lakes, ponds, and marshes. It is an environment capable of supporting vast numbers of waterfowl and has been called the duck factory of North America. This unique wetland niche is a legacy of the most recent glacial ages. When the vast ice sheet retreated northward, gouging the earth with boulders and abandoning hunks of underground ice to melt, it left behind a topography rife with small, water-filled depressions. Over time, plants such as arrowroot and sago pondweed colonized the seasonally flooded lakes, while cattails and grasses grew into a sheltering habitat for dozens of wildlife species. A delicate balance of timely precipitation, warm summer temperatures, and poorly drained soils has maintained the prairie potholes since the last Ice Age.

The Everglades of southern Florida exist because of an interplay between a high water table and a gently sloping topography. This wetland once covered 600,000 hectares (1.5 million acres). Human industry—dredging, channeling, draining—has drastically altered and limited its extent, but the Everglades remain a fascinating corridor 160 kilometers (100 miles) long and 80 kilometers (50 miles) wide. Water slowly but steadily pours southward across

White pelicans cluster in wetland vegetation in the Everglades.

the lower half of Florida. From Lake Okeechobee (in the north) to the southern coast, the topography slopes at an almost imperceptible 5 centimeters (2.5 inches) per mile. Sawgrass is the dominant plant species, growing in soils rich with clay and calcium carbonate. Animal and plant species have evolved to cope with the Everglades' hydroperiod, which is characterized by marked wet and dry seasons and punctuated with longer periods of drought. Still more wetland environments merge with the Everglades at its margins. Brackish marshes and saltwater mangrove swamps dominate near the southern coast and extensive cypress swamps lie to the west.

The wetland delta created by the Peace and Athabasca Rivers, in northern Canada, constitutes a rich and productive habitat for many wildlife species.

In northern Canada, the Peace and Athabasca River Delta has formed at the juncture of two prodigious rivers, creating what has been called the largest freshwater delta in the world. Tremendous river volumes and spring floods fed by snowmelt in the Canadian Rockies have formed a wild wetland that once covered more than a million hectares (2.5 million acres). Floods routinely recharged and flushed the critical "perched basins" (lowlands that spread beyond the river banks). Sections of the delta provide a summer habitat for the last remaining flock of wild whooping cranes, a haven for the world's largest herd of free-roaming wood buffalo, and an essential source of food and shelter for millions of migratory water birds.

Common Wetland Types

Bog: A peat-accumulating wetland that has no significant inflows or outflows and supports acid-loving mosses, particularly sphagnum. Water comes mostly from precipitation. Some shrubs (heath family) and evergreens also grow in bogs

Bottomlands: Lowlands along streams and rivers, usually in the floodplain (land adjacent to the banks that becomes flooded when water overflows normal levels). Often forested, and sometimes called riparian wetlands or bottomland hardwood forests.

Delmarva or Carolina bay ("whale wallow"): An isolated, irregularly shaped or elliptical basin fed by rain or ground water, containing dark-colored acidic water. These basins may support trees or shrubs, and may dry up in late summer. They are found in coastal regions of the eastern United States, and their origin is uncertain.

Fen: A peat-accumulating wetland that receives some drainage from surrounding mineral soil and usually supports marshlike plants.

Marsh: A fresh, brackish, or saltwater wetland, vegetated mostly by herbaceous plants that grow up out of the water (emergents). Marshes are frequently or continually flooded and are often found on the edges of rivers, creeks, ponds, and lakes, in isolated depressions, and along coasts.

Mire: Any peat-accumulating wetland (commonly used term in northern Europe).

Moor: A high moor is a raised bog, and a low moor is in a basin or depression (European).

Muskeg: A large expanse of peatlands or bogs, particularly common in Canada, Alaska, and Siberia.

Peatland: Any wetland that accumulates partially decayed plant matter, or peat.

Playa lake: Temporary ponds formed in desert landscapes; characterized by internal drainage systems (common in the western United States). Vegetation is usually marshlike.

(continued)

Tundra peatland on a misty day along the coast of the Arctic Ocean in northern Alaska.

Susan Higgins

Subarctic peatlands form a scattered belt of wetland environments encircling the earth's northern latitudes. Low annual precipitation creates a cold desert environment, but wetland conditions persist because of poorly drained soils, underlying layers of permafrost, and cool temperatures that allow plant production to exceed decomposition. The thick, extensive mats of peat and moss that result provide food for herds of caribou, fuel for heat in regions often devoid of trees, and nesting habitat for cranes, geese, and dozens of other bird species. Northern Europe, Canada, Alaska, and Russia contribute some 3.5 million square kilometers (1.4 million square miles) of peatlands to the world.

Susan Higgins

Worldwide, salt marshes like this one in Maine make up much of the transition zone between oceans and continental uplands.

Coastal salt marshes form along ocean/land boundaries where gently sloping topography creates transition zones between continental uplands and the open ocean. In the United States, salt marshes provide a nourishing habitat for a staggering two-thirds of the commercial fish and shellfish harvest. Daily tides pulse through stands of cordgrass, aiding the dynamic ebb and flow of nutrients. Fish and other marine animals breed and spawn in the productive shallows. Crabs, oysters, and clams flourish in the mucky bottom deposits. Shallow water and dense vegetation create a buffer against hurricanes and other ocean storms.

Wetlands Classification Chart

Major Categories	General Location	Wetland Types
Coastal Wetlands:		
Marine (undiluted salt water)	Open coast	Shrub wetland, salt marsh, mangrove swamp
Estuarine (salt/freshwater mix)	Estuaries (deltas, lagoons)	Brackish marsh, shrub wetland, salt marsh, mangrove swamp
Inland Wetlands:		
Riverine (associated with rivers & streams)	River channels & floodplains	Bottomlands, freshwater marsh, delta marsh
Lacustrine (associated with lakes)	Lakes & deltas	Freshwater marsh, shrub and forest wetlands
Palustrine (shallow ponds & miscellaneous freshwater wetlands)	Ponds, peatlands, uplands, ground water seeps	Ephemeral ponds, tundra peatland, ground water spring oasis, bogs

Potholes: Shallow marshlike ponds in the midwestern United States and the prairie provinces of Canada.

Slough: A swamp or shallow lake in the northern and midwestern United States, or a slowly flowing, shallow swamp/marsh in the southeastern United States.

Swamp: A wetland vegetated mostly by trees and shrubs; often associated with rivers, slow streams, or isolated depressions.

Wet meadow: A grassland with waterlogged soil near the surface but without standing water for most of the year.

A wet meadow full of iris in Colorado.

Paul D. McIver

3 Wetland Functions

Wetland environments have been receiving greater attention in recent years, and there have also been increasing calls for their protection. Are these cries warranted? Why should we concern ourselves with wetlands? From an anthropocentric point of view, what do wetlands do for humans? How are wetlands important to global ecological health and biological diversity?

We have some answers, but they have too often become clear only with hindsight. Only after many wetlands have disappeared, and we have been struck by the consequences, has the importance of their contribution been revealed. When we begin searching for the causes of certain environmental problems, the trail of inquiry often leads back to wetland losses.

There are many obvious indications of lost wetland functions—increased flooding of lowlands, species that die out, muddy rivers—but other effects are subtle, invisible, or evident only after a long span of time. The atmospheric balance of oxygen, carbon, nitrogen, and sulfur is affected by the efficiency of wetlands. Some wetlands recharge critical but hidden ground water reservoirs. Remarkably preserved archaeological evidence quickly deteriorates when a wetland is drained. Other important wetland contributions may not yet be known ("Wetland Metaphors," p. 85; "Wetland Tradeoffs," p. 285).

Physical/Hydrological Functions

Flood Control

Many studies have confirmed the correlation between wetland losses and increased downstream flooding. Floods are an age-old threat to human enterprises, especially since lowlands offer attractive sites for settlement—with productive soils for agriculture, ready access to navigation routes, topography conducive to building—which are nonetheless vulnerable to the threat of periodic, damaging floods.

However, wetlands left in place can act as protective natural sponges by capturing, storing, and slowly releasing water over a long period of time, thereby reducing the impact of floods ("Runoff Race," p. 210; "Soak It Up!" p. 162). This runoff storage curbs river volume, reducing both the velocity and stage of floodwaters. Water stored in wetland soils is released steadily over weeks and months rather than in a sudden and uncontrolled pulse ("Wetland in a Pan," p. 212).

This railroad bridge near Glasgow, Missouri was washed out during the severe flooding in the Missouri and Mississippi watersheds in 1993.

Coastal Protection

Coastal marshes, mangrove swamps, and other estuarine wetlands act as effective storm buffers. Studies have concluded that more than half of normal wave energy is dissipated within the first 3 meters (3.3 yards) of encountering marsh vegetation such as cordgrass. Within 10 meters (11 yards) the destructive energy is completely absorbed.

Turbulent clouds with "waterspouts" (tornado-like funnels full of water) approach the Florida coast.

In vulnerable locations like Bangladesh and the eastern seaboard of North America, wetlands have historically played an important role in lessening storm damage.

The erosive power of tides is also dampened by wetland plants because their roots hold soil in place and their stalks reduce the destructive energy of waves and wind. In fact, dense plant growth traps additional sediment that gradually increases wetland acreage, providing further coastal protection. In vulnerable locations like Bangladesh and the eastern seaboard of North America, wetlands have historically played an important role in lessening storm damage. That role becomes starkly evident when wetlands are destroyed.

Ground Water Recharge

Wetlands' role in recharging ground water varies widely, but it is clear that wetlands often contribute to ground water and can be important in recharging aquifers. Variables such as soil permeability (the rate at which water can pass through) and porosity (the percentage of open pore space), wetland size, and local geology determine the significance of a given wetland to ground water recharge ("Water Under Foot," p. 204). A wetland site on impermeable clay, for instance, will have little potential for contributing to aquifers. On the other hand, a 1,080-hectare (2,700-acre) Massachusetts wetland was found to recharge a shallow aquifer at a rate of more than 8 million gallons per day.

Sediment Traps

Wetlands improve water quality by acting as sediment sinks, or basins. They are especially effective at trapping sediments in slow-moving water. Wetland vegetation slows water velocity, and particles settle out as current or tidal-flow speeds decrease.

The benefits of lessening the sediment load in bodies of water are many. To start with, water quality is improved. Pesticides, heavy metals, and other residues are buried, along with sediments, in layers of wetland soil ("Nature's Filter," p. 250).

Decreased turbidity (cloudiness due to sediment) allows sun-

Courtesy of Everglades National Park

22

©The Watercourse and Environmental Concern Inc. 1995

light to penetrate more effectively, encouraging the growth of phytoplankton and other tiny organisms that make up the base of the food web and add oxygen to the water through photosynthesis. Turbid water can lead to a host of problems—clogged gills in aquatic life forms, the burying of benthic organisms (microbial fungi and bacteria, and some larger invertebrates) that exist on the soil's surface, and alterations in the normal fluctuation of water temperature. Economic benefits that accrue from this wetland function include a reduced need for dredging in shipping channels and a slowing of siltation in reservoirs behind dams.

Atmospheric Equilibrium

Wetland plants produce oxygen through the process of photosynthesis. Excess nitrogen such as that contained in fertilizers is broken down in wetlands through a process known as denitrification. Atmospheric levels of carbon and sulfur, both of which have increased dramatically as a result of fossil fuel and peat burning, are lowered by wetlands' ability to act as sinks (natural catchment basins) and as environments capable of reducing these elements to harmless or inert forms. Although statistical evidence regarding wetlands' impact on atmospheric dynamics is scanty, we know enough to understand that it shouldn't be taken lightly.

Chemical Functions

Pollution Interception

Depending on the development along a watercourse, pollution in a watershed might include industrial effluents, fertilizers, sewage, and city storm runoff ("Wetland in a Pan," p. 212). For example, concentrations of nitrogen and phosphorus from fertilizers collect in large quantities in wetland habitats. Left untreated or free in the water, high levels of these nutrients cause eutrophication, an initial explosion of algal growth followed by a precipitous decline in plant life ("Nutrients: Nutrition or Nuisance?" p. 188). Pollution can harm wildlife habitat, kill fish, and reduce oxygen production, among other problems ("Recipe for Trouble," p. 199).

Wetlands handle pollutants in several ways. Plants take up and filter some ("Treatment Plants," p. 120). Others settle into the anaerobic soil strata and are chemically reduced over time. Still more are processed by bacterial action. One pollutant, phosphorus, sometimes binds with iron or calcium compounds in the water through a process known as co-precipitation. When wetlands are lost, pollutants they would have rendered harmless remain at large, free to move on into other aquatic systems.

Toxic Residue Processing

In developed areas wetlands receive their share of toxic residues. When heavy metal toxins such as selenium or lead wash down the watershed, they are often destined for a wetland stop. These residues, like pollutants, can be buried and neutralized in

Pollution can harm wildlife habitat, kill fish, and reduce oxygen production, among other problems.

Peat and Heavy Metal

Commercial peat moss may prove useful in mine cleanup and, possibly, in cleansing radioactive wastes at nuclear weapons plants.

The process has become known as "membrane-media extraction" and has been tested, among other places, in a cleanup project at the Asarco Globe Plant in Globeville, Colorado. Mine wastewater carrying heavy metals and other contaminants is strained through beds of peat and purified of arsenic, cadmium, lead, manganese, zinc, and selenium.

Early reports suggest that water that has been filtered through peat is clean enough to be discharged into a sewer system. Much of the retrieved metal is reusable. Tests at the Rocky Flats nuclear weapons plant near Denver indicate that membrane-media extraction might hold promise in removing radionuclides from wastewater.

This acid mine drainage is being discharged into a constructed wetland, where much of the metals waste will be filtered out.

Wetlands catch and filter pollutants: sediment becomes trapped among the plants or settles out of the water; excess nutrients are taken up and used by the plants; some toxic substances are caught and stored in the soil matrix.

soils; taken up by reeds, rushes, and other plants; and reduced through ion exchange ("Water Purifiers," p. 215).

However, large-scale or long-term additions of toxins will overpower a wetland's capacity. In fact, some toxins can be made more dangerous by undergoing chemical changes in a wetland (inorganic mercury can become the more potent and dangerous methylmercury, for instance). Often, toxins are only temporarily held by a wetland before being released again into a water body. While wetlands play a crucial part in protecting watersheds from toxins, their capacity and long-term ability to do so is limited.

Waste Treatment

Wetlands can be remarkably effective in treating controlled amounts of human and animal wastes. Peat is a very efficient filter, and mangrove swamps, salt marshes, and other wetlands have

Wetland plants can be used to process residential sewage, as in this septic tank system utilizing wetland vegetation near Signal Mountain, Tennessee.

also proven to be effective.

Several factors contribute to wetlands' performance in processing waste:

1. a high rate of biological productivity (see below) that leads to a large capacity for consuming waste

2. heavy deposition of sediments that bury waste

3. a high level of bacterial activity in sediment layers that breaks down and neutralizes waste.

Cities like Philadelphia and Calcutta, India, have incorporated wetlands into their wastewater treatment schemes for decades, with persuasive results. While it is important to pay attention to a wetland's capacity, these urban wastewater treatment wetlands have removed coliform bacteria and suspended solids, reduced the turbidity of wastewater by nearly half, and added tons of oxygen to the water every day on a sustained basis.

Biological Functions

Biological Production

Tremendous primary productivity (or the sustained yield of organic material, mostly vegetation) is a salient characteristic of wetlands. As a whole, they outproduce almost all other environments, often many times over. Tropical rain forests are the only ecological communities that come close to equaling wetlands' production levels. Wetlands cover only 6.4 percent of the earth's surface, yet they account for 24 percent of total global productivity.

Several factors contribute to this. Much wetland vegetation is made up of leafy perennials, so photosynthesis occurs with constant, inexorable efficiency. Many plants have evolved root systems able to take up and use inorganic nutrients. Flooding, tidal pulses, and heavy precipitation deliver and distribute large quantities of nutrients ("Nutrients: Nutrition or Nuisance?" p. 188).

Some wetland vegetation (wild rice, cranberries) is directly consumed by grazing animals or humans, but the lion's share of productivity comes in the form of dead and dying plants, or detritus. This forms the base of wetland food webs. Populations of larvae, protozoa, bacteria, and fungi live off detritus. They, in turn, are the food of fish, worms, birds, and other life further along in the energy web.

Habitat

From bacteria to beavers, crocodiles to Cajuns, wetlands are both home and supermarket for myriad residents. Biological productivity attracts life, namely, the many plants and animals that utilize wetlands for food, shelter, spawning, nesting, or predatory opportunities.

Eighty percent of all breeding bird populations in the United States, along with more than half of the protected migratory bird species, rely on wetlands at some point in their life cycle. Ninety-five percent of all U.S. commercial fish and shellfish species depends on wetlands to some extent.

A roseate spoonbill in the waters of an Everglades wetland.

A relatively small percentage of species, such as the muskrat, alligator, and marsh rat, are year-round wetland residents. Many more rely on wetlands during part of their daily, seasonal, or life cycles. Deer come to wetlands for water and food. Fish establish nurseries in shallow, nutrient-charged estuaries. Migratory birds stop in wetlands along flyways to rest and eat.

In some regions of the world, humans have also developed subsistence economies in wetland habitat. The Inuit of the Far North, Arabs who inhabit the delta of the Tigris and Euphrates watersheds, and some residents of the Amazon watershed have adapted their transportation, economies, and diets to flourish in wetland conditions.

Socioeconomic Functions/Benefits

Food

Wild rice and cranberries are examples of wetland crops that can be harvested and consumed directly. However, the greatest food contribution accrues from wetland soils that have been drained and turned into agricultural land or that are under cultivation during dry periods. Wetland soils are nutrient-rich, full of organic material, and generally less prone to erosion than other soils. They tend to be highly productive, especially in the first de-

Wetland soils are nutrient-rich, full of organic material, and generally less prone to erosion than other soils.

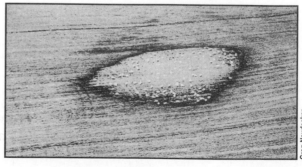

A temporary wetland with migrating swans and ducks in cultivated farmland.

cade of planting. Drained wetland soils in the United States, taken as a whole, produce more than 25 percent of all major crops, a monetary value of roughly $9 billion. Throughout the world, wetland soils consistently outperform other cultivated land.

Of course, once wetlands are permanently drained, the conditions that created productive soils are lost, along with benefits like recreation, fish habitat, and pollution interception. In addition, wetland soils are chronically vulnerable to flooding. When these considerations are added to the equation, the cost/benefit analysis becomes much more complicated.

Commercially Important Fish, Bird, and Animal Populations

Trapping fur-bearing animals for their pelts, harvesting fish and shellfish for food, and recreational fishing and hunting are all activities that depend heavily on wetland habitats and contribute tremendous economic benefits to the global economy.

Alligator, muskrat, mink, and nutria skins and furs amounted to a $1 billion American crop in 1980. In 1988 commercial fishing added $1.7 billion to the U.S. gross national product. Significant wetland habitat loss leads to lowered species populations and, therefore, lower yearly harvests.

courtesy of George Wuerthner and the Greater Yellowstone Coalition

Hunters and anglers pour billions of dollars into license fees, transportation, lodging, guide services, and the like. For instance, as long ago as 1969 a California estimate of direct and indirect income from anglers put the average cost of one salmon to fishermen at $18.11. U.S. Fish and Wildlife Service figures show that 5.3 million waterfowl hunters spent $638 million in 1981 alone.

Fuel

For centuries, peat has been harvested, dried, and burned. In areas without fossil fuels or extensive forests, peat is the most viable local energy source. Finland, Ireland, and the former Soviet Union are responsible for more than 95 percent of world peat production, but Canada, the United States, and other countries are

Peat Mines

Peat development requires two conditions: a positive water balance (greater precipitation and inflow than evapotranspiration and runoff), and a surplus of organic accumulation over decomposition. Cool, moist climates like those found in northern latitudes are ideal for the accumulation of peat. Although primary production (the accumulation of detritus) is fairly low in northern climes compared to other wetland environments, decomposition is even more depressed, so layers continue to develop and thicken.

Much of northwestern Europe is conducive to the development of peat. For thousands of years, residents of that part of the world have been mining the vast peat deposits that carpet the landscape. Traditionally, the peat-cutting tool of choice was a two-sided spade. Slices of wet peat, rich with organic (and combustible) material, were removed, laid out to dry, and then burned to fire furnaces and heat homes.

Although manual peat harvesting continues, industrial mining techniques depend on giant peat-shaving machinery. Peat is removed to dry, then collected in a crumbled or powdered state. This powder can fuel furnaces, factories, and power stations; be compressed into flammable pellets and briquettes; or be liquefied to make industrial fuels.

In the United States, Minnesota has looked into the economics of mining its considerable peat reserves (400,000 hectares, or 1 million acres). Calculations suggest that peat could supply the state's energy requirements for 30 years or more.

considering mining peat more aggressively as well. Given the high cost of fossil fuels, peat offers an attractive and profitable alternative. In modern times peat has been mined, reduced to powder, and burned at electrical power generating stations. Pellets and briquettes are also produced for fuel. Worldwide, minable peat reserves have been estimated at 420 million hectares (1 billion acres).

Paul D. McIver

A small-scale peat mining operation in South Park, Colorado.

The environmental impacts of peat mining, on the other hand, are considerable. For all practical purposes, peat is a nonrenewable resource. Peat mining can result in compromised local water quality, unchecked storm runoff, and the destruction of habitat that has taken thousands of years to evolve. Areas such as the Norfolk Broads in England have been heavily impacted by centuries of continuous peat extraction.

Wetland herbaceous vegetation such as the water hyacinth also has potential as an energy producer. A 1,000-hectare (2,500-acre) hyacinth plantation in a warm climate could produce 10^{12} BTU (British Thermal Unit, roughly equal to 250 calories) of methane every year. As a side benefit, that same plantation would be capable of removing the excess nitrogen in the wastewater from a large city on an ongoing basis.

Timber and Fiber Harvest

Prolific growth rates and dense stands of vegetation make wetlands attractive areas for wood and fiber industries. Salt hay, for instance, has been an important harvested crop in the northeast-

courtesy of South Florida Water Management District

Wetland timber harvesting in Florida.

ern United States and in other areas of the world for generations. Wetland timber stands along the Mississippi watershed and along the watersheds on the south Atlantic coast were estimated to be worth $8 billion in 1979. Total U.S. timber reserves in wetland settings come to some 22 million hectares (55 million acres).

Although draining and clear-cutting have been the wetland timber-cutting norm until recently, more advanced silvicultural practices like selective cutting and vigorous replanting have now been initiated in some areas, with good results. Any achievement of sustainable harvests will be due, it now appears, to rapid tree growth rates.

Mangrove swamps in tropical and subtropical regions (especially Asia) have been heavily cut at a pace that cannot be sustained. In the Philippines nearly 50 percent of all mangrove areas were cut between 1967 and 1976.

Recreation, Aesthetics, and Education

The recreation, aesthetics, and educational benefits of wetlands are tough to quantify, but they are no less compelling for that. Of the three, recreation is the most tangible, but even that benefit is lumped with hunting and fishing, while such things as bird-watching, canoeing, and walking are often unaccounted for. It was estimated that 107 million people took advantage of wetland-related recreational activities in 1985. In that year hunting, fishing, and nonconsumptive wildlife-related activities were valued at $55 billion.

courtesy of United States Fish and Wildlife Service

That aside, wetlands serve as biological laboratories and educational field stations with the potential to handle thousands of students learning lessons in natural history, cultural heritage, and other disciplines. They are attractive sites for research as well, because they tend to be compact in area and diverse and complex in nature.

Artists, photographers, bird-watchers, and those who seek the

Ancient Ancestors in Florida

When peat deposits near Cape Canaveral, Florida, were drained for a housing development, workers were startled by bodies that began appearing—lots of very old bodies. What they had stumbled across was a Native American burial ground more than 7,000 years old.

Archaeologists think the deceased had been wrapped in woven mats and staked, along with a variety of implements and artifacts, to the bottom of what was then a shallow pond. The pond was gradually sealed by peat deposits which effectively halted further decomposition ("People of the Bog," p. 266).

More than 150 individuals have been recovered, many of them children. Clothing, intact artifacts, even the contents of individuals' stomachs have been preserved well enough to study and interpret. The surviving fabrics, far and away the oldest ever found in eastern North America, are of great interest to the archaeological community.

Draining was stopped, and most of the area, called the Windover Site, has been resealed pending careful examination.

refreshment of outdoor settings are all drawn to wetlands. That attraction is an unquantifiable benefit, but certainly no less valuable than fuel supplies or animal pelts.

Cultural Heritage and Archaeological Evidence

The same anaerobic wetland conditions that create thick layers of organic material also act to retard the processes of decomposition at archaeological sites ("People of the Bog," p. 266). Artifacts, clothing, and even human remains are unbelievably well preserved. Cultural information about dietary nuances, clothing materials, and building styles are available for study in wetland sites. Once removed from the anaerobic setting, these materials quickly decompose and are lost without careful preservation. Precise pollen dating, dendrochronology (tree-ring dating), and radiocarbon dating allow for accurate reconstruction of cultural history and archaeological sequences.

The archaeological site known as Monte Verde in the Andes Mountains of South America was sealed in oxygen-deprived beds of peat. Leftover food (nuts, fruits, remains of paleocamel), pieces of wood and ivory, flesh from a mastodon, and even a child's footprint are freshly preserved there. Most startling, this site may predate the earliest verified evidence of people in the western hemisphere by thousands of years.

Wetlands As Home

One of the most visible and spectacular attributes of wetland environments is their quality as habitat for plants and animals ("Wetland Habitats," p. 87). Even casual observers can't avoid the most blatant evidence of functioning wetland habitat—great flocks of waterfowl, crisscrossing animal tracks in mud, the drone of insects in the air, impenetrable vegetation ("Wet 'n' Wild," p. 99).

The loss of wetland habitat is also quite noticeable, due to the predictable decline in species and population levels. Flocks of birds become greatly diminished, fish aren't caught in customary numbers, and freshly beaver-chewed stumps no longer gleam along stream banks. By the time this evidence appears, it is likely that other, less obvious wetland processes have already ceased or been curtailed.

The seasonally flooded wetlands along the Central Valley of California once provided habitat for 40 million waterfowl. Since the 1940s, however, efforts to convert wetlands to agricultural land through dam-building and draining have shrunk this habitat dramatically. Presently there is sufficient wetland habitat for only 5 million waterfowl.

In a wetland, as in a tropical rain forest, species competition is fierce and life strategies and adaptations amazingly complex. For sheer productivity, consider a salt marsh, which is capable of amassing 10 tons of organic matter for every half-hectare (one acre) annually. The presence of water, along with great concentrations of nutrients, encourage dense and rapid plant growth. Detritus ("Nature's Recyclers," p. 226; "A Rottin' Experiment," p. 245) feeds the zooplankton, fungi, larvae, and bacteria at the base of the food web. These, in turn, become prey to other life forms along the various energy pathways.

Life in a wetland, although full of rewards, is not without challenges. In many cases plants and animals have to succeed in conditions that are both terrestrial and aquatic. Water and soils are

Themes

- Wetland habitats
- Life-strategy challenges posed by wetlands
- Protist adaptations
- Plant adaptations
- Animal adaptations and strategies
- Species interactions
- Endangered species habitat
- Energy web dynamics

Recommended Activities

- "Wetland Habitats"
- "Jumping Jehoshaphat"
- "Tracking Plants and Keeping Track"
- "Nature's Recyclers"
- "A Rottin' Experiment"
- "Marsh Market"
- "Marsh Mystery"
- "Wetland Weirdos"
- "Wetland Wheel"
- "Salt Marsh Players"
- "Wet 'n' Wild"
- "Whose Clues?"
- "This Plant Key Is All Wet!"
- "Life in the Fast Lane"

Wetland Havens for Endangered Species

While wetland habitat accounts for a mere 3.5 percent of the land area of the United States, roughly half of the more than 200 animal species identified as endangered or threatened depend on wetlands for their survival. Nearly 75% of endangered or threatened bird species rely on wetland habitats, and more than 25% of threatened or endangered plant species exist in wetlands.

The dusky seaside sparrow, a former resident of Florida marshes, became extinct in 1987 due, in large measure, to the destruction of its habitat. Whooping cranes were brought to the brink of extinction by hunting, habitat loss, and pesticide poisoning. They are on a very slow path to recovery, with a current world population of roughly 150 wild birds. Trumpeter swans, Kemp's Ridley sea turtles, and bladderpod plants are among the forms of life that depend, at least in part, on wetland habitat, and whose existence hangs in the balance.

Wetland species are involved with other life forms in a complex ecology. Take slackwater darters, for example. These tiny riverine fish require small marshy areas associated with ground water seeps to spawn. They travel to these shallow waters to lay their eggs on a single species of rush. The darters refuse other vegetation, even if it is similar. The breeding grounds become home for the larvae during the critical four to six weeks before they move into their home streams.

We have only a vague understanding of the relationships that make up the web of wetland life. If one wetland habitat is lost, what species are affected?

A Sampler of Threatened & Endangered Wetland Species

Mammals
red wolf - coastal wetlands, Louisiana
   and Texas
Florida panther - floodplains,
   southeastern United States
Amargos vole - inland marshes,
   California
harvest mouse - salt marshes, California

(continued)

often highly saline and full of other concentrated minerals. Plants must find ways to root themselves in soil that has little or no oxygen (anaerobic) and to flourish in flooded environments. Animals must cope with aquatic environments often laden with salts, cycles of drought and flood, and stiff competition, on top of the usual rigors of hunting food, finding adequate shelter, and successfully continuing their species.

The Protists

At the most basic level, protists are simple, one-celled organisms (algae, bacteria, etc.) that lack the ability to change habitats and are forced to respond metabolically to wetland stresses. Without available oxygen (a common wetland circumstance, especially in sediments), organisms are compelled to find substitute molecules to facilitate respiration and to act as electron acceptors (oxygen is normally the terminal electron acceptor that facilitates the oxidation of organic molecules).

Some protists have the ability to capitalize on oxygen when it is available and switch to inorganic ions when it is lacking. Others have developed strategies to exist in a constant anaerobic state. Members of the genus *Desulfovibrio*, for instance, use sulfate instead of oxygen as a terminal electron acceptor. That respiratory process produces sulfides, lending the characteristic "rotten egg" odor of many marshes. Various wetland bacteria have adapted to use ammonia, sulfide, or ferrous ions as their energy suppliers.

High concentrations of salt create the danger of osmotic shock and toxicity for bacteria and other cells. Single-celled wetland organisms can accumulate concentrations of potassium to prevent osmotic invasion by salt ions in the surrounding environment. Organic compounds such as glycerol can also be concentrated within cell walls to resist the pressures of salt.

Vascular Plants

Vascular plants (species in which the phloem transports sugar and the xylem transports water and salts) are far more complicated than protists, and utilize a much wider range of adaptive strategies ("This Plant Key Is All Wet!" p. 123). More than 1,200 plant species make their homes in freshwater environments in the United States alone. Worldwide, thousands of species utilize fresh- and salt-water environments ("Wetland Wheel," p. 129). From water hyacinths to massive cypress trees, all have evolved ways to thrive in wetlands.

On a community level, plants interact through competition, parasitism, cooperation, and symbiosis. All life forms compete in the hunt for space, food, air, shelter, and the continuation of their species. The result, in a wetland, is an amazingly intricate and dynamic ecological web, with plants at the hub ("Tracking Plants and Keeping Track," p. 138).

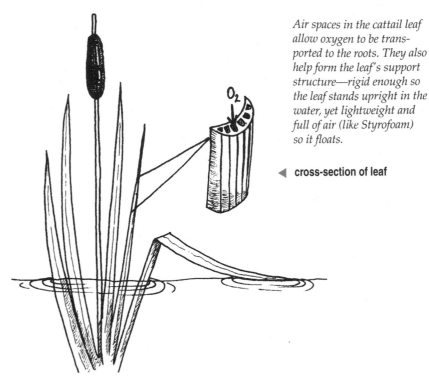

Air spaces in the cattail leaf allow oxygen to be transported to the roots. They also help form the leaf's support structure—rigid enough so the leaf stands upright in the water, yet lightweight and full of air (like Styrofoam) so it floats.

◀ **cross-section of leaf**

The subtleties of species' development and interaction are complex and ingenious ("Wetland Weirdos," p. 94). Complicated oxygen-transport mechanisms in plant stems and protective barriers against excessively saline surroundings are two of the many adaptations vascular plants employ to capitalize on wetland habitat while surviving its stresses.

The roots of wetland plants are routinely subjected to anaerobic conditions. In response, the plants have evolved air spaces, or aerenchyma, throughout their roots and stems to allow oxygen molecules to diffuse from aerial (emergent) portions to underwater roots. As much as 60 percent of a wetland plant's mass can be

Cattails are one of the most common and widespread wetland plants. They provide food and shelter for wildlife, and often are the most visible indication of a wetland's location.

Susan Higgins

Birds
Cape Sable sparrow - marshes, Florida
Mexican duck - inland marshes, New Mexico
Aleutian Canada goose - lakes and marshes, California, Oregon, Washington
American peregrine falcon - coastal wetlands, United States
whooping crane - prairie and coastal wetlands, south-central United States
California black rail - salt marshes, California
Eskimo curlew - coastal wetlands, Texas

Reptiles
American alligator - swamps and marshes, southeastern United States
bog turtle - bogs, northeastern and southeastern United States
San Francisco garter snake - coastal wetlands, California

Amphibians
Wyoming toad - temporary pools, Wyoming
Vegas Valley leopard frog - springs, Nevada
Texas blind salamander - cave waters, Texas

Fishes
Devil's Hole pupfish - desert springs, Nevada
Pahrump killifish - spring-fed pool, Nevada
Big Bend gambusia - desert springs, Texas
unarmored three-spine stickleback, rivers - California
Apache (Arizona) trout - mountain streams, Arizona

Insects
delta green ground beetle - vernal pools, California
Oregon silverspot butterfly - coastal marshes, Oregon, Washington

Plants
Eaton's quillwort - pond and stream edges, northeastern United States
umbrella sedge - pools and depressions, southeastern United States
cylinder spikerush - shallow water, Texas
California pitcher plant - bogs and marshes, California
violet-flowered butterwort - bogs and savannas, Alabama, Florida, Mississippi

Shrubs
beautiful pawpaw - wet flatwoods, Florida
bog spice bush - shrub bogs, North Carolina, Louisiana, Mississippi

Emergents, Floaters, and Submergents

Most wetland plants, especially in marsh ecosystems, can be classified as emergents, floaters, or submergents ("This Plant Key is all Wet!" p. 123). In some cases, plant types cluster in sharply defined zones corresponding to specific water depths. For example, cattails root themselves in the shallow margins, lilies float in moderate depths, and bladderwort and pondweed lie submerged in the deepest water. More often, however, plant types don't form crisp boundaries and instead, intermingle throughout a wetland.

Emergents such as cattails, pickerelweed, arrowhead, golden club, and many sedges extend above the water's surface, growing in water up to 2 meters (6.5 feet) deep. Air spaces in the plants' structure transport oxygen from above-water portions to root systems. Thick stands of emergent growth offer nesting sites, camouflage, and important sources of food for many wetland animals. Muskrats feed on the underground sections of cattails, and dabbling ducks feast on the storage nodes of arrowhead roots (known as "duck potatoes").

Floaters include plants like lilies and water hyacinth, which are rooted in bottom muck, and free-floating species such as duckweed, which reproduce asexually by forming large mats of plantlets with thousands of tiny dangling water roots. In water of moderate depth, these plants can completely cover the surface of a pond. Floaters utilize stomates, or tiny openings on the top of floating leaves, to facilitate gas exchange. Stems or stalks are often spongy and inflated, for buoyancy.

Submergents include pondweeds, milfoils, water celery, and bladderworts. With few exceptions, they live entirely underwater. Bladderworts extend only their flowers above the water surface, and water celery's flowers rise to the surface in order to pollinate. Bladderworts are carnivorous, with tiny bladders on their

(continued)

honeycombed pore space (two to seven percent is common for terrestrial species).

Certain plants can make morphological responses to sudden flooding as well. The rapid stem growth of rice and other species allows a greater percentage of their structure to reach aerobic conditions as water levels rise. Some plants can quickly add to their root systems, seeking out aerobic environments when the original roots are oxygen-deprived.

Several woody trees (cypress, willow, mangrove, etc.) are successful wetland residents. Their adaptations include adventitious "prop roots," full of pores called lenticels, that extend above the flooded or tidal zone and supply oxygen to submerged roots. Cypress "knees" (knobby root growths extending above the water level) and mangrove pneumatophores (air roots) are similar adaptations.

Oxygen diffusion from the emergent portions to the root systems of wetland plants may actually be prolific enough to produce a certain amount of soil oxidation around the roots. In a soil profile, it's common to find rust stains around roots (oxidized rhizospheres) where oxygen has escaped into the soil horizon.

The nutrients found in wetland soils would be inaccessible to most upland plants, which require oxygen to efficiently absorb elements such as nitrogen, sulfur, and phosphorus. Wetland plants, however, are capable of maintaining their metabolic rates in saturated environments and have evolved a variety of coping mechanisms so that nutrient absorption is unimpeded. These include an elevated tolerance for elements such as sulfur or manganese; the ability to shunt excess nutrients to parts of the plant (vacuoles, vascular tissue) where they won't retard the metabolic process; and the capacity (in some species) to directly absorb such wetland products as ammonium.

In addition, many wetland plants have developed the capacity to respire anaerobically, thereby reducing their need for oxygen. To varying degrees, vascular plants share metabolic strategies with the protists, including the use of substitute electron acceptors (such as sulfate) and the development of protective barriers against toxic accumulations of substances like ethanol.

Plants in saline environments often develop barriers in their outer layers to block salt from entering the organism. Others are able to secrete excess salt through salt glands. Marsh grasses, for instance, are often covered with crystalline salt secretions.

Because plants aren't very mobile, we don't generally think them capable of escape and avoidance tactics. However, subtle versions of these strategies are important to many plants. By using selective timing, some wetland plants produce seeds in dry seasons. Others have evolved buoyant seeds that float to a terrestrial margin to take root or seeds that germinate while the fruit is still attached to the parent plant. Plants often escape the rigors of heavy flooding by becoming dormant, and therefore less susceptible to oxygen deprivation, during the high-water season.

Wetland Animals

Species adapt to their environment in countless ways, and a complete catalog of those adaptations is beyond our scope. It is no overstatement to say that every plant and animal in every wetland has evolved coping strategies. The webbed feet of beaver and muskrat, the oarlike legs that keep water striders afloat on a pond's surface, the black fly larvae that live only in oxygenated water, and the mosquito larvae that pierce the air pores of plants to tap oxygen supplies: all are formulas for wetland success.

Compared to plants and protists, animals are more mobile and complex in their adaptive responses to wetland conditions. In addition to biochemical and physiological strategies, animals react behaviorally to cope with obstacles ("Wetland Weirdos," p. 94).

Coping with Low Oxygen Levels

1. Gills cover a variety of physical and behavioral adaptations that allow species to maintain a healthy oxygen level. Fish gills bring blood to the body surface, where oxygen transfer takes place across a thin layer of skin. Black fly larvae use spiracular gills, or canals beneath the skin, across which oxygen diffuses. Mayflies rely on blood gills located on their abdomen. Beetles and many other bugs actually carry oxygen tanks with them in the form of air bubbles that are often held under their wings or trapped in hair on their abdomens.

submerged leaves that inflate suddenly in response to the movements of minuscule aquatic creatures. Prey is sucked in through the bladder opening and then digested.

courtesy of United States Fish and Wildlife Service; photo by Dan O'Neal

Wetland vegetation, whether submerged, floating, or extending above the water's surface, has developed a myriad of adaptations and strategies to cope with the presence of water.

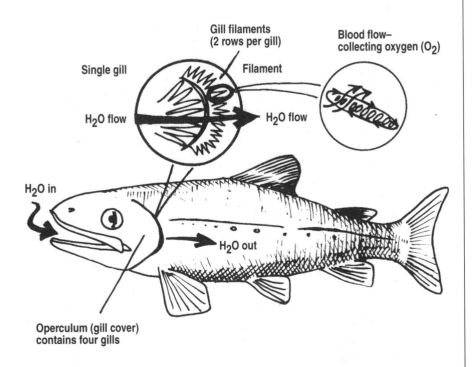

Gill filaments (2 rows per gill)

Blood flow– collecting oxygen (O_2)

Single gill   Filament

H_2O flow H_2O flow

H_2O in

H_2O out

Operculum (gill cover) contains four gills

2. Internal structural changes include the development of an exceptionally powerful heart, an increased density of blood vessels, or a super-efficient circulatory system.

3. Oxygen-binding compounds, most commonly the iron compound hemoglobin, are essential for capturing and releasing oxygen molecules during the process of respiration. In wetland animals this process has to be extremely efficient to take advantage of diminished oxygen supplies. Substitute oxygen-binding compounds such as copper are used by crayfish and other species, producing distinctive blue blood.

4. Periods of low-oxygen stress cause behavioral responses in some creatures. Decreased activity levels lower the need for oxygen, so many animals enter a quiescent state when oxygen is lacking. When oxygen is plentiful, as during low tide in a tidal marsh, animals such as the fiddler crab feed and move actively. Once high tides return, fiddlers scramble for their burrows, where they remain inactive and consume very little oxygen.

Maintaining an Osmotic Balance

Aquatic life must adjust its internal chemistry in response to its surroundings. Aquatic animals take in water, salt, and minerals as needed, but block out toxic excesses of the same. This is called maintaining an osmotic balance. In simplistic terms, osmosis is the process by which concentrations of materials (usually suspended in fluid) pass through membranes to areas with lower concentrations. Simple organisms are usually osmoconformers, meaning that their internal cell chemistry mimics the osmotic concentrations in their surroundings.

More complicated forms of life like shrimp, crab, and fish cope in a variety of behavioral and physiological ways to maintain their osmotic equilibrium. These species have to be flexible since their surroundings can change dramatically and abruptly, as with the ebb and flow of tides. Two of the most common physiological adaptations are impervious body surfaces like turtle shells and snake skins, which allow certain species to regulate their internal environment, and excretory organs like kidneys, nasal glands, antennal glands, and specialized gills, which remove excess water and concentrations of salts or other minerals.

Successful Reproductive Strategies

1. Periods of reproductive dormancy allow some cysts (small sacs that enclose certain organisms during their dormant or larval stage) and eggs to wait out unfavorable periods (usually drought) to hatch when conditions improve. Dormancies of 20 years or more have been documented in some drought-resistant protozoan cysts, and some eggs can remain dormant for a year or two.

2. Animals adapt their life cycles so that they emerge at times most likely to favor optimal temperatures, food availability, stream velocity, and other environmental benefits. Some animals use environmental cues such as salinity or sunlight to trigger egg releases or larval development. Other species have no larval stage, so they can more immediately take advantage of good conditions.

3. Asexual reproduction allows other wetland animals (and plants) to react quickly to environmental conditions. The rapid cell division of simple species like the amoeba gives them the ability to respond immediately to changes in the environment.

Methods of Dispersal and Migration

Many animals (not just birds) respond to their environment by moving regularly and with purpose. Wetland species are no exception. Leeches attach themselves to duck feet or turtle shells to hitch a ride. Insects fly to new homes. Frogs hop from pond to pond. Fish travel widely in ocean and stream currents.

Even organisms that are incapable of locomotion use winds, currents, or animal hosts to disperse themselves. Many eggs, cysts, and plant spores travel so efficiently that they have colonized the world.

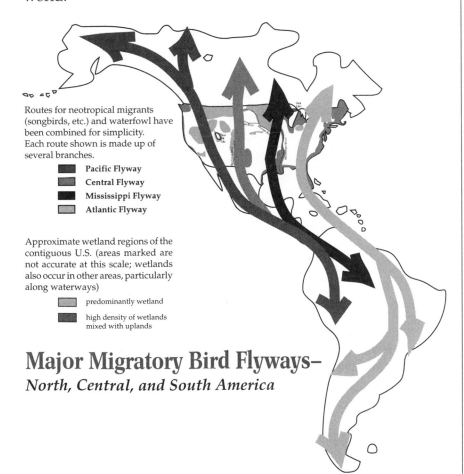

Routes for neotropical migrants (songbirds, etc.) and waterfowl have been combined for simplicity. Each route shown is made up of several branches.

■ Pacific Flyway
■ Central Flyway
■ Mississippi Flyway
■ Atlantic Flyway

Approximate wetland regions of the contiguous U.S. (areas marked are not accurate at this scale; wetlands also occur in other areas, particularly along waterways)

■ predominantly wetland

■ high density of wetlands mixed with uplands

Major Migratory Bird Flyways–
North, Central, and South America

Gators & Gator Holes— A Boom & Bust Lifestyle

American alligators living in the Florida Everglades are most comfortable with plenty of water around them. How, then, do they cope with the regular droughts that afflict their habitat?

Like crayfish and salamanders, alligators are capable of aestivation (a torpid state during summer months), and can endure long periods of drought inside their mud dens.

Alligators also survive dry periods by creating their own microwetlands. By lashing their tails and digging with their feet and snouts, alligators create pools that become tiny marshes called gator holes. These holes provide an environment that serves other species as well. Lilies, arrowheads, and cattails quickly grow in gator holes, while flowers and shrubs take root in the excavated dirt. Birds nest in the new growth. Fish, snails, and turtles move in alongside the gator, carrying on their life cycles while they wait for the rains to replenish the Everglades.

Other opportunistic species are inevitably drawn to gator holes. Marsh rabbits come to feed on succulent vegetation. Raccoons rob eggs from turtles' nests. Herons wait motionless in the shallows for their prey. Birds like the wood stork time their nesting patterns to take advantage of dry cycles, so that when they have young to feed, they can easily find fish concentrated in confined wetlands like gator holes.

When water returns to the Everglades the animals redistribute themselves, and the American alligator is free to roam until the dry cycle comes around again.

courtesy of United States Fish and Wildlife Service; photo by Dick Bailey

Beavers—Wetland Movers & Shakers

Beavers are the rodent industrialists of many wetland settings ("Wetland Weirdos," p. 94). Their ability to topple trees and construct dams out of mud and branches gives them the power to create new or expanded wetlands.

Beavers' front teeth are powerful gnawing tools capable of downing a 15-centimeter (six-inch) diameter tree in ten minutes. Beavers' gnawing teeth extend outside their lips in order to keep wood splinters and chips out of their mouths. These four teeth grow continuously, and gnawing action is required to balance the growth rate. Clear eyelids allow beavers to see under water, and specialized nostril valves keep water out.

Bark, twigs, leaves, and roots are beavers' dominant food, and the animals are able to consume more than a kilogram (roughly three pounds) in one meal. These large rodents live in earth burrows with underwater entrances along river banks or in lodges with living quarters above the water level in ponds and marshes.

Local wetland hydrology can be drastically affected by the activity of beavers, whose dam-building often floods extensive lowlands. When food supplies become depleted at one dam site, beavers will frequently move upstream to build another dam, thus creating a string of wetlands along a watercourse.

Marypat Zitzer

Responses to Environmental Change

1. Wetland amphibians and many reptiles hibernate through winter. Snakes, toads, turtles, and other species burrow under leaf litter or mud until longer days, greater warmth, and/or returning water bring them out of their torpor.

2. Aestivation is similar to hibernation in that it involves lowered metabolic activity. Most often, aestivation is a response to heat and drought, and isn't necessarily part of a regular yearly pattern. Alligators in southern wetlands survive periods of extreme drought by digging protected mud dens, and drastically reducing their metabolism once inside.

3. Many animal species adjust to the daily, or diurnal, changes in their environment. Turtles sunning themselves to raise their body temperatures and crabs waiting out high tide in their burrows to conserve oxygen are using diurnal strategies ("Salt Marsh Players," p. 165).

Wetland Interactions

It's easy to single out a species and study its behavior or structure as if it existed in isolation. But the more we understand about the complexity of environments, the more it becomes clear that interdependence, cooperation, competition, and other dynamics make ecosystems true societies ("Whose Clues?" p. 104), not communities of independent residents ("Wet 'n' Wild," p. 99).

Habitat Niches

Deer coming to a marsh to browse and drink, flycatchers chasing insects from a perch on a branch, fish finding nursery space in

an estuary, herons pacing shallows in search of fish, blue-winged teal resting along migratory routes, and plants seeking the optimal balance of sunlight, water, and nutrients are only a few of the competing, and interacting, users of a wetland ("Wet 'n' Wild," p. 99).

Think of the ways humans in crowded cities adjust their patterns to minimize competition and conflict. Varied work shifts, maximized living space in high-rise apartments, and shopping at odd hours are all ways of dealing with overcrowding and limited resources. Wetland inhabitants employ similar tactics to concentrate their efforts productively while avoiding costly conflicts ("Salt Marsh Players," p. 165).

courtesy of Everglades National Park

This anhinga has just caught its wetland meal. As usual for this species of diving bird, the main course will be fish.

A great many species of birds feed on insects, for example, but some feed only during very specific periods of the day, or at a narrowly defined altitude, or on a few exclusive types or sizes of insect. Loons and grebes nest at the wet edges of water bodies, while swans build platforms away from shore. The various species of perching birds nest at different levels in the forest. Leopard frogs flourish in full sunlight and open water, while wood frogs prefer the cool, shady margins of ponds. Mallards and pintails feed in the bottom muck in shallow water, while loons, grebes, and mergansers chase after fish at greater depths.

Vegetation height and density, temperature gradients, water levels, food diversity, daily and seasonal fluctuations, and soil types all combine in vibrant, humming, synchronized concert to create the symphony that is a healthy and flourishing wetland.

Food and Energy Web

Wetland species literally feed off each other ("Marsh Market," p. 109). Plants produce energy from sunlight, water, and nutrients. When plants die they form the detritus that tiny bacteria, fungi, and zooplankton feed on. Worms, snails, small fish, and crustaceans consume these simple organisms, and are prey to larger

Energy Web—Freshwater Stream

The food chain concept is too linear and simplistic to describe the real world of wetland interaction. That interaction is much more like a web, with pathways of energy crisscrossing in a complicated drama ("Marsh Mystery," p. 116).

Producers, the primary foundation of an energy web, are mostly algae and other green plants, along with some forms of bacteria. The plants and animals that eat other plants and animals are the web's consumers. Herbivores eat plants, carnivores feed on meat, and omnivores consume a combination of plants and meat, as well as detritus (dead organic matter).

As food progresses through the pathways of a wetland society, it leaves behind a significant percentage of its original energy. As a result, fewer members of a given species can be supported at each stage. A section of stream may support millions of bacteria, but only several dozen adult fish and a single pair of belted kingfishers.

In a freshwater stream the producers are plants such as watercress, moss and diatoms, and other algae. These, along with detritus from decomposing plants and animals, form the basic food resource. The tiniest residents—caddis fly larvae, bacteria, fungi, zooplankton, and others—feed on the producers and detritus. Minnows and crayfish consume the smaller consumers and are gobbled up in turn by larger fish, turtles, and kingfishers. Otters, osprey, bald eagles, and a few other large animals then take their share. Finally, the consumers die, decompose, and themselves become part of the detrital base of the energy web.

Plant & Animal Ingenuity

When we think of species' adaptations and coping behaviors the most obvious examples come to mind—beavers constructing dams, bald eagles plucking fish from a pond, carnivorous pitcher plants luring insects into their watery traps. But the interactions and strategies that operate on a more subtle level are even more incredible.

Take the lowly skunk cabbage, resident of red maple swamps and other wetlands. Skunk cabbage's ability to convert stored food directly into heat allows it to begin flowering despite nighttime temperatures below freezing. The plants' relative warmth also helps spread their distinctive odor, which attracts the pollinating insects critical to their survival.

Birds in the heron family have adopted some amazing hunting techniques. The snowy egret flies just above the water and dangles one foot to stir up the fish on which it preys. The Louisiana water heron spreads its wings and sticks its head under first one, then the other. Biologists suspect that its wings shade the water and attract fish into their illusory protection.

Marsh and swamp rabbits, residents of the hardwood swamps in the southern United States, have evolved fascinating strategies to facilitate their survival. Swamp rabbits have widely splayed feet that enable them to stay on top of wet ground and are such accomplished swimmers that they often elude predators by submerging themselves, leaving only their nostrils exposed. Female marsh rabbits can reabsorb developing embryos into their placentas, when flooding that might imperil their young occurs during the breeding season.

The mysterious complexity of wetland life is both a source of wonder and a testimony to the ingenuity of all species.

fish, herons, snakes, turtles, and raccoons. The cycle continues when birds, mammals, large fish, and other wetland consumers die and the products of their bacterial decomposition enrich the soils that feed the plants.

Predator/Prey Dynamics

The constant and inexorable process of birth and death is essential to the continued health of an environment ("Life in the Fast Lane," p. 152). Humans who "prey" on fish, shellfish, or cranberries are no different than otters eating trout, worms devouring nutrients, or falcons plucking songbirds from shrubbery. In a balanced environment predators and prey evolve a system of checks and balances that maintains species diversity and sustainable population levels. If fish populations aren't culled by birds, mammals, and larger fish, their numbers can grow until their own food resources are threatened. If minks don't prey on muskrats, the rodent population can explode, decimating the marsh vegetation in a few short years.

5 How People Manage Wetlands

We tend to notice the physical and behavioral adaptations species evolve to fit into their environment. But all species also manipulate their environment to make it conform to their needs. Beavers build dams to create wetland ponds and marshes. Muskrats build homes out of wetland reeds. Fiddler crabs dig burrows in tidal flats to hibernate or escape predators. Yet no species comes close to human beings in the ability to alter the environment. It is a basic human drive to improve one's lot. Once the essentials of life (food, shelter, financial security) are assured, we work toward improving our comfort, material wealth, recreational opportunities, and leisure time. These improvements often have environmental implications. In the short span of history since the Industrial Revolution, powerful technologies, broad-scale schemes, and exponential global population growth have led to unprecedented environmental manipulation.

We have built upon and paved over thousands of wetlands. Our dams and irrigation systems have created and removed wet-

Themes

- Human manipulation of wetlands
- Historic wetland decline
- Benefits of sound management
- Wetland law and policy
- The "takings" issue
- Management objectives
- Management options (restoration, acquisition, etc.)
- Case studies: Mississippi flood; Colorado Delta

Recommended Activities

- "Marsh Mystery"
- "Recipe for Trouble"
- "Water Under Foot"
- "Over Hill and Dale"
- "Hydropoly!"
- "Wetland Tradeoffs"
- "A Drop in the Bucket"
- "Regulation Rummy"

Mark Kraus

Hackensack Meadowlands, New Jersey.

lands on a massive scale. By adding pollutants to a watershed, we tax wetlands' capacity to filter impurities and function normally ("Marsh Mystery," p. 116; "Recipe For Trouble," p. 199). Wetlands have been drained for centuries to create agricultural fields and building sites.

Historically, dredging and draining have been a common wetland fate.

Even without humans, wetlands are constantly in a state of flux.

Even without humans, wetlands are constantly in a state of flux. A river meanders across its valley, leaving an oxbow-lake wetland behind. Over many years a pond fills in with vegetation, slowly turning into a peat deposit. Climates gradually shift and either shrink or enlarge existing wetlands. Ocean levels fluctuate, drowning some wetlands and establishing others. In areas with little topographic relief, a drought may completely wither a wetland pond that was brimful only a few months earlier.

Human intervention has dramatically increased the rate of environmental change. Between 1780 and 1980, a period of dramatic population growth and economic progress, 47 million wetland

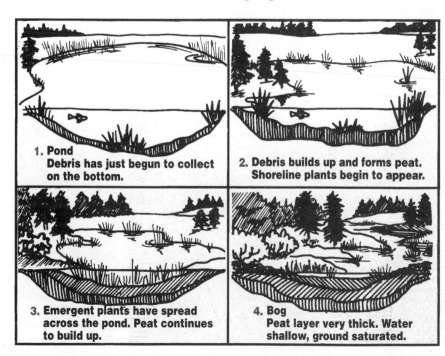

1. **Pond**
Debris has just begun to collect on the bottom.

2. **Debris builds up and forms peat.** Shoreline plants begin to appear.

3. **Emergent plants have spread across the pond. Peat continues to build up.**

4. **Bog**
Peat layer very thick. Water shallow, ground saturated.

hectares (117 million acres) disappeared in the United States, most of it as a direct result of policies that promoted draining. Wetlands that covered an area almost the size of California were lost in two centuries, an eye blink of geologic time.

Between 1964 and 1968, 50,000 hectares (125,000 acres) of prairie pothole wetlands were drained in the states of Minnesota, North Dakota, and South Dakota alone. In the 200 years ending in 1980, California lost 91 percent of its wetlands, Connecticut lost 74 percent, Missouri lost 87 percent, and even the relatively unpopulated state of Nevada lost 52 percent.

Regardless of the debate over economic benefits and environmental responsibility, the net result of human activities on wetlands has been a precipitous drop in their extent worldwide. Puerto Rico has lost 75 percent of its mangrove wetlands, which once covered 24,000 hectares (60,000 acres). In little more than a decade the Philippines lost fully half of its mangrove wetlands to timber harvests. During the decades of economic expansion in the United States, 120,000 to 200,000 hectares (300,000 to 500,000 acres) of wetlands disappeared annually—an area nearly the size of Delaware every three years.

Though humans are, in many ways, no different than any other species competing to survive, we alone are numerous and powerful enough to have a dramatic cumulative impact on the world environment. Fortunately, we are also intelligent enough to be aware of our impact.

Much of our wetland management has been undertaken with the best of intentions. Wetland destruction hasn't been the result of a sinister plot, but rather of countless innocent moves based on good motives—decisions made to create jobs, to expand cities, to insure economic progress, to feed people ("Over Hill and Dale," p. 220). The highway engineers who bisect a wetland don't intentionally disrupt the hydrology of that marsh. The farmer who drains his pothole lakes doesn't mean to bring about a decline in

Major highways cut through the Everglades in Florida.

History of Major Wetland Regulations in the United States

Year	Regulation
1991	Wetlands Reserve Program
1989	North American Wetlands Conservation Act
1988	No Net Loss Policy
1986	Emergency Wetland Resources Act
1985	"Swampbuster" provisions in Food Security Act
1977	Floodplain Management–Executive Order 11988
1977	Protection of Wetlands–Executive Order 11990
1976, 1990	Water Resources Development Act
1974	Federal Aid to Wildlife Restoration Act
1973, 1977	Flood Disaster Protection Act
1972	Coastal Zone Management Act
1972, 1982	Federal Water Pollution Control Act, amended to become the Clean Water Act *Section 404*–dredge & fill permits *Section 402*–pollution discharge elimination system *Section 401*–water quality certification *Section 303*–water quality standards *Section 208*–water quality planning
1969	National Environmental Policy Act
1968	Land & Water Conservation Fund Act
1967	Fish & Wildlife Coordination Act
1934	Migratory Bird Hunting Stamp Act
1929	Migratory Bird Conservation Act
1899	Rivers & Harbors Act

A Glimpse of the National Wetlands Regulation Maze

Clean Water Act, Section 401

Focus

Aims at maintaining water standards for discharge materials dumped in wetlands

Overseeing Agencies

Environmental Protection Agency; state agencies

Rivers & Harbors Act, Sections 9 & 10

Focus

Oversees discharges of solid wastes and construction in navigable waters, including wetlands

Overseeing Agency

U.S. Army Corps of Engineers

Clean Water Act, Section 404

Focus

Issues permits for all dredge and fill activity on U.S. waters, which include most wetlands

Overseeing Agencies

U.S. Army Corps of Engineers; Environmental Protection Agency; U.S. Fish & Wildlife Service

National Environmental Policy Act (NEPA)

Focus

Discloses the effects of federal actions on wetlands

Overseeing Agency

Federal permitting agency

Coastal Zone Management Act

Focus

Develops plans overseeing coastal management issues

Overseeing Agency

Department of Commerce

(continued)

the wild mallard population.

Each decision, taken singly and in a local context, is understandable. These kinds of choices have been made by humans for millennia, and are the kinds of decisions made routinely (even if instinctively) by all other species. It is the cumulative impact of our projects that is unprecedented.

There are compelling reasons to manage wetlands with a long-term commitment. All of the beneficial functions outlined in chapter 3—from flood control to aesthetic refreshment—are enhanced by good management and compromised or lost under poor management. Managed carefully, wetlands will continue to be an essential component of watershed integrity. Managed poorly, wetlands will be degraded or lost, and myriad environmental problems may ensue.

Philosophically at least, we have begun to appreciate the need for wetland stewardship, and that appreciation is reflected in political decisions. The Food Securities Act of 1985 carried a "swampbuster" clause that cut off subsidies to farmers who transform wetlands into croplands. Federal permits are now required before any dredging can proceed or any pollutants can be dumped in wetlands (Sections 404 and 401 of the Clean Water Act). The Emergency Wetlands Resource Act earmarked millions of dollars each year for national wetland acquisition. As an example of international cooperation, the United States and Canada signed the North American Waterfowl Management Plan in 1986, which mandates the acquisition and restoration of wetlands critical to the maintenance of waterfowl populations. Many private associations and conservation groups are active in raising funds, expanding wetlands, and furthering educational efforts on wetlands' behalf.

These efforts are major departures from past management practices. The Swamp Land Act of 1849 typifies the former approach to wetland law and policy. It gave states a free hand over wetland reclamation projects and contributed to an era of tremendous wetland losses. In a reference to this act, the Supreme Court revealed a glimpse of the old attitude:

"If there is any fact which may be supposed to be known by everybody and therefore by the courts, it is that swamps and stagnant waters are the cause of malaria and malignant fevers, and that public power is never more legitimately exercised than in removing such nuisances."

Despite the recent shift in attitude, wetland management is plagued by persistent problems. To begin with, wetlands are regulated through a fragmented array of laws and acts and a variety of agencies. Separate sets of rules and governing agencies operate at the federal, state, and local levels.

Portions of wetlands and wetland activities are not covered under some laws, like the Clean Water Act. A 1991 Government Accounting Office study concluded that Section 404 of the Clean

Water Act covers only 20 percent of the activities that damage wetlands. While Section 404 is commonly thought of in terms of wetland protection, its true focus is the discharge of dredged or fill material into regulated waterways.

Murky and sometimes overlapping statutory definitions make it difficult to determine which wetlands are covered under which law and what human activities are subject to control. This confusing situation, coupled with lack of funding, has made the enforcement of laws problematic. Surveillance to detect unpermitted or illegal activities has been spotty. Because jurisdictions sometimes conflict, even reported crimes can fall through the cracks and escape investigation.

Some government agencies now charged with wetland protection were historically on the other side of the fence. Until recently, the U.S. Army Corps of Engineers, Natural Resources Conservation Service, and Bureau of Reclamation all facilitated wetland drainage. On the other hand, the U.S. Department of the Interior (specifically, the U.S. Fish and Wildlife Service) was charged with protecting wetland waterfowl habitat. Each of these agencies (and others) currently oversee some portion of wetland regulation.

The global state of affairs is even more difficult. The various regions of the world and individual nations within those regions have different and sometimes opposing goals. As a result, international cooperation is still in its infancy. The 1971 Ramsar Convention (Ramsar, Iraq) made a start in this direction by initiating a Convention on Wetlands of International Importance. Since that time, 74 countries have signed on, and a global office has been established in Switzerland. By 1993, 582 Ramsar wetland sites totaling 37 million hectares (92.5 million acres) had been designated.

Worldwide, agricultural conversion has been by far the greatest single cause of wetland loss. In the conterminous United States, 87 percent of wetland losses can be attributed to agricultural conversion. Although this percentage appears to be dropping, urban growth and other pressures are increasing. Two-thirds of the world's population live on coastlines, and the pressure for housing and urban development there is tremendous. The ditching, levees, and drainage projects taken on in the interests of flood control are responsible for more wetland losses. Industrial expansion, transportation corridors, and navigation projects all contribute their share.

The clamor for raw materials, building sites, urban expansion, and agricultural development is loud and clear. The call for wetland preservation, although growing, is often overwhelmed by the cry of those who have reasons to make wetlands useful.

To complicate matters, wetland preservation is rarely an economic benefit, from the landowner's point of view ("Hydropoly!" p. 260). While the broader ecosystem may be better off for wetland preservation, the landowner loses property that might other-

Floodplain Management Program

Focus

Regulates activities that have potential impact on flood levels, with indirect jurisdiction over wetlands

Overseeing Agencies

Shared by all government agencies

"Swampbuster" provisions in Food Security Act

Focus

Denies subsidies to farmers who drain wetlands for crops

Overseeing Agencies

U.S. Department of Agriculture; Natural Resources Conservation Service

On the state and local levels, things get more complex yet! Cities, counties, and states usually have their own sets of regulations and policies governing environmental impact statements, endangered species protection, pollution control, construction permitting, and so on. At every level this network of law, policy, and jurisdiction makes the development of a coherent approach to wetland management a real challenge.

The "Takings" Issue

The "takings" issue revolves around a clause in the Fifth Amendment to the Constitution which states, "nor shall private property be taken for public use without just compensation." It is clear that private lands appropriated for such uses as parking lots, highway interchanges, or parks are covered by this clause.

However, landowner use of most wetlands is simply restricted by protective laws regarding draining, dredging, and so on. In these cases, landowners are limited in the use of their property, even though their land hasn't been designated for public use. Has this land been "taken"? Some property owners think so. In fact, they have felt strongly enough about it to go to court.

A number of court cases have found that even substantial regulation does not constitute a taking. Further, landowners who are able to derive some economic benefit from their total property holdings are not covered by the Fifth Amendment clause, even if the most profitable use of their land is not allowed. For instance, a farmer who is prevented from draining wetlands in a field would not be entitled to compensation, since the rest of his property is in agricultural use.

In the last generation there have been some 400 wetland regulatory court cases. The issue of takings was raised in at least 200 of these. However, in only approximately a dozen cases have wetlands regulations been ruled to be a taking. Furthermore, the vast majority of those cases were decided before 1985, and successful takings cases have been very rare since then.

There are significant gray areas in legal interpretation. Factors like a site's susceptibility to flooding, an area's ecological importance, and restrictions that derive from environmental hazards make each case unique. As long as private ownership conflicts with interests perceived as being for the greater public (or environmental) good, the takings issue, and its court cases, will persist.

(continued)

wise be turned into profitable cropland, real estate, and so on. This issue has spawned a number of "takings" suits in which landowners sue the government or managing agency for compensation for their loss ("Wetland Tradeoffs," p. 285).

In many ways, wetland management is as elusive as wetland

Property development alongside wetlands in this Maine salt marsh.

Susan Higgins

definition. Wetlands are, by nature, environments prone to drastic fluctuations and commonly exist as vaguely delineated transition zones between distinct, well-defined ecosystems. Management schemes must therefore take both a macro and micro approach. The big picture includes oceans, the atmosphere, the global water cycle, and entire watersheds. The small (even microscopic) picture zooms in on bacteria, fungi, tiny crustaceans, fish, and even the levels of carbon or oxygen in plant stems.

Understanding and coping with the factors involved in wetland health is not unlike the challenge faced by meteorologists.

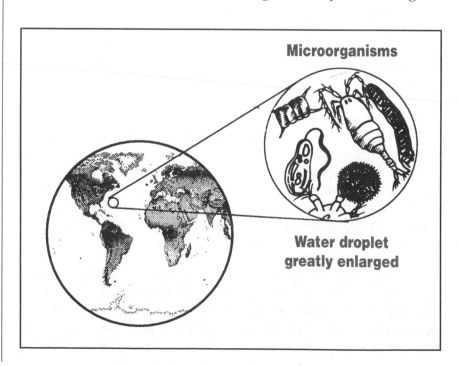

Microorganisms

Water droplet greatly enlarged

Unpredictable events and an ever-changing scene make wetland management as difficult as the forecasting of hurricanes. If you work out a scheme to manage a wetland during its flooded season, for instance, your plan may not be appropriate when things are dry. If you enhance a wetland for its permanent wildlife residents, you may make it unsuitable for migrating or seasonal species. Simply keeping a wetland wet may not be enough. The timing of flooding and drought cycles, and the seasonal changes in a wetland's water depth (its hydroperiod) are critical to the entire spectrum of interactions that take place there.

It's clear that wetland management requires an impressive juggling act. Environmental protection, resource production, recreational use, and aesthetic appeal all have to be considered simultaneously.

The most common objectives driving wetland management plans include ("Hydropoly!" p. 260):

1. maintaining water quality

2. erosion reduction

3. flood protection

4. pollution control

5. enhancing green zones in urban areas

6. maintaining habitat integrity and species diversity

7. furthering recreation and aesthetic benefits for humans

8. resource production (food, fiber, fodder)

9. establishing educational/scientific laboratory sites.

What are Some Management/Stewardship Options?

Mitigation/Creation

Mitigation is the strategy by which a wetland destroyed by a project (highway or dam construction, mining, etc.) is replaced with a comparable human-made wetland in the same region. Mitigation has received increased attention ever since no net loss of wetlands became government policy, and several of these "swaps" have been attempted in California and elsewhere. Wetland creation isn't an entirely modern phenomenon. Artificial wetlands in the form of rice paddies have been created in Asia for centuries, and groups like Ducks Unlimited and the U.S. Fish and Wildlife Service have been in the business of wetland habitat creation for half a century or more.

Wetland creation, however, is tricky science; successful outcomes are by no means assured. As in any environmental manipulation, layer after layer of natural interaction must be considered. Since wetlands are such dynamic ecosystems, it isn't enough to simply make an area wet and then leave it alone. The specific hy-

A Case Synopsis

Loveladies Harbor, Inc. vs. United States

Loveladies Harbor and the government of the United States have been fighting a court battle over a 12.5-acre parcel of land in New Jersey since 1982.

Development on the Loveladies property was begun well before the 1972 enactment of the Clean Water Act's Section 404 permit requirement. In 1981 the company received a state permit to develop the parcel of land, but in 1982 the U.S. Army Corps of Engineers denied the Section 404 permit.

Loveladies Harbor unsuccessfully challenged that denial through the courts until they pursued a takings claim in the Court of Federal Claims. In 1990 they were awarded $2,658,000 in compensation. The government appealed, but in June of 1994 a three-judge panel of the Federal Circuit affirmed the compensation award, with interest.

At this writing the United States is seeking a rehearing, with the support of several environmental groups.

drology, which often involves a cyclical ebb and flow of water, is crucial. Soil, vegetation, topography, and energy webs each impact the potential for success in wetland creation. Long-term study and monitoring are essential to the process of creating self-sustaining wetlands.

Restoration

Restoration is a fancy term for undoing what we have already done. Negative consequences from wetland losses are sometimes dramatic enough to convince us to try to restore the wetlands and their beneficial functions.

In the best cases, restoration requires little more than plugging drainage pipes and allowing the normal hydrologic regime to reestablish itself. At the other extreme, wetlands that have long been buried beneath parking lots and shopping centers are essentially irretrievable.

Most projects fall somewhere between these extremes. If the water regime can be regained, the potential for successful wetland restoration is much improved. Wetland experts have said that if the hydrology is right, the rest will follow.

Even so, it is almost impossible to fully duplicate a lost wetland's complex chemical and biological matrix. Precise balances of salinity and acidity, for example, are extremely difficult to target. From soil composition to the pathways of the energy web, the restoration of compromised natural balances presents formidable challenges. Any restored ecosystem will differ from the original, but can still be a valuable and functioning environment.

In the best cases, restoration requires little more than plugging drainage pipes and allowing the normal hydrologic regime to reestablish itself.

Wetland enhancement projects underway in Montana.

Some goals for successful restoration projects:

1. Restore the hydroperiod (i.e., water flow, flood, or tidal regime).

2. Reestablish the proper wetland topography (shifts in sea level, changes in watershed hydrology, or water diversion may actually

require that the new wetland topography be different from the original).

3. Isolate or control changes in the watershed that may impact restoration.

4. Control outside contamination before it enters the site.

5. Control invasion of undesirable wetland plants (native and non-native).

6. Control wildlife (geese, muskrats, beaver, nutria, wild hogs, and carp are some of the organisms that could destroy the chances of successful restoration).

7. Plan for the impacts of human use (people can be just as damaging as wildlife or undesirable plant species).

8. Choose native plants that:

a) will grow successfully in the new hydrologic regime (not necessarily those historically on the site)
b) are found in wetland communities with a similar hydrology
c) are commercially available (although wild plants are usually cheaper than nursery varieties, collection can be detrimental to natural sites).

9. In your restoration zeal, don't break any laws! Permits are frequently required for aspects of restoration work.

10. Never stop asking questions and seeking assistance. Restoration can be very complicated, but there are often a host of local experts willing to help.

Enhancement
See chapter 6.

Acquisition
The most direct approach to wetlands preservation is to buy wetlands outright. The Nature Conservancy, Ducks Unlimited, and other organizations pursue this strategy, as do some land grant and conservation corridor programs at the local level. Federal agencies such as the Emergency Wetlands Reserve Program actively pursue the direct purchase of millions of dollars worth of wetlands. Even individual landowners can create easements or corridors or make donations to land trusts.

Once acquired, wetlands normally need a continued management effort. Limited hunting and trapping may be necessary to control wildlife populations; invasive plants are often a problem; and simple enhancement steps (see chapter 6) may greatly increase wetland functions and benefits.

A Management Sampler—*Two Case Studies*

In the two scenarios that follow, management involves a deli-

The most direct approach to wetlands preservation is to buy wetlands outright.

cate balancing of a combination of strategies. Both of these watersheds include vast ecosystems and are home to millions of people. Decisions are complex, fraught with consequences, and terribly complicated by the political process ("Hydropoly!" p. 260; "Regulation Rummy," p. 270; "Wetland Tradeoffs," p. 285).

The Colorado River Delta

In 1922 Aldo Leopold (author of *A Sand County Almanac*) spent several weeks camping in the Colorado River Delta near the Sea of Cortez in Mexico. Leopold's journal is full of references to bobcats, wolves, coyotes, deer, wading birds, and waterfowl by the thousands; he describes an abundance of life set in lush wetland vegetation, in a landscape laced with channels, bays, estuaries, lagoons, and marshes:

"Every evening a great flight of cormorants comes into the lagoon from the north, and every morning they go out. Around camp, in camp, and in fact all over are incredible numbers of quail. Also many doves. A few ducks fly over the lagoon.

This night a beaver kept slapping the river right by camp. Sounded like a large heavy boulder plumping into the water. We have a grass bed and sleep with great comfort."

Goats drink from the last of the Colorado River in Mexico.

Since that time the river delta has essentially dried up. The Colorado River watershed is managed and controlled until it disappears. For significant periods, no water reaches the sea. Even when a little survives the gauntlet of irrigators, thirsty cities, and reservoir evaporation, it is a muddy, salt-laden, pesticide-laced trickle.

The Colorado River, along with tributaries that make up a watershed the size of France, is harnessed to a heroic task. These waters, flowing through a landscape otherwise arid and sere, supply the needs of more than 20 million people and 800,000 hectares (two million acres) of farmland. The watershed serves seven states and two countries in a basin covering 634,400 square kilometers (244,000 square miles).

"Every evening a great flight of cormorants comes into the lagoon from the north, and every morning they go out. Around camp, in camp, and in fact all over are incredible numbers of quail. Also many doves. A few ducks fly over the lagoon.

This night a beaver kept slapping the river right by camp. Sounded like a large heavy boulder plumping into the water. We have a grass bed and sleep with great comfort."

-Aldo Leopold

In 1922, the same year as Leopold's trip, the Colorado River Compact established water allocation among seven western states. Since then the Colorado has been plugged by dams, funneled into vast canals, pumped into irrigation systems, diverted to provide drinking water for cities, and run through some 30 hydroelectric plants. A 1944 treaty with the Mexicans belatedly guaranteed them 1.5 million acre-feet every year. But the water reaching Mexico is often so saline (a result of repeated irrigation) that it far exceeds potable levels.

Allocation figures are based on an annual flow of 16.5 million acre-feet, but since 1930 the Colorado has averaged only 14 million. Evaporation from reservoirs behind scores of dams accounts for an additional loss of two million acre-feet. Until now, several states have consistently underused their allocations to make up this inherent shortfall.

Traditionally, 80 percent of the Colorado River's water has been diverted for irrigation. With burgeoning urban centers like Las Vegas, Nevada demanding a greater share of the remainder, it is only a matter of time before the waters of the Colorado are completely withdrawn. For the delta, that day has already come. An oasis rich with wetland life only two generations ago has long since been turned into an arid ghost of the place Aldo Leopold enjoyed.

Wetlands and Flood Control on the Mississippi River

The year 1993 will long be remembered as the year of the Great Mississippi River Flood. Week after week, rains kept swollen tributaries out of their banks and saturated the systems of earthen levees. The Mississippi River finally overtopped its containment walls, breached levees, and sent unprecedented floodwaters raging through towns, covering field after cropland field with silty water.

Billions of dollars have been spent keeping the Mississippi from flooding over its banks and from making natural migrations across its floodplain. As long ago as the early 1700s, elaborate systems of levees and channels were established along this watershed. Levees and channels, by definition, deny the associated floodplain its water. Most of the ten million hectares (25 million acres) of wetlands lost along the Mississippi floodplain since 1780 have been settled or turned to agriculture. The river itself has been elevated and straightened, thereby increasing the velocity of the current and exacerbating the potential for flood damage. The stage was set for the 1993 disaster, when artificial controls were overwhelmed, and the security that people had come to take for granted was abruptly stripped away.

Since then, arguments have raged over wetlands' capacity to lessen flood damage. Wetland scientists claim that an acre of wetland will retain two acre-feet of flood water. Conservative estimates place the 1993 flood surge at about 22 million acre-feet. If these experts are correct, a simple calculation reveals that roughly

The Colorado River disappears into the sand a few miles south of the Mexican border.

4.5 million hectares, or 11 million acres of wetland would have been required to soak the 1993 flood up. Advocates of wetland flood control assert that retained wetlands would have softened much of the effect of the flood, and that people wouldn't have been lured into settling on the vulnerable floodplain in the first place if it hadn't been for the security offered by "flood-proof" levee systems.

Some water managers refute the practicality of the wetland approach. They argue that wetlands, too, would have been overwhelmed by the volume and severity of the 1993 flood (a one-in-500-years event, by some estimates). Further, they point to the logistical difficulties involved in relocating cities and farms and reestablishing former wetlands.

The argument continues, but no one can deny the staggering costs of the Mississippi watershed strategy. Billions of dollars were spent on the system of dams, levees, and artificial channels. Billions more are required for disaster relief, rebuilding, and repairs.

Floods are natural events that will occur no matter what controls are in place, but most parties agree that wetlands play at least some role in flood control.

Floods are natural events that will occur no matter what controls are in place, but most parties agree that wetlands play at least some role in flood control. The U.S. Department of Agriculture's Natural Resources Conservation Service (NRCS) is charged with rehabilitating more than 3,200,000 hectares (eight million acres) of flood-damaged farmland. The option of converting much of this acreage to wetlands is enticing, especially in light of the high cost of returning it to crops.

The Emergency Wetlands Reserve Program has embarked on an ambitious effort to convince flooded farmers to enroll appropriate acreage in the wetland reserve. Qualifying land (much of which, historically, was wetland) could reach totals of more than 40,000 hectares (100,000 acres). The rewards of these re-established wetlands might include flourishing wildlife, cleaner water, and reduced crop- and flood-insurance claims. After the 1993 flood, crop-insurance claims alone totaled nearly $1 billion!

courtesy of United States Army Corps of Engineers

Amphibious aircraft were what the St. Joseph, Missouri, airport needed during the 1993 flooding!

52

Action for Wetlands

One hundred years ago, a voice raised in defense of wetland preservation would have been a lonely sound indeed. Now there is a growing chorus of concern. Growing numbers of farmers in the prairie pothole region are choosing to save their wetlands rather than drain them. Urban centers are considering using wetlands as green space or as a component of sewage treatment facilities. Landowners are enhancing and restoring small wetlands. Politicians, the media, and private citizens are all starting to tune in to wetland issues. The combined membership of environmental organizations that preserve and protect wetlands—The Nature Conservancy, Ducks Unlimited, the Sierra Club, the Izaak Walton League, and others—numbers in the millions.

Scores of newspaper stories, magazine articles, newsletters, and books are devoted to wetland advocacy. Programs like the Environmental Protection Agency's "Adopt-A-Wetland," the Izaak Walton League's "Wetland Watch," and the U.S. Fish and Wildlife Service's "Partners For Wildlife" have actively promoted wetland enhancement and protection.

Themes

- Gathering wetland information
- Getting involved on wetlands' behalf
- Wetland enhancement strategies
- Educators and wetlands
- Wetland field trip
- Wetland sampling kit
- Interdisciplinary approach to wetland study

Recommended Activities

- "Let the Cattail Out of the Bag!"
- "Regulation Rummy"
- "Introducing Wetlands"
- "Over Hill and Dale"
- "Tracking Plants and Keeping Track"
- "Water We Have Here?"
- "This Plant Key Is All Wet!"
- "Hear Ye! Hear Ye!"
- "Helping Wetland Habitats"
- "Get Involved!"

Greg Neudecker

Wetlands and development co-exist in this overview of Montana landscape.

National Wetland Inventory Maps

Known collectively as the National Wetland Inventory (NWI), these maps are similar to the topographic quadrangles used by hikers, bikers, and other outdoor enthusiasts. They are produced by the U.S. Fish & Wildlife Service (FWS) and distributed by the U.S. Geological Survey. NWI maps correspond geographically to topographic maps and go by the same names (usually the largest community or most prominent landform on the sheet). Whereas topographic maps provide information about the lay of the land (elevation base lines), the primary information in the NWI is the identification of wetland areas.

The FWS uses the following wetland classification system:

Marine: saltwater tidal wetlands (e.g., beaches, coral reefs)

Estuarine: estuarine and brackish water tidal wetlands (e.g., salt marshes, tidal rivers, mangrove swamps)

Riverine: flowing fresh water wetlands (e.g., along water channels)

Lacustrine: nontidal wetlands fringing deep, standing water (e.g., lakes, deep ponds)

Palustrine: wide variety of inland, nontidal wetlands (e.g., swamps, marshes, bogs, shallow ponds).

(continued)

National Wetland Inventory maps are valuable tools in any organized attempt to study or identify wetland areas.

This is evidence of a significant shift in public attitude. Teachers, students, and citizens play a critical role in the process of wetland education and stewardship.

This chapter focuses on concrete steps that citizens, teachers, and students can take to gather information, involve themselves in the wetland political debate ("Hear Ye! Hear Ye!" p. 253), and study and enhance wetlands directly.

A Citizen's Wetland Action Guide

Inform Yourself ("Get Involved!" p. 310)

1. Send for a National Wetland Inventory Map, produced by the U.S. Fish and Wildlife Service and sold by the Earth Science Information Center of the U.S. Geological Survey. To order one for your area, call 1-800-USA-MAPS or send a check (made out to USGS-DOI) to USGS, ESIC, 507 National Center, Reston, VA 22092.

2. State wetland maps are often available through state fish and wildlife service and county soil and conservation district offices. Remember that each mapping office has its own set of criteria and target audience, so the maps may not always correspond.

3. Soil maps drawn by soil and conservation districts over the last half century indicate likely wetland sites. Any areas marked "poorly drained" or "very poorly drained" point out potential wetlands.

4. Join local and national groups concerned with wetland stewardship. Their newsletters are full of information (see Resources, p. 326).

5. Research local wetland vegetation and wildlife species. Government offices like state departments of natural resources, the U.S. Fish and Wildlife Service, and the U.S. Environmental Protection Agency may be able to provide field guides or wetland species inventories. University science departments may also be helpful. Field guides to plants, birds, and animals are available in libraries and bookstores.

6. Call the Environmental Protection Agency Wetlands Hotline (1-800-832-7828) for sources of wetland information and a list of state contacts.

7. Contact the U.S. Fish and Wildlife Service or U.S. Department of Agriculture to investigate federal and local wetland preservation programs.

Involve Yourself

1. Stay abreast of community wetland issues and attend permit hearings and important land use meetings ("Hear Ye! Hear Ye!" p. 253).

2. Make presentations about the importance of wetland functions and/or take field trips to local wetland sites with school groups,

landowners, bird-watchers, and other citizens. Firsthand observation of a wetland can leave a powerful impression. Activities like fishing, clamming, and bird-watching will add fun to the learning experience.

PUBLIC HEARING TODAY

3. Once you have identified your local wetlands, several courses of action are possible:
• organize a cleanup effort to remove trash (and have a picnic afterward)
• encourage people who own land near wetlands to consider conservation easements or land donations. Organizations like The Nature Conservancy, the Trust for Public Land, and local land trusts are experienced in these transactions
• coordinate a wetland enhancement project ("Helping Wetland Habitats," p. 288)
• promote wetland nature centers or sanctuaries in partnership with local conservation groups.

4. Support wetland conservation by buying federal duck stamps and wildlife conservation stamps.

5. Contact government representatives about local wetland management topics. Address letters to: (senator), U.S. Senate, Washington, DC 20510 and (representative), U.S. House of Representatives, Washington, DC 20515.

6. Get involved in the federal and state permitting processes. State environmental agencies publish regulation guidelines. Public review and comment by local citizens are integral parts of the permitting process in Section 404 of the Clean Water Act ("Regulation Rummy," p. 270).

Some Wetland Enhancement Basics

In pristine settings wetlands do perfectly well on their own without any "help" from well-intentioned humans. As any management professional will tell you, the most well-meaning tampering can lead to unforeseen side effects. It may seem beneficial to introduce exotic species, stock fish in a pond, or alter the flow of water, but these sorts of actions may start a chain of consequences that results in harmful effects such as eutrophication or species invasion.

Also, what appeals to us may not be what is best for a wetland and its inhabitants. Too often, enhancement is for the benefit of human beings rather than the ecosystem. We might hanker for a

Each of these five major groups is subdivided into smaller classes, and each wetland is described by a code that can be interpreted with the legend (key) on the map. For example, a wetland with the code P-FO-1-H is a Palustrine, Forested, Broad-leaved Deciduous tree, Permanently flooded wetland. In other words, this is a freshwater forested wetland that has some surface flooding all year and a predominance of deciduous trees. The code R-4-SB-2 means Riverine, Intermittent, Stream bank, Sandy bottom. This is a stream with a sandy bottom that dries up during part of the year. There are many more combinations.

These maps provide an excellent opportunity to utilize (or teach) map-reading skills while investigating local wetlands and are a valuable resource for showing students where a variety of local wetlands can be found. Using NWI maps, teachers and students can locate the wetlands closest to the school, each student's home, and so on.

NWI maps are based on aerial photo interpretation and ground sampling. Much of the country has been mapped. The maps can be ordered on paper or mylar, and versions with both wetland and topographic information are sometimes available. All maps show the location of local roads, prominent buildings, and bodies of water.

fish pond in the middle of a marsh, but that pond will almost certainly change the marsh hydrology and have other consequences.

Study a wetland for indications of the need for enhancement. Look for a lack of plant diversity, signs (or lack thereof) of wildlife, evidence of erosion or sediment (cloudiness) in the water. These clues will point to the most beneficial enhancement steps.

Include your community in the enhancement process. Enlist the help of Scouts, 4-H, an Audubon Society chapter, or local engineering or construction firms to expand community involvement in the project. Be sure to obtain appropriate permissions from landowners or government agencies before starting to work.

With this advice in mind, consider the following:

Vegetation Plantings

Vegetation has a stabilizing effect on wetland soils and improves water retention and pollution filtering. Wildlife use vegetation for food, shelter, and building materials. However, if your wetland already has dense plant growth, it is probably a mistake to add more. Don't force vegetation on parts of a wetland that are natural clearings. Study the site for signs of erosion and other damage caused by vegetation loss, and be sure to select native plants that would normally appear in that wetland. (Garden centers and plant books are good sources of information.)

Removal of exotic or noxious vegetation may also be appropriate. County extension offices have information on these plants, as well as recommendations for removal. **Herbicides should be used with great caution, especially near water.**

courtesy of Coastal Zone Management, Cape Cod Regional Office, Massachusetts

Creating Buffer Zones

Wetlands merge into the surrounding environments gradually. If it is possible to enlarge the buffer zone around a wetland, it is almost always beneficial to do so. Don't establish lawns or build right to the edge of a wetland. If lawns or cultivated areas are already there, consider letting a border area return to its natural state.

It may be necessary to plant appropriate native species in reclaimed buffer zones.

Exclude or Limit Domesticated Animals and Pets

Horses, cattle, and free-roaming dogs and cats are foreign species in a delicate wildlife matrix. Spring is a particularly vulnerable time for wetland species. If exclusion of pets is impossible, ask pet owners to put bells on cat and dog collars, and take steps like wrapping sheet metal around tree trunks to keep cats from climbing after birds.

Wildlife control may be necessary as well. Unchecked populations of carp, geese, nutria, and other species are capable of decimating a wetland.

Restrict Off-Road Vehicles

Wildlife Habitat Additions

Birdhouses, nesting boxes and platforms, and feeding stations will attract birds to a wetland. Local birding organizations can offer advice about species-specific structures. Tree stumps, dead

A worker grades an embankment at a wetland near a Montana highway.

The Section 404 Permitting Process

1. Applicant completes engineer Form 4345 and submits it to the district office of the U.S. Army Corps of Engineers.

2. After processing, a public notice is issued.

3. Thirty-day comment period, open to review by:
   - U.S. Army Corps of Engineers
   - individuals and special interest groups
   - local agencies
   - state agencies
   - federal agencies

4. Public hearing (in some cases), during which factors such as the following may be assessed:
   - economics
   - aesthetics, recreation, and environmental concerns
   - historic value
   - flood control
   - water quality and supply
   - food and resource production
   - navigation

5. Application either approved or denied.

6. If approved, applicant signs off and returns form.

7. Permit issued.

Interdisciplinary Approaches to Wetlands

The most obvious avenue to wetland study is through the scientific disciplines. But there is wonderful potential in wetland sites for lessons in geography, social science, writing, photography, and other fields. Here are some ideas to start with.

Political Science/Economics

Almost every significant wetland area has been the subject of the permitting process, landowner conflicts, or arguments between economic developers and conservationists. Have a class debate the economic benefits of development versus the benefits of preservation. Look at the short-term and long-term pictures. Take a field trip to explore the significance of a wetland's values and to study the effects that development might have (or already has had). Have the class go through a mock permitting process (see p. 57) and compare their results with the actual outcome, if possible. If there is a current controversy over a wetland, research news clippings, attend town meetings, and make a wetland field study to amass pertinent information.

Writing/Photography/Art

Take a "journaling" field trip to a wetland. Have students find a quiet spot to sit still and observe the surroundings. Encourage them to spend at least 20 minutes just observing, then have them describe their surroundings, their feelings, the weather. They should use input from all their senses. Students who enjoy drawing can illustrate their journals. A photography class can conduct a similar field trip and create a wetland photo album or slide show. Follow up with visits at different seasons and different times of day.

snags, and small brush piles offer shelter, perching sites, and homes for birds and other animals. A few strategic placements (one per hectare, or two per acre) can help attract wildlife (see "Helping Wetland Habitats," p. 288).

Trails and Boardwalks

These access corridors encourage human enjoyment of a wetland while restricting traffic to specific strips. A trail around the periphery of a wetland will be less disruptive than one into the center. Boardwalks are necessary where natural trails become rutted with overuse and where abundant water makes walking difficult. During the breeding and nesting seasons, it may be prudent to limit or close off access.

A Blind

Simple blinds built either in a tree or on the ground can allow people to "disappear" from the view of birds and other wildlife and quietly observe wetland residents.

More intrusive "enhancement" measures such as fish stocking, aggressive landscaping, and extensive planting are complicated and delicate operations that should be attempted only in cases of severe wetland degradation. Even then, expert consultation and assistance is a must.

Susan Higgins

An Educator's Action Guide

Educators are in a pivotal position to promote awareness of wetland functions and benefits. Teachers, refuge managers, park interpretive staff, and nature center workers come in contact with large numbers of people and can have more impact on public awareness than most citizens.

Besides, why study diagrams on a blackboard in a stuffy classroom when a nearby wetland has it all in living color, waiting for your class to arrive? The student who digs a soil profile hole to discover the characteristics of the soil horizon, is far more likely to

Mark Schilling, a wetland educator, leads a WOW! *workshop for a group of teachers.*

Alice Hanley

remember that experience than the student who studies a text-book diagram ("Wet 'n' Wild," p. 99). It may even be possible for a class to create its own wetland in the classroom ("Wetlands in the Classroom!" p. 80; "People of the Bog," p. 266), then establish a site on school grounds (see Planning and Developing a Schoolyard Wetland Habitat, appendix).

Find a Wetland to Study

1. Use map sources listed on p. 329 to locate prominent wetlands in your area.

2. Brainstorm a list of local wetland sites with students. Remind them to consider water, soil, and vegetation when thinking of likely places (see chapter 2).

courtesy of Coastal Zone Management, Cape Cod Regional Office, Massachusetts

History

Study a local wetland through the historic record. Research old accounts of settlers, explorers, and early travelers to see how the wetland was viewed, and how it was utilized over time. How did the Native Americans in your region use it? What did they call it? Has there been resource exploitation there? Is there still? How has the local view of the wetland evolved, or has it? Was it a barrier to settlement? A benefit to the local economy?

Jump ahead 50 years and imagine how things will have changed in your region. What role will the wetland play then? How might people view it?

Take a field trip and explore. Look for cultural artifacts. Encourage the class to imagine coming upon it for the first time and having to cross it or look for a place to build.

Math

Conduct a mapping exercise to chart the extent and topography of a wetland. Calculate plant density by taking sample plot censuses and extrapolating. Use math to figure stream velocity, acidity levels, and water quality. Figure the percentage of wetland area on a Wetland Inventory Map.

Social Studies/Geography

If a local wetland has been a dumping ground, organize a clean-up field trip and then make a trash study. How long has trash been dumped there? What sorts of things do people discard there and why? Can you detect the time periods of heaviest dumping?

Brainstorm ways that a wetland can become a community resource such as a wildlife-viewing blind or nature trail. Encourage the class to develop a proposal for wetland improvements to present to city or county commissioners.

3. Potential wetland study sites include:
- the edges of ponds, streams, and permanent bodies of water
- tidal zones along coastlines
- topographic depressions that are typically wet and muddy long after rains
- temporary bodies of water that are wet for weeks at a time
- drainage ditches that are frequently wet
- sites with obvious wetland vegetation (cattails, rushes, etc.).

4. Don't overlook urban and suburban locations for wetland islands. Even construction sites may offer newly dug ponds used to filter and control runoff. Wetland plantings in such places can be very helpful.

Paul D. McIver

Riparian wetland habitat in eastern Colorado.

Some Field Trip Tips

1. Visit the wetland at least once before the class trip to work through travel and parking logistics, the feasibility of planned activities, and landowner permissions.

2. If students don't know each other, make name tags.

3. Have enough leaders and planned activities to keep everyone busy.

4. Make alternate plans for bad weather.

5. Plan pre-visit activities that will prepare students and post-visit activities to follow up. Making the sampling equipment is a good pre-visit exercise and will familiarize students with sampling devices. See pp. 62-67 and "Wet 'n' Wild," p. 99).

6. Hand out a list of items for students to bring (see p. 61).

7. Review the itinerary and your expectations with the group beforehand, and again when you arrive at the site.

8. Bring a camera, binoculars, and a simple first-aid kit.

9. Consider alerting local media about your field trip. Students enjoy the attention and publicity.

The Sentinel Daily News • Friday, May 13, 1994 • **C3**

Fiddler's Run Hosts Young Discoverers
Fifth Grade Students Explore Wetland Preserve

Dante Bradford, 11, left, and Timothy Andrews, 10, of Rays Point Elementary immerse themselves in their study of the creek at Fiddlers Run marsh.

10. During the field trip, schedule pauses to discuss problems and findings and to allow for food or bathroom breaks.

11. If possible, plan several wetland visits. The first will provide an introductory experience, while subsequent trips will expand and reinforce concepts.

Student Checklist
- wettable shoes/boots (waders are ideal, but not always available)
- a change of clothes and shoes
- appropriate weather gear (jacket, rain gear, hat, sunglasses)
- insect repellent, if necessary (nonaerosol)
- rubber gloves (optional— for bottom sampling)
- appropriate clothing (quick-drying materials like polyester and nylon are better than wool and cotton)
- bag lunches (marked with students' names)
- trash bag

If possible, plan several wetland visits. The first will provide an introductory experience, while subsequent trips will expand and reinforce concepts.

A Basic Wetland Sampling Kit

High-quality sampling equipment can cost thousands of dollars, an investment that makes wetland study prohibitive for most school budgets.* Fortunately, low-cost devices can be constructed at minimal expense using common household materials and other inexpensive supplies. Students can help gather materials and construct sampling gear themselves. The exercise will heighten student interest, acquaint students with the equipment's operation, and assure that they have a personal investment in the field trip's success.

Use the following devices in conjunction with such activities as "Water We Have Here?" "Wet 'n' Wild," and "Tracking Plants and Keeping Track." Even simple sampling tools add an important information-gathering component to wetland field trips and help students appreciate the complexity and variation inherent in wetland systems.

*If extensive wetland study over a period of years is planned, you may consider purchasing a Munsell™ soil color book and a soil probe from Ben Meadows Co., Inc., P.O. Box 80549, Chamblee, GA 30366 (800/628-2068). These items range in price from $50-$100.

Instructions for Making Simple Wetland Sampling Equipment

The following material has been adapted from booklets prepared by the Tennessee Valley Authority and is used here with their permission. The original artwork was produced by Claudia Denton.

Deep Water Sampler
(for collecting water at desired depths)

Materials
- 1 clear plastic milk or beverage bottle, preferably with handle
- nylon rope (long enough for sampling desired depths)
- rubber stopper (to fit bottle)
- eyehook bolt/screw (large enough for rope to pass through)
- drill with 1/4-inch bit
- electrical or duct tape
- small rock
- scissors
- yardstick

Directions
1. Drill hole in rubber stopper, screw in eyehook, and tie rope onto the eyehook, leaving a 15- to 20-centimeter (6- to 8-inch) tail.

2. Attach tail of rope to bottle handle or around bottleneck. If you wrap around the neck, use tape to secure the rope in place.

3. Use yardstick to mark 30-centimeter (1-foot) increments on the rope, starting at the mouth of the bottle. Mark increments with pieces of tape.

Deep Water Sampler

4. Cut a 60-centimeter (2-foot) piece of rope to tie around the rock. Secure the rope with rock attached around the base of the bottle with tape.

How To Use

Lower the bottle gently to the desired depth, making sure the stopper is in place. A sharp tug on the line will pop the stopper out, and the bottle will fill with water. Wait several minutes and gently pull the bottle up. Empty the contents into a clean sampling jar and store in an ice-filled cooler until you can perform the water quality tests. Don't store more than 24 hours.

Deep Water Sampler

Secchi Disk
(for measuring the turbidity, or clarity, of water—see "Water We Have Here?" p. 174)

Plankton Samplers
(for collecting plankton—see "Wet 'n' Wild," p. 99)

D-Net
(for collecting aquatic invertebrates and fish)

Materials
- 4 pieces of nylon netting 25 centimeters x 30 centimeters (10 inches x 12 inches)
- 2.5-centimeter (1-inch) bias tape or equivalent fabric scrap 100 centimeters (40 inches) long
- thread
- scissors
- sewing machine
- wire coat hanger
- wire cutters
- drill with 1/4-inch bit
- broom handle or wooden dowel a bit more than 1 meter (4 feet) long
- pliers
- duct tape

Directions

1. Cut netting into four triangular pieces 25 centimeters (10 inches) high with 30-centimeter (12-inch) bases and sew together as shown.

2. Cut a 100-centimeter (40-inch) strip of bias tape or fabric to make casing and sew onto net opening, leaving casing open to insert wire frame.

3. Take a wire coat hanger and untwist, slip into net casing, and retwist. Cut twisted stem of hanger to two inches with wire cutters.

4. Drill hole in broom handle or dowel and insert stem as shown.

5. Take one of the remaining pieces of coat hanger, cut it, and bend it in a U shape as shown.

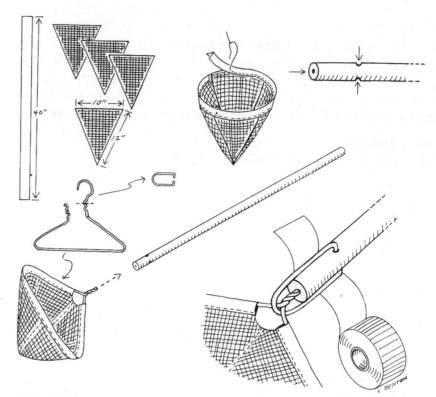

6. Drill shallow holes on opposite sides of the handle, push in the ends of U-shaped hanger as shown, and wrap with tape.

How to Use

   Place the net firmly on the stream bottom, making sure the net is flowing downstream. A second person standing upstream should scrub rocks and/or dig into the stream bottom in front of the net. Since slippery rocks, broken glass, or other sharp objects may be on the bottom, make sure participants are wearing sturdy shoes and that they take care with their footing. Invertebrates will be swept into the net. Use a scooping motion to lift the net out of the water. Deposit the contents of the net into a sampling jar or pan.

Plastic Bottle Dredge
(for collecting invertebrates in bottom mud)

Materials
• plastic bottle with handle and screw-on lid
• scissors or sharp knife
• large nail
• oven mitt or protective glove
• matches or lighter

Directions
1. Screw the lid on securely. Cut bottle as shown.

2. Using a hot nail (as shown), poke holes in the plastic bottle. Make sure to use protective glove or mitt when handling the hot nail (teacher may want to handle this step).

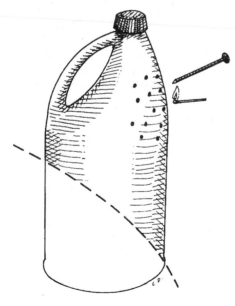

Plastic Bottle Dredge

How to Use

Holding the bottle handle, scoop up bottom sediments. Empty contents of dredge into a sieve (or into a wide-mouth plastic jar for storage). To collect any organisms, use a hose or bucket of water to wash away sediment. Use forceps to remove any remaining organisms from the sieve and store them in a sampling jar or pan.

Algae Sampler
(used in streams to collect attached algae)

Materials
- 4 microscope slides
- 1 brick
- waterproof adhesive
- fishing line
- bobber
- scissors

Directions

1. Tear off eight small pieces of waterproof adhesive and roll into balls about the size of peas.

2. Attach microscope slide to brick by placing two pieces of adhesive on each end of slide, then pressing firmly onto the brick until stuck tightly.

3. Repeat with remaining three slides.

4. Tie one end of the fishing line around the brick and the other end to the bobber (the bobber will mark the brick's location under the water).

How to Use

Place brick flat on the bottom in relatively clear, shallow water. (In waters with heavy silt, orient the brick on its end so sediment won't quickly cover slides.) Leave for two to four weeks before collecting, at which time you should find algae growth on the slides. When transporting and storing the brick, don't let the slides dry out. Carry in a bucket with water from the stream and store in a cooler filled with ice. Don't store more than 24 hours.

Wire Basket Sampler
(for collecting a representative sample of invertebrates by providing a surface for them to colonize)

Materials
- 75-centimeter x 75-centimeter (30-inch x 30-inch) piece of window screening
- tin snips
- yardstick
- wire or heavy nylon thread
- scissors
- rocks

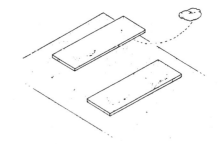

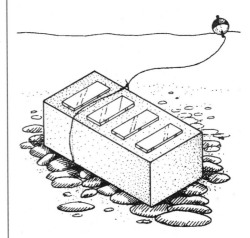

Algae Sampler

Directions

1. Use tin snips to cut screen into shape shown.

2. Fold up sides and sew together with wire or nylon thread.

3. Fill basket with fist-sized rocks.

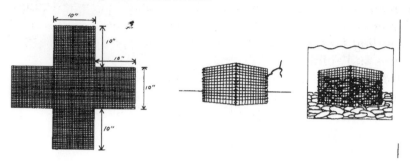

How to Use

Place or lower the sampler to desired depth and hold in place with a stake or heavy rock. Leave for three to six weeks. To collect the organisms, raise the sampler slowly with a dip net underneath to catch any loose organisms. Put the sampler into a bucket or tub, open it, and empty out the rocks. To remove clinging organisms, rinse the sampler and scrub each rock with a stiff brush. The sample can be concentrated using a sieve and then stored in a sampling jar. To store/preserve the sample, replace the water with a 70 percent ethanol preservative (NOT rubbing alcohol).

Dip Net
(for collecting aquatic invertebrates and small fish)

Materials
- wire kitchen strainer with handle
- broom handle or wooden dowel 1 meter, 30-centimeters (4-feet) long
- electrical or duct tape
- scissors

Directions

1. Mount strainer on broom handle with tape as shown.

How to Use

Move the net from side to side in the water with a sweeping motion, working your way deeper into the mud or gravel at the bottom, or scoop up swimming invertebrates and fish. Periodically empty the contents of the net into a sampling pan. Check the net for movement and remove organisms with forceps.
WARNING: Some states require permits to use nets to trap fish. Check with your state wildlife agency before your field trip.

Underwater Viewer
(for viewing aquatic organisms—see "Wet 'n' Wild," p. 102)

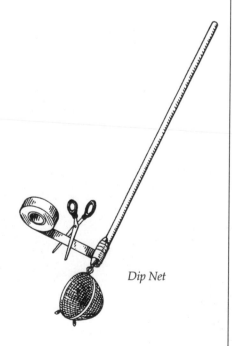

Dip Net

Miscellaneous Sampling or Study Supplies

Hand Lens: for magnifying small aquatic plants and animals in the field

Cooler: for preserving water samples and live fish

Sampling Pan: for sorting and counting aquatic invertebrates

Thermometer: for measuring water temperature

Sampling Jars: for collecting water samples and storing aquatic plants and animals

Eyedropper: to remove small specimens from water samples

Forceps: for removing and studying larger specimens

Probe: for manipulating and dissecting specimens

Hand Lens

Cooler

Sampling Pan

Thermometer

Sampling Jars

Eyedropper

Forceps

Probe

II
Part

The Activities

Section

1

So This Is a Wetland!

A series of activities designed to introduce general wetland concepts and definitions. These are good activities to choose from when beginning a wetland study unit.

Introducing Wetlands

Grade Level
K-12

Subject Areas
Biology, Art,
Earth Science, Math,
Social Studies, Music

Duration
Variable

Setting
Classroom and
outdoors

Skills
Depends on activity
chosen

Charting the Course
Try "Let the Cattail Out
of the Bag!"and "Wetland
Metaphors" after this
activity, then explore
details about wetland
functions, plants, animals,
soils, and issues through
other *WOW!* activities.

Vocabulary
wetland, environment,
hydric soils, hydrophytic
plants, marsh, swamp, bog

Summary

What is a wetland, anyway?

Before getting into the nitty-gritty of wetland studies, your students may need an introduction to wetlands, or even to the outdoors, on a more casual level. This collection of warm-ups and icebreakers will get you started.

Objectives

Students will:

- become aware of the characteristics of a wetland and learn that wetlands are defined by the presence of water, specialized soils, and hydrophytic plants.

- become comfortable in outdoor settings and use their senses to observe nature.

Materials

Materials vary. See the following individual icebreaker ideas.

Making Connections

Students may have heard the term *wetland* and many may have visited wetland sites. However, they may not know exactly what wetlands are. The series of icebreakers that follows will orient students to wetland environments and provide ways to assess students' present knowledge, interest, and preconceptions.

Background

With the help of legends, fictional stories, and the film industry, wetlands have been touted throughout history as mosquito-breeding, malodorous wastelands fit only for monsters and other unsavory creatures. For kids, that translates into "stinky" and "scary." Today, as we gain more

knowledge of the beauty and benefits of wetlands, we are drawing the line between make-believe and reality, and the monster images are fading.

So, what is a wetland, anyway? Wetlands are basically *wet lands*. They are often transition zones between dry lands and deep water, but some are more isolated. The most common types of wetlands are swamps, bogs, and marshes. Students may know other types by a variety of names: mire, fen, moor, muskeg, prairie pothole, bottomland, riparian wetland, wet meadow, slough, playa lake, and Delmarva bay. What these have in common is what defines them as wetlands: *water*, *special soil*, and specialized plants called *hydrophytes* (water loving). The interactions of these three characteristics are what make one kind of wetland distinct from another. See chapter 2 for additional information.

Some interesting facts about wetlands:

- Water is present at or near the ground's surface all or part of the time, even for as few as seven consecutive days.

- Depth, duration, and frequency of flooding vary from wetland to wetland.

- Wetlands may be tidal or nontidal (unaffected by oceanic tides) and may contain fresh, salt, or brackish water.

- Wetlands may be any size or shape, from a low spot in a field that covers a few hundred square feet to an expansive marsh that covers several hundred square miles.

- Wetlands are found on every continent except Antarctica and in every climate from the tropics to the tundra. They may be in coastal or inland areas, along ponds or rivers, in agricultural fields, or even in cities.

- Wetlands may be pristine natural areas or may have been "built" by people. Many have been disturbed, to one degree or another, by human activity.

- Wetlands provide many benefits. (See chapter 3.)

Procedure
Warm Up
Ask students to describe what they think wetlands are, and what makes them unique. Make a list of wetland characteristics on the board to revise later as students learn more. (See "Getting Oriented," next page.)

The Activity
Choose from the following icebreakers for a fun introduction to wetlands (age group varies).

Note: The Likes and Dislikes, Treasure Hunt, and Use Your Ears icebreakers focus on becoming familiar with the environment in general, and are not specific to wetlands.

Wrap Up and Action
Ask students to review the list they made on the board and revise it based on what they have learned.

Have students create a Wonders Of Wetlands display. In it, they can identify qualities of wetlands (likes and dislikes) and describe why people might want to visit a wetland.

Assessment
Have students:

- identify factors that define a wetland.

- compare their thoughts and feelings about wetlands before and after they were introduced to them.

Extensions
Once students are comfortable with their surroundings, you can plunge into more specific learning by continuing on to other *WOW!* activities or organizing a field trip.

Resources
Mitsch, William, and James Gosselink. 1993. *Wetlands.* New York: Van Nostrand Reinhold.

National Geographic 171, no. 3 (March 1987).

The Icebreakers:
Likes and Dislikes
(Materials: paper and pencil)

Have each student make a list of things that he or she likes and dislikes about the environment. Because the term *environment* may mean different things to different students (e.g., a neighborhood, the yard at home, the world, or even the school building—the immediate environment), let them choose their own definitions. After students have made their lists, ask a few to report what they have written and to describe or define the environment they called to mind. Answers will vary widely.

Take the class outside for ten minutes. For the first five minutes, have the students look around and write down five things they see that they like and five that they dislike. Spend the last five minutes sharing responses. There are no right or wrong answers. Return to the classroom and ask the students to write a poem or short story about one thing they'd like to change about the environment and how they would go about making that change. Display their work on a bulletin board.

Treasure Hunt
(Materials: creative prizes, treasure map)

What better way to overcome uneasiness in an unfamiliar environment than to search for something rewarding? Hide things that students will drool over among bushes and trees, trees, under rocks, in the soil, etc.

Be creative. Some ideas: "coupons" for a class film or video on a Friday; a free bonus point on the next test; a snack; or, for younger students, a position as line leader for the day or tangible treasures such as neat erasers and pencils, stickers, or a coloring book. Make treasure maps to the different prizes or leave a trail of clever clues. The kids will have so much fun, they'll forget where they are!

Use Your Ears
(Materials: nature tapes)

Take the class on a brief trip to two different outdoor settings such as a city and a forest, a busy street and a park, or the school grounds and a field trip site.

Have them sit quietly with eyes closed and listen to the sounds, taking note of what they hear.

After a designated length of time appropriate to the age group, have them share what they heard. Compare and contrast the sounds in the two sites.

Which did they find more pleasing?

Another way to tune your class in to the sounds of nature is to listen to recordings.

Try *The Solitudes Series* tapes, available from nature and specialty stores or The Moss Music Group, Inc., 48 West 38th Street, New York, NY 10018.

The series includes Volume 1, "By Canoe at Loon Lake/Dawn by a Gentle Stream"; Volume 4, "Among the Ponds and Streams of Niagara Falls"; Volume 6, "Storm and Night on a Wilderness Lake"; and Volume 7, "Night in a Southern Swamp/Don't Feed the Alligators."

Can your students identify the sounds? Do they have a mental picture of the place the recording was made? Ask the students to speak or write a poem about how the tape(s) made them feel.

Getting Oriented
(Materials: paper and pencils)

1. Ask each student to write down the name of a **type of wetland** (e.g., marsh).

2. Ask them to write an example of an **animal** they associate with any type of wetland.

3. Ask them to write an example of a **plant** they associate with any type of wetland.

4. Ask them to write at least **two adjectives** or short phrases to describe any wetland.

Sample Student Reply
- Wetland type: *Bog*
- Wetland animal: *Beaver*
- Wetland plant: *Cattail*
- Wetland adjectives: *Damp, full of animals*

5. After students complete these steps, survey them item by item (i.e., ask for answers to step one, then to step two, and so on). There is no need to get each and every student's answer, but it is helpful to get a thorough picture. For example, after asking several students what type of wetland they wrote down (step one), you might ask the rest of the class, "How many others wrote down swamp?" or "How many of you wrote down an answer that hasn't been given yet?" Or, after several answers to step four, ask, "How many others wrote down an answer that has to do with the smell of a wetland?" In this way, you and the class will get a good feeling for the variety (or lack thereof) of answers. Make a table of the answers on a chalkboard or overhead.

The answers will illustrate preconceptions or misconceptions related to wetlands and highlight the particular areas that could be better understood through subsequent instruction. If replies include, for example, *buggy swamps that smell,* the challenge is clear. It is likely that students will suggest a greater variety of animals than plants, yet it is plants that are the most reliable indicators of the presence of wetlands. Government regulations use certain plants as indicators of legal wetlands, but do not use animals.

Marsh Soup
(Materials: spoons and cups)

Send younger students off, cup and spoon in hand, in a small, designated wetland area. Ask them to bring back a delicious cup of "marsh soup" full of colorful and odorous ingredients! This takes some imagination, since many will not find mud and plants particularly appetizing. If students are very young, remind them that this is just pretend—no tasting! This is an opportunity for a self-conducted sensory introduction to the wetland.

Get Messy!
(Materials: old clothing, mud, art paper)

Yes! Children need to experience the sights and sounds of wetlands firsthand to really appreciate them. Ask students to dress in old clothes for their wetland adventure. Let them get a real feel for the mud—have them scoop up a handful! What does it feel like? How does it smell? Bring paper for mud finger paintings or let the kids draw mud designs on themselves. If mud is not readily available, make a few buckets of your own. And have fun!

Wetlands—
A Changing Image

Wetlands have been given a bad rap. Many students may find that the idea of studying wetlands brings very unsettling thoughts of monsters, muck, and squishiness to mind. So why not begin the unit by addressing those thoughts and studying how others have perceived wetlands throughout history?

Mystery Topic
(Materials: package of rice, bag of mud, toy frog or alligator, photo of seafood [shrimp or crab], shells, nature tapes, wetland poster)

For several days before you begin a wetlands unit, display a new clue about wetlands each day. See if the students notice, then see if they can guess what the "mystery topic" is. You might bring in a package of rice, a bag of mud, a toy frog or alligator, a picture of some seafood, a clam or oyster shell, or a tape of bird songs or other natural sounds—anything that has to do with wetlands. On the last day, hang up a wetland poster (with the title covered). Then, on the first day of the unit, use the poster to introduce the topic. For poster information, see p. 328.

What Do You Think?
(Materials: paper and pencils)

Find out what kind of prior knowledge students have about wetlands. Expand on the Warm Up by asking them to write a poem or short paragraph about wetlands and how wetlands make them feel. Try the activity again after studying and visiting wetlands. Have students' attitudes changed?

Wetlands Around the World
(Materials: paper and pencils, library resources)

Many cultures throughout history have evolved around wetlands, which exist on every continent except Antarctica. Have students research and report on how different societies worldwide have used wetlands for food, housing, and economic gain. Two good sources of information are *National Geographic* and encyclopedias.

Ideas for Topics:

• Cajuns of coastal Louisiana's Atchafalaya Swamp and the lumber industry.

• Archaeologists in the United States and Europe who study ancient bodies preserved in peat deposits; early humans and their cultural practices.

• Use of peat in gardening, as insulation, and as an energy source—United States, Russia, Ireland, Germany, Belgium, The Netherlands, Denmark.

• Rice production—Thailand and other Asian countries.

• Mangrove wetlands as a source of timber and other resources— the Malay Archipelago, East Africa, Central and South America.

• Use of salt marshes for livestock grazing, hay production, and thatching for roofs—Europe, British Isles, United States (New England).

• The cranberry industry— northern United States (New Jersey, Massachusetts, and Wisconsin).

• Irish folktale about the will-o'-the-wisp, strange lights that led people astray on the bogs. The lights are actually produced by methane gas, also called swamp or marsh gas, which can catch fire briefly when released from many wetlands as a product of their chemical reactions.

• Colonial America, where towns and cities grew up around rivers for transportation and trade.

Fact or Fiction?
(Materials: newspapers, magazines, videotapes)

Read stories and newspaper and magazine articles about wetlands, and watch movies that explore wetlands themes (or settings). Use at least two sources to obtain contrasting views. Discuss and compare the ways wetlands were presented. Which are fact and which are fiction? Do students agree with the ways wetlands are depicted in these works? For suggestions, see p. 326.

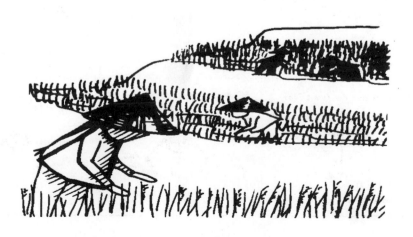

Lift Up Your Voices
(Materials: musical recordings, listed below)

Sing songs about wetlands. An old favorite is given below. If you don't know the tune, make one up! Or play recordings for students to sing along with. *Romp In the Swamp*, upbeat songs for all ages by Billy "B." Brennan, includes "Along the Coast," "The Bog Jogs," and "Wild Wetlands." Available from Jensen Publications, 2770 South 171st Street, New Berlin, WI 53151. For younger children, try "Freddie the Fly-Eating Frog" from the tape *Monsters in the Bathroom*, by Bill Harley. Available from Round River Records, 301 Jacob Street, Seekonk, MA 02771.

Rattlin' Bog
(an add-on song, like "The Twelve Days of Christmas")

Chorus:

Hey, ho, the rattlin' bog,
Bog down in the valley-o,
Hey, ho, the rattlin' bog,
Bog down in the valley-o.

Well in this bog, there was a *tree*,
A rare *tree*, a rattlin' *tree*,
A *tree* in the bog
And the bog down in the valley-o.

(Chorus)

Well on this tree, there was a *limb*,
A rare *limb*, a rattlin' *limb*,
A *limb on the tree and a tree* in the bog
And the bog down in the valley-o

(Chorus)

And on this limb, there was a *branch*,
A rare *branch*, a rattlin' *branch*,
A *branch on the limb and a limb on the tree and a tree* in the bog
And the bog down in the valley-o

(Chorus....)

Add: twig, leaf, bug, smile, and so on—let kids think of more.

Jumpin' Jehoshaphat
(Materials: crayons, markers, heavy construction paper)

Students can make paper frogs that really jump when pressed on the back end like a tiddly-wink. Follow the directions below to make Jehoshaphat, the Jumping Frog. Color Jehoshaphat with crayons or markers and make a wetland out of construction paper for him to jump into. You may want to set up a frog jumping contest to see whose Jehoshaphat is the best jumper!

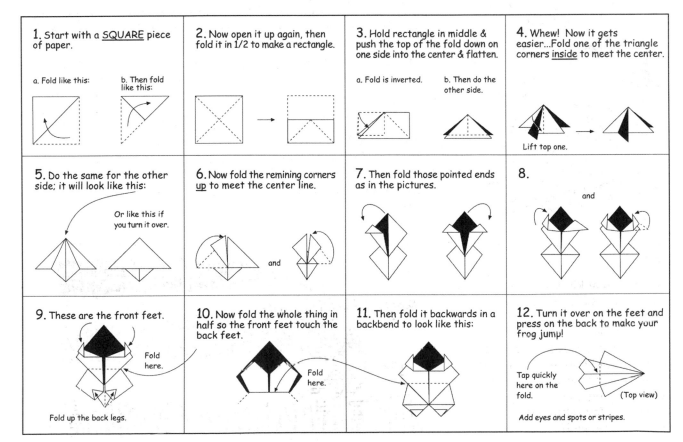

1. Start with a <u>SQUARE</u> piece of paper.
   a. Fold like this: b. Then fold like this:

2. Now open it up again, then fold it in 1/2 to make a rectangle.

3. Hold rectangle in middle & push the top of the fold down on one side into the center & flatten.
   a. Fold is inverted.   b. Then do the other side.

4. Whew! Now it gets easier...Fold one of the triangle corners <u>inside</u> to meet the center.
   Lift top one.

5. Do the same for the other side; it will look like this:
   Or like this if you turn it over.

6. Now fold the remining corners <u>up</u> to meet the center line.
   and

7. Then fold those pointed ends as in the pictures.

8.
   and

9. These are the front feet.
   Fold here.
   Fold up the back legs.

10. Now fold the whole thing in half so the front feet touch the back feet.
    Fold here.

11. Then fold it backwards in a backbend to look like this:

12. Turn it over on the feet and press on the back to make your frog jump!
    Tap quickly here on the fold.   (Top view)
    Add eyes and spots or stripes.

What's Wrong With This Picture?

Each of the four pictures below has a mistake in it—there is something that doesn't belong in the scene or something that isn't real about the drawing. Can students find what's wrong with each picture? Use these to pictures to begin a discussion about wetlands and the myths or misconceptions people have about them.

Answers:

Top left—Alligators are not naturally found in wetlands in the city. Also, there are mountains in the background, and alligators are a southern species found mainly in coastal South Carolina, Georgia, Florida, Louisiana, etc. *Top right*—Most swamps are too shallow and/or too densely wooded for a sailboat to pass through. *Bottom left*—Ponds are too small, shallow, and fresh to have a whale in them. There is a type of wetland called a Delmarva or Carolina bay (see p. 18) that some people call a "whale wallow," but this last name probably has little to do with whales. *Bottom right*—Venus flytraps *are* carnivorous plants, but they are only a few inches high and eat insects, not people. (They only eat people in horror movies!)

Springo!

(Materials: copies of the Springo! cards)

Use this "bingo" card to help young students concentrate on looking for things that live and grow in a wetland. This game works well when the class is walking along a boardwalk or the edge of a wetland. You can play the game any way you like, but here are two suggestions. (If you're not playing in spring, you might just call it "wetland bingo."):

Make copies of this card, cut the squares apart, and rearrange them to make three or four different cards (optional). Have students work in groups, with adult leaders. Groups that spot one of the items (or something similar, or an animal sign, such as a footprint), should shout "SPRINGO!" and point it out for all to see. Then everyone can mark off the item on the cards. Try to find as many as possible.

Or, make copies of the card, cut out squares, and use 9 of the 12 squares to make cards that are 3 squares by 3 squares. Have the groups find items until they have marked off a horizontal, vertical, or diagonal line, the shape of a *T* or *L*, or the whole card. The first group to make the designated pattern shouts "SPRINGO BINGO!" and wins.

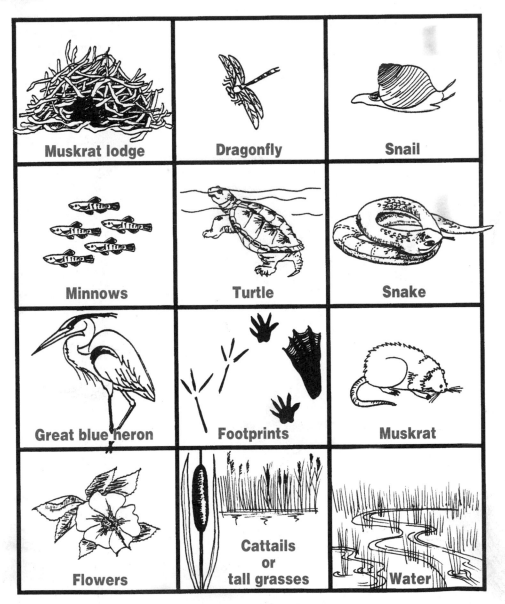

Let the Cattail Out of the Bag!

Grade Level
K-6

Subject Areas
Earth, Physical, and
Life Sciences

Duration
10 minutes to 1 hour

Setting
Classroom or outdoors

Skills
Observing, interpreting

Charting the Course
This activity provides an introduction to wetlands and can be used in conjunction with "Introducing Wetlands," p. 71. Follow this activity with activities that examine specific aspects of wetland soil, water, and plants. "Wetland Weirdos," for instance, takes a look at species adaptations.

Vocabulary
cattail, wetland

Summary

Students prepare for some of the sensory experiences they may encounter on a visit to a wetland when they explore a "touchy-feely" bag full of wetland objects.

Objectives

Students will become aware of some sensory qualities of wetland inhabitants.

Materials

Sample wetland artifacts are listed here; you can add your own, too. If there isn't a wetland nearby for collecting these items, you might find some through seafood markets, biological supply companies, local nature centers, or even a government agency that works with natural resources. Most staff members tend to collect odds and ends, which they may be willing to loan or donate.

- *a bag, such as an old pillowcase or sturdy paper bag*
- *cattail stalk and flower (fuzzy "hot dog" part)*
- *feather*
- *shell (clam, oyster, scallop, mussel)*
- *crab claw or dried shell*
- *wetland mud (in a baggie; smells like rotten eggs)*
- *turtle shell*
- *fur (small piece, pelt, or stuffed specimen—muskrats, beavers, and other mammals have fur)*
- *flower (wetlands have many beautiful ones; avoid endangered species)*
- *tap water (in a small container)*
- *leaves (grasses, wetland trees, etc.)*
- *a toy frog, fish, insect, duck, etc.*
- *snake skin*
- *bird's nest (only one that has fallen from a tree)*

Making Connections

Wetlands are full of fascinating plants, animals, and microscopic aquatic life. Students' curiosity about wetlands will be awakened when they feel the textures and shapes of special wetland objects. This hands-on learning game encourages an appreciation of the uniqueness of wetlands.

Background

Wetlands cover about six percent of the earth's surface. They can be found in every one of the United States and on all continents except Antarctica. They are found in rain forests, river deltas, coastal swamps, peatlands, salt pans, cranberry bogs, river estuaries, salt tidal flats, moist alpine tundra, and wet river bottom forests.

To be a wetland, an area must have three characteristics during most of the growing season: hydric (saturated) soils, water-tolerant plants, and enough water to either saturate the soil or cover the land to a shallow depth. A variety of plants and animals make their home in this unique environment, often with adaptations that help them thrive in wet conditions.

Procedure

Warm Up

Introduce wetlands to the class with the help of a colorful wetland poster (see Resources, p. 328).

The Activity

1. **Call a volunteer to the front of the room. Blindfold the volunteer and ask her to reach into the bag and remove one object, or**

place one object in her hands. **The object should be held out for the class to see.** Younger students may need a reminder to put hands over mouths so they don't give away the object's identity.

2. **Ask the volunteer to feel (and smell, if appropriate) the object, then describe her sensations to the class. Provide descriptive words to choose from if the volunteer needs help. The volunteer may then try to guess what the object is. If necessary, the class may help.**

3. **Remove the blindfold so the volunteer can see the object, then ask the class to locate it or something similar to it on the poster.**

4. **Repeat for several volunteers and objects.**

Wrap Up

Ask students to review all of the objects they felt in the bag. Which ones were plants? Which ones were animals?

Ask students why they think the objects in the bag belong in a wetland. Would any one of the objects appear in a dry area? Why or why not? Do students have a wetland in their area, or have they ever been to one? Have them describe the wetland and the plants and animals found there.

Assessment

Have students:

• describe a wetland.

• identify plants and animals that live in a wetland.

Extensions

Go to a wetland near your school and have students create their own grab bag of one or two objects (avoid gathering endangered or rare species). Take the bags back to the classroom and ask them to "let the cattail out of the bag" with their classmates.

Have students lead each other on a blind walk in a wetland. Each blindfolded student should be led by a student who is not blindfolded. The seeing students present the blindfolded students with the sounds, smells, and tactile sensations wetlands provide.

Resources

Niering, William A. 1985. *Wetlands*. Audubon Society Nature Guides. New York: Alfred A. Knopf, Inc.

Wetlands in the Classroom!

Grade Level
K-8

Subject Areas
Life Science, Biology, Art

Duration
Teacher's discretion

Setting
Classroom

Skills
Gathering and organizing
information

Charting the Course
After creating your own
wetland community, try
other introductory activities
such as "Let the Cattail Out
of the Bag," "Introducing
Wetlands," "Wetland
Metaphors," "Marsh Mar-
ket," and "Wet 'n' Wild."

Vocabulary
wetland, adaptations, cypress
swamp, cypress knees,
marsh, cattail, fiddler crab,
brackish water

Summary
*What better way could there be to
study wetlands than to have one right
in your classroom!*

Students create a "life-size"
cypress swamp or display, or
nurture wetland plants and
animals in an aquarium or
terrarium.

Objectives
Students will:

- gain greater insight about what
  makes up a wetland.

- describe a wetland community
  as a whole.

Materials
- *pictures or posters of wetlands and
  wetland plants and animals (see
  resource list, p. 326),*
- *reference books*

For Part I:
- *large rolls of colored bulletin board
  paper or posterboard*
- *egg carton cups*
- *fishing line*
- *construction paper*
- *tape*
- *scissors*
- *crayons*
- *markers*
- *paint and brushes*
- *scraps of tissue paper, yarn, and
  fabric*
- *ladder*

For Part II:
- *10- to 20-gallon (36- to 76-l)
  aquarium*
- *filter*
- *bubbler*
- *screening for container cover*
- *aged tap water*
- *sea salt mix from an aquarium store*
- *gravel, sand, or mud*
- *plants (preferably not taken from a
  wetland but purchased from a*

*nursery that sells wetland plants.
See page 304 for a listing.)*
- *animals collected by students or
  purchased from a biological supply
  company*
- *food for collected animals*

Making Connections
Any of us may be faced with
significant decisions that ultimately affect wetlands. Our
ability to make sound choices
depends on the understanding
factors that allow wetlands to
thrive. Sometimes it isn't until we
define all parts of the big picture
that we begin to understand the
importance and function of all the
puzzle pieces. By investigating the
components of a cypress swamp
and a terrarium or aquarium,
students gain a greater appreciation of the interactions among the
various biological and physical
components of an ecological
community.

Background
The Cypress Swamp: There are
different kinds of swamps. A
swamp may contain trees or
shrubs, and certain species may
predominate. A cypress swamp
supports primarily bald cypress
trees.

Bald cypress trees have needles,
like pine trees, but they are
deciduous, meaning the needles
drop off in the fall. Cypress trees
can grow in standing water and
have developed unusual adaptations for living in such a situation.
The bases of the trees are fluted or
buttressed for aeration and better
support. Bald cypress trees also
have "knees," extra roots that
grow up out of the water that may
aid in oxygen gas exchange.

Cypress swamps can be found on the East Coast from Florida to Delaware; along the Gulf Coast to eastern Texas and northward into Arkansas and Tennessee; and in the Mississippi Valley to southern Illinois and Indiana.

Although cypress swamps seem widespread, many people are unfamiliar with these areas of timeless beauty. Spanish moss seems to drip from tree limbs, creating an eerie atmosphere in the darkness beneath the tall, looming trees. The scene is serene, but not quiet, as a green heron "lurks in the shadows of button-bushes rimming tea-colored pools; painted turtles bask on mossy cypress knee islets; and warblers, vireos, wrens, and bullfrogs join in a chorus accompanied by the rattling drum of pileated woodpeckers" [*Quote above from "Knee Deep" in* Virginia's State Parks . . . Your Backyard Classrooms, *Virginia Department of Conservation and Recreation, Richmond, VA.*]

Aquariums and Terrariums: An aquarium is a glass-sided tank or bowl in which fish or other living animals are kept. A terrarium is a glass container, usually enclosed, for growing and displaying plants. Learn how to build them in Part II of this activity.

Procedure

To create your own cypress swamp, use the diagram and instructions below.

In addition to or as an alternative to building a wetland scene, construct and maintain a wetland aquarium or terrarium. You can have a fresh, brackish, or salt-water wetland living right where your students can watch it every day!

Warm Up
Show the class pictures or posters

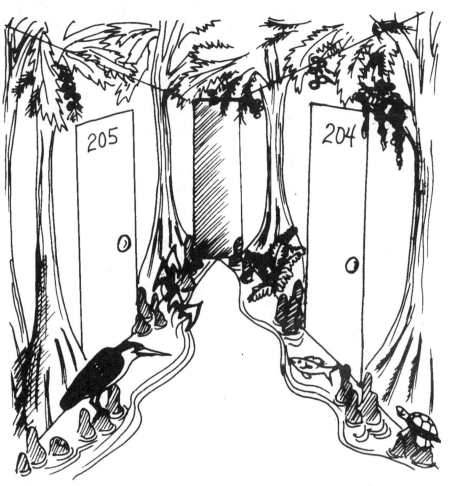

of different types of wetlands, including the cypress swamp, or have them research wetlands on their own. The choices include saltwater or freshwater marshes, bogs, swamps, bottomlands, mangrove swamps, potholes, and even wetlands created by beaver dams. Ask students to identify the components that differentiate cypress swamps from other wetlands. What would they need to build their own wetland?

The Activity

Part I: *The Cypress Swamp*

1. **Explain that the class will be working together to create a large scene of a wetland, complete with plants, animals, and (of course) water.** Students may want to vote on the type of wetland to depict.

2. **Help the students make a list of all the plants and animals they could include in their scene. Let the students choose the parts they wish to create. Use the following list as a guide:**

• *The Swamp Backdrop*
Line the school hallway with a cypress forest! Use the large rolls of colored bulletin board paper to cut out life-size tree trunks that stretch to the ceiling. Make the trunks about one foot wide at the top and flared at the bottom. Tape the tops of the trunks to the walls and the bottoms of the trunks to the floor about a foot from the walls, so they stand out. Extend the tops of the trees onto the ceiling and make some branches that hang down. The leaves are needlelike, and round, green "cones" dangle from the limbs.

• Knees

Cut brown paper into the shape of cypress knees or make paper cones; tape the knees to the floor so they stand erect. (You may have to make cardboard supports for flat paper knees.) Place the knees all around the bases of the trees. The "caps" of the knees are usually rounded and often red or orange. Make little caps for the knees with paper or painted egg carton cups.

• Water

Use dark blue or black paper to represent acidic water. Cut paper to form a meandering river that runs along the floor at the edges of the hallway. Trees and knees should look as though they grow out of the water. Leave walking room in the center of the hall.

• Animals

Cut out life-size construction paper or posterboard animals and decorate them with various craft materials. You might use crayons, markers, paint—even scraps of tissue paper, yarn, and fabric. Be creative and make some animals three-dimensional. Tape them in appropriate places in the scene.

Ideas: wading birds such as green or great blue herons and a rookery (a group of heron nests in the tree branches), pileated woodpeckers, wood ducks, barred owls, kingfishers, songbirds, snapping or painted turtles and bullfrogs in the water or on the knees, brown water snakes, alligators (southern swamps only!), sunfish or pickerel, insects (dragonflies, butterflies), raccoons, mice, white-tailed deer. Smaller birds and insects can "fly" through the scene if hung from the ceiling with fishing line.

• Plants

Fill in the understory (the vegetation growing under the trees) with lots of plants. Make these out of

Freshwater Marsh

anything that will help make them look interesting. Some of the plants that grow in cypress swamps are: arrowhead (also called duck potato), lizard tail, buttonbush, Virginia chain fern or cinnamon fern, Jack-in-the-pulpit (only in the drier parts, not right in the water), rushes and sedges, swamp rose (a shrub), Spanish moss, etc.

The diagram will help you plan your swamp or any other kind of wetland. Let the students add their own ideas to make the display exciting!

Part II: *The Aquarium and Terrarium*

1. **Plan to set up an aquarium or terrarium that represents a type of wetland you have nearby. Before starting an aquarium or terrarium, have students contact a local public aquarium, wildlife park, zoo, or nature center for information on animal care.**

2. **You may want to take students to a wetland to see how it is "put together" and to collect specimens for the tank. (See the activity on observing and collecting aquatic animals, p. 99.)** What kind of water is in the wetland? (If you are planning a small tank,

you may want to take back a bucket or two of water.) What is the ground like? What kinds of animals live here? Have students make lists, notes, and drawings to help plan the tank. Other tips:

• **Keep it clean.** If you plan a very shallow wetland, you may not need a filter, but you should still insert an aerator (bubbler) hose into the water and change the water frequently. If your tank is at least one-fourth full of water, a filter will help keep it clean. The type of filter you use will determine which kind of material you should place on the bottom of the tank. An under-gravel (biological filtration) filter works quite well with gravel, but fine particles such as sand or mud will clog the filter.

For these materials, use an outside filter with charcoal or angel hair.

• **Your tank does not have to be full of water.** In fact, your wetland representation will be better if the tank is only partially filled. Some sample tanks are shown. Keep in mind the kinds of plants and animals you want and the kind of habitat in which they live. For example, fiddler crabs are air-breathers and will drown if kept underwater all the time! Some plants survive better in only a small amount of water, while others need to be submerged. Your trip and some field guides will help you choose the proper water level.

• **Use good judgment when taking things from a wetland.** If the property is protected (Nature Conservancy or National Wildlife Refuge land), do not take any living things. If there are only a few specimens of a certain kind of plant, leave them all there. If you are in the middle of a marsh full of *Spartina* or cattail, it is probably okay to dig up a few plants to take with you. **Always ask property owners before a visit.**

• **Be gentle with animals and be sure to provide safe, covered transportation containers (with air holes). Take only a few of each animal; they will die if overcrowded.** Note where each was taken, so that it can be returned to its home later. To provide bacteria to keep the system healthy, collect a few rocks and/or a fat stick or two from the water. The hardiest specimens will be some small fish, aquatic insects, and other invertebrates such as crabs and grass shrimp. The return of the creatures is an important part of the lesson.

• **Try to minimize trial and error in your feeding program.** Consult field guides and reference books, or a public aquarium, zoo, wildlife park, or nature center to learn what the animals eat in the wild. Use these foods if possible, comparable foods if not. Crabs, minnows, and other scavengers will eat bits of fish, shrimp, clam, etc., or an occasional earthworm. Improper feeding can make the animals unhealthy or cause some to become food for others! This is a lesson in food webs, but you might find yourself with a nearly empty tank. Most animals will not eat for a few days after capture, and many will normally go a day or two without eating at all. Some animals may not appear to be eating, but remember that oysters, anemones, and many small creatures will feed on tiny bits of leftovers floating in the water—they're the clean-up crew! However, they can only handle so much. Excess leftovers will become poisons if left in the tank for more than a day.

• **Keep fiddlers fit.** Keep only fiddler crabs and maybe a snail or two in the tank. Use an aquarium, large bowl, or dish pan with sides high enough to prevent escape and cover the container with screening. Fill the tank with about 10 centimeters (4 inches) of water, tilt it up on one end, and pile sand or mud up on the high sides so the crabs can construct their burrows out of the water. If you do not use natural salt water, let tap water age (dechlorinate) overnight, then mix in sea salt according to the package directions for a salinity of about 7-10 parts per thousand. A third alternative is to add 28 grams of table salt to 4 liters of water (approximately 5 teaspoons of salt per gallon of water). Change the water at least once a week. Feed the fiddlers by placing a pinch of commercial fish food or a small piece of meat, shrimp, oyster, or clam into the water. Don't be surprised if your specimens eat each other! Keep handling to a minimum, and remain very still when observing so the crabs will come out of their burrows. [*From "Fiddling Around with Fiddlers" by Heidi Koerfer and John E. Dille,* Science and Children, *February 1987. Used with permission of National Science Teachers Association, 1840 Wilson Blvd., Arlington, VA 22201-3000.*]

• **A Terrarium (Ter-RARE-rium).** Many unusual and rare plants grow in bogs. If you'd like to make a bog, you will need a

Salt marsh with fiddler crabs

Bog

sphagnum moss "floor." You might wish to include a few carnivorous plants (your students can feed them with dead insects). Contact the following for carnivorous plants and a teachers' guide to keeping them: Michael Szesze, Arthur Storer Planetarium, Dares Beach Road, Prince Frederick, MD 20678, or call 1-301-535-2904.

Wrap Up and Action

Have students choose a wetland component and present it to the class, identifying its relation to other wetland elements. Instruct students to lead a tour through the wetland or construct interpretive signs that describe aspects of the wetland. Invite other classes to view the classroom terrariums and aquariums.

Assessment

Ask students to:

• identify an element of a wetland and describe its function.

• write an interpretive sign for a wetland nature trail.

• conduct a tour of a mock wetland.

• create and manage a wetland aquarium or terrarium.

Extensions

Try creating different types of wetlands (bogs, marshes, etc.), or make a diorama.

Resources

The Audubon Society Nature Guide series includes *Wetlands* (New York: Alfred A. Knopf, 1985), by William A. Niering. This book is an excellent reference for the cypress swamp activity. The introduction contains descriptions and photographs of several different types of wetlands, and the body is a field guide to a wide variety of North American wetland plants and animals.

Regnier, K., M. Gross, and R. Zimmerman. 1992. *The Interpreter's Guidebook: Techniques for Progress and Presentations.* Stevens Point, WI: University of Wisconsin, Stevens Point Press.

Wetland Metaphors

[From "Wetland Metaphors" in Aquatic Project WILD, *Western Regional Environmental Education Council, 1992. Adapted with permission.]*

Grade Level
1-12

Subject Areas
Environmental and Earth Science

Duration
30-40 minutes

Setting
Classroom

Skills
Analyzing and interpreting

Charting the Course
Try "Marsh Mystery," "Treatment Plants," "Soak It Up!," "Wetland in a Pan," and others for a more detailed look at wetland functions.

Vocabulary
wetland functions, habitat, filter

Summary

What is a home, a sponge, and a strainer all at the same time?

Consider a selection of common objects as physical metaphors for natural wetland functions.

Objectives

Students will:

• describe characteristics of wetlands.

• appreciate the importance of wetlands to wildlife and humans.

• identify ecological functions of wetlands.

Materials

• *A Mystery Metaphor Container (e.g., large pillowcase, bag, or box) that has an opening just large enough to allow students to reach inside to retrieve an object without seeing the contents*
• *sponge*
• *small pillow*
• *soap*
• *egg beater or mixer*
• *small doll cradle or pictures of nursery items*
• *sieve or strainer*
• *paper coffee filter*
• *bottle of antacid tablets*
• *small box of cereal or wild rice*
• *3-inch x 5-inch cards with magazine pictures representing other wetland functions (see chart at end of activity)*

Making Connections

Citizens in our rapidly developing world should understand the benefits of wetlands as resources for humans and other species. This activity brings those benefits to life and encourages a new appreciation of the many important roles wetlands play.

Background

Wetlands provide critical benefits to plants, animals, humans, and the total environment. (See chapter 3.)

Most wetlands, with their abundance of food, vegetative cover (shelter), and water, are rich with diverse wildlife species. Coastal and inland marshes, for example, are the breeding, resting, and wintering habitats for thousands of migratory birds, including ducks, geese, swans, shorebirds, herons, and other wading birds. Many species of fish and shellfish that have important commercial and recreational use reproduce and spend part or all of their life cycle in fertile wetlands. A wide variety of reptiles, amphibians, insects, and crustaceans also breed and live in wetlands. Many mammals depend on wetlands for food, shelter, and water.

Wetland vegetation is highly beneficial. Plants absorb nutrients and help cycle them through the food web. They keep water's nutrient concentrations from reaching toxic levels. Plants produce oxygen through photosynthesis, and they are an important food source for other life forms.

Wetlands have a unique ability to purify the environment. They are extremely effective natural filtering systems. For instance, they trap and neutralize sewage waste, allow silt to settle, and promote the decomposition of many toxic substances.

Wetlands mitigate the harmful effects of sudden and seasonal variations in the water supply. When runoff from rain and spring thaw is high, wetlands retain excess water, allowing it to drain into streams and rivers and permeate the soil gradually. Healthy wetlands are buffer zones that prevent flooding and erosion. In drier periods, they hold precious moisture long after open bodies of water have disappeared.

As remarkable and resilient as wetlands are, they do have limits. Wetland functions can be compromised when portions are drained and filled for other uses. When a wetland is lost, the effects on wildlife, humans, and overall environmental quality can be significant. Although many wetlands are protected by federal and state laws, there is still a need to create a greater awareness of the importance of wetlands as unique and essential ecosystems.

Procedure

Warm Up

If necessary, provide the class with background information on the natural functions of wetlands and their value as wildlife habitat (See chapter 3.) Use "Wetland in A Pan," p. 212, if you need to give a demonstration. Introduce wetlands though posters, pictures, stories, etc. How do the students feel about wetlands? Do they think wetlands are important? Why? Discuss students' answers and make a list of "pros" and "cons" on the board.

The Activity

1. **Tell students that they are going to expand the "pros" list through the use of** *metaphors.* **Explain that a metaphor represents a thing or idea through another thing or idea, such as in "a tree is a home," "the world is a stage," or "books are windows of thought." Ask students to provide examples of other metaphors.** The household objects

in this activity are tangible symbols of wetland benefits.

2. **Divide the class into groups of four or five. Ask a representative from each group to choose an item from the Mystery Metaphor Container. Each group must decide how the object could represent what a wetland is or does.** All items in the box have something to do with wetlands.

3. **Allow time for students to discuss their answers in groups before each group presents its object and ideas to the class.** Examples are given in the chart below, but students may come up with other clever ideas.

Wrap Up and Action

As students report to the class, discuss each idea and invite others to add their ideas. Add to the list of "pros" on the board. At the end, ask the class to summarize the major roles that wetlands perform. Have students' attitudes and understanding changed since they started the activity?

Assessment

Have students:

- use metaphors to relate the many functions of wetlands to everyday objects.

- identify reasons wetlands are important.

Extensions

Have students prepare displays or short demonstrations on the benefits of wetlands or prepare a wetlands benefits booklet, each student contributing one page.

Resources

Mitsch, William J., and J. G. Gosselink. 1993. *Wetlands.* New York: Van Nostrand Reinhold.

(*Note to Teacher:* Use the chart below to help prepare your Mystery Metaphor Container, although metaphors other than these might be offered by students.)

Object:	Metaphoric Function
Sponge	Absorbs excess water caused by runoff; retains moisture for a time even if standing water dries up (sponge stays wet even after it has absorbed a spill)
Pillow or bed	A resting place for migratory birds
Egg beater	Mixes nutrients and oxygen into the water
Cradle	Provides a nursery that shelters, protects, and feeds young wildlife
Strainer	Strains silt and debris from water (keeps water supply clean)
Coffee filter	Filters smaller impurities from water (excess nutrients, toxins)
Antacid	Neutralizes toxic substances
Cereal, rice, picture of garden	Provides nutrient-rich foods for wildlife and humans
Soap	Helps cleanse the environment
Picture of zoo	Habitat for diverse wildlife
Picture of resort or motel	Resting or wintering place for migrating waterfowl

Wetland Habitats

[*Adapted from "Classifying Habitats of the Chesapeake Bay" in* The Changing Chesapeake *pp. 19-22, with permission of the National Aquarium in Baltimore.*]

Grade Level
6-12

Subject Areas
Ecology, Life Science

Duration
45 minutes

Setting
Classroom

Skills
Organizing, analyzing, interpreting

Charting the Course
Prior to using this activity, try some of the icebreakers in "Introducing Wetlands." Once students have learned about the various types of wetlands, have them try "Tracking Plants and Keeping Track" and "Wet 'n' Wild" to survey the plants and animals living in those habitats.

Vocabulary
classification, habitat

Summary

This activity uses a flow chart to introduce and sort out the common types of wetlands.

Objectives

Students will classify wetlands based on their characteristics.

Materials

- *copies of Wetland Habitats Flow Chart*
- *copies of Habitat Cards*
- *pictures of wetlands (magazines, books, posters)*
- *paper and pencils*
- *map of the United States (optional)*

Making Connections

Many people are unfamiliar with wetland habitats. Before you begin exploring the topic with your students, find out what they already know and think about wetlands. Once students are more comfortable with their surroundings, you can plunge ahead into more specific learning. Students learn to use a flow chart, a valuable classification tool, and sharpen their observation skills.

Background

A habitat is the place where an animal finds food, water, shelter, and space in a particular arrangement. Wetlands offer a wide variety of habitat types for many species of wildlife. (See chapters 2 and 4.)

An area does not always have to be wet to be considered a wetland. Many wetlands are covered by water only during the rainy spring season. Others are regularly or infrequently flooded by tides, while others may be covered by water most or all of the time. (See chapter 2, p. 14).

Some wetlands have salty water, while others are wetted by freshwater streams, rivers, ponds or lakes, or rainwater. Differences in salinity and wetness, as well as slope, elevation, and climate, cause differing plant communities to develop. Wetlands are classified, in part, by the type of water, frequency and degree of inundation, and types of vegetation most prevalent there.

Procedure

Warm Up

Discuss the preceding, using pictures of wetlands as examples. Define habitat. Explain that students will be using a flow chart to identify ten wetland types by the habitats they provide. Review the use of a flow chart and practice as a group with one of the pictures.

The Activity

Have students, working individually, in pairs, or in threes, use the Wetland Habitats Flow Chart to identify the ten wetlands described on the Habitat Cards. Advanced students may be able to identify photographs using the flow chart. They will have to infer the salinity by the types of plants shown.

Answers: 1. sandy beach, 2. shrub swamp, 3. aquatic plant bed, 4. wet meadow, 5. mud flat, 6. tidal freshwater marsh, 7. forested wetland, 8. seagrass bed, 9. bog, 10. salt marsh

Wrap Up

Ask students to name different types of wetlands. What kinds of plants grow there? Is the water salty or fresh? Do students think they could classify a real wetland on a visit? Have them try!

Assessment

Have students:

• describe several types of wetlands.

• identify qualities that might distinguish one type of wetland from another.

Extensions

Using a map of the United States, have students discuss where the different wetland types might appear.

Areas of high wetland density in the contiguous United States. What kinds of wetlands are they?

Approximate wetland regions of the contiguous U.S. (areas marked are not accurate at this scale; wetlands also occur in other areas, particularly along waterways)

Wetland Habitats Flow Chart

Carefully read each of the habitat cards, then use this flow chart to identify each habitat. Start at the left side of the page at the first box. There are two boxes connected to that box—choose the one that matches the description on the card. Then move on to the next set of boxes, following the lines, and make another choice. Continue until you reach the name of the habitat described on the card. Can you identify all ten habitats?

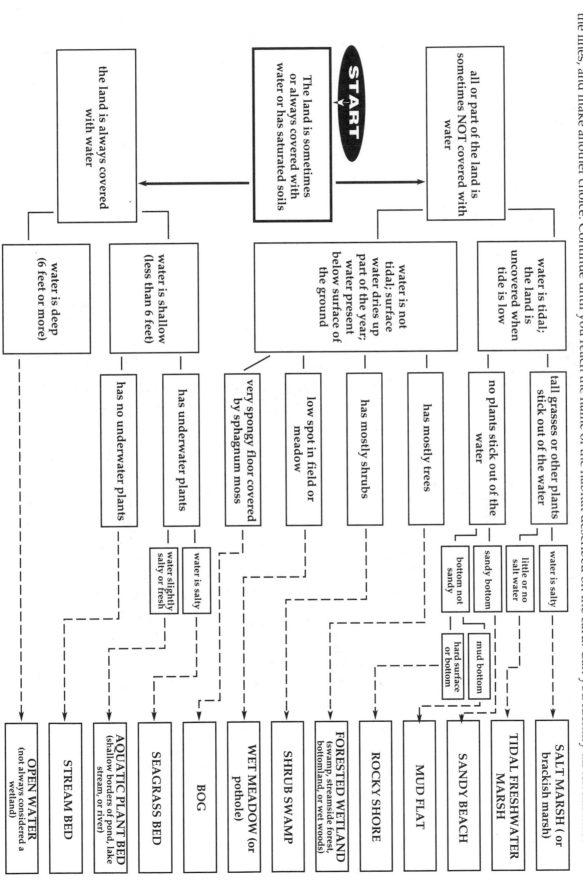

Habitat Cards

1. During storms, the waves push grains of sand into ever-changing patterns. During low tide the animals that live among the sand grains feel the summer heat or the winter cold. Shore birds search along the water's edge for these animals and for bits of food that wash in from the water. No plants grow here.

2. Scrubby, low-growing thickets of shrubs grow here, in places that may have started out as wet meadows. You might find these places near the coast, or where lakes, streams, rivers, marshes, and forested swamps overflow. They are not always covered with water. This type of wetland offers good habitat for fish, reptiles, amphibians, and many other animals.

3. In the shallow borders of ponds, lakes, rivers, and streams, where there is good light and the water has little salt, underwater plants and plants with floating leaves grow. Some of these plants are valuable food for many kinds of water-fowl including ducks, geese, and swans. All make places for little fish and other animals to live and feed. These plants slow water movement and protect the soil on shores and banks from erosion.

4. Depressions in the ground may fill with rain and ground water and stay wet for several days or weeks. Landowners often mow or plow around these spots to avoid getting tractor wheels stuck in the soft ground. On spring evenings, these puddles seem alive with the high-pitched calls of spring peepers (tiny frogs) looking for mates among the rushes and sedges that grow here. In the heat of the summer, these places usually dry up.

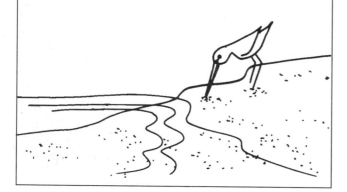

Habitat Cards

5. Fine particles of dirt make mud when they settle out of the water. Where the water is very shallow, the muddy bottom is uncovered at low tide. While this area may not look like home to many animals, and few or no plants grow here, lots of creatures live down in the mud. Watch for hungry shore birds searching for them in the mud.

6. Tall grasses and other kinds of plants grow up out of the water. The water contains little or no salt, but the push of incoming tides is strong enough to raise the water level in the river. The ground is sometimes flooded and sometimes dry or exposed. The plants provide food and places to hide for many kinds of animals including fish, invertebrates, muskrats, and lots of birds.

7. Where trees grow in low-lying areas, the ground may hold water for part of the year. In the spring, many beautiful wildflowers grow here, and frogs and salamanders find wet places to lay their eggs.

8. In salty bays or at the ocean's edge, two kinds of plants may grow under the shallow water. They can only live where it is shallow because they are rooted on the bottom and need light to make food. The plants are eaten by many animals, and many of them find safe places to live among the plants. These plants protect the shore and reduce the muddiness of the water by slowing the waves.

Habitat Cards

9. Old lakebeds and other low areas that fill with rainwater sometimes accumulate layers of partially decayed plants called peat. At first glance these places might look dry, but their moss-covered floors actually hold a good deal of fresh water just below the surface. The ground here feels very spongy. Some shrubs and evergreen trees also grow above the sphagnum moss. In these unusual conditions, many unique, beautiful, and rare plants and animals can be found.

10. Along the shore where the water is salty, tall grasses grow up out of the water. Tides move in and out, but some places are flooded only during storms and very high tides. When the tough plants here die, they break down in the water to form little particles called detritus. Many animals eat detritus by filtering it out of the water.

Section

2

The Wetland Community (plants and animals)

A series of exercises and activities that will help students understand critical wetland issues such as habitat niche, plant and animal adaptations, wetland delineation, plants' role in filtering pollutants, identifying and classifying plants, and more.

Wetland Weirdos

[Cattail activity adapted from Hanging On to the Wetlands *(book one) by Irwin Slesnick and David Newton, Bellingham, WA, p. 16; Beaver activity adapted from* Virginia's State Parks . . .Your Backyard Classrooms, *Virginia Department of Conservation and Recreation, Richmond, VA.]*

Grade Level
4-12

Subject Area
Ecology, Biology, Botany, Environmental Science

Duration
40-60 minutes for each activity

Setting
Classroom and field

Skills
Gathering, interpreting, and applying information

Charting the Course
Once students have studied these sample plant and animal adaptations, try some of the other activities in The Wetland Community section. They will provide a closer look at plant collection, animal tracking, and functions of both plants and animals in a wetland environment.

Vocabulary
adaptations, cattails, emergent, aerenchyma, xylem, phloem

Summary

Investigate the structure of a cattail, read about beavers, then create a specially adapted creature!

Objectives

Students will recognize that plant and animal adaptations can be inferred from observations of organisms' physical structures.

Materials

- *copies of student pages*
- *magnifying lenses*
- *dissection scopes and tools (scalpel, probe) for older students*
- *cattails*
- *craft supplies*
- *pencils*
- *stuffed beaver, if possible*

Making Connections

The study of plant and animal adaptations sharpens observation and critical thinking skills while increasing awareness of valuable species.

Background

Adaptations: Adaptations are specialized characteristics that plants and animals have developed over time in response to environmental pressures. Adaptations may be physical features or specialized behaviors. These tools enable the plant or animal to survive in specific conditions, such as the wet or alternately wet and dry conditions in wetlands. Within the wetland habitat, some species have adapted to living in the wettest parts, while others are more suited for the driest areas.

Adaptations come in many forms. For example, they might help an animal compete for specific kinds of foods; enable locomotion in air, water, and trees, and on land; or provide protection through color (blending in with surroundings), armor (as with the turtle), or the ability to fight or flee. Plant adaptations provide means for obtaining oxygen, nutrients, water, sunlight, and other necessities.

Cattails: Cattails are emergent plants (they stick up out of the water). The part that looks like a cat's tail or a hot dog is the female flowering structure, and there is a thinner male structure above it during the early part of the growing season. If you pull the flower apart, you will find thousands of fuzzy white things that blow around. Each one contains an ovary (the thin, tan bulb in the center of the white fluff) halfway up a little stalk. If the ovaries are pollinated (by wind, gravity, insects, birds), they soon become fertilized seeds with a bulb at the tip. Cattails reproduce by seed germination and through use of underground horizontal stems called rhizomes. In the classroom, it may take three weeks or so to germinate seeds. Keep them wet—a zippered plastic bag will help!

Long, narrow leaves are attached at the base of each plant, overlapping each other and surrounding the stem. The bundle of leaves and stem near the cattail's roots form the shoot, the white part of which is edible and tastes a bit like cucumber. If you cut a cross section of the shoot, you will see what looks like a slice of a bunch of celery; the leaves overlap each other, making almost a spiral pattern.

The leaves have vertical channels filled with a starchy material that is part of the vascular system of the plant. They contain xylem and phloem, which transport water and nutrients during growth and metabolism. If you cut a piece of a mature leaf several inches up the leaf, the cut surface will be D-shaped and will show a honeycomb structure that helps strengthen and support the leaves.

A stem supports the cattail's flowering bodies. A stem cross section reveals a pattern of holes that have two functions. The holes in the center of the stem, and some in the individual blades, are air-conducting vessels called aerenchyma. They transport oxygen down to the roots, since there is little oxygen in wetland soil for roots to take up. Only wetland and aquatic plants have this adaptation. In plants with floating leaves, aerenchyma help make the stems buoyant. The holes arranged around the outside of the stem are water-conducting vessels closely bound with fibers that provide support for the stem.

Beavers: See Beaver Tales student page.

Procedure

Warm Up

Begin with a general discussion of adaptations. Do students already know what they are? Do people have adaptations? Explain that the most unique human adaptations are the ability to walk upright and the opposable thumb. Have students imagine or try doing things without the use of their thumbs (tape or tie thumbs to palms and try writing or eating), or while walking on "all fours." Would they be able to throw a baseball this way?

Ask students to name animals or plants that are specially adapted to living where they do. For instance, camels and cacti live in dry climates and have adaptations for conserving water; fish have gills for breathing underwater; and birds have multitudes of adaptations, particularly their specialized bills and feet.

The Activity

In these activities, students will be looking closely at two species that are adapted for life in wetlands: cattail and beaver.

Part I

1. **For the cattail investigation, collect or have students collect several cattails.** Be sure all cattails are collected from dispersed locations, and that all parts of the cattail are gathered. *Permission from landowners is a must.*

2. **Have students conduct their own studies using the Cattail Investigation student page. Explain the procedure before they begin and leave time at the end of class for sharing discoveries.**

3. **After students have studied the plant's structure and have answered the questions, discuss the answers together.** What other methods could they have used to find out the correct answers? (Visit the library, ask plant specialists or wetland scientists.)

Part II

1. **Give students copies of the Beaver Tales student page to do on their own.** Try to have a stuffed beaver or beaver model on display.

2. **After students complete the questions, invite them to imagine and list the characteristics of a beaver that are adapted to living in a desert instead of a pond.** Younger students may use a paper bag and any other materials they wish to make a puppet of the "desert beaver." Have them show or list as many adaptations as they can.

3. **Have students present their lists or creations as part of a group discussion. If you have a beaver pond nearby, arrange for students to visit and investigate.** Beavers are most active at night, but you will still see signs of activity during the day.

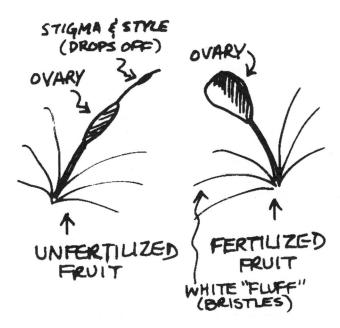

STIGMA & STYLE (DROPS OFF)

OVARY

OVARY

UNFERTILIZED FRUIT

FERTILIZED FRUIT

WHITE "FLUFF" (BRISTLES)

Wrap Up and Action

Ask students to summarize ways that cattails and beavers are adapted to their environment. Have them think about other wetland plant and animal adaptations (e.g., water lilies, which have adapted by floating on water; pitcher plants and cranberries, which can survive in a bog's acidic environment; and so on).

Have students imagine an organism (plant or animal) that lives in a place with a strange climate and unusual landscape, and create a story or drawing about this organism and its environment. Students should identify ways in which the organism has adapted to the environment. Ask them to include as many details as they can.

Assessment

Have students:

• analyze the parts of a cattail and, from their observations, infer the functions of plant parts.

• describe the functions of various beaver body parts.

• describe how beavers and cattails have adapted to their environment.

• create an organism and explain its adaptations to its environment.

Extension
Nature in Your Neighborhood

Are there animals in your neighborhood that have developed special adaptations or behaviors for living among people? Write a poem or story about one of the animals you have observed close to home, or choose one from the list below:

dog or cat   housefly
pigeon   raccoon
sparrow   human
mouse or rat   squirrel

Notes:

Cattail Investigation

Collect some cattails to study. You will find them growing in fresh or slightly salty water along creeks, rivers, ponds, lakes, and wet roadside ditches. You will need the whole plant: roots, if you can get them, stalk, leaves, stem, and the "cat's tail" at the top. Gather one plant for every four to six students—you will be able to share plants to study, so do not take *all* of the cattails growing in one area!

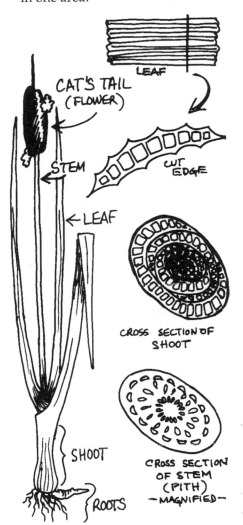

CAT'S TAIL
(FLOWER)

LEAF

STEM

← LEAF

CROSS SECTION OF SHOOT

SHOOT

CROSS SECTION OF STEM (PITH) —MAGNIFIED—

ROOTS

← FRUITS ↘

1. Carefully examine all parts of the plant and how they are arranged. On another sheet, draw a picture of each part.

2. Pull off one of the leaves. Where are the leaves attached to the stalk? Are both sides of the leaf the same? Is the leaf flat or does it have some thickness? Write your answers below.

_____

_____

3. Cut the leaf crosswise (see diagram) and look at the cut edge with a magnifying lens. What's inside cattail leaves that makes them hard to tear?

_____

_____

4. Cut a thin slice of the shoot and draw it on the back of this page. The shoot is edible, so taste a piece! Describe the taste. What do you think the white, spongy stuff inside is for?

_____

_____

5. The stem holds the cat's tail up. Cut the stem crosswise, then cut a thin slice off the cut end. Observe the slice with a dissection scope. Draw a picture of the slice's middle, or pith, on the back of this sheet.

6. What do you think the holes in the pith are for? (*Hint:* Wetland plants grow in wet soil that has no oxygen, and plants' roots need oxygen.)

_____

_____

7. Carefully pull some of the fuzz from the cat's tail. These are ovaries and fruits. Are they all the same? What differences can you see? (Use a magnifying lens.)

_____

_____

8. When ovaries are pollinated, they soon become fertilized seeds that will grow new plants. Put some of the different fruits between layers of wet paper towels and seal in a plastic bag that zips closed. Which of the fruits start growing after a few weeks?

_____

_____

9. Why do you think cattails make so many fruits?

_____

_____

10. How might cattail seeds be pollinated? How are seeds spread?

_____

_____

Beaver Tales

If you lived in a wetland, what kinds of special body parts or tools would you need to survive? The beaver is one of many wetland-dwelling creatures equipped with a variety of unique, and even weird, adaptations. The beaver's lifestyle requires specialized physical features and behaviors.

If you spent most of your life in the water or on wet ground, you'd get "goose bumps" pretty quickly! To keep itself from getting cold, the beaver has a thick layer of fur consisting of a fine undercoat and long, protective guard hairs. Add to this a thick layer of fat under the skin. It also has a built-in radiator, a special kind of circulation that brings heat to its legs, feet, and tail!

Sebaceous glands produce oil, which waterproofs the beaver's fur. The beaver also has musk sacs called castor glands which produce an oil the beaver uses to mark its territory. This oil has also been used to make some perfumes and medicines.

The second claw on each beaver's hind foot is split and used like a comb to keep the fur groomed for maximum water repellency. The webbed hind feet provide propulsion through the water. The outermost toes on the front paws are modified for grasping, much like the human thumb, and are used for holding food and working on dams. The long front claws are adapted for digging. The broad, flat, leathery tail is not used for scooping up mud, as shown in many cartoons. It actually serves as a propeller and rudder (for steering) when the beaver is swimming. The tail also supports the animal when it sits upright to gnaw on a tree. When danger is near, the beaver slaps its tail on the water's surface as a signal to others.

This animal's characteristic large front teeth grow continuously, keeping pace with the constant wear from gnawing on wood. These teeth project past the beaver's lips so it can gnaw, chew, and swallow underwater without choking. To seal out water during dives, the beaver's ears and nose have special flaps and the back of its mouth closes. It can stay under water for up to fifteen minutes! A beaver's eyes have nictitating membranes, also called third eyelids, which serve as underwater goggles. Though the beaver's vision is weak, its hearing and sense of smell are acute. It finds most of its food (tree bark and soft vegetation such as grasses, ferns, mushrooms, leaves, stems, and roots of water plants) by smell.

The beaver's remarkable behaviors have led many people to consider the animal highly intelligent, but most of these behaviors are probably instinctive.

The beaver is quite an engineer! It responds to the sound of running water by building dams of mud and wood chips to stop the flow. Small trees, branches, and twigs are stored in the mud at the bottom of their home ponds as supplies for winter, when the pond freezes. Large trees are gnawed until they topple, bringing the more tender parts at the top within reach. Leftovers are used to build the lodge. Lodges are intricate, with many rooms and underwater entrances. These unique behaviors have made the beaver a very successful survivor. Many species depend on the beaver's talents, since beaver ponds are home to many kinds of plants and animals.

After reading the information, write answers to the questions below on notebook paper.

1. Does a beaver freeze when the water is cold or frozen? Explain.

2. How do a beaver's toes help the animal survive?

3. Why would a beaver bury sticks and logs in the mud under water?

4. Why do beavers cut down large trees that are too tough to eat?

5. Is a beaver a good swimmer? Why?

6. Name some animals that might be attracted to an area after beavers have moved in.

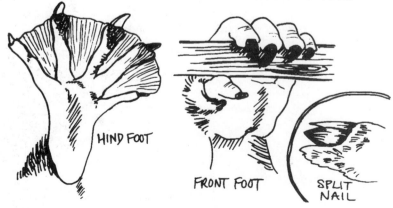

HIND FOOT

FRONT FOOT

SPLIT NAIL

Wet 'n' Wild

Grade Level
K-12

Subject Areas
Biology, Ecology, Art

Duration
5-90 minutes outdoors, depending on grade level; 30-60 minutes to complete field guide pages

Setting
Classroom and wetland

Skills
Gathering, organizing, and interpreting information

Charting the Course
This is a super activity for learning about wetland communities. It can be tied in nicely with "Tracking Plants and Keeping Track," which asks students to collect and record plant specimens. "Wetland Weirdos" has students look at special adaptations in wetland plants and animals.

Vocabulary
habitat, endangered species

Summary

Many people think wetlands are dangerous places full of mosquitoes, monsters, and poisonous snakes. Let your students see firsthand that the creatures living in wetlands are ones we enjoy, need, and want to protect. Students will collect and observe wetland animals and make a wildlife field guide.

Objectives

Students will describe the living and nonliving components of wetland habitats.

Materials

- copies of Wet 'n' Wild Mini Field Guide
- paper, pencils, clipboards
- colored pencils, felt-tip pens, or crayons
- collecting equipment (see Equipment for Collecting Critters for specific materials needed)
- "wettable" clothes and shoes or boots, change of clothes
- field guides

Making Connections

Careful field collection techniques support an appreciation of adaptations unique to wetlands animals. Skillful observation and proper data collection and recording methods are critically important to good field technique.

Background

Wetlands are so often depicted as dark, dangerous places full of undesirable creatures that many of us tend to believe it! However, even skeptics who visit wetlands will admit that they are actually beautiful places full of interesting and beneficial animals.

The kinds of animals in a wetland depends on the type of wetland, the plants that grow there, and the quality of the water (salty or fresh, clean or polluted). Field guides to wetlands, ponds, mammals, fish, insects, birds, and wildflowers, (see Resources, p. 327) are helpful identification tools. Some of the common wetland fauna are shown in the Wet 'n' Wild Mini Field Guide on p. 103.

A habitat is the place where an animal finds food, water, shelter, and space, in the arrangement that suits its needs. Different animals often require different habitats, though many may share the same habitat. The habitat for a

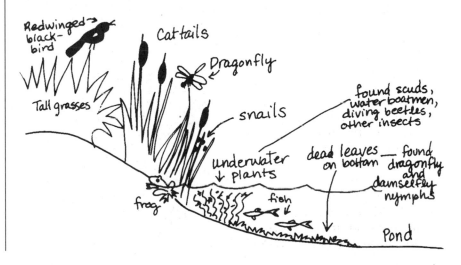

fish is water; for a bear, the woods; for a whale, the ocean; and for an earthworm, the soil. Even within the same class of species, habitat requirements can vary: some fish live in salt water, others in brackish or fresh water; some prefer moving water, others stay where it is still.

An animal may occupy a specific area within a habitat, often called its microhabitat. Some microhabitats are very specific. For example, the green salamander, an Appalachian species, lives among shaded, lichen-covered rocks with crevices that allow it to stay cool and moist. It is very discriminating about the types of crevices it chooses. The crevices must interconnect throughout the rock habitat and cannot be too dry or too wet! Because the green salamander's microhabitat is so specific, it is an endangered species—there aren't enough suitable places these days for this animal to call home.

When resources in an area are limited, animals must diversify to reduce competition. Animals may share habitats, but each species has its own place (microhabitat or niche) within that setting.

Procedure

Warm Up
Explain that animal identification is valuable, but the observation of animals' behavior and location may be even more important.

Tell the students they will be going outside to investigate a wetland habitat and the animals that live in it. Ask for a definition of habitat and list the four components (food, water, shelter, and space) on the board. Ask them for some examples. Use the fish example to get more complicated—ask if all kinds of fish live in the same kind of water.

Ask the students why animals adapt to living in particular places. Have them imagine how it would be if all class members lived in the same house. They may suggest that it would be crowded or that there would be a long line for the bathroom. If the refrigerator only holds enough food for, say, ten people, what would happen at mealtimes? Some might start fighting, and some would eventually move out. Ask if they think animals could all live in the same type of habitat.

Describe the wetland so students know what to expect. Read through the Wet 'n' Wild Mini Field Guide and note the animals that might be found in a local wetland. Point out the few that might give a painful bite if handled (an asterisk [*] appears by these animals' names). Tell students to keep these animals inside nets, pans, etc., for safe observation.

Make or gather equipment (see p. 102 of this activity or chapter 6) and demonstrate its use before going outside.

The Activity
1. **Ask the students to work in teams during the field trip. Instruct each team to collect and observe different animals that live in the wetland and make notes for their classroom field guide about those animals. Review these collection tips with students:**

• Be gentle when handling any living thing. Prepare for squirming critters to avoid dropping them in surprise. Hold animals in a relatively low-stress environment (e.g., keep water animals in water, keep salamanders moist).

• Begin the "hunt" around the edges of the area, then work your way in. Look high and low, behind and under, all around.

• Approach the area quietly and slowly so the animals won't be scared away. When wading, try to keep your shadow behind you to avoid announcing your approach.

• Place animals in containers appropriate to their size and behavior. Ice cube trays filled with water work nicely for many aquatic insects. A shallow pan with a half-inch or so of water will hold small fish and larger aquatic insects. Use a deep bucket with only a few inches of water (and a lid, if possible) for holding frogs. Baby food jars with holes punched in the lid work well for terrestrial insects and other small critters.

• Stress the importance of returning rocks, logs, plant matter, and creatures back to their original location.

• Review your safety rules: depth to which wading is allowed, buddy system, and so on, as appropriate to site and age level of students.

2. **Ask students to jot notes about the following while observing and collecting (to be used later to complete the field guide):**

• *What color is the specimen?*

• *What is its size and shape?*

• *Where, specifically, was it found, and what was it doing?*

• *How does it move?*

• *How does it breathe?*

• *Where are its mouth, eyes, legs, nose, ears? (The last two are often hard to see.)*

3. **Have each team make a simple sketch of the area, and mark on the drawing the location of the microhabitats where animals**

were found. The sketches will be part of the field guide. Students can use symbols or different colors to show landmarks such as water, grassy area, fallen tree, forest. The diagram may be an aerial view or a cross section (side view showing the waterway and its bottom). Youngest students and students who are inexperienced in making a diagram may need to practice by drawing a "map" of the classroom (the habitat) and marking each student's "microhabitat" (seat or desk) before the field trip.

Wrap Up and Action

Have students complete their field guide pages indoors. Assemble the guide and make photocopies for everyone. Students can color their own copies. Suggest that students share their guide with friends to test its effectiveness.

Assessment

Have students:

• identify some animals that live in and use wetlands.

• describe the habitats of these animals.

Extensions

Key out each of the species described in the field guides and identify genus and species.

Make a similar field guide for wetland plants.

Resources

A good guide to freshwater critters is the *OBIS Pond Guide*, available from Delta Education, 1-800-442-5444.

Equipment for Collecting Critters

Homemade equipment (students can help):

Insect net or plankton tow. You will need nylon stockings, heavy wire or old coat hangers, old broom handles or 1-inch wooden dowels, duct tape, needle and thread or yarn. Cut the legs off of the nylons and save. Bend the wire to form a circle and a straight "neck." Tape the neck securely to the end of the stick. Stretch the stocking over the loop, roll the edges to encase the wire, and sew. Use this net to catch insects on land, or scoop it lightly along the surface of the water to catch tiny water animals.

Water viewer. You will need coffee cans with both ends removed, rubber bands, plastic food-wrap, and duct tape. Stretch plastic wrap tightly over one end so it is taut and smooth and you can see clearly through it. Use a rubber band to hold the wrap in place, then tape it to the can. Hold the viewer with the wrapped end in the water. Look through the top and you'll be able to watch what goes on under the surface!

Sieve. Stretch metal screening on an embroidery hoop. Secure edges with duct tape. Make several of these using different gauges of screening. Scoop mud and leaf litter into the sieve, rinse thoroughly with water, and see what you find! Run a sample through a stacked sieve (sieves with larger mesh on top) to catch as much as you can. Pick out critters and place in observation pans.

Equipment to buy, find, or borrow:
Assorted kitchen strainers and sieves.

Long-handled dip nets. Scoop things out of the water or drop over top of frogs, dragonflies, etc.; jiggle and shake in underwater weed beds to loosen hiding animals.

Seine with weighted bottom (ends attached to stakes). Wade into flowing water and hold net bowed across the flow, or walk through still water dragging the net behind. Be sure bottom of net is on bottom. Splash, stomp, and stir water to scare animals into net. Scoop net up flat, draw up its sides, and lay it on the ground. Pick through carefully.

Cast net. Toss out, let drop, haul in with rope (takes practice).

Short dip nets. Used with aquariums.

Minnow trap. Set in flow of waterway. Leave for 30 minutes or so before pulling in.

Observation and holding containers:
Plastic ice cube trays (white) filled with water

Baking pans, porcelain or plastic pans, or basins

Five-gallon buckets with lids

Baby food jars, with holes punched in lids

Bug boxes (plastic box with magnifying lens in lid)

Milk carton observation pans

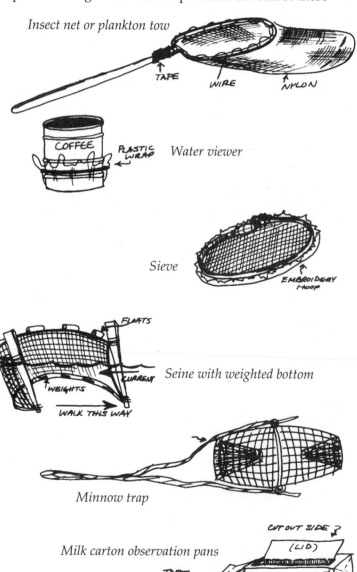

Insect net or plankton tow

Water viewer

Sieve

Seine with weighted bottom

Minnow trap

Milk carton observation pans

* Available from a bait and tackle shop or biological supply company. See also chapter 6, p. 62.

Wet 'n' Wild Mini Field Guide

Most animals listed here are found in freshwater wetlands, though some may be found in brackish or saltwater wetlands. For some salt marsh ideas, see the "Salt Marsh Players" cards, p. 170.

Aquatic Insects and Their Kin: Dragonfly, damselfly, stonefly, mayfly, alderfly, dobsonfly, cranefly, caddis fly, mosquito, and others, found on and above water; their larvae (nymphs) found in the water. Water-dwelling adults and larvae: water boatman, predacious diving beetle*, giant water bug*, water strider, backswimmer*, whirligig beetle, crayfish, sideswimmer, water mite.

Other Insects and Their Kin: Horsefly, deerfly, butterfly, moth, tick, spider*

Fish: Mudminnow, killifish, various sunfishes, pickerel, darter, catfish. Others in salt water.

Amphibians: Frog (green, bull, pickerel, leopard, carpenter, wood, green tree, spring peeper), salamander.

Reptiles: Skink (small lizard), turtle (bog, snapping,* mud, painted, wood, spotted, musk, terrapin* [brackish water]), snakes (brown, ribbon, water*), alligator* (southern United States).

Birds: Wide variety of ducks, geese*, wading birds (herons, etc.), hawks and eagles*, owls*, songbirds (such as red-winged blackbirds and woodpeckers), shore birds (coastal).

Mammals*: Raccoon, fox, shrew, meadow vole, mouse, mink, muskrat, nutria, beaver, river otter, deer, moose (northern United States).

* May bite if handled.

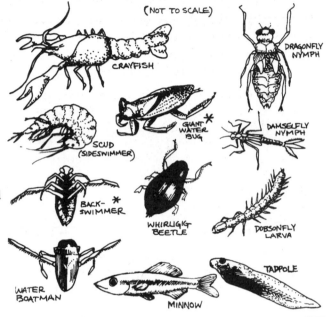

Sample Field Guide Sheet

Save paper. Make two copies of the blank field guide sheet below. Place the two together on an 8 ½ by 11-inch piece of paper, then photocopy and cut into individual sheets. Students may jot notes on the back.

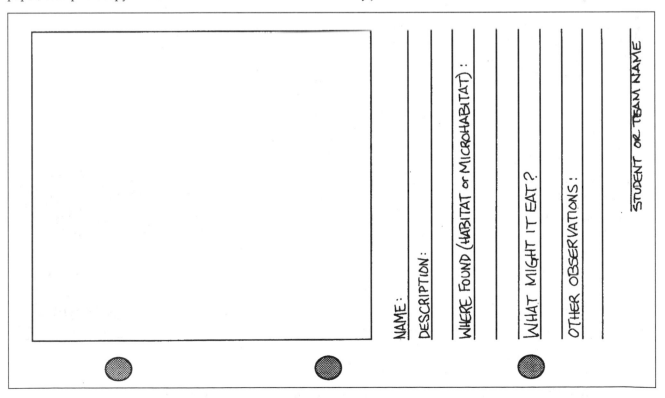

Whose Clues?

[From "Whose Clues?" in Virginia's State Parks . . . Your Backyard Classrooms, *pp. 64-67]*

Grade Level
K-12

Subject Areas
Biology, Ecology

Duration
1 hour

Setting
Classroom and wetland

Skills
Interpreting information

Charting the Course
While looking for signs of animals, students might want to collect samples and make a field guide ("Wet 'n' Wild"), study animal adaptations to wetlands ("Wetland Weirdos"), or play clue game to identify different wetland types ("Wetland Address").

Vocabulary
scat, carnivore, omnivore, sign

Summary

Putting together evidence (clues) to solve a mystery is fun, and it's also part of a scientific approach to problem-solving. Students look for and try to identify animal tracks and other signs of wildlife. They make inferences about the source of the signs and the circumstances under which they were left.

Objectives

Students will:

• observe and identify clues to make inferences about the types of wildlife present in an area, as well as their behavior.

• describe some interrelationships between animals and their environment.

Materials

• *brightly colored ribbon or flagging tape (two 1-foot [0.3 m] pieces per student)*
• *ice cream sticks (two or more per student)*
• *copies of "Whose Clues?" student pages (one per team)*
• *clipboards, paper, pencils*
• *poster-sized piece of absorbent paper and rags or old towels (optional for younger students)*
• *pictures of various animal clues, glue or tape, blank cards (optional)*

Making Connections

Often people walk through a field or forest and they don't "see" any wildlife. This activity sensitizes students to a variety of ways to detect the presence of wild animals and their habitats. Firsthand observation of clues in the field is a critical step in biological research and assessment.

Background

The prospect of a class trip to a wetland or other natural setting may inspire students to envision scenes from *National Geographic* specials or Disney films—a muskrat diving underwater just beyond the grasp of a swooping red-tailed hawk, a beaver gnawing down a birch sapling, an otter in hot pursuit of a bluegill, or fledgling wood ducks plopping comically into the water from their nest cavity in an old tree. Though these scenes occur daily in natural areas, they are seldom witnessed, especially by crowds of enthusiastic youngsters. However, all animals leave behind clues to their activities: what they've been eating and where they've been walking, running, resting, and rearing their young. When a group of sharp-eyed youngsters starts searching an area for these signs, fascinating discoveries are sure to follow.

Tracks, among the most obvious clues of an animal's presence, are most easily found in the soft mud or sand near puddles, ponds, or waterways. Each type of animal leaves a distinct footprint distinguished by the number of toes, claw marks, size, and pattern of the tracks.

Other marks are not always as distinctive as tracks, but they may still be important clues. For example, claw marks on smooth bark indicate where squirrels, opossums, or raccoons have been climbing. Narrow trails or pathways indicate the regular routes of deer, rabbits, or raccoons. A worn place on the bank of a creek or pond might indicate the place where beavers or otters regularly come ashore. Otters leave "sliding boards" in the bank where they slip down into the water. Muskrats dig connecting pathways and tunnels in the marsh mud that are often visible when the water level is low.

Animals leave abundant evidence of what and where they have been eating. Deer and other browsers snip off tips of twigs and branches. Squirrels drop stripped pine cones and nutshell fragments. Small, freshly covered or overturned patches of leaves and soil might indicate where a squirrel or chipmunk has stashed or recovered nuts. Scattered feathers or tufts of fur show where a predator captured or devoured a bird or mammal.

The form and contents of droppings, also called scat, can reveal a lot about the types of animals living in an area and what they've been eating. The scat of plant-eating animals tends to be small and uniform in size and composition. Scat of carnivores and omnivores tends to be larger and may contain hair, bones, and undigested seeds.

Not everything that looks like a dropping is necessarily scat, however. Among birds of prey such as owls, not all of the indigestible parts of a meal pass through the digestive tract. Instead, these birds regurgitate pellets of fur and bones about the size of the end of a thumb. These pellets often accumulate under a favorite roost.

Roosts of other birds might be recognized by white splatters from their droppings on the ground under trees, just as on statues,

lampposts, and windowsills. Another sign of a resting place may be compressed vegetation in a thicket where animals such as deer have been lying.

Many animals, especially birds, build nests when they're ready to raise young. Although most nests will be hidden, a few can usually be spotted. Songbirds' nests are typically tucked away in thickets or in the leafy cover of trees. The nests are made of a variety of materials such as grasses, spider webs, straw, hair, and bark. Large birds of prey such as hawks, eagles, and osprey build nests of sticks high in the treetops (osprey also build on buoys and channel markers over water). Woodpeckers excavate holes in dead trees or limbs and nest within the hollow. Wood ducks are also cavity nesters, though they find natural cavities to use. Muskrats build lodges of cattail stalks and mud. These look like small beaver lodges, which are made of mud, branches, and vegetation. A marsh wren's spherical nest is

cleverly concealed among the tops of cattails and reeds—but which is the real one? The wren builds several "dummy" nests to fool predators!

Some animal homes, such as beaver and muskrat lodges, may be used year-round. If you approach an area quietly, you may get a glimpse of an animal as it ducks into its home and out of sight.

Procedure
Warm Up
Before the trip, visit the area and select a good site for the activity—one with soft ground and the greatest diversity of habitat as possible.

In class, describe the area and brainstorm the types of animals that might live there and clues those animals might leave behind. Make a list on the board.

Divide the class into small teams. Have each team make two flags (foot-long pieces of ribbon taped to ice cream sticks) per student.

Explain that teams will search for animal clues at the wetland and mark the clues with the flags. Leaving the flags in place will allow everyone to study how and where clues were left. After the search time, each team will take the class on a tour to show its flagged clues. Each team member will talk about two clues, giving the team's inferences about the student page questions.

The Activity
1. **At the wetland, review the search procedure and hand out copies of the student pages for teams to read before starting off. Define search area boundaries, taking into consider-**

ation the age of the students and the diversity of the sites.

2. **Set a search time limit of 10-20 minutes. Have each team search within its designated area for two clues per student, or as many as possible. There may only be a few clues per site. As they are found, clues should be marked by poking a flag into the ground or tying it to a nearby branch. Team members should plan their answers to the student page questions.**

Wrap Up and Action

After the search time, regroup and take the tour, as described above. Remove the flag after each clue is presented. Encourage all students to offer alternative explanations of a clue. A few specimens may be collected for the classroom, if desired (leave scat where found).

Assessment

Have students:

- identify different signs animals leave behind.

- present or draw examples of scat and tracks.

Extensions

Make a Mud Print poster! Have younger students make their own mud prints with hands (or shoes, if reluctant), first in the ground, then on a big piece of absorbent poster paper. Bring old rags or towels to wipe hands clean. Students can write their names on the poster next to their prints. Make a neat design and bring it back as a souvenir!

Carefully pick through owl pellets to retrieve the rodent and bird bones inside. Carolina Biological Supply (1-800-334-5551) offers pellets and diagrams of skeletons that students can use to identify bones and skulls. Students might

try to put the skeletons back together.

Adapt student pages to make picture-and-question flash cards with identifications written on the back. Ask students to identify the animal signs.

Notes:

Whose Clues?

1. *What kind of a sign is it?* (Track; scat; evidence of feeding such as a gnawed branch; actual remains such as a bone, feather, or shed skin; a nest; a pathway or tunnel; other sign.)

2. *What type of animal do you think left the sign?*

3. *What was the animal doing when it left the sign? How can you tell?*

4. *When you look at the scat or owl pellets, can you tell what the animal had been eating?* (Neat stuff can be found by examining pellets or poking around in scat with a stick. Most wild animal scat is relatively odorless.)

5. *For each of the above questions, how could you find out if your answers are correct?* (Use the back of this sheet or an extra sheet if you need more space.)

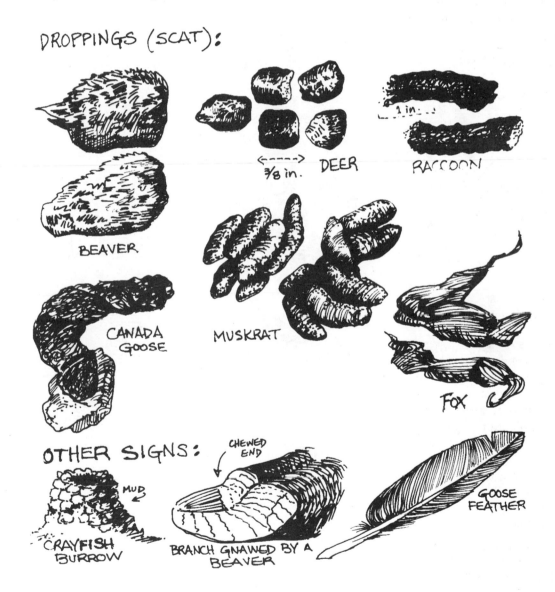

DROPPINGS (SCAT):

⅜ in. — DEER

1 in. — RACCOON

BEAVER

CANADA GOOSE

MUSKRAT

FOX

OTHER SIGNS:

CRAYFISH BURROW — MUD

CHEWED END — BRANCH GNAWED BY A BEAVER

GOOSE FEATHER

Whose Clues?

Footprints (tracks)

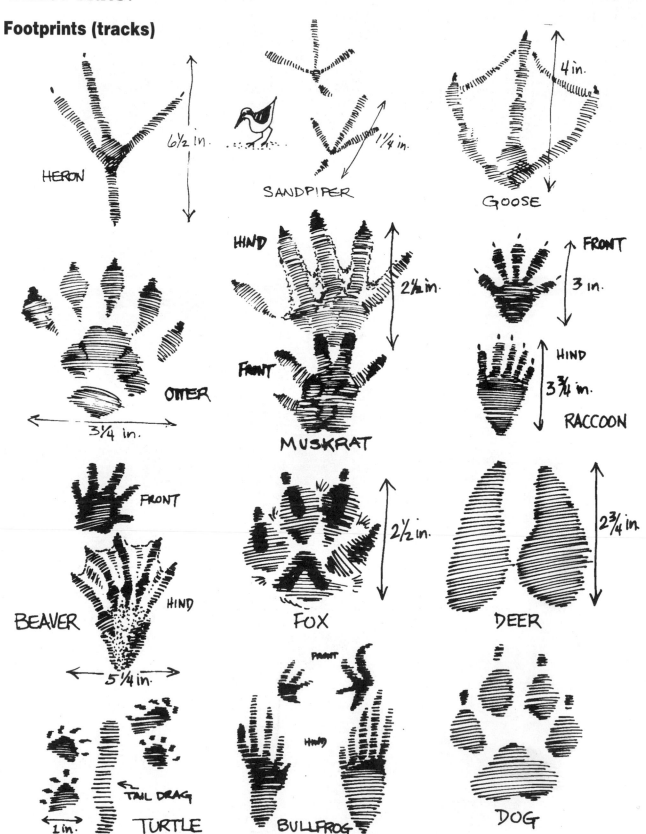

HERON   6½ in.

SANDPIPER   1¼ in.

GOOSE   4 in.

HIND   FRONT   2½ in.

OTTER   3¼ in.

FRONT   MUSKRAT

FRONT   3 in.

HIND   3¾ in.   RACCOON

FRONT   BEAVER   HIND   5¼ in.

FOX   2½ in.

DEER   2¾ in.

TURTLE   1 in.   TAIL DRAG

FRONT   BULLFROG   HIND

DOG

Marsh Market

Grade Level
2-8

Subject Areas
Ecology, Biology

Duration
Part I: 40 minutes;
Part II: 40-60 minutes

Setting
Classroom

Skills
Gathering, analyzing, and
interpreting information

Charting the Course
Advanced students may do
"Marsh Mystery," a lesson on
bioaccumulation. You may
also play the "Marsh
Munchies" game to learn
more about nutrients and
energy flow.

Vocabulary
herbivore, carnivore,
omnivore, insectivore,
predator, prey, producer,
consumer, decomposer,
food web

Summary

Students construct a "living"
wetland food web, then create
their own web by tracing components of their lunches.

Objectives

Students will:

- appreciate the interdependence
of the organisms, including
humans, involved in a food web.

- make the connection between
the importance of natural
resources and the ways we
impact them.

Materials

- *large ball of string or yarn*
- *large file cards or strips of paper*
- *students' lunches or lists of every
item each student ate in a recent
meal*
- *drawing paper and markers*
- *tape*

Making Connections

Wetland habitats provide the
necessities of life: abundant food
source, adequate water supply,
space to live and grow, safe cover
for resting and nurturing young.
Without wetlands, we would not
have many of our own sources of
food and income. Your students
may be surprised to find out how
many familiar things we derive
from wetland resources.

This activity introduces the
importance of wetland community. This study of interactions of
organisms in a habitat leads to an
understanding of our own roles
in, and potential effects on, the
environment.

Background

A wetland is a great marketplace
of food sources. The vast number

of plants growing in a healthy
wetland form the basis of this food
web. (A food web is a complex
system of many food chains.)
Resident and visiting animals can
find a wide array of food choices
in a wetland, whether they eat
plants, animals, or both. A wetland with a great diversity of plant
life will attract higher numbers
and more species of animals.

Plants are called primary producers because they supply food at
the lowest level of a food chain.
It takes an enormous number of
individual plants to support the
other parts of the web. Wetland
habitats are extremely productive
in terms of plant life.

At the next level of a food chain
are primary consumers: plant-
eaters or herbivores. Primary
consumers include rabbits, mice,
deer, and certain other mammals,
some insects and fish, and ducks,
geese, and certain other birds.

Primary consumers are eaten by
secondary consumers, or carnivores (meat-eaters). This group
includes predators such as birds
of prey, some snakes, foxes, wild
cats, and people. Secondary
consumers are eaten by tertiary
consumers, which may be predators or scavengers such as turkey
vultures, crabs, and sometimes
people. Note that these categories
are very broad and general. Many
animals fit into more than one
group, and there are more complex levels of the web.

Any of the food web components
mentioned above can be broken
down by decomposers, organisms
such as bacteria and fungi that
reduce dead plant or animal
matter into smaller particles. A
decaying plant, for example, will

be broken down into nutrients that enrich the soil. This process supports the growth of more plants.

People are also part of the wetland food web! Many regional economies depend upon wetland foods. Are you a seafood lover? Oysters, shrimp, bluefish, flounder, and other popular, commercially important fish and shellfish are produced in wetlands, especially coastal marshes. Waterfowl, deer, and other game species that visit wetlands provide a source of food and income. Wetland mammals such as beaver, mink, and muskrat are valued for their fur—and muskrat is even becoming a popular gourmet dish. Cattail shoots, wild rice, and many other wetland plants that grow in wetlands are edible. Next time you get the munchies, visit a wetland for a snack!

Procedure
Warm Up
Have the class discuss the concept of a food web—what animals eat and who eats them. Introduce or review the terms herbivore, carnivore, omnivore, insectivore, predator, prey, producer, and consumer. Have older students

discuss the flow of energy from primary producers through tertiary consumers and decomposers (see diagram).

The Activity
Part I: *Make a "Living" Wetland Food Web*

1. **Make a list of plants and animals (birds, mammals, reptiles, amphibians, fish, insects, and other invertebrates) that live in or use wetlands. Assign items on the list to students and have them research the animals' food habits and predators. Then place the animals in a chart of "carnivores," "herbivores," etc.**

2. **Write the name of each plant and animal on the list on a separate card or strip of paper. Tape the cards or strips on the board and ask students to select one name. Have students stick their selection on their clothing.**

3. **Have the class stand in a circle. Select a "plant" to begin the web and give that student a ball of string. Ask him to wrap the end once around his hand, then pass the ball to an organism that eats his plant, connecting the one who is consumed to the consumer. This student should wrap**

the string around her hand and pass the ball either to an organism that eats her organism or to her own organism's food source. Remember that many of the plants and animals should be connected to several others; if a student receives the ball of string a second time (or more), he should pass it to a student he hasn't already passed it to. As the activity progresses, those who researched the organisms involved can help decide where to pass the string. Continue in this manner to create a "living" wetland food web.

4. **Once the web has been completed (all possible connections have been made), have the students shift around until the web is taut. Have students discuss the fact that sometimes a plant or animal's role in the web may change, or disappear entirely.** What effect would this have on the web?

Use the following scenarios to describe what can happen to parts of the web when the wetland habitat is disturbed. With each description, have the students decide which organism would be affected by the change first (suggested answers appear in parentheses). Have the student wearing this sign tug on the string. Anyone who feels the tug should raise her or his free hand. Have each of these students tug on the string, and so on. When the third scenario has been covered, have the class sit down and discuss the web.

Scenarios:
• It is raining. A lawn-care company's truck skids and crashes near the wetland, spilling hundreds of gallons of weed killer. The rain washes the chemicals into the wetland (plants).

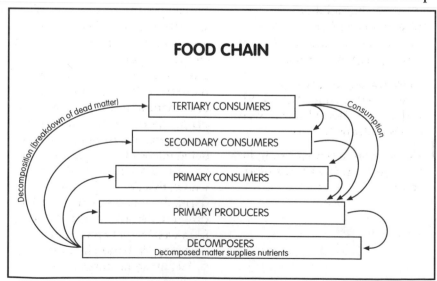

FOOD CHAIN

TERTIARY CONSUMERS

SECONDARY CONSUMERS

PRIMARY CONSUMERS

PRIMARY PRODUCERS

DECOMPOSERS
Decomposed matter supplies nutrients

Decomposition (breakdown of dead matter)

Consumption

• A stream is blocked by a huge pile of dumped garbage. The part of the stream that usually flows through the wetland dries up (fish).

• The wetland is destroyed when someone buys the land and builds a shopping mall there (everything).

Part II: *What's For Lunch?*

1. **Ask the students to take out their lunches (don't eat them now!) or list foods eaten at a recent meal. Have students draw self-portraits at the top of a piece of paper. Below this, have them draw and label pictures of each item in their meal and label each one (or draw a circle for each item and write the item's name inside).** Be sure to include all items; i.e., instead of "sandwich," list or draw "ham," "cheese," "mayonnaise," "whole wheat bread," and so forth.

2. **Decide what each item is made from.** What is cheese? Where do frozen peas come from? What went into the can of soup? Break down each component of the meal, tracing each ingredient to its most fundamental sources. For example, mayonnaise is made of eggs and vinegar. Eggs come from chickens, which eat grain, which grows in the soil. Chickens come from eggs which come from chickens . . . let's not get into that. Vinegar can be made from apples, which grow on trees, which need air, soil, sun, and water.

3. **Students should label the consumers and the producers in the diagram. Ask which category shows up most.** There should be more primary producers, since the foods were probably made from or raised on primary producers. Explain that it takes a lot of grain to raise one cow, and many primary producers to support the higher levels of a food web!

4. **Ask students to imagine that one of the natural resources in the diagram has been depleted. Have them choose one and put an X beside it. Then go through the food web and put an X beside each item they would not have without that resource.** Would their meals have been the same? Would they lose things they need, things they just like to have, or both?

Wrap Up and Action

Ask students to describe ways that the food web might be affected by a change in one of its links. Help students understand that a change in the availability of even one food source could affect many wetland residents. Stress that parts of an ecosystem are interconnected and interdependent, and every link is vital to the health of the whole.

Assessment

Have students:

• identify animals and plants in a wetland food web and describe their role (carnivores, herbivores, omnivores, insectivores, etc.).

• describe interrelationships among wetland organisms (consumers, producers, decomposers, predator, prey).

• demonstrate how several components in a wetland food web can be affected when even one is disturbed.

• draw a diagram identifying how their own lunches fit in a food chain.

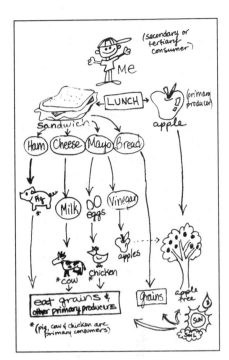

Extensions
Nature in Your Neighborhood
Take a trip to a nearby wetland or other natural area. Observe, list, and diagram the components of the area's food web. You may not see many animals, but look for signs that they were there—droppings, footprints, feathers, nibbled leaves and twigs, remnants of a meal (bones, fur, etc.), even a tunnel or other pathway.

You may find signs that people are part of this food chain. Fishing line caught in trees or shrubs and empty shotgun shells on the ground can be signs of human predation. Does this area offer other natural resources that people need, use, or want? Are there signs that resources here are being misused, or cared for? Do you see ways in which the food web in this area might be harmed? What can you do to help preserve the resources and the food web? See chapter 6, or "Helping Wetland Habitats," p. 288, for some ideas.

The Wetland Gourmet

Grade Level
K-12

Subject Areas
Home Economics, Social Studies, History

Duration
Variable

Setting
Kitchen and classroom

Skills
Gathering and applying information

Charting the Course
Students can study plants and animals used in this activity in "Tracking Plants and Keeping Track" and "Wet 'n' Wild." See Procedure for other connections.

Vocabulary
edible plants, productivity

Summary
How would you like to dine out in a wetland? Persimmon pudding and a wetland salad bar? Give them a try!

Students go to the kitchen to discover the fruits of a wetland.

Objectives
Students will:

• appreciate wetland environments as incredible food sources.

• tune up their cooking skills!

Materials
Materials will depend on ingredients needed for the gourmet feast; see recipes on next pages.

Optional for the Warm Up:
• *a persimmon*
• *a bag of white or wild rice*
• *fresh or canned blueberries*
• *fresh or bagged cranberries*
• *mint tea*
• *cattail shoots, watercress, beach peas, or other wetland salad ingredients*
• *a can of crab meat*
• *a can of turtle soup*
• *a muskrat pelt*

Making Connections
Many items that end up on the dinner table originate in wetlands. This activity asks students to examine the "root" of our culinary bounty, and, in doing so, discover the wealth and productivity of wetlands.

Background
Wetlands offer many foods that provide humans and other species with essentials for survival. Even salt, a necessary food preservative in Colonial times, used to be "mined" from salt marshes. People can find a wide variety of edible plants in wetlands, as well as fish and game. Ducks, geese, deer, muskrats, and numerous species of fish and shellfish such as crabs, shrimp, and crayfish abound in wetland settings. In the South, even alligator has become a delicacy.

Procedure
Warm Up
Describe a meal of crab cakes, roast duck with cranberry sauce, and blueberry pie. What is common to every course of this meal? The ingredients came from wetlands! Can students come up with other wetland meals?

As an option, present the food items on the materials list and ask students where the items came from. Lead a discussion on the productivity of wetlands. (See chapter 3, p. 25.)

The Activity
1. **Have a wetland festival in the classroom and invite other classes! Have students make displays; perform the salt marsh play (p. 165); play a tape of wetland, lake, ocean, and even rain forest (yes, they're wetlands, too) sounds to set the mood (see pp. 71, 329); and offer a variety of wetland taste treats listed in this activity.** Students and parents can make some things and bring them in. Many of these recipes can be cut into tidbits and served as hors d'oeuvres. Have older students make a few of these recipes in home economics cooking classes. **Be sure to check with parents about any allergies students may have to shrimp or other foods.**

Wrap Up and Action
Take pictures of the taste treats and make a class cookbook

complete with recipes, photos, and written comments from festival participants!

Assessment

Have students:

- make a meal using materials from a wetland.

- create a wetland cookbook, identifying wetland food sources.

Extensions

Choose one of the plants or animals used in the recipes below, identify its Latin name, and write a short report on that species. Note its locations, uses, physical characteristics, adaptations, and so on.

Research diets from Colonial times or Native American cultures and identify wetland dietary staples from different parts of the United States.

Persimmon Pudding

[*From* A Lighthouse Window: Recipes and Recollections from the Chesapeake Bay Maritime Museum (*in St. Michaels, Maryland*). 1989. Easton, Maryland: Waverly Press.]

Persimmons, also called "sugar plums," are most abundant in the southeastern states. The trees grow along streams, roadsides, fields, and sandy bottomlands. They are a food source for foxes, raccoons, opossums, skunks, and birds. Collect the soft, orange fruits well after fall frost or they'll make your mouth pucker! Press pulp through a colander.

2¼ cups flour
1 teaspoon allspice
½ cup sugar
½ teaspoon salt
1 cup packed dark brown sugar
2 cups persimmon pulp
1 teaspoon baking powder
1 cup buttermilk
1 teaspoon baking soda
2 eggs
1 teaspoon cinnamon
whipped cream for garnish

1. Combine all ingredients except whipped cream in large bowl. Mix at low speed just until batter is smooth.

2. Spread batter in two greased 9 x 9 inch baking pans; level batter with spatula. Bake at 350 degrees for 60 minutes or until a toothpick inserted in the center comes out clean.

3. Serve warm or cool, and garnish with whipped cream.

Blueberry Grunt

Much more pleasing than its name indicates, this sweet dessert can be made in the classroom by even the youngest of students (with supervision, of course). The blueberry is a very common shrub found in forested wetlands, shrub swamps, bogs, and even wet overgrown fields. The similar-looking huckleberry can be substituted in this recipe. The sauce makes a delicious topping for pancakes or ice cream, as well.

Sauce:

4 cups blueberries
1½ cups sugar
2 Tablespoons lemon juice
2 lemon rinds, grated
½ teaspoon cinnamon
½ teaspoon salt
3 cups water

Dumplings:

1 cup sifted flour
¼ cup sugar
2 teaspoons baking powder
½ teaspoon salt
3 Tablespoons shortening or margarine
⅓-½ cup milk

1. Combine sauce ingredients in a heavy saucepan. Bring to a boil, then reduce heat and simmer 5 minutes. Remove from burner and set aside.

2. Sift dry ingredients together into a bowl. Cut in shortening until crumbly. Add enough milk to make a sticky dough; do not overmix.

3. Simmer sauce again until bubbly. Drop dough from greased spoons onto the surface of the sauce. Cook uncovered 10 minutes. Cover tightly and cook 10 more minutes without lifting the lid!

Wild & Wonderful!

Wild rice is a flavorful and colorful change from that plain, white standby. It goes well with lots of foods, especially the wetland recipes. By the way, white rice is grown in wetlands, too. They're called rice paddies!

Cranberry Ice

[*From* Betty Crocker's Cookbook. *1986. Racine, Wisconsin: Western Publishing Company, Inc. Reprinted with permission of General Mills, Inc.*]

Cranberries grow in bogs in cooler climates such as those in the northern states of Massachusetts, New Jersey, and Wisconsin. The ones you find in the grocery store have been cultivated by cranberry growers. Most people are familiar with cranberry sauce and cranberry juice, but this treat is a bit more unusual—and it's one that's as good *for* you as it is good (cranberries are a good source of vitamin C)!

1 pound cranberries
2 cups water
2 cups sugar
¼ cup lemon juice
1 teaspoon grated orange peel
2 cups cold water

Cook cranberries in 2 cups of water until skins are broken, about 10 minutes. Rub the berries through a sieve to make smooth pulp (discard skins). Stir in sugar, lemon juice, and orange peel. Stir in 2 cups cold water. Pour into square baking dish, 8 x 8 x 2 inches. Freeze until firm, stirring several times to keep mixture smooth. Let stand at room temperature 10 minutes before serving. (If you like, you can spoon the partially frozen mixture into ice cube trays and insert popsicle sticks to make cranberry pops.)

Wet Your Whistle!

Try a variety of drinks made from wetland plants. Mint, cranberry, and hibiscus teas are available in many grocery and specialty stores.

Have you ever heard of Moxie® soda? It's an "old-fashioned" drink that's sort of in between ginger beer and root beer. This zippy soda is made from a beautiful wetland wildflower called gentian. It's still sold in many stores in New England and perhaps other areas. Aromatic bitters, a flavoring used in cooking and cocktails, is also made from gentian.

Wetland Salad Bar!

Just for fun, think about eating a salad made of the many different edible plants that grow in wetlands. If you want to taste any of these, make certain that you collect the correct plant (the ones listed here are easy). Use Peterson's *Guide to Edible Wild Foods* or another reliable guide for help. From freshwater wetlands, collect young cattail shoots or stalks, peeled and sliced (taste like cucumber); fiddleheads (buy these in the store); wild leeks or ramps, sliced; watercress leaves, whole or chopped. From the seashore, find beach peas (cooked); glasswort, also called pickleweed or sea pickle (salty!); chopped sea lettuce (a seaweed); sea rocket leaves; and for a tart/sweet addition, beach plums and rose hips. A healthy combination! Top off with your favorite dressing.

Mini Maryland Crab Cakes

This bite-sized treat is made from the sweet meat of the blue crab. The crab's Latin name, *Callinectes sapidus*, means "beautiful, tasty swimmer." To those who have seen this leggy crustacean steamed and seasoned fire-red, only the "tasty" part might seem fitting. But anyone who has ever seen a blue crab dancing sideways in the water or slipping secretly through a bed of aquatic plants at a wetland's edge surely understands the origin of the name.

1 pound "lump" crab meat (claw meat will do, too)
1 cup bread crumbs
2 eggs, beaten
2 Tablespoons mayonnaise
1 Tablespoon spicy mustard
1 teaspoon horseradish
2 Tablespoons chopped parsley
2 teaspoons seafood seasoning (for crab or shrimp) **OR** ¼ teaspoon each of celery salt, celery seed, ground mustard, and black pepper, and [optional] ⅛ teaspoon paprika, ⅛ teaspoon mace (optional)
1 finely crushed bay leaf
1 teaspoon Worcestershire sauce
oil for frying

Mix all ingredients together in a bowl. Taste and correct seasonings. Form mixture into bite-sized balls or cakes (about a half-inch thick). If mixture is not sticky enough, add a bit more mayonnaise. Heat oil in skillet; add cakes. Fry until golden brown, turning only once. Blot on brown paper bags or paper towels and serve hot or cold (tartar sauce optional).

Wetland Critters

Though many people today oppose the use of animals in food and other consumer products, it is important for students to understand that animals have supplemented human diets and incomes since prehistoric times. Hunting, trapping, and fishing are a part of our cultural and economic past.

Duck, Duck, Goose!

Waterfowl hunting has provided a source of food and income throughout history. Look in a favorite wildfowl cookbook for some savory ways to prepare a holiday meal.

Terrapin and Snapping Turtle

These reptiles have been included because of their historical popularity as epicurean delights. The diamondback terrapin and its purportedly delicious eggs were once hunted to near extinction in their tidal (brackish) marsh habitat. Today, with stricter hunting regulations, its numbers are more plentiful; its popularity as an entree has diminished enough to allow it to thrive. Snapping turtle, also used in soups, is found in fresher waters. The preparation of these unusual treats is so laborious (not to mention gruesome) that those interested in tasting them might be better off turning to the canned variety of soups available in the gourmet section of the grocery store!

Tail Kabobs??

Sure! Use the tail meat of one of three popular wetland creatures: shrimp, crawfish, or alligator. Just skewer peeled shrimp, crawfish, or chunks of alligator meat with cherry tomatoes, slices of onion and green or red pepper, mushrooms, and pineapple. Marinate, if you like, in lime juice or Italian dressing, then grill over hot coals. Serve on a bed of wild rice. A great summer treat!

Marvelous Muskrat

Originally trapped for its soft pelt, the muskrat has historically provided many people with a source of income, food, and clothing. Today, the muskrat has become a delicacy often euphemistically called "marsh rabbit" or "marsh hare" to tempt potential buyers with something a bit more appetizing.

Muskrats are quite prolific and are voracious eaters. They can decimate a marsh of its vegetation if their numbers are not controlled. With trapping for furs in decline, people in many regions are helping to keep muskrat populations at reasonable levels by including these rodents in their diets. If you'd like to try muskrat, you may find it in a gourmet butcher shop or a seafood market or roadside stand in a region with many fresh or brackish marshes. You could also inquire at a national wildlife refuge or state wildlife management area (they often hold an open trapping season for muskrat control and could put you in touch with a trapper). Two ways to prepare muskrat are fried, like chicken, or stewed with a variety of vegetables.

There's Something Fishy About This Pizza!

That's because one of the toppings is fish! Why not? Many of our favorite food-fish are born and raised in wetlands. Try rockfish (striped bass), bluefish, catfish, perch, pickerel, salmon, or any other fish. Sauté the meat, then break it into pieces and use it with your favorite pizza recipe! If you like this one, try clams, oysters, shrimp, or blue crab.

Marsh Mystery

Grade Level
5-12

Subject Areas
Environmental Science, Government

Duration
30-45 minutes for each of two parts

Setting
Classroom

Skills
Interpreting and applying information

Charting the Course
See "Treatment Plants" and "Marsh Market" for other activities on food webs and nutrient uptake.

Vocabulary
bioaccumulation, toxin, producer, consumer, pesticide

Summary
Students read a mystery story and, to solve the mystery, play a game that demonstrates bioaccumulation.

Objectives
Students will:

• be introduced to the concept of bioaccumulation.

• discuss factors contributing to pollution of resources.

Materials
Based on a class of 25; adjust numbers to fit class size.
• *25 paper plates or large paper strips for labels*
• *tape or string*
• *scissors*
• *magic markers*
• *32 red construction paper tokens (2-inch squares)*
• *copies of The Mystery of Sandy Bottom Creek (optional)*
• *copies of Possible Solutions for New Port City and Cedarville (optional)*

Making Connections
Many students recognize signs of pollution when they see litter or a smoggy sky. They may not realize that the consequences of pollution are not always easy to see. Students in some areas may have heard warnings about contaminated seafood; others may have learned about DDT and how it has affected various plants and animals. Understanding the process of bioaccumulation helps students appreciate the potentially far-reaching impacts of local pollution.

Background
Bioaccumulation or biological magnification is the process by which pollutants build up in the bodies of consumers in the food web. An example: plants (primary producers) are sprayed with a pesticide. Insects (primary consumers) eat the plants and ingest the pesticide. Some die, others are eaten before the pesticide kills them. A bird or other animal (secondary consumer) eats several insects, thereby taking in the pesticide. This consumer's body now contains a quantity of pesticide equal to the amount taken in by an insect multiplied by the number of insects and plants it ate. A predator or scavenger (tertiary consumer, or third in the chain) now eats a few of the secondary consumers, and the pesticide is further concentrated in its body.

This is how we sometimes destroy entire populations of wildlife and can endanger human health as well. For example, before the pesticide DDT was banned, bald eagles were driven nearly to extinction from its effects.

Procedure
Warm Up
Ask students what happens when certain toxic substances are introduced into the food web. Read The Mystery of Sandy Bottom Creek to the class (you

may want to give them copies so they can read along). On the board, draw a map of the situation as you read.

The Activity

1. Ask students if they can solve the mystery. How did the boy become ill? Could it be from something he ate? Give the students this hint: There is a man in New Port City who earns his living by catching fish in the Johnstown River and selling them to markets throughout the region.

2. Explain that each student will represent a component of the King's Folly marsh ecosystem. Give students paper plates or strips and have them label their plates or strips as follows: four students are cattail plants, one is a muskrat, one is a mouse, one is

an eagle, ten are shellfish, five are small minnows, two are large bass, and one is a person. Have the students tape their labels to their clothing or tape loops of string through them so they can be worn like a necklace. (For older students, you may want to assign animal identities and diagram the proceedings on the board.)

3. Start at the "bottom" of the food web to try to uncover clues to this mystery. Remind the group that it is known that the pesticide did get into the water that flows through King's Folly Marsh on its way to New Port City, and that the class members represent things that live in the marsh.

4. Ask the cattails (primary producers) what they need to survive (soil, water, sunlight, air). Tell them that as cattails take up water, they are also taking in the pesticide. Give each of the cattails three tokens (red squares) to represent the pesticide concentration they contain. Have them tape the squares to their plates or labels.

5. Ask which of the animals would eat the cattails? Cattails that are eaten by the muskrat should give their tokens to the muskrat; those eaten by the mouse should give their tokens to the mouse. (All the cattails should be eaten.) How many tokens do each of these animals now have? Since the mouse and muskrat ate the cattails, anything in the plant tissue was also eaten, and is now in their bloodstreams and bodies.

6. Ask who would eat these animals? Have the muskrat and mouse give all of their tokens (12) to the eagle, who now has this much of the pesticide in his

body. Have the eagle tape the 12 tokens to his label. This is enough to kill him.

7. Now give each of the shellfish two tokens. Explain that shellfish feed by filtering tiny bits of plant and animal material out of the water. In this way, they also have taken in some of the pesticide.

8. Ask which of the remaining live animals would eat these shellfish. Have the minnows eat two shellfish each and take in their pesticide tokens.

9. Next, have the bass eat all of the minnows and take their tokens.

10. The person (perhaps someone living in New Port City who caught fish from the Johnstown River or bought fish from the fish merchant) then eats the two bass, takes in all 20 tokens and tapes them to his label. Ask if this is enough to make a person ill. Explain that this is a simplified demonstration of a natural process called bioaccumulation or biological magnification. Substances that accumulate (build up) in organisms work their way through the food web.

11. Ask students to review the process by describing what happened in the demonstration. Read the story again. Make a list on the board of all the clues to the mystery and have the class answer the following:

How did the people get sick? Bioaccumulation of the pesticide caused the sickness. The sick people ate fish caught in the Johnstown River. These fish fed in the marsh, a drainage area for the Cedarville farms, before they moved downstream to the river. Some of the contaminated fish were sold in New Port City, while others were sent to a market in the state to the north.

Why didn't the people in Cedarville get sick? Cedarville kids fished and swam in Sandy Bottom Creek north of town, upstream from the runoff from Cedarville farms. King's Folly Marsh is downstream from the farms, and so was contaminated when the pesticide washed down and accumulated in its sediment (silt and soil), water, plants, and fish. If the citizens of Cedarville had eaten the marsh fish, they would have become sick, too.

Why didn't the water test show dangerous levels of pollutants? The marsh filtered out some of the pollutants, so the water that flowed on to the Johnstown River was not badly contaminated. The marsh wasn't able to filter out all of the pesticide, however, so the chain of bioaccumulation began.

When pollutants wash away, are they really away? Is the problem gone? Is the presence of the marsh part of the problem? No! Discuss the benefits of having the marsh there (helps filter pollutants; provides food and cover for valuable animals—animals that give us food and jobs, and animals we just enjoy seeing.) If people did not pollute, problems such as the one in the story would not occur.

Wrap Up and Action
Ask students if this situation could happen in their neighborhood. Have them research their community to find potential sources of pollution that could accumulate in the environment. Have students consider possible solutions to the problems they discover. Students may ask:

• How does the local landfill dump control leakage of chemicals? Does the community offer separate hazardous waste collection and storage?

• Do farmers in the area use buffer strips (areas of trees, shrubs, or even wetland vegetation between tilled land and waterways) or other methods to filter farm runoff?

• Are methods of filtration used on runoff from streets and parking lots? (One method uses stormwater management ponds that allow sediment and attached chemicals to settle out of the water.)

• How can I work to prevent pollution? Organize a community-wide planting day to add a buffer zone (filtering area) to the edges of waterways, or even around parking lots. Plant a wetland! (See Appendix.) Encourage friends and neighbors to keep pollutants off the land and out of waterways by using and disposing chemicals carefully and according to package directions. Some chemicals break down rapidly into harmless, common compounds. Read labels to find out about products' safety and contact the manufacturer for information if necessary. Become more aware of how certain chemicals react in the environment and purchase and use the safer ones. That is, be a wise consumer!

Assessment
Have students:

• diagram how pesticide runoff can contaminate food sources.

• propose and evaluate solutions to a seafood contamination problem.

Extensions
What could people in the story do to solve their problem? Give students copies of the possible solutions listed below. Ask students to take the different roles mentioned in the story (one health official, several townspeople, the sick boy's mother, etc.) and decide which solution each would prefer. Discuss these solutions and others that the students propose. With some guidance, this could turn into a healthy debate.

Have students vote on the solutions or work together to propose a compromise. Advanced students may wish to debate and vote on solutions at a mock town meeting. The class will probably be divided over these issues. How are issues like these settled in real life?

The Mystery of Sandy Bottom Creek

Sandy Bottom Creek, a small tributary, flows through a rural town called Cedarville. The people of Cedarville are mostly farmers who have worked the land since the area was settled in the late 1600s. Cedarville is a small community. Its residents know each other well and often work together to protect the area's resources.

In the summer the children of Cedarville swim and fish in Sandy Bottom Creek just north of town, at a spot where the water is deep. Cedarville residents say, "Many a summer supper came to our table from the idlings of our youngsters! Seems Sandy Bottom's been feedin' our families since time began."

The creek flows through a great marsh on its way out of town. This marsh is called King's Folly Marsh because, before the area was settled, the King's men (English soldiers) took a shortcut through the marsh on their horses and got stuck in the mud!

King's Folly teems with animals and is alive throughout the year with colorful insects, herons, egrets, ducks, muskrats, and many kinds of fish. Last year the Cedarville town picnic was held just outside the marsh, since the scenery there is so beautiful.

This fall, the citizens of Cedarville are up in arms about an alarming and mysterious set of circumstances. It all started when a health official came from New Port City, an urban area bustling with industry and port activities that lies downstream (south) of Cedarville, where the creek joins the Johnstown River. The official said a small boy had become quite ill in New Port City, and a test showed dangerous levels of a pesticide byproduct in his blood. Cedarville farmers use this pesticide in their crops. The case is a mystery: the boy has never visited Cedarville and has never even left his neighborhood in New Port City.

New Port City's drinking water was tested, and not a trace of the pesticide was found. The unfiltered water from Johnstown River was tested. A small amount of the pesticide was found, but this was expected since runoff from Cedarville farms is known to contribute small quantities of pollutants to Sandy Bottom Creek. So how did this poison get into the boy's blood?

In the state north of Cedarville, several people have also reported mild cases of a similar disorder. Yet Cedarville is the only town in the region that uses the pesticide.

The town has called a meeting to discuss the problem. The citizens are concerned about their responsibility in the matter and also worried that they won't be able to use this chemical anymore to protect their crops. They feel this pesticide is the best one ever developed. They've used it for two years and there has never been a problem. Has there been some mistake?

No illnesses were reported during the summer, when people were eating the tomatoes and corn grown in Cedarville, and none of the crops were shipped out of state. If the pesticide is making people ill, why haven't the people who have eaten crops grown in Cedarville been affected? No one in Cedarville has gotten sick—though one man did report finding a dead eagle near his farm south of town.

Possible Solutions for New Port City and Cedarville

1. Make the man in New Port City stop catching and selling fish there. How would this affect the man?

2. Stop all fishing in the Johnstown River and Sandy Bottom Creek. Who would this affect and in what ways?

3. Make the farmers in Cedarville stop using the pesticide. What should they use instead? Have someone play the role of the pesticide manufacturer.

4. Install good pesticide management practices on the farms. Plant wide strips of trees, shrubs, and other plants along the borders between farm fields and waterways to trap eroding soil and pollutants. Who would pay for this to be done?—the farmers or the town, state, or national government? Many of the farmers would lose a piece of their cropland for this purpose. How would they be compensated (repaid) for the cropland lost?

5. Write new or stronger laws to regulate the use of pesticides near waterways. What would the regulations say? How would each of the characters react to these new laws?

6. Have the Health Department or other government agency of New Port City test the water and the fish periodically for toxic levels of pollutants. They should then publish a notice or warning to let people know when to avoid the fish or the water. Would this cause undue alarm in the citizens? What would happen to merchants who sell fish in the city?

7. Do not let the children of Cedarville fish in or near King's Folly Marsh. Make sure they continue to fish upstream from the marsh. Is this an effective means of avoiding contaminated fish? Why or why not? Is this the best approach to natural resource management? Is this treating the symptom or its cause?

8. Fill in King's Folly Marsh and make it a landfill (dump), since pollutants are going there anyway. What effect would this have on the environment and its inhabitants (people, too)?

Treatment Plants

[From "Treatment Plants" in Discover Wetlands]

Grade Level
2-12

Subject Areas
Biology, Environmental Science

Duration
Set up a day ahead; 30 minutes for demonstration and discussion

Setting
Classroom

Skills
Gathering and interpreting information

Charting the Course
Compare this activity with "Marsh Mystery," which studies pollution intake by animals.

Vocabulary
pollutant, capillary action, toxin

Summary
Going up?

Demonstrate the uptake of pollutants into plant tissues.

Objectives
Students will:

• describe how plants remove pollutants from the water.

• analyze the limitations of this ability when wetlands are overloaded with pollutants from the surrounding land.

Materials
• *fresh celery stalks, with leaves*
• *2 beakers or jars*
• *red or blue food coloring*
• *water*
• *paring knife*

Making Connections
Many people do not realize that plants are vital to the health of our water supply. In fact, wetlands and their plants are an increasingly popular alternative for filtering wastewater from homes, schools, factories, and businesses. This activity helps students appreciate wetland plants' natural ability to help keep our water supply clean.

Background
Healthy wetlands perform some very important functions in the cleansing of polluted runoff and wastewater. Pollutants include petroleum products, heavy metals, pesticides, industrial wastes, excess nutrients (such as nitrogen and phosphorus) from household or commercial use, and even litter. The soil layer and the tangle of stems, leaves, and roots in a densely vegetated wetland impede the flow of water and act as a natural sieve. As a result, the water that is processed by a wetland usually enters an open body of water in a much cleaner state. Not surprisingly, a growing number of communities around the world are using wetlands as part of a comprehensive waste-water treatment program.

Wetlands also provide a flood control benefit. The wetland zone along the edge of a stream, river, or pond can temporarily capture and hold floodwaters. The excess water is released gradually from wetlands and the destructive effects of sudden storm surges are avoided. Similarly, when a heavy load of pollutants enters a wetland, the wetland can hold the pollutants for a while and release them into nearby bodies of water slowly. This often minimizes or prevents the harmful effects that would result if most of the pollutants entered the water within a short period of time.

The soils and plants in a wetland can capture and hold, maybe even use and change, many pollutants. Because of the relatively slow movement of water through a healthy wetland, plants form a barrier that allows many sediments and suspended pollutants to settle down to the soil level. Larger floating materials, such as litter, often get caught in the vegetation as well. All these pollutants are buried as new soil materials settle over them. Soil particles often bind with pollutants and prevent them from moving into an open body of water, thus protecting the quality of water. In some cases, the microbiological activity in the soil can actually render pollutants harmless.

Wetland plants play other roles in the preservation of water quality. During plant metabolism, plants draw water, air, and nutrients through their root system. In the daytime, plants use carbon dioxide and produce oxygen during photosynthesis. At night, plants produce carbon dioxide during respiration. Much of this gas exchange occurs through pores (stomata) on the plant surface. These pores also allow water to escape to the atmosphere as vapor (transpiration); some minerals are excreted during this process.

As plants draw water into their roots they also take in nutrients for metabolic activities. Wetland plants can metabolize excess nutrients from human activity, thus protecting the open water bodies that receive wetland runoff. The cattail is a prime example of a wetland plant that will readily use these available nutrients. Of course, there are limits to what a wetland can do, and it is possible to so overload a wetland with nutrients that eutrophication results.

Plants also take up toxic materials when they draw water from their environment. Toxins are stored until the plants excrete them or die. The toxins are then rereleased into the water and soils of the wetland, where they may be captured by other plants, or bind with soil particles. Even so, some pollutant materials do find their way through the wetland and into our rivers, streams, and ponds.

Procedure
Warm Up
Ask students what they think happens when pollutants such as toxic chemicals and garbage flow through a wetland. Explain what happens.

The Activity
Note: Prepare steps one and three one day prior to the lesson. Repeat these steps in front of the class to show how the demonstration was prepared.

1. **Add several drops of food coloring to a water-filled beaker or jar. In class, explain that the food coloring represents pollution by a toxic substance such as a pesticide. Let students suggest other toxic substances.**

2. **Ask the students to imagine that the water is flowing through a wetland and the celery stalks are the many plants (cattails, sedges, grasses, etc.) growing there .**

3. **Cut off the bottom half-inch of the celery stalks and place the stalks in the water overnight. Over time, the colored water will travel via capillary action up the stalks, showing how plants can absorb pollutants with the water they "drink." The colored water may or may not be visible on the outside of the stalk. Cut off 1-inch pieces of the celery and hand them out for students to**

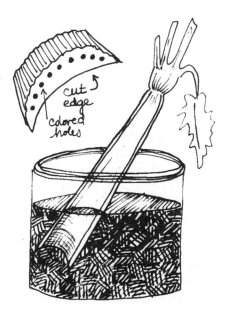

study closely. They will see colored dots on the cut surface. Explain that these are vertical, water-filled channels in the celery seen in cross section.

4. **Discuss what happens to pollutants when they pass through a wetland.**

Wrap Up
Ask students:

How do wetland plants help purify water?

Why is the water remaining in the beaker still polluted?

Where does the water go after uptake into the plant?

What happens to the pollutants?

Why can't we dump all of our waste into wetlands?

Assessment
Have students interpret the role plants play in water purification.

Extensions
Nature in Your Neighborhood
Lots of pollutants run off of the land from construction sites, streets, highways, and the communities in which we live. Sometimes ditches or stormwater management ponds are built to filter polluted runoff and excess rainwater from these sites. These ponds are often planted with wetland plants to aid in the filtering. As the runoff and rainwater rest before flowing on, many of the pollutants, especially soil particles, settle to the bottom and the cleaner water drains off from the top.

Is there a stormwater management pond near where you live? Find one in a safe spot, away from speeding cars. If it is fenced off, stay outside of the fence. Visit the pond on a dry day and again just after a heavy rain. Is there a difference in the appearance of the water in the pond and/or the water washing into the pond? Where is the water flowing from and where do you suppose it is going? You may be able to see water leaving the pond—is this water cleaner? It should be!

This is how natural wetlands work. In fact, this *is* a wetland—a human-made one. If the pollutant load is managed with care, the pond will evolve into a beautiful wetland for all to enjoy! For assistance in finding a pond, contact your highway department, office of public works, or one of the groups listed on p. 330.

Notes:

This Plant Key Is All Wet!

Grade Level
3-12, parts labeled as appropriate

Subject Areas
Life and Environmental Sciences

Duration
30-60 minutes

Setting
Classroom and wetland

Skills
Organizing

Charting the Course
For some easy plant identification in the field, use the "Wetland Wheel."

Vocabulary
dichotomous keys, classification

Summary
What's in a name?

Use a flow chart key to classify students, then use dichotomous keys to identify wetland plants.

Objectives
Students use a flow chart or dichotomous key to classify plants or other objects.

Materials
- *pictures of wetland plants*
- *copies of the Kid Key Tree, What Type of Plant Is It? and Key to Emergent Plants student pages, as appropriate*
- *construction paper, scissors, markers, tape (grades 3-6)*
- *scissors*
- *markers*
- *field guides (optional, see p. 326)*
- *hand lenses*

Making Connections
People use classification skills when they select what clothes to wear, organize compact disks by music type, or decide which books to read. In the sciences, classification systems are used to organize abundant and complex information. Learning how to use a dichotomous key encourages the development of decision-making skills and provides a glimpse of the world of scientific classification.

Background
Wetland plants make special adaptations to the wet and often harsh conditions in which they live (see "Wetland Weirdos," p. 94). These specially-adapted plants thrive, assisting in the proper functioning of wetlands by improving water quality and providing food and cover for numerous species of animals.

Above all, wetland plants are truly unique and fascinating, and they are part of what makes wetlands so beautiful!

Plants are often used to identify an area as a wetland, but an area remains a wetland even if the plants are removed (as long as wetness and wetland soils remain). Learning to identify wetland plants can be fun. It can also be complicated, but we'll leave that to the trickier aspects of plant identification. If you and your students learn to recognize a few common plants, you're on the way to knowing a wetland when you see one! To identify plants, students will need to know the following:

- A dichotomous key provides a series of opposing choices leading to the identity of an unknown.

- A plant does not always look the same—it may change with the seasons. In winter, most soft plants die back, though some (e.g., cattails) leave behind woody stalks. Many trees and shrubs do not have leaves in winter, though some do (needles are leaves). A plant that keeps its leaves all winter is an evergreen. A plant that loses its leaves is deciduous.

- Many plants do grow flowers, even if we do not call the plant a flower. Flowers appear before fruits develop, and seeds come from the fruits. Even lawn grass grows flowers if it's not mowed.

- Leaves and twigs are arranged in different patterns on different plants. They may be opposite, which means that they grow out of the same place on the stem, but on opposite sides. Alternate leaves also grow on alternate sides of the stem, but at alternating elevations along its length. Whorled leaves grow out of the same place on the stem all the way around, like the spokes of a wheel.

• Leaves may be simple (one leaf per stem) or compound. A compound leaf has several leaflets on a stem arranged in the shape of a hand (palmate) or a feather (pinnate). Individual leaves may also have palmate or pinnate patterns.

• The shape and edges of leaves are important identifying features. Leaves may be round, oval, long, pointy, lobed, etc.; edges may be smooth (called entire), hairy, toothed (jagged, like a steak knife), wavy, etc. Look very closely!

Some features of plants and their leaves:

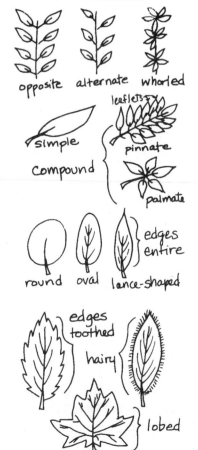

Procedure

Warm Up

Show students pictures of different types of plants. Ask them to describe some of each plant's features. What does it look like? What shape is it? How tall is it? What kind of leaves does it have? What color is it? Does it have flowers? Is it herbaceous (soft) or woody (twigs and stems are rigid like shrub or tree branches)? Where might it grow? (It may be difficult to determine some of these characteristics from a picture.) Have students describe each plant in as much detail as possible.

The Activity
Part I

Have students in grades 3-6 practice using a flow chart by choosing a partner and "identifying" him or her using the Kid Key Tree on p. 125. Remember, this is an example of a flow chart, not a dichotomous key.

Part II

What Type of Plant Is It? demonstrates how to use a dichotomous key. Have students in grades 5-7+ use the key as directed on the student page. *Answers:* A. tree, B. aquatic plant, C. vine, D. emergent plant, E. shrub, F. emergent plant.

Part III

The Key to Emergent Plants student page will introduce students in grades 6-12 to the use of a dichotomous key. There are many more kinds of emergent plants; others may fit the descriptions in this key. Make photocopies of the drawings to be identified with the key. (This key may also be used, along with field guides, at a freshwater wetland to help identify some species of

emergent plants.) The plants shown with this key are also used on the "Wetland Wheel," p. 129. *Answers:* A. Duck potato, B. Cattail, C. Bulrush, D. Soft rush, E. Iris, F. Tearthumb, G. Hibiscus, H. Wild rice, I. Jewelweed, J. Phragmites, K. Skunk cabbage

Wrap Up and Action

When students have had ample practice using the key(s), go out to a wetland and try to identify some of the plants.

Assessment

Have students:

• classify each other using a flow chart

• classify plant types using a dichotomous key

Extensions

Students who have learned to use flow charts and dichotomous keys will be raring for a plant identification field trip! Remember, the keys provided in this activity are certainly not complete! Hundreds and hundreds of plants grow in wetlands, and plant populations differ from region to region. On your wetland visit, bring along copies of the Key to Emergent Plants and some field guides (see Resource, p. 327). Your students may become frustrated if they choose common weeds. Try to visit the site before the class does to look for easy-to-recognize wetland plants like those in the key. You can steer students to the plants that will give them more success. Disturbed or stressed places (along a highway or in a heavily developed area), may only support *Phragmites* (common reed), since it usually takes over once it becomes established. Your pre-trip visit will alert you to this fact.

Kid Key Tree

Make a Kid Key Tree on a wall or bulletin board in the classroom, using the diagram below as a model. Have students pair up. Give each student a construction paper cutout of a leaf. Ask students to write the name of their partner on their leaf. Have partners use the Kid Key Tree to identify each other based on physical features: gender, hair color and appearance, and eye color. Modify the classification scheme, if these features of your students are not varied. You might use clothing to classify students (e.g., "wearing pants," "wearing a skirt," "wearing stripes," "wearing print," and so on. Be sure the students avoid insulting or embarrassing descriptors such as "fat," "dumb," "ugly," etc. Have students work to the smallest branch on the tree and attach their leaf at the end. When the activity is complete, all students in the class will have been "keyed out" and the tree will be full of leaves.

Mangrove trees like this one, grow in wetlands in Florida and other tropical areas.

[*Tree classification scheme from "Keying Out Trees" in* Nature Scope: Trees Are Terrific, *copyright 1992. Reprinted with permission of the National Wildlife Federation.*]

What Type of Plant Is It?

This is a practice key that will help you to learn to use a dichotomous (di-KOT-uh-muss) key. The word dichotomy means "division into two." A dichotomous key divides the task of identifying something into a series of questions that are based on physical features. Each set of questions offers opposing answers to choose from. As you make choices and eliminate others, you eventually find out the name of the mystery item. Use this key to identify the types of plants pictured below.

1. Are stems or other parts of the plant woody and rigid, like a tree?

Yes. . . . . . . Go to 2.

No. . . . . . . .Go to 6.

2. Is the plant growing above the ground but leaning on other plants?

Yes. . . . . . . It is a **VINE**.

No. . . . . . . .Go to 3.

3. Is the plant growing above the ground and standing on its own?

Yes. . . . . . . Go to 4.

4. Is the plant 20 feet tall or taller?

Yes. . . . . . . It is a **TREE**.

No. . . . . . . .Go to 5.

5. Does the plant have more than one main stem?

Yes. . . . . . . It is a **SHRUB**.

No. . . . . . . .It is a sapling (young) **TREE**.

6. Is the plant a soft (herbaceous) plant, like grass?

Yes. . . . . . . Go to 7.

No. . . . . . . .Start over.

7. Is the plant growing in open water that is always there, such as a pond, lake, or permanent stream?

Yes. . . . . . . Go to 8.

No. . . . . . . .Go to 10.

8. Is the plant growing completely under water, freely floating on the surface, or does it have floating leaves?

Yes. . . . . . . It is an **AQUATIC PLANT.**

No. . . . . . . .Go to 9.

9. Is the plant growing with roots and part of the stem under water, but the rest sticking up above the surface?

Yes. . . . . . . It is an **EMERGENT PLANT.**

No. . . . . . . .Go to 10.

10. Is the plant growing in soil that is saturated, wet, spongy, or appears to have been wet at one time (remember that wetlands are not always covered by water)?

Yes. . . . . . . It is an **EMERGENT PLANT.**

Write the plant type on the dotted line in each block.

A. _ _ _ _ _ _ _

B. _ _ _ _ _ _ _

C. _ _ _ _ _ _ _

D. _ _ _ _ _ _ _

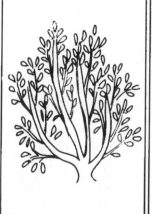

E. _ _ _ _ _ _ _

F. _ _ _ _ _ _ _

Key to Emergent Plants

Instructions: You will be given pictures of plants to identify with this key. Begin at number 1 and choose the phrase that best describes the plant you wish to identify. Then move to the number indicated and choose again. When you come to a name, you've found the plant. If neither one of the pair of phrases fits the plant, either go back to the last choice made and make another, or go back to number one and start over.

1. Plant is a grass or is grasslike. . . . . Go to **2.**

Plant is not grasslike, but is a flowering, soft (herbaceous) plant . . . . Go to **5.**

2. Plant is a grass (has hollow, jointed stem) . . . . .Go to **3.**

Plant is grasslike (does not have a jointed stem) . . . . Go to **4.**

3. Leaves stick out of both sides of the stem, "head" bushy or feathery . . . . **Phragmites.**

Very long leaves grow up from water, "head" sparse and droopy . . . . **Wild rice.**

4. Plant is a sedge (stem has edges, is triangular) . . . . **Bulrush.**

Plant is a rush (stem is round, no edges). . . . . **Soft rush.**

Plant is not a sedge or a rush . . . . Go to **5** or **1.**

5. All or most leaves grow up from the bottom of the stem . . . . Go to **6.**

Leaves arranged along stem . . . . Go to **8.**

6. Leaves long and narrow . . . . Go to **7.**

Leaves arrow-shaped . . . . **Duck potato.**

Leaves wide and rounded . . . . **Skunk cabbage.**

7. Leaves feel flat; blue or violet flower . . . . **Iris (Blue Flag).**

Leaves more "fleshy," has brown "hot dog" near top . . . . **Cattail.**

8. Leaves simple and alternately arranged . . . . Go to **9.**

Leaves simple and oppositely arranged or needlelike *not* included in key.

9. Leaf edges toothed . . . Go to **10.**

Leaf edges not toothed, leaf arrow-shaped, stems prickly. . . . . **Tearthumb.**

10. Plant soft and nearly droopy, small orange or yellow flowers . . . . **Jewelweed.**

Plant more erect, some stems woody, leaves pointier, almost lobed, large white, pink or red cup-shaped flowers . . . . **Hibiscus.**

[Adapted from Field Guide to Nontidal Wetland Identification *by Ralph Tiner, Jr. 1988. Maryland Department of Natural Resources, Annapolis, MD, and U.S. Fish and Wildlife Service, Newton Corner, MA.]*

Key to Emergent Plants

A.

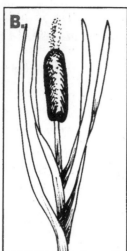
B.

C.

D.

E.

F.

G.

H.

I.

J.

K.

Wetland Wheel

Grade Level
4-12

Subject Areas
Botany, Environmental
Science, Art

Duration
One hour

Setting
Classroom

Skills
Organizing and analyzing

Charting the Course
Use this activity as a supplement to the dichotomous keys in "This Plant Key Is All Wet!" to identify plants on a wetland field trip. You will need to review characteristics of plants with your students. Follow this activity with "Tracking Plants and Keeping Track," a field exercise in plant sampling and herbarium preparation. Special wetland plant adaptations are examined in "Wetland Weirdos."

Vocabulary
dichotomous key, plant identification

Summary
How about a quick and easy way to identify plants in your local wetland?

Students construct a Wetland Wheel with all the answers!

Objectives
Students will classify selected wetland plants and learn to recognize those plants indigenous to wetlands.

Materials
- *copies of wheel pieces and instructions*
- *several pairs of scissors with pointed blades*
- *straight pins*
- *paper fasteners*
- *paste or glue sticks*
- *transparent contact paper to laminate each piece of the wheel (optional)*
- *colored pencils (optional)*
- *colored ribbon or tape*
- *stapler (optional)*

Making Connections
Students may have noticed many different types of plants and flowers in a field, on a mountaintop, or in a wetland. They may have wondered about the names of those interesting plants. Creating and using the Wetland Wheel sharpens observation and classification skills and helps students recognize wetland areas more readily.

Background
See the background section in "This Plant Key Is All Wet!" (p. 123) and "Tracking Plants and Keeping Track" (p. 138).

Procedure
Warm Up
Ask students what types of plants they would expect to find in a wetland. Can they name a wetland tree, shrub, and vine, and an emergent plant and aquatic plant? How do they think these plants have adapted to a wet environment? What features make wetland plants unique?

Note: The species used in this activity are more common in the eastern United States and are most often found in fresh or slightly brackish water. However, some of these plants are common in most areas of the country. If you are visiting a salt marsh you will need to use a field guide. Since many species could not be included here, field guides will help in any case (see Resources, p. 327).

The Activity
Part I

Hand out the materials needed to construct the Wetland Wheel and give each student a copy of the How to Make a Wetland Wheel instruction card. Have them make a wheel.

You may want to white-out the numbers on the plant wheel to make identification more challenging. If your students are younger, it may be helpful to lightly color each of the five major groups of plants with unique colors to aid in plant identification. To do so, lightly color all the wedges on the large wheel marked "Emergent" and all the corresponding wedges on the small wheel with matching numbers with the same color. Choose a different color and do the same for each of the other plant groups. Have your students use the colors to match the wedges correctly. Similarly, you could leave the numbers on the wedges as an aid to younger students.

Part II

Try to scout the field site and find the plants you want to use before doing this activity. Or, ask a naturalist who is familiar with local wetland vegetation to tell you which of the plants found on this wheel you might encounter at your field site. Plan to use only those plants you have prechosen on your field trip. Have the class look at pictures of the plants before the trip so that they will be more familiar with them in the field. When you arrive with your students, use a tape or ribbon to indicate the plants they are to identify with the wheels—without telling them the names of the plants.

Wrap Up

Have students discuss what they found. Was it easy to use the wheel? How might it compare with using a field guide? Encourage them to keep a tally of plants they have identified.

Assessment

Have students:

* construct a Wetland Wheel.

* use a Wetland Wheel to "key out" a wetland plant.

Extensions

Students can create a Wetland Wheel for any type of wetland. Have them research plants that might be on a Wetland Wheel for a New England bog, a North Dakota prairie pothole, a Florida cypress swamp, and a Missouri River riparian wetland.

After they have keyed out some wetland plants, have them create an herbarium of selected, common species (see p. 138).

Have students find out Latin names for plants they key out. Using the "What's Its Name" list on p. 137. Look up these plants in field guides.

Notes:

How to Make a Wetland Wheel

1. Glue each *direction piece* to a manila folder or piece of tagboard. As a nice added feature, cover both sides of each piece with the contact paper. Cut through all thicknesses along the solid outline. Cut out the pie-shaped section in each direction piece to make a window. Place the pieces back to back, match them up, then glue or staple them together across the top only.

2. Carefully cut out *each of the four wheels* along the solid outline.

3. Poke pinholes in the center of each of the two large wheels, then use the pin to line up the two wheels back to back. Glue the wheel pieces together, back to back, so that centers match. Remove the pin. Cover both sides of the large double-sided wheel and each smaller one-sided wheel with contact paper, if desired.

4. Match the side of the large wheel #1 that has trees, shrubs, and vines with the small wheel #1 that has illustrations of trees, shrubs, and vines (numbers 1-16, if you have kept the numbers). Align the small wheel with the large wheel so that the edge of the small wheel lines up with the inside circle on the large wheel. Gently push a paper fastener through the center of the small wheel, then the large wheel. Now match small wheel #2 (emergents and aquatics, numbers 17-32) with the other side of the large wheel; thread it onto the paper fastener. You should now have a two-sided wheel. Remove the paper fastener, keeping the three wheels in alignment.

5. Slide the wheels between the two halves of the direction piece. Adjust the wheels and direction piece halves until all the centers line up. The outside edge of the large wheel should fit just behind the top edge of the window. Gently push the paper fastener through the top half of the direction piece, all three wheels, and the bottom half of the direction piece.

6. Fasten the paper fastener, and your Wetland Wheel is ready to use!

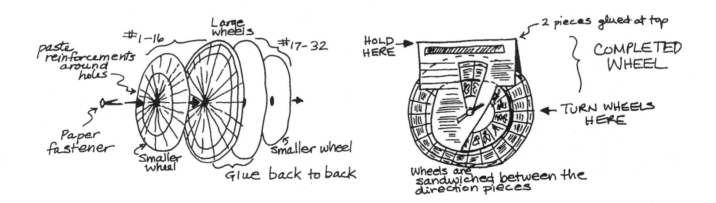

Direction Piece

Cut along solid outline.

Wetland Wheel
A Wheel-y Fun Way to Learn Wetland Plants!

What TYPE of plant is it? ⇨

Description of plant: ⇨

Cut out window

What is its NAME? ⇨

What does it look like? ⇨

Directions:

1. Find a wetland plant to identify.

2. Turn the small wheel until you find a picture that looks like the plant.

3. Turn the large wheel until you find a description that matches the plant. This will give you the name of the plant!

Hint: If your wheel has numbers, be sure the choices you line up in the window have the same number!

Remember to look closely at the leaves and stem arrangement of each plant!
Leaf edges may be:
• entire (smooth)
• toothed (jagged) or wavy
Leaves may be:
• simple (one part)
• compound (many parts [leaflets]):
   pinnate = like a feather
   palmate = shaped like a hand
Leaf shape may be:
• round, oval, oblong, egg-shaped, etc.
• lance-shaped (long, pointy) or tapered
• lobed (edges curve inward in places, almost dividing leaf into parts)
   Leaves may be arranged along the stem so that they are:
   • opposite
    • alternate
      • whorled
         (like spokes of
          a wheel)

Large Wheel #1
Photocopy and cut one (1) per Wetland Wheel.
(Paste to Large Wheel #2, back to back.)

Cut along solid outline.

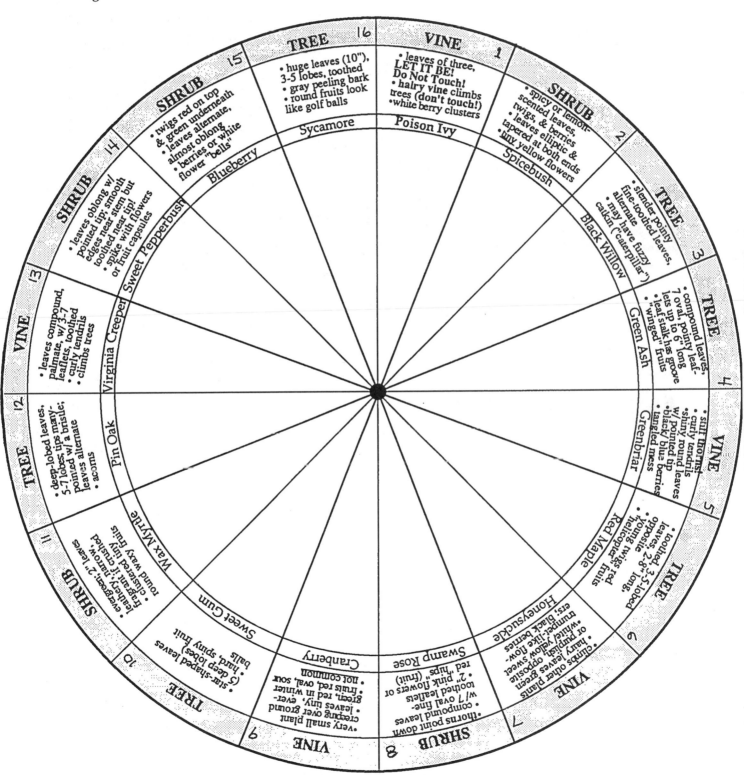

The wheel is divided into 16 numbered segments:

16 TREE — Sycamore
- huge leaves (10"), 3-5 lobes, toothed
- gray peeling bark
- round fruits look like golf balls

1 VINE — Poison Ivy
- leaves of three, LET IT BE! Do Not Touch!
- hairy vine climbs trees (don't touch!)
- white berry clusters

2 SHRUB — Spicebush
- spicy or lemon-scented leaves, twigs, & berries
- leaves elliptic & tapered at both ends
- tiny yellow flowers

3 TREE — Black Willow
- slender pointy, fine-toothed leaves, alternate
- may have fuzzy catkin ("caterpillar")

4 TREE — Green Ash
- compound leaves, 7 oval, pointy leaf-lets up to 6" long
- leaf stalk has groove
- "winged" fruits

5 VINE — Greenbrier
- stiff thorns!
- curly tendrils
- shiny round leaves w/ pointed tip
- black/blue berries
- tangled mess

6 TREE — Red Maple
- leaves opposite 2-3-5-lobed
- toothed, 2-8" long
- young twigs, red
- helicopter fruits

7 VINE — Honeysuckle
- climbs other plants
- hairy leaves, opposite
- white/ yellow sweet or purplish flow-ers; black berries
- trumpet-like flow-ers

8 SHRUB — Swamp Rose
- thorns point down
- compound leaves w/ 7 oval fine-toothed leaflets
- 2" pink flowers or red "hips" (fruit)

9 VINE — Cranberry
- very small plant creeping over ground
- leaves tiny, ever-green, red in winter
- fruits red, oval, sour; not common

10 TREE — Sweet Gum
- star-shaped leaves (5 deep lobes)
- hard, spiny fruit balls

11 SHRUB — Wax Myrtle
- evergreen 2" leathery, narrow, fragrant if crushed
- clustered tiny round waxy fruits

12 TREE — Pin Oak
- deep-lobed leaves, many-5-7 lobes tips w/ a bristle; pointed w/ a bristle
- leaves alternate
- acorns

13 VINE — Virginia Creeper
- leaves compound, palmate, w/ 3-7 leaflets, toothed
- curly tendrils
- climbs trees

14 SHRUB — Sweet Pepperbush
- leaves oblong w/ pointed tip; smooth edges near stem but toothed near tip!
- spike with flowers or fruit capsules

15 SHRUB — Blueberry
- twigs red on top & green underneath
- leaves alternate, almost oblong
- berries or white flower "bells"

Large Wheel #2
Photocopy and cut one (1) per Wetland Wheel.
(Paste to Large Wheel #1, back to back.)

Cut along solid outline.

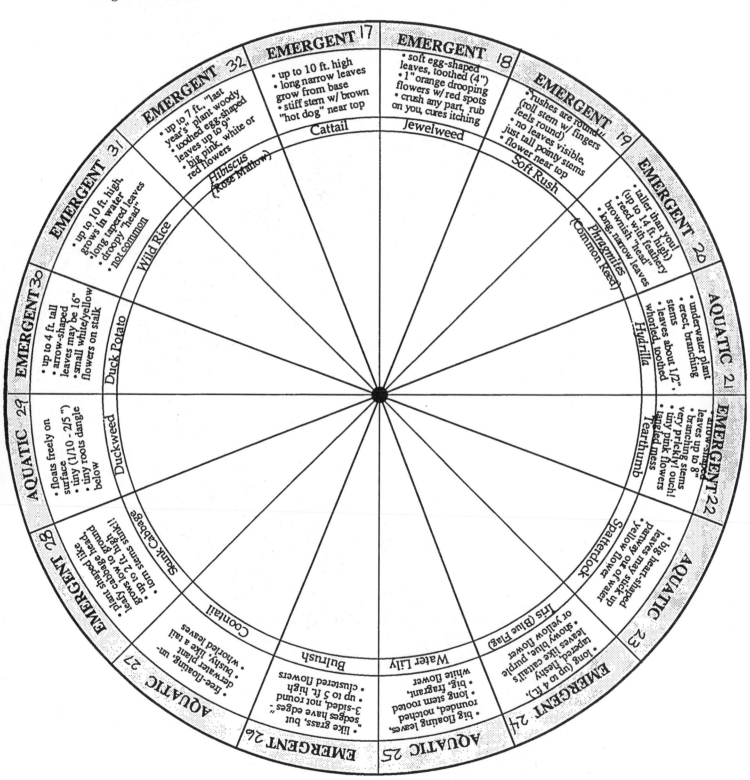

EMERGENT 17
- up to 10 ft. high
- long narrow leaves grow from base
- stiff stem w/ brown "hot dog" near top

Cattail

EMERGENT 18
- soft egg-shaped leaves, toothed (4")
- 1" orange drooping flowers w/ red spots
- crush any part, rub on you, cures itching

Jewelweed

EMERGENT 19
- rushes are round! (roll stem w/ fingers feels round)
- no leaves visible, just tall pointy stems
- flower near top

Soft Rush

EMERGENT 20
- taller than you! (up to 14 ft. high)
- brownish "head"
- long, narrow leaves

Phragmites (Common Reed)

AQUATIC 21
- underwater plant
- erect, branching stems
- leaves about 1/2", whorled, toothed

Hydrilla

EMERGENT 22
- arrow-shaped leaves up to 8"
- branching stem
- very prickly stems
- tiny pink flowers
- tangled mess
- tangled mess ouch!

Tearthumb

AQUATIC 23
- big heart-shaped leaves may or out of water
- yellow flower
- part way in

Spatterdock

EMERGENT 24
- long (up to 4 ft.), fleshy tapered, like cattail's leaves
- showy blue, purple or yellow flower

Iris (Blue Flag)

AQUATIC 25
- big floating leaves, rounded, notched
- long stem rooted
- big, fragrant, white flower

Water Lily

EMERGENT 26
- "like grass, but sedges have edges"
- 3-sided, not round
- up to 5 ft. high clustered flowers

Bulrush

AQUATIC 27
- free-floating, underwater plant
- bushy, like a tail
- whorled leaves

Coontail

EMERGENT 28
- leafy cabbage-like plant shaped head, grows low to ground
- up to 2 ft. high
- torn stems stink!

Skunk Cabbage

AQUATIC 29
- floats freely on surface (1/10 - 2/5")
- tiny roots dangle below

Duckweed

EMERGENT 30
- up to 4 ft. tall
- arrow-shaped leaves may be 16"
- small white/yellow flowers on stalk

Duck Potato

EMERGENT 31
- up to 10 ft. high.
- grows in water
- long tapered leaves
- droopy "head"
- not common

Wild Rice

EMERGENT 32
- up to 7 ft., "last year's" plant woody
- toothed egg-shaped leaves up to 9"
- big pink, white or red flowers

Hibiscus (Rose Mallow)

Small Wheel #1 (trees, shrubs, and vines)
Photocopy and cut one (1) per Wetland Wheel.

Cut along solid outline.

Smaller Wheel #2 (aquatics and emergents)

Photocopy and cut one (1) per Wetland Wheel.

Cut along solid outline.

What's Its Name?

Use this reference list of plant names when looking up plants in field guides or other reference books. Common names often differ from region to region, so use the latin names (*Genus, species*) to locate plants in books. These plants are used in the Wetland Wheel and dichotomous keys.

Type of Plant	Common Name	Latin Name
Aquatic	Coontail	*Ceratophyllum demersum*
Aquatic	Hydrilla	*Hydrilla verticillata*
Aquatic	Spatterdock	*Nuphar lutea*
Aquatic	Water Lily	*Nymphaea odorata*
Aquatic	Duckweed	*Spirodela polyrhiza*
Emergent	Hibiscus or Rose Mallow	*Hibiscus palustris (moscheutos)*
Emergent	Jewelweed	*Impatiens capensis*
Emergent	*Phragmites* (Common Reed)	*Phragmites australis*
Emergent	Skunk Cabbage	*Symplocarpus foetidus*
Emergent	Duck Potato (Arrowhead)	*Sagittaria latifolia*
Emergent	Cattail	*Typha angustifolia (latifolia)*
Emergent	Soft Rush	*Juncus effusus*
Emergent	(Green) Bulrush	*Scirpus atrovirens*
Emergent	Wild Rice	*Zizania aquatica*
Emergent	(Halbred-leaved) Tearthumb	*Polygonum arifolium*
Emergent	Iris or Blue Flag	*Iris versicolor*
Shrub	Sweet Pepperbush	*Clethra alnifolia*
Shrub	Spicebush	*Lindera benzoin*
Shrub	Blueberry	*Vaccinium corymbosum*
Shrub	Wax Myrtle	*Myrica cerifera*
Shrub	Swamp Rose	*Rosa palustris*
Tree	Sycamore	*Platanus occidentalis*
Tree	Red Maple	*Acer rubrum*
Tree	Sweet Gum	*Liquidambar styraciflua*
Tree	Pin Oak	*Quercus palustris*
Tree	Green Ash	*Fraxinus pennsylvanica*
Tree	Black Willow	*Salix nigra*
Vine	Poison Ivy (*Do not touch!*)	*Toxicodendron radicans*
Vine	Virginia Creeper	*Parthenocissus quinquefolia*
Vine	Greenbriar	*Smilax rotundifolia*
Vine	(Japanese) Honeysuckle	*Lonicera japonica*
Vine (trailing plant)	Cranberry	*Vaccinium macrocarpon*

Tracking Plants and Keeping Track

Grade Level
5-12

Subject Areas
Life Science, Environmental Science

Duration
Teacher's choice; may be conducted yearly as a continuing project

Setting
Classroom and wetland

Skills
Gathering, organizing, and analyzing information

Charting the Course
See "This Plant Key Is All Wet!" and "Wetland Wheel" for more wetland plant identification activities.

Vocabulary
herbarium, inventory, community, transect, quadrat, invasive plant

Summary
Use two sampling methods to collect specimens, then preserve, organize, and display the collection.

Objectives
Students will:

• name and identify wetland plants.

• practice sampling procedures used in taking plant inventories.

• describe a plant community based on species collected.

Materials
• *colored flagging or traffic cones*
• *notebook (see directions in Background)*
• *plant press (see directions in Background)*

For each team:
• *plastic baggies*
• *pruning shears*
• *scissors*
• *Hula-Hoop® or five yards of string*
• *paper, pencils, clipboard*
• *3-inch x 1-inch (7.6 cm x 2.5 cm) paper strips*
• *tape*
• *field guides (see Resources, p. 327) and "Wetland Wheel," (p. 129)*
• *Transect/Quadrat Data Chart student page*

Making Connections
This is not just an exercise in identifying plants, but a lesson in how to collect, organize, and keep information. Used from year to year, it can be a means of monitoring a wetland's species in order to better care for it as changes occur.

The lesson also illustrates the importance of collections such as herbariums, which systematically record and preserve an area's species. Herbariums exist worldwide, and some are very old. They offer fascinating insights and information to botanists, anthropologists, authors, and many others.

Background
Plant diversity makes wetlands valuable to both wildlife and humans. A wide variety of plants offers good habitat for many animals—there are simply more options for food and cover (places to hide).

In disturbed wetland areas (those altered by development or stressed by poor land use or pollution), we often find invasive plants such as *Phragmites* (frag-MITE-teez), the common reed. *Phragmites* multiplies very quickly through rhizomes, underground stems that grow horizontally and send up new shoots. It tolerates stressful conditions better than other plants, and so eventually outcompetes the other plants in an area. The ecological value of a stand of *Phragmites* is subject to debate. Very few animals find it a good food source, though it does offer cover. It also helps to slow erosion and trap sediments. Wetlands are far healthier, however, when inhabited by a variety of plant species more natural (native) to the area.

Plants are indicators of the health of a wetland and the quality of its water. Ecosystems generally change slowly, so sudden, drastic change indicates disturbance, and warns us to take steps to maintain a wetland's health. Species inventories and monitoring help us recognize problems when they first occur.

Sampling

Scientists use several methods of sampling. In this activity, the class uses two: linear transects and quadrats. Quadrats are normally square (hence the name), but this activity uses Hula-Hoops® since they are easier to obtain. The quadrat method is a type of random sampling. The entire site to be sampled should be divided into areas marked by flagging or cones, and team of students should be assigned to each area.

Linear transects: Students should "draw" lines across the sampling area at five or more equal intervals, using string to form the lines. Then they will identify plants along the line. For this activity, it is not necessary to identify every plant along the transect. Students may instead:

• count and record the number of different plants they see along each line, tallying all plants touching the string or hanging over or under it within one foot on either side

• tally each type of plant (tree, shrub, vine, emergent, or aquatic plant; see key, p. 126)

• identify the most common (most numerous) plants along the transect and note any unusual ones.

Quadrats: Students toss a hoop so that it lands anywhere within the quadrat area. To make the sampling truly random, students should close their eyes while tossing (the rest of the team should stand behind the tosser). Once the hoop has landed, no one may touch it, unless it is caught on something. The team then works together to count and identify plants that are *rooted* within the hoop. Again, students may tally different plants, the types of plants, or the most

common plants. Have each team repeat this process at least five times, or until they feel they have accurately sampled their area.

Collecting specimens: Students will collect a few specimens for the class herbarium (see below). Make sure that specimens are not rare or endangered species. Review the characteristics used to identify a plant (see pp. 123-124). Since stem or leaf arrangement and other features are all used in keying out plants, merely collecting leaves is not enough. A good specimen includes enough stem to show leaf arrangement and any flowering structures or fruits. Snip these carefully from the plant with shears, use 3-inch x 1-inch slips of paper and tape to label each specimen with the plant name or number and transect or quadrat number, and seal in plastic baggies until they can be pressed. Record where the plants were found (water's edge, along a path, etc.) and any other observations. Plants may be keyed out and labeled in the classroom to save field time.

Plant Presses and Preparing the Herbarium

Plant presses should be prepared before the trip. Two plans are suggested below. Both methods call for a stack of newspapers and several pieces of blotter paper and corrugated cardboard (approximately 8 inches x 10 inches).

Place two pieces of blotter paper on top of one piece of cardboard; this is one layer. Repeat the layering until you have one layer for each specimen you will collect. Specimens are placed between folded pieces of newspaper, with leaves, stems, and flowers spread out flat. Place one newspaper-wrapped specimen between the two pieces of blotter paper in each layer. Then:

Method One: Sandwich all layers between two cardboard endpieces. Use two adjustable straps or belts to hold the press together tightly, or weight the stack down with books, bricks, or a cinder block.

Method Two: Cut two square or rectangular pieces of 1-inch-thick wood. The pieces can be any size—12 inches x 12 inches works well. Drill holes in the four corners of both pieces and insert 12-inch bolts through the holes. The top piece should slide up and down the bolts easily. Use wing nuts as fasteners. Place all layers of papers and plants between the two pieces of wood and screw top down tightly.

Pressing plants: Leave the tightly closed press in a sunny, warm, dry place for at least a week. After a few days, however, open the press and check the newspaper and blotter paper. If it is very moist, replace it or add several pieces of newspaper to absorb more moisture. Do not remove the plants until they are completely dry, i.e., they do not droop when lifted from the press.

Herbarium notebook: Use heavy stock paper such as watercolor or manila paper and a three-ring binder. On the left-handed pages, attach the plant specimens. On the opposite pages, fill in the following information: common name, Latin name, description of the plant, where it grows (type of habitat and range), where and when the specimen was collected (and by whom), and any special observations. Include students' data charts and any maps of the sample plots in the notebook.

Procedure

Warm Up

Ask students to describe the community in which they live or the school community. They might describe the physical appearance of their neighborhood, the buildings, location of businesses, etc., or they might describe the people who live there. The school community might be described as a group of male and/or female students of a certain age range who live in a particular geographic area. Faculty and staff are also part of the school community.

Tell students they will be going to a wetland to study its plant community. Why is it important to identify a plant community? Point out that many of our medicines, foods, and other products come from plants. Though scientists have studied most plants that grow in the United States, only a small percentage of the world's vegetation has been identified. There may be medicinal plants we don't even know about!

Review methods of sampling (transects and quadrats) and collection (plant presses and herbariums). Discuss the importance of organized, accurate record-keeping and review how herbariums accomplish this.

The Activity

Part I

1. **At the wetland, divide the class into teams and hand out equipment. Remind the students that this activity is a step toward protecting the area. They should be careful to "tread lightly" on the wetland while they are there. Locate spots that offer easy access and identify and avoid areas that could be harmed by foot traffic.**

2. **Have students use the quadrat and transect sampling methods described in the Background and note what they find. Have half the class use transects and half use quadrats, but let everyone have a chance to try both methods. Use the Transect/Quadrat Data Charts to record findings.**

Part II

1. **Ask students to name the five most common plants in the sample areas studied in Part I.**

2. **Have students go back and collect one good specimen of each of the five plants. They should collect only one sample of a plant per team. *Caution them to take a sample only if the plant is abundant. Otherwise, they should sketch the plant and leave it there.* Stress the type of sample needed (do not rip out entire plant).**

3. **In the classroom, have students preserve the specimens and prepare pages for the classroom herbarium as described in the Background.**

4. **After the specimens have dried, students can affix them to the herbarium pages.**

Wrap Up

Students can use their findings to describe the plant community of the investigated site. Tell them the data they collected for the herbarium notebook will be used to monitor the wetland from year to year. Their data can be compared with the work of previous and future classes to help keep track of the wetland's health. The record should make sudden changes noticeable, and classes can try   to track down the source of the changes. If changes are caused by human activity, have students work together to do what they can to reverse the problem.

Assessment

Have students:

- sample plants using the quadrat or transect method.

- inventory plants in a sample to identify a wetland plant community.

- assemble collected plants in an organized fashion, creating an herbarium notebook.

Extensions

Advanced students may draw a simple map of their sample area on graph paper, marking where each transect or quadrat was taken.

Record data in this chart, keeping notes and making observations of plants identified as well as dominant plants.

Transect/Quadrat Data Chart

	Transect or Quadrat #				
	1	2	3	4	5
Type of Plant	Number of Plants Counted				
Tree					
Shrub					
Vine					
Emergent					
Aquatic					

Run for the Border

[Adapted from "Marsh March" in Virginia's State Parks . . . Your Backyard Classrooms.*]*

Grade Level
5-12

Subject Areas
Ecology, Biology

Duration
1 hour, plus 30 minutes for discussion

Setting
A wetland near your school

Skills
Gathering, organizing, analyzing, and interpreting information

Charting the Course
Activities that help students collect and identify plants could precede this activity. See "This Plant Key Is All Wet!" "Wetland Wheel," and "Tracking Plants and Keeping Track."

Vocabulary
delineation, hydrology, indicator species, uplands, wetlands

Summary

It is not always easy to tell where wetlands begin and end. In this activity, students will look at the most obvious indicators of the wetland/upland border—changes in plant communities and different degrees of wetness.

Objectives

Students will:

• make the observations necessary to infer where wetland boundaries exist.

• define obvious differences in plant communities.

• describe conditions for wetland existence.

Materials

• *"wettable" footwear for all*
• *photographs or specimens of various plants*

For each team:
• *Wetland Investigations student page*
• *clipboard*
• *pencil(s)*
• *trowel*

Making Connections

Students may have walked in a wetland without knowing it. This activity asks students to stop, observe, and make inferences. Observation is key to learning, regardless of the discipline. The ability to recognize wetland boundaries is essential to wise land-use decisions.

Background

Where does a wetland begin and end? Sometimes it is hard to tell where the boundaries lie, since wetlands may gradually fade into upland at one limit, and into a waterway at the other. Scientists delineate (draw the boundaries of) wetlands by looking closely at the plants, soils, and "wetness" in the area. Generally, when wetland plants (certain species used as wetland indicators), wetland soils (see p. 231), and a certain degree of wetness prevail, the area is called a wetland; when these things do not prevail, the area is called an upland. There is a very fine line between the two. (See chapter 2.)

The conditions of an area—soil type, slope, climate, amount of sunlight, and hydrology (wetness)—determine which plants will grow there. The many plants that share an area characterized by certain conditions are known as a plant community. Plant communities are usually obvious—a forest is one type of community, a field is another; a cluster of cattails and rushes is a community distinct from one dominated by shrubs.

Students do not have to be skilled in identifying plant species—they only need to recognize physical differences among plants. To many people, all plants look alike; a bit of practice distinguishing between plant types may be in order. (See the key on p. 126.)

Procedure
Warm Up

Tell the students that they will be going to a wetland to investigate how it is organized. Review the observation sheet and discuss how students will use it (they will work in teams). Then, have students practice distinguishing between pairs of photos or samples of plants (even houseplants). Ask: Is this plant the same as this one? Why not? Ask students to describe both plants in as much detail as they can.

Discuss the things plants need and "prefer" for growth. Use houseplants as an example: some require direct sunlight, others grow best in shade, and some need more water than others. Ask: Would a cactus grow in a wetland? Would a water lily grow in the desert? Why not?

Explain that these are the sorts of things students should keep in mind when making their observations and looking at changes in plant communities. By making these observations, they will be determining where edges or borders of the wetland lie.

Review the Investigation student page. Explain that scientific observations are descriptions of what we actually see, hear, feel, taste, or smell. We make inferences, on the other hand, when we use logic, or even guesses, to interpret or explain our observations. One set of observations may lead you to many inferences, or to none.

Note: This activity is merely a lesson in observation and in understanding that wetland conditions are not always obvious. Accurate wetland delineation is something best left to wetland science professionals. Students' inferences on boundaries need not be proven right or wrong.

The Activity

At a nearby wetland, divide the class into teams of four. Ask each team to make observations using the Wetland Investigations student page. Explain that it suggests where students might direct their observations in order to make logical inferences about the wetland later on.

Wrap Up and Action

After all observations are complete, ask students to work together to complete the Wetland Investigation student page. Have them summarize ways they can identify wetlands. Review their observations and inferences with them, using the Investigation Guide. Suggested answers are listed below.

Investigation Information

1. *Where do you think the upland ends and the wetland begins?* The upper limits of wetlands are usually marked by changes in vegetation and soil. In many marshes, there is a clear transition from trees and shrubs to tall, grasslike plants such as cattails, sedges, and rushes. The vegetation changes are less clearly defined on the upper edges of forested wetlands such as swamps. There, soil color and moisture might be the best clues. Unless it has rained very recently or there has been a prolonged dry spell, wetland soil will be noticeably wetter, often squishy or even inundated. (For soil colors, see "Do You Dig Wetland Soil," p. 231.)

2. *Does the wetland have another boundary? If so, what is it?* The lower limit will usually be the adjacent waterway. Some wetlands may be bounded on all sides by uplands, others will seem to stretch on indefinitely.

3. *What conditions seem necessary for a wetland to thrive?* By finding the upper and lower limits to a wetland, students can infer conditions wetlands require, such as the abundance of water (but not deep water or swiftly moving water like currents or waves).

4. *Where might the wetland be changing or experiencing destruction?* In the geologic time frame,

wetlands are dynamic places that undergo rapid change. Trapped sediments (whether natural or increased by human activities) can fill wetlands. Rising sea level can flood coastal wetlands, and erosion can wash them away. Of these forces, only erosion may be readily apparent. Erosion is most easily observed along the lower limits of wetlands bordering swift tidal creeks, streams that flood during heavy rains, open bays, or rivers.

Human activity can cause a variety of changes in wetlands. Some of the more observable human activities and their possible effects are:

• Damming the waterway downstream might flood wetlands.

• Damming the waterway upstream might dry up the wetland.

• Drawing water from the waterway for irrigation, or from ground-water supplies for too many wells, might dry the wetland up.

• Cutting a ditch across a wetland might drain it.

• Pushing dirt onto a wetland, as in construction site preparation, might fill it in and destroy it.

• Dramatically disturbing the soil on the nearby upland might fill the wetland with sediment.

• Repeated wakes from excess boat traffic could destroy a marsh through erosion.

5. *What indicates that the wetland might be part of an aquatic food web?* See if students observed the abundance of dead plant material (detritus), which is most obvious in marshes. Detritus is one of the basics of a food web. Point out that most of the detritus along the waterway edge is likely to be

washed into the waterway and into other connected bodies of water.

Students might deduce the importance of wetland plants as a major component of an aquatic food web. They may also have observed animals feeding in the water, or muskrat-chewed plant stumps.

6. *What indicates that the wetland is important to terrestrial and aquatic animals?* Benefits to wildlife can be inferred from observations of wetland animals such as fiddler crabs, turtles, snakes, insects, and birds, as well as their signs, such as droppings, tracks, and nests (see "Whose Clues?" p. 104). Other benefits can be seen by noting animal food sources such as whole plants, seeds and fruits, and other animals.

Assessment

Have students:

• name three factors to consider when delineating wetland boundaries (soils, hydrology, plants).

• define the differences between uplands, wetlands, and open bodies of water.

• identify conditions necessary for wetlands to exist.

• draw a food web that includes wetland organisms.

Extensions

Have students discover a wetland near their homes by making observations and inferring the boundaries of that wetland. If possible, loan cameras to students so they can create a class scrapbook of "Wetlands I Have Known."

Resources

Mitsch, William J., and James G. Gosselink. 1993. *Wetlands.* New York: Van Nostrand Reinhold.

Wetland Investigations

Wetland Observations

1. Are all the plants in the wetland the same type of plant? If not, how many types are there?	5. Is the same amount of water visible everywhere? Is the soil everywhere equally damp?
2. Are they distributed evenly, randomly, in clumps, or in some pattern?	6. Are some types of plants usually found close to the water or in the dampest soil?
3. Are some types always found close together?	7. Are some types of plants never found close to the water, or found only in the driest soil?
4. Are some types never found close together?	8. Use the back of this sheet for any other observations that might help your team answer the investigation questions, below.

Investigation Guide

Investigation Questions	Relevant Observations	Inference (Possible Answer)
1. Where do you think the upland ends and the wetland begins? How can you tell?		
2. Does the wetland have another boundary? If so, what is it?		
3. What conditions seem to be necessary for a wetland to thrive?		
4. Where might the wetland be changing or experiencing destruction by nature or humans?		
5. What indicates that the wetland might be part of an aquatic food web?		
6. What indicates that the wetland is important to terrestrial and aquatic animals?		

Wetland Address

[Adapted from "Water Address," Project WET Curriculum and Activity Guide. 1995. Used with permission of The Watercourse and the Western Regional Environmental Education Council.]

Grade Level
5-10

Subject Areas
Life Science, Ecology, Geography, Language Arts

Duration
60 minutes

Setting
Classroom

Skills
Analyzing and gathering information

Charting the Course
Activities like "Introducing Wetlands" and "Wetland Habitats" should precede this lesson to orient students to wetland environments. Following this lesson, activities such as "Salt Marsh Players" and "Wetland Weirdos" will help illustrate adaptive strategies for wetland survival. "Wet 'n' Wild" addresses the larger issues of habitat and species communities.

Vocabulary
adaptation, wetland, hibernate

Summary

In times of drought I can survive by creating my own small wetland; what's my wetland address?

Students identify plants and animals and their wetland habitats by analyzing clues that describe their adaptations, characteristics, and other species trivia.

Objectives

Students will recognize wetland adaptations and characteristics of some plants and animals.

Materials

- set of Wetland Address Cards for each group of students (can be mounted on cardboard for durability)
- pencils and paper for scoring
- pictures or photographs of organisms listed on clue cards (optional)
- 3-inch x 5-inch index cards
- map of world (optional)

Making Connections

Most children have seen pictures of cranes and alligators, beavers and pitcher plants. One thing common to all these organisms is that they live in or use wetland environments. Learning about these species helps students appreciate the variety of remarkable strategies for wetland survival.

Background

Since three quarters of Earth is covered with water, many plants and animals live in wetlands such as bogs, swamps, and marshes. To survive in these water-dominated habitats, living beings have special features, or adaptations. Developed over time, these adaptations help wetland residents make full use of available nutrients and energy, protect their species against enemies, and cope with different climates.

There are many examples of how animals and plants are suited to live in wetland environments. For example, fish have streamlined bodies and fins to help them maneuver through water. Ducks have webbed feet for swimming and oily feathers to keep from getting soaked. Other organisms have developed ways of breathing while their bodies remain under water. Water lilies anchor themselves on the bottom of ponds and lakes, but send their large leaves to float on the surface to gather light and oxygen.

Behavior patterns are also examples of ways animals have adjusted to wetlands. Migration patterns of birds correlate with wetland areas like prairie potholes, which they utilize for food and resting spots. When the water dries up in a pond, some species of frogs bury themselves in the mud and can hibernate for years while waiting for the rains to return. These are just a few of the countless examples of plant and animal wetland adaptations. (See chapter 4.)

Procedure

Warm Up

Discuss the importance of adaptations to species' success. What is the longest time students can remember going without water? How would they survive in an environment that lacks oxygen? While some organisms can live without oxygen, and some without light, all living things need water, nutrition, shelter, and other necessities.

Have students list different wetlands around the world (rice paddies, prairie potholes, salt marshes, etc.) and compare the characteristics of these areas. Ask students to list plants and animals they think might be found there, and to describe how these life forms might have adapted to live in and make use of their habitat.

Review the concept of adaptation. Ask students if they have pets or plants that have special adaptations. Fish have many physical adaptations for living in water. Some students may have a cactus or an air plant growing in their homes. Dogs such as spaniels or retrievers are adapted for swimming. What adaptations make these dogs good water dogs? Students may have noticed webbed feet and oily hair, both of which make it easier for the dog to swim.

The Activity

1. **Tell students they're going to play a riddle game in which they try to guess an organism's identity and "wetland address." Arrange students in groups of three to four.**

2. **Hand out a set of the enclosed clue cards to each group. Instruct students not to look at the cards before the game starts.**

3. **Explain that each card lists four adaptations, characteristic features, or trivia facts about a certain wetland plant or animal. Based on the clues, students will try to guess the plant or animal and the wetland type or location in which it is usually found.**

4. **Each group should pick one student to start as their reader. This student will read clues, one at a time and in any order, until someone else in the group can guess the name of the organism**

and where it lives (peatland, swamp, marsh, etc.). Answers are listed at the bottom of each card. If photos of the organisms are available, have students place the image on a map of North America to indicate where it lives.

5. **The student who comes closest to guessing both the name of the organism and its wetland address receives points based on the number of clues that were read before he or she got the answer. Assign one student in each group to be scorekeeper and to keep track as follows:**

Only one clue read = four points

Only two clues read = three points

Three clues read = two points

All four clues read = one point

6. **The student who correctly guessed the previous wetland riddle (or came closest) becomes the new reader and begins the clues on the next card. Continue the game until all cards have been read.**

Wrap Up and Action

Discuss how adaptations enable organisms to live in their environment. Have students summarize the adaptations encountered in the game. Remind students that there are thousands of plants, animals, and other organisms not included in this activity, and each one has many adaptations. Have them visit the library and view videos to research additional organisms' adaptations, and then make clue cards for their own game. The game can then be played with new cards, and groups can swap sets for longer sessions. Encourage students to play with friends and family.

Assessment

Have students:

- identify an organism and its wetland environment based on a set of clues describing adaptations, unique features, and characteristics.

- explain how adaptations enable plants and animals to live in diverse wetland environments.

- create clue cards for different organisms and other wetland habitats.

Extensions

Students can create a new organism that could live in an odd location on Earth, in an environment of the future, or in a fictional wetland environment on a different planet. Have them imagine special features or behaviors the organism would need to live in this environment. Encourage them to be creative. They should write a detailed description or draw an explicit picture of the habitat, how the organism blends into the environment, and how it has adapted. Have students critique each other's designs and provide suggestions for improvement. The portraits and descriptions can be posted in a "Wetland Address" gallery. The display should include a description of the organisms and their adaptations. The "Wetland Address" game could be adapted to include these new organisms.

K-2 Option

Show children drawings or magazine pictures of plants and animals that have various wetland-related adaptations. Discuss ways the plant or animal lives in wetlands. Cut each picture into strips and place each cut up picture in a separate envelope.

Divide the class into small groups and give each group an envelope. A student in each group pulls out one strip of paper at a time and tries to guess what the plant or animal is. If she cannot guess, she pulls out a second piece, and so on until she figures out the organism. The group then summarizes the special features or adaptations that help the organism live in its environment. The groups can trade envelopes to continue the activity.

Resources

Attenborough, David. *The Living Planet*. Boston: Little, Brown & Co., 1984.

Parker, Steve. *Pond and River*. New York: Alfred A. Knopf, 1988.

Parker, Steve, and Jane Parker. *Migration*. New York: Gloucester Press, 1990.

Notes:

Wetland Address Cards

• I have dense, oily fur, webbed hind feet, and ears and nostrils that close when under water.

• I sink green branches into my pond to retrieve in winter for food.

• I use my wide tail as a paddle.

• I build a home in water with sticks, and it has an underwater entrance.

Answer: **Beaver** - lives in streams, ponds, and rivers

• I can be found on the surface of water.

• I have six wax-coated feet.

• I stand with legs splayed to distribute my weight so I won't break through the water's surface.

• I appear to glide across the water's surface.

Answer: **Pond skater** - lives in ponds and quiet water

• My fur makes me look like a shaggy buffalo, but I am actually a member of the goat family.

• I am one of the few mammals to live full time in my high Arctic home.

• My hair is a fine wool that hangs in long skirts almost to my feet and insulates me through the harsh northern winters.

• I have plate-like horns plastered against my skull, with sharp tips to ward off my most dangerous natural enemy, the wolf.

Answer: **Musk ox** - resident of the tundra peatlands of northern Canada and Greenland

---

• I am the largest reptile in North America.

• I can either dig a mud den, or create a small wetland by lashing my tail and digging with my feet and snout, in order to survive periods of drought.

• My eyes are on top of my head, so I can lie submerged and still see above water.

• My skin is a tough, protective leather shield, prized for boots and luggage.

Answer: **American alligator** - an endangered species living in the Everglades of Florida and other wetlands throughout the south-eastern United States

---

• I grow in swamps and am known for my smell.

• I share my name with a mammal, also known for its strong odor.

• I am able to turn energy into heat, so I can warm myself and start spring growth even when night temperatures are still below freezing.

• My flowers may appear before the last ice of winter melts away, and they smell much sweeter than my leaves, which are responsible for my less than attractive name.

Answer: **Skunk cabbage** - found in shady swamps throughout North America

---

• I grow in peat bogs.

• My common name comes from the shape of my leaves, which remind people of something you pour water out of.

• Although I am a plant, I catch and eat insects.

• Sugar-scented pools of water lure my prey, and downward-pointing hairs on my leaves keep insects from climbing to freedom.

Answer: **Pitcher plant** - found in North American peat bogs

Wetland Address Cards

• I am an exotic species (brought to North America from somewhere else). In my case, I came from Argentina.

• I was brought here for my valuable fur, but either escaped or was let free from fur farms, and now live in wetlands in at least 15 U.S. states.

• At first glance I look like another wetland resident who is known for building dams, but the biggest visual difference between us is our tails. Mine is short and stubby.

• I am nocturnal, or active at night, and chew up wetland plant foods much like a muskrat.

Answer: **Nutria** - introduced from South America at the turn of the century, but now lives successfully in the wild from Texas to Alabama, North Carolina to Maryland, and Oregon to Washington, as well as in other states

• In flight my wingspan is 7 1/2 feet across, and I am the tallest North American bird.

• Although I once inhabited a much more widespread area, I now nest in a few isolated Canadian bogs every summer, and migrate south to the Texas coast every winter.

• Not many years ago I was almost extinct due to pesticide poisoning, hunting, and habitat (wetland) destruction. My entire species was down to less than 50 individuals. I am still endangered, but am making a slow comeback.

• At times, and especially during courtship, I dance wildly on long, stilt-like legs.

Answer: **Whooping crane** - an endangered species that summers in Wood Buffalo National Park, Canada, and winters in Aransas National Wildlife Refuge, Texas

• My names describes what I do best, which is to catch fish.

• I live near water, and you'll see me perched where I can watch for my favorite food.

• I am often heard before I am seen, and once you hear my loud, rattly alarm call, you'll never mistake me.

• Like terns, I dive headfirst from the air into the water.

Answer: **Belted kingfisher** - found throughout North America near rivers, streams, and ponds

Extend this activity by having students research other wetland wildlife and make Address Cards for them. Groups can then exchange cards and keep playing activity rounds. Possible species to start with include: mallard, Canada goose, cattail, bullfrog, mosquito, dragonfly, mink, moose, crayfish, water lily, great blue heron, turtle, salamander, venus fly trap. Come up with more of your own!

Part II

1. Tell students they are going to participate in a scavenger hunt to simulate this race against time. Explain that they are organisms living in a newly formed temporary wetland.

2. Have students count off by fives. Tell all number ones to write the word *predator* on a piece of paper and pin it to their shirts. Predators, which eat insects and other organisms, include frogs, salamanders, and turtles. The rest of the students are prey organisms, such as insects, crustaceans, etc.

3. Tell students the temporary wetland will dry up in a specified amount of time. Players must search their school or playing field to acquire what they need to survive. The amount of time will depend on the size of the school or playing field and the distribution of items. Start with a 10-minute time limit.

4. Distribute Scavenger Hunt (Prey) and Scavenger Hunt (Predator) student pages and plastic cups to students. The four main categories are water, shelter, food, and a partner (a mate). Students must obtain all items in one category before they can begin to fill the next. That is, all items in one category must be brought to the classroom and initialed on the scavenger sheet. The first three categories can be completed in any order, but all three must be completed before students can identify a partner.

5. Warn students that they must avoid predators while scavenging. If they are tagged by a predator, they become the food of the predator. The prey must stop searching and travel with the predator.

6. After students acquire partners, they return to the classroom and have their scavenger sheets finalized. All students must return once the allotted time has elapsed.

7. Set the timer and release students. Departures of predators and prey should be staggered to give the prey time to scatter. Prizes can be awarded to students who return within the time limit.

Wrap Up and Action

Discuss the outcome of the scavenger hunt. What might be the fate of organisms that do not obtain what they need before the wetlands dry up? Have students summarize the challenges of living in temporary wetlands. Explain that, despite such limited time, one advantage over permanent water bodies is that food and shelter are generally more accessible, with predators less common.

Have students discuss the results of their local temporary wetlands study. What organisms did they find? Did any wetlands dry up during the study period? How might their results relate to the scavenger hunt? Have students discuss how wetlands could benefit their community. Why might people want to eliminate temporary wetlands? Compare students' comments in class discussion, to identify differing points of view. Local governments or state resource agencies may be interested in students' findings.

Assessment

Have students:

• record observations of physical and biological elements of a temporary wetland over time.

• describe the benefits and

challenges of life in a temporary wetland.

• research and write a paper identifying how temporary wetlands benefit a community.

Extensions

Compare the longevity of several wetlands during the same season. Explain differences.

Students may be interested in researching how human actions can protect or endanger temporary wetlands.

Read *Neighborhood Puddle* to students and have them write a story about their temporary wetlands.

Resources

Braus, Judy, ed. 1987. *NatureScope: Let's Hear It for Herps!* Washington, D.C.: National Wildlife Federation.

Caduto, Michael. 1990. *Pond and Brook: A Guide to Nature in Freshwater Environments.* Hanover and London, England: University Press of New England.

Downer, Anne. 1992. *Spring Pool: A Guide to the Ecology of Temporary Ponds.* New York, N.Y.: Watts.

Mitsch, W. J., and J. G. Gosselink. 1993. *Wetlands*, 2nd ed. New York, N.Y.: Van Nostrand Reinhold.

Project WILD. 1992. Activities "Micro Odyssey" and "Puddle Wonders." From *Aquatic Project WILD.* Bethesda, Md.: Western Regional Environmental Education Council.

Waters, John F. 1971. *Neighborhood Puddle.* New York, N.Y.: Frederick Warne and Co., Inc.

Temporary Wetland Data

Wetland name_____

Student name_____

Location_____

Date/time	H$_2$O temp	Diameter	Depth	Animals	Plants

Scavenger Hunt (Prey)

Water Teacher initials_____	Three cups of water
Shelter Teacher initials_____	A toothpick and some soil
Food Teacher initials_____	Four pieces of food (one hard candy, one piece of chocolate, one peanut, one cracker)
Partner Teacher initials_____	A partner (the first student you see who has found water, shelter, and food)

Scavenger Hunt (Predator)

Water Teacher initials_____	Three cups of water
Shelter Teacher initials_____	A toothpick and some soil
Food Teacher initials_____	Eight pieces of food. The actual food items (hard candy, chocolates, peanuts, crackers) count as one piece each. Students (prey organisms) represent two pieces of food each. You can scavenge eight pieces of food or four prey students, or any combination of food pieces and students to equal eight pieces. (For example, three prey students and two pieces of food equal eight pieces.)
Partner Teacher initials_____	A partner (the first student you see who has found water, shelter, and food)

Section

3

Drip, Drop, Dribble, and Splash! (water)

Activities that relate to the role of water in the wetland picture. These include water-related wetland functions, filtration experiments, demonstrations of erosion, and plant productivity.

A Drop in the Bucket

[Adapted from Project WET Curriculum and Activity Guide. *Used with permission of The Watercourse and the Western Regional Environmental Education Council.]*

Grade Level
6-8

Subject Areas
Earth Science, Mathematics, Geography

Duration
1 hour

Setting
Classroom

Skills
Gathering and organizing information

Charting the Course
Students should review percentages before they begin this activity. This would be a good activity to try just after the introductory activities in "So This is A Wetland!" Other activities that explore fresh water availability include "Water Under Foot," "Over Hill and Dale," and "Water We Have Here."

Vocabulary
salt water, fresh water

Summary

What is abundant and rare at the same time?

By estimating and calculating the percent of available fresh water on Earth, students understand that this resource is limited and must be conserved.

Objectives

Students will:

• calculate the percentage of freshwater available for human use.

• explain why water is a limited resource.

Materials

For each group:
• *2 colors of construction paper*
• *scissors*
• *sheets of white paper*
• *markers*
• *water*
• *copies of Water Availability Table*
• *student page*
• *1000-ml beaker*
• *100-ml graduated cylinders*
• *small dish*
• *salt*
• *freezer or an ice bucket*
• *eyedropper or glass stirring rod*
• *small metal bucket*
• *globe or world map*
• *newspaper articles related to water quality, quantity, and distribution*

Making Connections

Students may know Earth is covered mainly by water, but they may not realize that only a small fraction is available for human consumption. Learning that water is a limited resource helps students appreciate the need to use water resources wisely, including protection of wetlands and watersheds.

Background

Ironically, on a planet extensively (71 percent) covered with water,

---

Water Availability Table
(for Instructors)

Total water (100%) on Earth divided among all people (based on a world population of 6 billion people)
> = 233.3 billion liters/person

Minus the 97% of each share (233.3 billion liters) that contains salt (oceans, seas, some lakes and rivers)
> leaving 7.0 billion liters/person

Minus the 80% of this 7.0 billion that is frozen at the poles
> leaving 1.4 billion liters/person

Minus the 99.5% of the 1.4 billion that is unavailable (too far underground, polluted, trapped in soil, etc.)

> leaving 7.0 million liters/person available in lakes, rivers, streams, wetlands, and ground-water aquifers

this resource is one of the main limiting factors for life on Earth. The Water Availability Table summarizes the major factors affecting the amount of available water on Earth. If all the clean, fresh water was distributed equally among people, there would be about 7.0 million liters (1.8 million gallons) per person. Amazingly, this is only about 0.00003 percent of the total water on Earth.

On a global scale, only a small percentage of water is available, but this percentage represents a large amount per individual. The paradox is that for some, water may appear plentiful, but for others it is a scarce commodity. Why are some people in need of more water? Geography, climate, and weather affect water distribution. Land and water use for agriculture, industry, and homes affect the quality and quantity of available fresh water. These uses can have cumulative affects on soils, watersheds, and wetlands, hindering their ability to hold and filter water.

Procedure

Warm Up
Tell students they are going to estimate the proportion of drinkable (potable) and non-potable water on the planet. Have students work in small groups. Instruct them to draw a large circle with a marker on a white sheet of paper. Offer them two sheets of different-colored construction paper. One color represents potable water; the other represents the rest of the water on the planet.

Tell students that they will be tearing the two sheets of paper into a total of 100 small pieces. Ask them to estimate how many pieces will represent potable

water and how many pieces will indicate the rest of the water on the planet. Instruct each group to tear up their paper and arrange the 100 pieces within the circle so that these pieces reflect their estimates. Have groups record the number of pieces for potable and remaining water.

The Activity
Note: For simplicity, measurements have been retained in metric.

1. **Show the class a liter (1000 ml) of water and tell them it represents all the water on Earth.**

2. **Ask where most of the water on Earth is located (refer to a globe or map).** Pour 30 ml of the water into a 100-ml graduated cylinder. This represents Earth's fresh water, about 3 percent of the total. Put salt into the remaining 970 ml to simulate water found in oceans, unsuitable for human consumption.

3. **Ask students what is at the Earth's poles.** Almost 80 percent of Earth's fresh water is frozen in ice caps and glaciers. Pour 6 ml of fresh water into a small dish and place the rest (24 ml) in a nearby

freezer or ice bucket. The water in the dish (around 0.6 percent of the total) represents non-frozen fresh water. Only about 1.5 ml of this water is surface water; the rest is underground.

4. **Use an eyedropper or a glass stirring rod to remove a single drop of water (0.003 ml). Release this one drop into a small metal bucket.** Make sure the students are very quiet so they can hear the sound of the drop hitting the bottom of the bucket. This represents clean, fresh water which is not polluted or otherwise unavailable for use, about 0.00003 percent of the total! This precious drop must be managed properly.

5. **Discuss the results of the demonstration.** At this point many students will conclude that a very small amount of water is available to humans. However, this single drop is actually a large volume of water on a global scale. Have students use the Water Availability Table student page to calculate the actual amounts.

Wrap Up and Action
Remind students of their earlier guesses at how much water on

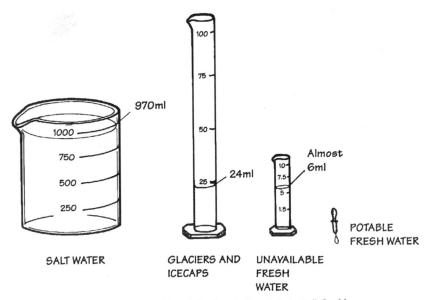

SALT WATER · GLACIERS AND ICECAPS · UNAVAILABLE FRESH WATER · POTABLE FRESH WATER

Illustrations in this activity done by Laurie "gigette" Gould

Earth is available to humans and compare these estimates to the actual percent available. Have students explain their reasoning for their initial estimates. How would they adjust their proportions? (One-half of one of the pieces of paper represents potentially available water [0.5 percent]. Only one small corner of this half [0.00003 percent] is actually potable water.)

Ask students again if enough water is currently available for people. If the amount of usable water on the planet is divided by the current population of approximately 6 billion, 7.0 million liters of water is available per person. Theoretically, this exceeds the amount of water a person would require in a lifetime. So, why does more than one-third of the world's population not have access to clean water? Discuss the main factors affecting water distribution on Earth (e.g., land forms, vegetation, proximity to large bodies of water). Other environmental influences affect availability of water (drought, contamination, flooding). In addition, wetlands and watershed integrity contribute to the retention of water, making more water available for use. Students can also consider that other organisms use water, not just humans.

Assessment

Have students:

• determine the proportion of Earth's potable water.

• calculate the amount of water available for human use.

• develop a television commercial outlining reasons why water is a limited resource.

Extensions

Students can calculate how much

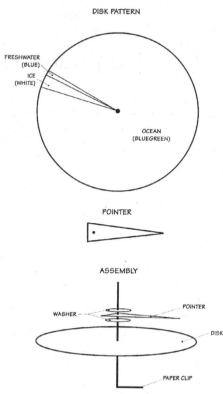

water they might use in their lifetime. Provide them with the following instructions: Keep track of how much water they use in one day. (The average person in the United States uses about 50 gallons [190 l] per day.) Multiply daily use by 365 days and then by 70 years (estimated life span). How does this compare to the 1.8 million gallons (7.0 million liters) available to them? (This applies to direct water use only.)

Students can identify areas of the globe where water is limited or in excess and discuss the geographical and climatic qualities contributing to these conditions. For example, large variations in precipitation occur within states. (Death Valley receives as little as 2 to 5 inches [5 to 12.5 cm] per year; only 100 miles [160 km] away, mountain ranges receive more than 30 inches [76 cm] per year.) These variations dramatically impact people, plants, and other animals.

Students can investigate sources of local surface water runoff by studying National Wetland Inventory or topographic maps (see pp. 54, 329 for more information). They may also contact the U.S. Geological Survey or the American Water Resources Association for information on aquifers.

K–2 Option
Conduct the first four steps of the activity. (If beakers are not available, use approximate volumes with 1 gallon [4 liters] of water representing all water on Earth. Of this, 1 fluid ounce [30 milliliters] is fresh water, and all but one small drop of the fresh water is frozen at the poles.) To help students appreciate these proportions, have them participate in the following activity. Construct, or have students make, spinners. (Make the disk, pointer, and washers out of sturdy cardboard.) Give each child a copy of the Water Chart. Children spin the pointer and color a box of the table in the appropriate row to indicate where the pointer landed. Which row of the table do students think will fill up first?

Resources

Miller, G. Tyler, Jr. 1990. *Resource Conservation and Management*. Belmont, Calif.: Wadsworth Publishing Company.

Goldin, Augusta. 1983. *Water: Too Much, Too Little, Too Polluted?* Orlando, Fla.: Harcourt, Brace, Jovanovich.

Hammer, Trudy J. 1985. *Water Resources*. New York, N.Y.: Watts.

Pringle, Laurence. 1982. *Water: The Next Great Resource Battle*. New York, N.Y.: Macmillan.

Water Availability Table

Water quantities	Amount available in liters/person	Percent of total water on earth
All the water on Earth	233.3 billion	100%
Only the fresh water		3%
Only the non-frozen fresh water		0.6%
Available fresh water that is not polluted, trapped in soil, too far below ground, etc.		0.00003%

Water Chart

K-2 Option

Soak It Up!

Grade Level
3-9

Subject Areas
Earth Science, Geography

Duration
1 hour

Setting
Classroom and outdoors

Skills
Gathering, organizing, and analyzing information

Charting the Course
Students should participate in "A Drop in the Bucket" to learn about the importance of wetland habitats. An understanding of water storage ("Runoff Race" and "Wetland in a Pan") supports this activity. "Do You Dig Wetland Soil?" provides a good follow-up to this activity.

Vocabulary
ground water, surface water, water table, runoff

Summary
Students increase their understanding of wetlands when they use a household sponge to demonstrate how wetlands capture, store, and release water.

Objectives
Students will:

• describe how some groundwater and surface-water wetlands are fed.

• identify areas in their community that may be wetlands.

Materials
• *jug of water*
• *blue food coloring*
• *shovel or hand trowel*

For each group:
• *two thick sponges*
• *scissors*
• *cardboard*
• *5-inch x 8-inch piece of cardboard covered with foil*
• *paper cup*

Making Connections
An understanding of wetland formation helps us determine where wetlands may occur. This knowledge is useful in making wise land-use decisions.

Background
Wetlands form in a variety of places, under a variety of circumstances. Some of the places may seem surprising: along edges of rivers, streams, lakes, and ponds; in low-lying woods; in roadside ditches designed to collect rainwater runoff; in low spots in fields; even on mountains and hillsides where snowmelt and rainwater run constantly.

Numerous combinations of soil types, water sources, and topography lead to the formation of wetlands, but the common denominator is always water. Wetlands are *wet lands*. When we understand where water comes from and how and where it flows, we can predict where wetlands will form. The source of water for a wetland is either surface water, ground water, or both. This activity will investigate both sources.

Some wetlands are fed by precipitation and surface water. Wetlands are formed when runoff and rainfall collect at the base of a slope or when surface waterways such as rivers overflow and saturate the surrounding land. When it rains, much of the water that hits the ground runs over the surface of the land through the force of gravity, eventually collecting in the low spots. Some of these low spots are (or become) waterways—rivers, streams, ponds, lakes, bays. The land along the edges of these waterways is often low-lying as well and often becomes saturated.

Saturated land is usually a wetland. When a waterway overflows, as it might during a heavy rainstorm, low-lying banks and shores become flooded. These areas are the waterway's floodplain. Floodplain wetlands may be marshes, fields, or even forests since a floodplain may extend several miles beyond the edge of the water, depending upon topography. However, not all of the area within a floodplain may be actual wetland at any given time.

At the base of any sloping land, rain and runoff can collect and saturate the soil, essentially forming a wetland. Some examples are: in mountain valleys where snowmelt collects; meadows at the base of a hill; and stormwater management ponds (a constructed feature built to collect and filter runoff).

In areas where the water table is high, ground water often seeps into pore spaces in the soil near the surface, forming a wetland. This ground water may have originally run downhill from uplands, seeped from waterways, or collected in confined areas to form the wetland. Slope wetlands are formed where ground water comes to the surface along sloping land. Many ponds and streams are fed in this way by ground water as well as by rainfall and surface water. Thus, wetlands may receive water from both above and below the ground.

Procedure

Warm Up

Ask the class to name some local areas they know of that are always muddy. Ask them to picture these places and guess where the water comes from or why it stays where it does. One example might be the ground below a rainspout, where water often collects.

Tell students that wetlands may form in areas where 1) rainwater and/or ground water collect; 2) the ground is concave and water collects on top of an impervious layer (e.g., a pond); or, 3) waterways overflow their borders.

The Activity

1. **Divide the class into small working groups. Hand out supplies. Have each group create a pond or depression in one sponge, by cutting away a small circle in the center of the sponge.**

Do this by folding the sponge in half and cutting out a half-circle, making sure not to cut all the way through to make a hole. In the same way, each group should make a stream or river in the second sponge. Have them cover the bottom of the cutaway portion with a strip of cardboard, which represents the waterway's bed. *Note:* If your students are younger, prepare the sponges ahead of time.

2. **When all of the models are ready, give the groups paper cups of colored water to pour into the waterways. Have students tilt the stream sponge to allow water flow and watch and describe what happens.** The water will be absorbed into the banks of the waterways and seep into the surrounding ground, creating wetland conditions. Students may pick up spills with the sponge, too, just as wetlands are fed by and store ground water from below.

3. **To illustrate that wetlands are also fed and formed by surface water, describe how rainwater that lands on a hill or slope runs downhill by the force of gravity. Have each group use the 5-inch x 8-inch foil-covered cardboard piece to represent a hillside. The bottom of each piece should rest on a sponge and the other end should be held up. Have groups pour water onto the foil near the top of the slope and describe what happens.** Water should collect in the sponge at the base of the hill until the sponge is saturated; some water may seep out, away from the hill.

4. **Now that the sponges are saturated, repeat step two.** The waterways should overflow, demonstrating flood-plain wetlands. This is also surface water.

Wrap Up

Have students identify the water sources that feed wetlands and summarize how wetlands regulate surface-water runoff.

Take the group on a walk around the school or community to find a body of water. Bring along a shovel or hand trowel. From the edge of a pond or stream, ask students to walk to the farthest spot away from the water where they think water has seeped into the ground. Dig a few holes and investigate the moisture content of the soil. Ask whether or not it could be a wetland. Are they surprised at what they find?

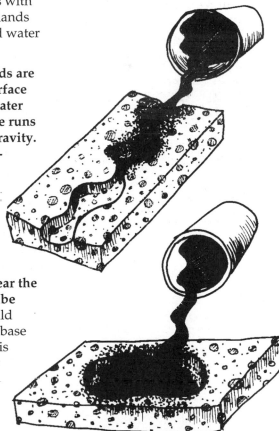

Assessment

Have students:

- identify sources of water in wetlands.

- investigate nearby soils and conclude whether or not the area could be a wetland.

Extensions

If students collect soil samples, have them determine how much water the samples contain. This is done by comparing the weights of samples before and after drying. (Remove water from soil samples by setting them in the sun until they are dry, or baking them in an oven at 150 degrees C [300 degrees F] for 30 minutes.)

Notes:

Wetlands often occur in a depression or basin in the land, with edges that slope up to the elevation of the surrounding ground:

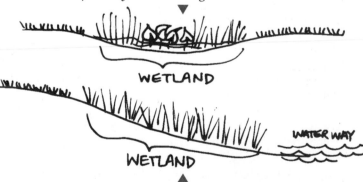

If the bowl is very shallow, the wetland probably occurs throughout the basin.

Sometimes this basin is shaped like a bowl. If the bowl is deep, the wetland is usually found on the sloping edges of the bowl—e.g., the edges of the pond.

Sometimes the basin is just the low area at the base of a slope. The slope can be steep or gradual. The lowest end of the slope is underwater, and is then called the bottom of the waterway. Wetland plants are often found growing along the slope that forms the waterway's shoreline. If the water is salty, the wetland is called a salt marsh.

Salt Marsh Players

Grade Level
3-6

Subject Areas
Ecology, Fine Arts, Language Arts

Duration
1 hour

Setting
Large classroom

Skills
Analyzing, interpreting, applying, and presenting information

Charting the Course
"Wetland Address" identifies how plants and animals adapt to wet environments. Other wetlands ecosystems are explored in "Life in the Fast Lane," and "People of the Bog."

Vocabulary
adaptation, salt marsh, habitat

Summary

How would you react if, for a part of each day, your house was covered with water?

Students role-play how organisms adapt to life in a salt marsh—a coastal, marine habitat that is alternately flooded and drained by tides.

Objectives

Students will:

• demonstrate how various salt marsh plants and animals adapt to environmental conditions.

• recognize various plants and animals that live in salt marshes.

Materials

• *photos, slides or a video of salt marshes and organisms that live in the salt marsh (optional)*
• *copies of The Salt Marsh Players Character Cards (make duplicates for larger classes)*
• *4-inch x 6-inch (10x15 cm) index cards*
• *glue*
• *scissors*
• *string*
• *2 cardboard tubes (paper towel)*
• *blue cloth, or a piece of blue ribbon approximately 12 to 20 feet long (4 to 6 m) and 1-foot (30 cm) wide (use the paper towel tubes to roll the cloth like a scroll)*
• *soap bubble bottle and bubble maker*

Making Connections

People see, hear of, and read about salt marshes and other wetlands in the media. Some students may have visited coastlines where salt marshes exist. Students may also have learned how certain species adapt to various conditions. By physically enacting behavioral strategies of salt marsh organisms encountering high and low tides, students are introduced to the complex and interrelated world of animal and plant adaptations.

Background

Salt marshes are grassy wetland habitats that occur within temperate estuarine environments. In the United States, marshes exist on the Atlantic and Pacific coasts and the shores of the Gulf of Mexico. They are part of the intertidal zone (the area between high and low tide) and are flooded once or twice a day by incoming tides.

The dominant plants of a salt marsh include grasses and algae. These plants die seasonally and regenerate, adding tremendous amounts of detritus (decaying organic matter) to the food chain. Scavengers and bacteria break down the detritus into nutrients and minerals. These provide the nutritional foundation for a complex food web, including fish, crabs, shellfish, and larger animals.

The pulsing action of tides delivers and distributes nutrients that plants and animals can consume. The comings and goings of tides also pose great challenges to salt marsh life. Regularly, a salt marsh is flooded with salt water during high tide. When the tide recedes, the land becomes exposed, and fresh water runoff often flows through the marsh. Not only are organisms exposed to varying degrees of moisture but also changes in salinity and temperature.

These variations produce an obvious distribution of plants and animals that are adapted to specific conditions within the marsh. This situation is called zonation and is often described as:

High Marsh—covered briefly each day by the tides, and

Low Marsh—beneath the level of the tide for many hours each day.

The area that is never exposed to the air is called the subtidal zone. Both the high marsh and low marsh comprise the intertidal zone.

The variability of the salt marsh environment requires residents to adapt, both physiologically and behaviorally. Changes in physiology, like marsh plants' ability to excrete salt, have evolved over long periods of time. Behavioral responses, like crabs burrowing into the mud at low tide, allow animals to adapt quickly to changes in the environment.

Some salt marsh species, like marsh snails, move away from incoming water. Others retreat into underwater burrows and remain inactive during high tides. Still others adjust their activities to suit the varying degrees of salinity or temperature. Salt marsh residents may have to adapt to both aquatic and terrestrial conditions within the same day!

The Salt Marsh "Stage"
Shown at low tide; arrows show movement as tide rises

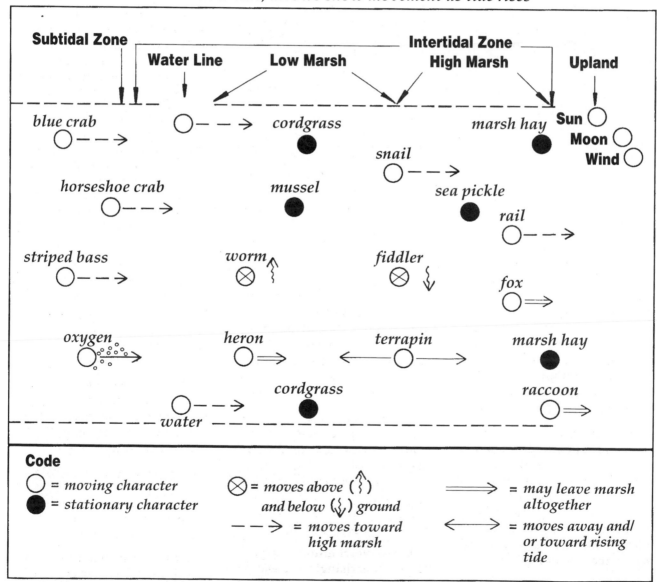

Illustrations in this activity by Laurie "gigette" Gould

Procedure

Warm Up

Ask students to list human behavioral responses to environmental change. What do we do in response to heat or cold? How do we prepare for a flood, cope with lack of food, or respond to physical pain?

Have the class brainstorm some obvious behavioral adaptations of common animals to the environment (pet dogs begging for scraps from the table, cattle seeking shade, birds migrating away from winter conditions).

Describe, display pictures of, or show a video of salt marshes and the organisms that reside there. Have students list some basic characteristics of the salt marsh and some plants and animals they think may live there. Explain that the marsh is flooded by the tide each day. Have students list ways they think plants and animals might adapt to life in the salt marsh.

The Activity

1. Hand each student a Salt Marsh Player Character Cards, string, and a large index card. Provide tape, glue, and scissors. Ask students to read the cards. Have them glue the pictures to one side the index cards and the descriptions to the other, punch two holes, and thread the string so the cards can be worn around the neck.

2. Designate a section of the classroom, at least 12 feet (4 m) x 15 feet (5 m). One end of the area will be a body of water (subtidal zone); and the other end is upland. The marsh is located between the two. Low marsh lies near the subtidal zone and high marsh near the upland.

3. Ask the water character to unroll the scroll of water and take a place at low tide (see diagram). Tell her to read her cards aloud and to make gentle wave motions with the fabric.

4. Ask, "What makes waves?" Have the student holding the wind card read about making waves, then make blowing sounds, dancing around while the waves move.

5. Taking turns, all the plants should read their Salt Marsh Players Character Cards and move into the appropriate area of the marsh. Each animal character does the same. Fish and blue crab live in the water, moving forward and back with the tides. The rest of the animals should take their low tide positions.

6. When all are in place, tell the wind to blow again. Ask, "What makes the tides move in and out?" Sun and moon should read their Salt Marsh Players Character Cards, then stand on chairs making circles above their heads with their arms, indicating a full moon and bright sun.

7. Have the oxygen character enter the water and read his or her Salt Marsh Player Character Card aloud. Tell students that wind churning the water helps mix oxygen into the water. Have the oxygen character blow soap bubbles while the wind howls.

8. Tell the characters to get ready to perform together. Remind students to notice what the other characters are doing. Announce that the sun and moon are high in the sky, the wind begins to blow, the waves start moving gently, and plants sway.

9. After several minutes, say, "The tide is rising!" The water character should walk very slowly toward the high marsh, with fish, crab, and oxygen following behind. Remind plants that since they are rooted in the ground, they must stand in place but should bend and sway in response to wind and water movement; plants should duck below the scroll of water as it passes. Animals should adopt high tide behavior (as described on their Salt Marsh Players Character Cards).

10. As the water reaches its high mark (just past the high marsh), announce that "It is high tide!" Ask the characters to explain their behavior briefly. Now reverse the sequence and have the water retreat back to low tide while players adjust their behaviors. The performance may be videotaped.

Wrap Up and Action

Have students write character sketches and locate materials from home to create costumes to dramatize the hardships and rewards of their existence. They may wish to do additional research. They should include ways that plants and animals adapt to the changing tides. They may be interested in learning how people adjust who live in tidal or storm-prone areas (houses on stilts, boats instead of cars, etc.).

Students may wish to choreograph a modern dance interpretation with their salt marsh players. This may be performed for school and community members.

Assessment

Have students:

• identify various plants and animals that live in salt marshes.

• enact the behavioral responses of salt marsh characters to tides.

- describe how various salt marsh plants and animals adapt to environmental conditions.

- write a sketch of a salt marsh player.

- design a costume to characterize a salt marsh player.

Extensions

Take a field trip to or show a video of a salt marsh and have students look for plants and animals from the play.

Classes might study other environments (rain forest, desert, tundra, etc.) and pinpoint the adaptations of plants and animals that live there. A class can develop a similar game for the residents of another environment, using seasonal change as the environmental factor, for example.

Resources

Mitchell, John G. 1992. "Our Disappearing Wetlands." *National Geographic* 182 (4) (October).

Mitsch, William J., and James G. Gosselink. 1993. *Wetlands,* 2nd ed. New York, N.Y.: Van Nostrand Reinhold.

Niering, William A. 1985. *Wetlands.* The Audubon Society Nature Guides. New York, N.Y.: Alfred A. Knopf.

The Salt Marsh Players Character Cards

Note: These characters represent the mid-Atlantic coast of the United States—species are different for other areas.

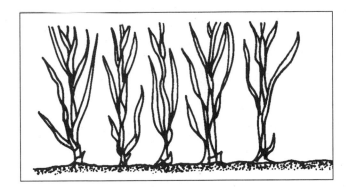

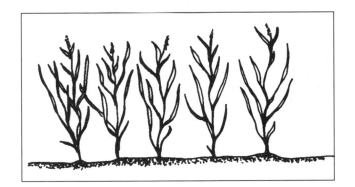

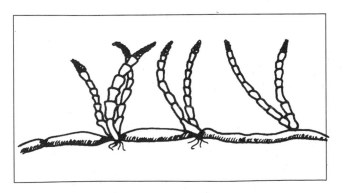

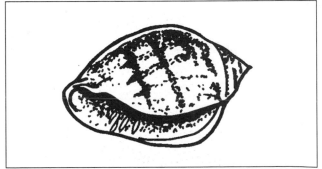

The Salt Marsh Players Character Cards

*(Make two or three copies of each plant)

Fiddler crab
(Uca pugnax)

I run about the marsh at low tide, searching for bits of dead plants and animals to eat, which I shove into my mouth with my one large and one small claw (females have two small claws). I am an air breather, so when the tide comes in, I plop down into my mud burrow and shut the "door" (a mud ball) so I don't drown!

Cordgrass*
(Spartina alterniflora)

I grow in the low marsh where the ground gets flooded by water for long periods of time each day. During the highest tides (spring tides), I might be completely underwater! Since I am a rooted plant, I can't move about except to sway with the breeze. I must tolerate sea water.

Blue crab
(Callinectes sapidus)

I am the tasty blue crab who comes into the marsh with the tide. Here, I find lots of oysters, fish, and many other creatures to eat. Since I breathe with gills, I must swim out of the marsh with the retreating tide. When I am "soft" (I shed my shell to grow), the marsh is a great place to hide from predators!

Salt meadow (salt marsh) hay*
(Spartina patens)

I am a grass, often called "marsh hay" because at one time I was harvested and fed to cattle. I grow in the high marsh where I get flooded for a few hours each day. When the wind blows, my neighbors and I sway softly, looking as though we were painted in watercolors. At low tide, we lie in swirly cowlicks, with roots still in the mud.

Horseshoe crab
(Limulus polyphemus)

I'm really not a true crab at all! Some think I am an odd, primitive creature. I stay at sea until a full moon in May, when it is time to lay eggs. Female crabs, with the smaller males in tow, swim ashore with the incoming tide, crawl onto the sand above the tide line, burrow, lay thousands of tiny eggs, then catch an outgoing tide a few days later.

Wind

I help the sun and moon drive the tide in and out. If I blow very hard, I can force the water to come in or go out farther than usual. I also add oxygen to the water, which helps make the water healthy and keeps plants and animals alive. Sometimes I can be very noisy as I sweep across the marsh!

Salt marsh snail
(Melampus bidentatus)

I prefer to live in the high marsh, since I am an air breather and don't like to be too wet. During low tide, I glide around the mud flats looking for algae and bits of dead plants to eat. As the tide comes in, I crawl up the stems and leaves of grasses to keep from drowning!

"Sea pickle" (saltwort)*
(Salicornia virginica)

I am a rather stiff, plump little plant that "crouches" down in the lower end of the high marsh, where I am alternately covered with water and exposed. I absorb a lot of salt water, which gives me my fleshy appearance. Considered a delicacy, sea pickles make a crunchy, salty addition to salads!

The Salt Marsh Players Character Cards

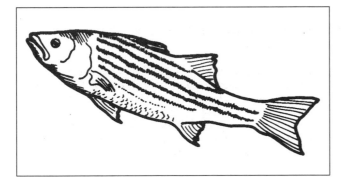

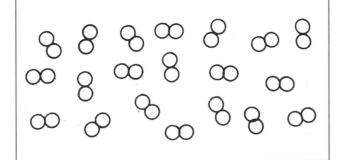

The Salt Marsh Players Character Cards

Sun

I am the sun and I help drive the tide! The sun's gravitational pull occurs as the Earth rotates daily on its axis. This causes the water to "pile up," making a high tide, and then later to pull away from shore, causing a low tide. I am about 30 percent responsible for the changing tide.

(You will stand on a chair and make a big circle above your head with your arms and "shine" over the marsh.)

Diamondback terrapin
(Malaclemys terrapin terrapin)

I am the only turtle that lives year-round in salty wetlands. I must breathe air, but I am really not affected much by tide, since I can swim to the surface and poke my head or nose out for a breath. I like to eat snails, crabs, worms, insects, and fish, so I go where the food is!

Moon

I am the moon and I am the major force driving the tide! I create a gravitational pull as I revolve around Earth. This causes the water to "pile up," making a high tide, or to pull away from shore, causing a low tide. I am about 70 percent responsible for the changing tide.

(You will stand on a chair and make a big circle above your head with your arms and "shine" over the marsh.)

Striped bass ("rockfish")
(Morone saxatilis)

Like many kinds of fish, I use the marsh as a nursery area, a protected place to raise my young (called "fry" or "fingerlings" at different stages). My tiny offspring dart in and out of the marsh plants as they move with the tides. (Remember, fish filter oxygen from water with gills!) These hungry youngsters find lots of food here.

Great blue heron
(Ardea herodias)

I am a large, beautiful bird that wades gracefully in the shallow water, hunting for food. With my long neck and long, pointed bill I snatch fish, crabs, water insects, and even small mammals out of the water. As the tide comes in, I move to higher parts of the marsh to stay in shallow water. Sometimes I just fly away.

Water
(H_2O, salty)

I am water and I am the tide! When it is time for the tide to rise, I move slowly into the low marsh, then up into the high marsh. At the high tide point, I stop and rest a minute, then turn in place and move slowly "out to sea."

(You will need a partner to help you make and move the strip of "water.")

Clapper rail
(Rallus longirostris)

I am an elusive, hen-like bird, often called the "marsh hen" because I live and nest in salt marshes. At low tide, I forage and probe my long bill into the mud, looking for fiddler crabs, worms and other small creatures, and seeds. High tide limits my territory to the high marsh, but here I can still eat snails that climb up grasses to escape the water.

Oxygen
(O_2 what a gas!)

Water must contain oxygen to support all the living things that live in it! As the tide moves in and out, I move along just behind the water line, showering all things I encounter with bubbles! Bubbles are made by carbon dioxide gas (which contains O_2) that animals exhale, or by the oxygen given off by underwater plants.

The Salt Marsh Players Character Cards

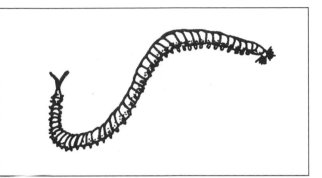

Sea worm (clam worm)
(Nereis succinea)

I am a colorful worm who burrows in the mud in the subtidal zone or in the low marsh, where I build a tube out of sand. When the tide is high and my tube is underwater, I look for food, such as the soft insides of clams, dead fish, or other small water animals. When the tide is low, I stay deep inside my tube.

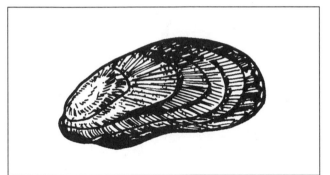

Ribbed mussel
(Geukensia demissa)

I am a bivalve, a two-shelled animal, like a clam. I live in mud in the low marsh, but half of me sticks above the mud. I can't move about. At high tide I open my shell a bit, take in water, and strain out oxygen and tiny plants and animals to eat. At low tide I close up tightly to hold moisture in my gills for breathing until next high tide.

Raccoon
(Procyon lotor)

Though I do not live in the salt marsh, I do come here to hunt for dragonflies, crabs, oysters, clams, fish, and other good bits of food. I am not fond of swimming, so when the tide rises, I leave the marsh for higher ground.

Red fox
(Vulpes vulpes)

I am a mammal who does not live in the salt marsh, but I do come here to hunt for rabbits, rodents, small marsh birds and eggs, and invertebrates. As the tide rises, I leave the marsh. I usually hunt in drier areas in winter.

Water We Have Here?

Grade Level
5-12; 2-4, with assistance

Subject Areas
Chemistry, Environmental Science

Duration
30-60 minutes each part, if used as separate activities; 15-20 minutes for each measurement taken in the wetland

Setting
Classroom lab and/or wetland

Skills
Gathering, analyzing, and interpreting information

Charting the Course
Water-quality tests can be done as part of several other activities. See "Recipe for Trouble," and "Nutrients: Nutrition or Nuisance?" and "Over Hill and Dale."

Vocabulary
salinity, turbidity, dissolved oxygen, acidity, pH, acid rain, nitrate, nitrite

Summary
Students perform a series of scientific measurements and tests on wetland water.

Objectives
Students will:

• measure and monitor water conditions (pH, temperature, salinity, dissolved oxygen, turbidity, rate of flow, and excess nutrients) in a local wetland.

• draw conclusions about a wetland based on water analysis measurements.

Materials
• copies of Water Data student page, p. 186 for grades 5-12, p. 187 for grades 2-4
• copies of student pages for the parameters studied
• clipboards, pencils, and paper
• copies of Water Data Analysis Information sheet, p. 185
• other materials, as listed in student pages

Making Connections
By measuring the physical characteristics of the water in a wetland, students become more aware of resources and how human actions affect them.

Background
There are many ways to monitor the health of a wetland. The presence of certain plant and animal species can be used as a barometer of wetland conditions. A look at the composition of wetland soils can also offer clues. However, the investigation of water itself offers a fundamental approach to the study of a wetland's well-being.

When the results of wetland water-quality parameter tests are documented, the data can be compared to data from other wetlands or data from the same wetland over time (particularly through a school year). The results can be correlated with other factors such as weather, watershed dynamics, and human activity. The exercises in this activity provide an opportunity for students to better understand how water samples differ, and how a number of factors combine to greatly influence wetland water quality. These factors can affect the ability of wetlands to perform valuable natural functions.

Procedure
Warm Up
What do students think they can study about water? Have them create a list of things they would study. What would the information they collect tell them about water quality? *Note:* If only one or two of the water-quality tests are conducted, you might want to focus the Warm Up discussion on these aspects. For example, ask students "Why do people measure pH?"

The following activities can be presented separately or together. For younger students, omit the more difficult parts of the activities (e.g., do the taste test for salinity, but not the dissolved oxygen test). Older students may carry the activities further by monitoring these water-quality parameters for several days, graphing results and correlating the data with weather conditions and with any noticeable polluting events (e.g., a rainstorm washes sediment in from a nearby construction site).

The Activity

1. **Introduce and discuss the water-quality parameters to be measured.**

2. Hand out student pages and review the measurement procedures.

3. **Have students conduct the test(s).**

4. **Discuss results. Use the Water Data Analysis Information sheet, if needed.**

Wrap Up and Action

Have students fill in the Water Data student page appropriate to their age group. If necessary, have them research what these parameters tell us. What influences the results? Do students think these conditions indicate a healthy wetland? Compare results with professional data.

Suggest things students can do to keep the water in their neighborhood healthy (e.g., improve conditions that change the pH, temperature, dissolved oxygen, turbidity, or rate of flow). Students may investigate:

Construction sites. How is erosion being controlled at construction sites? Look for silt fences (usually made of black mesh) or hay bales. Are they successfully trapping soil that is running off of the site?

Lawns. Ask your parents and friends what products they use for lawn care. Do they use fertilizer? Insecticides? Lime? These and other products change the pH of the water or add excess nutrients and poisons. Ask parents and friends to follow the directions on packages carefully, to use only as much as needed, and to avoid applying products before it rains (products will wash off even before they have a chance to work). Are there bare areas on the school lawn or at home? Students can plant grass or flowers or cover the spots with wood chips to prevent soil erosion.

Assessment

Have students:

• measure the parameters discussed in the student pages.

• interpret the results of the analyses.

Extensions

Acid rain is caused by excessive burning of fossil fuels such as coal, gasoline, and oil in our cars, homes, and factories. Reduce this form of pollution by being more conservative with these fuels. At home, turn the thermostat down five degrees and wear a sweater, or help your family install weather-stripping around doors and windows. Weather-stripping is inexpensive and comes in self-sticking rolls that are easy to apply. This will also help your family save money!

How many cars travel on your street or the street in front of school each day? Pick a point along the street and count the cars that pass the point during a 15-minute period. Multiply this number by four to get the number per hour, then multiply by 24 to get the average per day. Assume that each car travels 5 miles and produces 4 grams of nitrogen oxide (one cause of acid rain) per mile. The estimated amount of nitrogen oxide produced per day on the street equals the number of cars per day times 4 grams per mile times 5 miles. How many more streets are there in your neighborhood? [Formula reprinted from *Acid Rain Teacher's Guide*, with permission of National Wildlife Federation.]

How could you and your neighbors reduce the amount of nitrogen oxide produced? Try carpooling, walking, or riding a bike or the bus as frequently as possible. Combine trips to stores and pick up things for a friend while you are out. Maybe you and some friends could start a bicycle delivery service. Do small errands for people, make a bit of money, and improve air and water quality!

Measuring pH
Background

What substances do you think are acidic or basic (alkaline)? The measure of hydrogen ions (H+) in a solution is called the pH. A solution is more acidic when it contains more hydrogen ions. pH is measured on a scale of 0-14, where 0 is extremely acidic, 7 is neutral, and 14 is extremely basic.

Several factors contribute to the natural pH level of water and soils. For example, vegetation type and density, the underlying strata of rocks and soil, and the quality of waters flowing through the area will affect ground water and soil acidity. The pH range of natural systems under normal circumstances is typically between 6.0 and 8.0. This is the most favorable range for life, although some organisms can tolerate harsher conditions (e.g., plants and animals of highly-acidic peat bogs). The pH level of the water in wetlands is important to plant and animal life. Sudden, dramatic changes in pH could endanger the lives of young animals, in particular.

Human activity can change the level of acidity in watery environments. For example, air pollution

from automobiles and coal-burning utilities and factories contributes to acid rain. Sulfur dioxide (SO_2) and nitrogen oxide (NO_2) are emitted from tailpipes and smokestacks. When these compounds combine with water in the atmosphere, they form sulfuric and nitric acids (H_2SO_4 and HNO_3), which fall to the earth as acid rain, snow, hail, and fog. This precipitation mixes with surface water in creeks, rivers, ponds, and wetlands. The acidity of the water in wetlands can also be changed by other pollutants transported in runoff. On the other hand, the lime in agricultural and household products has an opposite, buffering or neutralizing effect. When limestone combines with water that has a pH of less than 8.0, it reduces acidity.

In general, naturally occurring organic acids from plants (sphagnum moss, several tree species, etc.) are weaker and less harmful to life than inorganic acids such as sulfuric acid. In fact, organic acids from plants can actually have a buffering effect on the inorganic acids that may have entered the system.

Note: Seawater has a natural buffering capacity because of the many salts it contains.

Materials

- *pH paper (Carolina Biological Supply 1-800-334-5551) or an acid rain test kit (Delta Education 1-800-442-5444)*
- *small jars or cups*
- *vinegar*
- *milk*
- *lemon juice*
- *ammonia*
- *tap water*
- *distilled water*
- *soda pop*
- *chalk*
- *baking soda*
- *aspirin*
- *antacid tablets*
- *safety goggles*
- *broom handle*
- *wire or string*

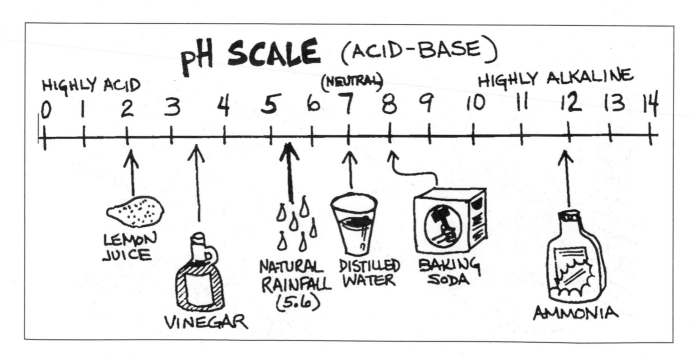

Measuring pH

(continued)

Procedure

1. Test and compare some common substances (lemon juice, vinegar, natural rainfall, baking soda, ammonia, and others), using the pH paper. Dissolve the solid items in distilled water. Draw a pH scale and use it to record and compare the results of each test. Distilled water has a pH of 7; lemon juice, pH 2; vinegar, pH 3.5; natural rainfall, pH 5.6; baking soda, pH 8; ammonia, pH 12.

2. A buffer is something that neutralizes acids and bases in solution. Chalk (calcium carbonate, $CaCO_3$), baking soda ($NaHCO_3$), and antacids act as buffers. Mix these with lemon juice and vinegar and test again. **Wear goggles for this part, and do not mix anything with the ammonia!** Some acid-base mixtures can produce dangerous reactions.

3. Rinse a glass jar with distilled water and leave it outside to collect rainwater. Measure the rainwater's pH. Is the rain in your area acidic or more neutral?

4. At a wetland site, collect small water samples from several different places (near shore, out several feet, etc.) and measure the pH. To sample beyond reach, tie string or wire around a jar and tie the jar to a broom handle or stick for dipping.

5. Use your results to answer the following questions:

• How does the pH of the wetland water compare to the pH of the rainwater?

• Do you think the rain has any effect on the wetland water? How can you tell? Test the pH of the wetland water right after it rains to see if it has changed.

• Are other factors affecting the pH of the water? Was the pH taken near the land different from the other measurements? Why?

How could you help reduce your contribution to acid rain? How about walking, riding a bike, carpooling, or riding public transportation whenever you can. You could even reduce the use of fossil fuels (coal and oil) by turning the heat down at home and school, insulating your homes, etc.

Measuring Temperature

[Adapted from Living In Water by Valerie Chase, National Aquarium in Baltimore.]

Background

What's the importance of temperature in a habitat? Most creatures that live in water are cold-blooded, so their body temperatures and metabolism and growth rates are determined (and limited) by the surrounding water temperature. Most can tolerate only a certain range of temperatures.

Dissolved oxygen (DO), necessary for the survival of aquatic life, is also dependent upon temperature. Cold water can hold more DO than warm water. All else being equal, warm water will support less life than cold.

The waterways around some power plants are affected by increased temperatures because water used to cool the plants' reactors picks up heat from the reactors before it is released into waterways. This is called thermal pollution. Some aquatic life cannot tolerate such an increase in temperature.

Materials

• *lab or aquarium thermometers*
• *tap water*

Procedure

1. Practice using the thermometers by testing hot, warm, and cold tap water.

2. At the wetland, take and record the temperature (T) of the water in several places. Do not hold the bulb end of the thermometer in your hand before taking the water temperature. To get a more accurate reading, keep the thermometer in place in the water for a minute or more. Compare temperatures taken in direct sunlight and in the shade, at the surface and one foot below it, in moving and still water.

3. While you record the water temperature, leave a thermometer out to take the air temperature. How does this compare to the water temperature? If the wetland is easily accessible, record both air and water temperatures every day for one to two weeks. Graph the results. Do you find a correlation between the two? Water requires more heat than either air or land for each degree of increased temperature. Bodies of water therefore change temperature more slowly and have more stable temperatures than land or air. Lakes and oceans warm adjacent land in winter and cool it in summer.

Measuring Salinity

[Hydrometer from Earth Science Activities for Grades 2-8 *by Marvin Tolman and James Morton, 1986. Used with permission of Parker Publishing Co., Inc., a division of Simon & Schuster, West Nyack, NY]*

Background

Salinity (the concentration of dissolved salts in the water) is an important factor in a habitat. Aquatic animals are adapted to living in certain salinity ranges. Sunfish, for example, are common in ponds and freshwater streams, but cannot survive in salt water. Animals that live in salty environments tend to be more tolerant of wider salinity ranges. Some species of fish migrate from salt to fresh water to spawn (reproduce).

Salinity is measured as a ratio of salts to water, and is expressed in parts per thousand (ppt), which means the number of units (parts) of salts per thousand units of water. There are three main categories of salinity: fresh water (0-0.5 ppt), brackish water (partly salty, or 0.5-30 ppt), and salt water (full seawater, greater than 30 ppt).

An estuary is a body of water that contains a number of salinity zones. Estuaries are partially enclosed by land and fed by freshwater rivers, and they open out into the ocean. With this wide range of habitats, estuaries support an abundance of life.

Salinity is affected by weather, especially at the surface of the water. During dry seasons, water evaporates, making salty water saltier (the concentration of salts increases). When it rains, salty water is diluted by the added fresh water. Do you enjoy fishing? After a heavy rain, look for freshwater fish in normally saltier water; during a drought, you may find exciting saltwater fish farther upstream than usual!

Salinity, like temperature, affects the amount of dissolved oxygen in the water. At high salinities, molecules of salts take up more space between water molecules, so there is less space for oxygen molecules.

Materials

- *table salt*
- *tap water*
- *1-liter beakers*
- *scale or balance that weighs grams*
- *lipstick tube caps*
- *several nails or screws, small enough to fit in lipstick tube cap*
- *clear cups or glasses*
- *grease pencil*
- *hydrometer, available from aquarium supply stores (optional)*
- *map of your state*

Procedure

1. Do a salt taste test. Mix table salt with tap water to make partly and very salty water to compare to fresh tap water. To taste, just dip a finger into a small cup of each solution. Do not drink the salty water!

You can also try mixing different concentrations of salt in parts-per-thousand ratios using this formula:

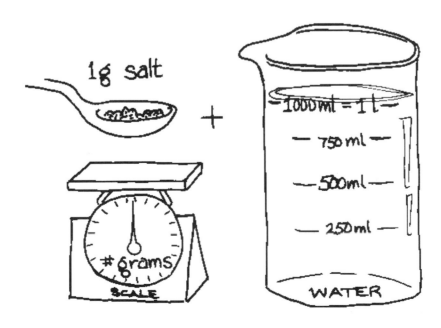

Measuring Turbidity

[Adapted from Project Estuary *by Gail Jones, North Carolina National Estuarine Research Reserve, and* Field Manual for Water Quality Monitoring *by Mark Mitchell and William Stapp, University of Michigan.]*

Background

What do plants need for growth? One answer is light. Because underwater plants need light too, and they die if they can't get enough, water clarity is an important factor in wetland habitats. Fewer plants means less food for many animals, and less production of oxygen from plants to help keep the water environment healthy. Young and otherwise vulnerable creatures find protection in beds of underwater plants. These plants also feed and protect many of the foods we eat, including fish, crabs, ducks, and geese.

When water is cloudy, it is said to be turbid. Turbidity is caused when sediment (soil and other particles that settle to the bottom) and other materials are stirred up in the water. When loose soil from construction sites, bare lawns, and eroding shorelines washes into a wetland, sediment levels rise. Excess nutrients in runoff promote the growth of algae, which also clouds the water. Rain, wind, waves, tides, animals, and various human activities can all stir up these suspended solids and increase turbidity.

Turbidity blocks the sunlight that is so vital to aquatic life. Fish, oysters, and other gilled creatures suffocate when their gills are clogged by sediment. Suspended particles absorb heat from sunlight as well, warming the water and decreasing DO.

A *Secchi (SECK-key) disc* is used to measure depth of light penetration, or turbidity. The deeper the disc is visible, the clearer and less turbid the water. Secchi discs are used in water that is fairly deep and slow or still.

Materials

• *lid from a large tin can (at least 6-8 inches [15-20 cm] in diameter)*
• *black and white waterproof paint*
• *drill or ice pick*
• *large eye bolt and nut*
• *heavy string*
• *tape measure*
• *permanent marker*
• *turbidimeter (optional)*
• *glass jars (optional)*

Procedure

1. List as many sources of sediment as you can. Try to use specific examples—things you have seen in the area or at home.

2. If the water in your wetland is slow-moving or still, construct Secchi discs as follows:

a. Paint the tin can lid white, then paint a large black X on top.

b. Punch or drill a small hole in the middle of the X and attach the string to the lid with the eye bolt and nut.

c. Mark off 0.5-meter (or 1-foot) increments on the string with the marker.

3. At the wetland, gently lower the disc straight down into the water until you can no longer see the X. Then, inch the disc back up until you can just barely see the X and hold the disc there. Reach down and grasp the string right at the surface of the water, and hold the string there while you pull the disk back out. Read the marking on the string to determine the depth to which light could penetrate. Compare readings from several places in the wetland.

Were some places more turbid than others? Were you able to see what caused the turbidity? *Hint:* Look for places where runoff and sediment are washing into the water from land. Are fish stirring up the water? Are you or your classmates standing in the water?

Note: If the water in your wetland is fast-moving, you may skip this part or use a turbidimeter, if there is one available to you. You could also use clear jars to collect running water at different places, let the jars sit until the solids settle out, and compare solids collected at the different sites by weight or volume.

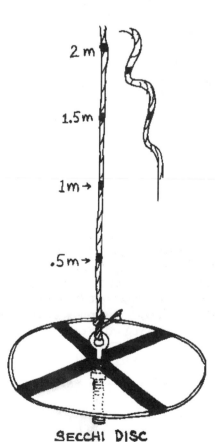

SECCHI DISC

Measuring Rate of Flow

Background

What happens to a nearby stream or other body of water when it rains, or has not rained for a long time? You may have noticed a change in rate of flow.

Rate of flow is a measure of how fast the water in a stream or other body of water is moving. Most flowing bodies of water (including the water in many types of wetlands) have varying flow rates. Reasons for this variation include precipitation (or lack thereof), spring thaws of snow and ice, and changes in the use of land in the watershed. During a dry season or drought, the flow may be greatly slowed by the lack of rainfall. Some bodies of water may become smaller or narrower than usual. Small streams may stop running altogether. (These are called intermittent streams, since they do not always flow.) Some bodies of water do not flow much at all and are nearly still.

Moving water typically carries many materials, including dissolved gases and salts (e.g., oxygen and sodium chloride), soil, mineral sediments, organic materials, nutrients, litter, and so on. As water travels through an area, it may deposit materials, pick them up, or both. This action provides important metabolic building blocks for aquatic plants and animals. In bodies of water with little or no flow (e.g., a pond), wind and animals' activities help mix in these materials.

As rain and runoff wash into a body of water, the rate of flow increases. Rushing floodwaters can be dangerous to people and property and can cause damage to the water itself. Soil and other pollutants are washed from the land. This input of sediment muddies the water, choking plants and animals. As the shoreline is carved away, valuable land and habitat are lost. Moreover, animals that are adapted to slow-moving water may not survive if the flow rate is greatly increased, particularly over a long period.

The combination of moving water and human development can seriously impact local watersheds. In areas with a great deal of pavement, water cannot penetrate the ground, so there is more runoff, which increases flow rate. On the other hand, parking lots, driveways, and sidewalks covered with gravel or wood chips instead of pavement allow some rainwater to soak into the ground. Runoff can also be slowed by a human-made, plant-filled buffer zone along a shoreline or water edge. A wetland performs this function naturally, providing a place where sediments and pollutants can settle out before runoff reaches the waterway.

Materials

- *2 stakes or sticks*
- *string*
- *measuring tape*
- *2 oranges of similar size and weight*
- *stopwatch or watch with second hand*

Procedure

1. At the wetland, measure at least a 5-yard (4.5-m) distance along the bank, where the water is visible. Measure 100 feet (30 m) if possible. Mark the length by setting the stakes in the ground at each end and connecting them with string.

2. Have a timekeeper stand at the upstream stake. Toss an orange into the water upstream of this stake. Begin timing as the orange floats by the stake (record the starting time, if using a wristwatch). Move to the other stake before the orange gets there, and stop the watch just as the orange passes the second stake. Record the time (subtract from the starting time, if using a wristwatch). Recover the orange if you can do so safely; otherwise, use the second orange to repeat the test for accuracy.

3. Now calculate the rate of flow.

Rate (r) x Time (t) = Distance (d).
So, $r = d \div t$.

Units should be expressed as feet per second, yards per minute, meters per second, etc., as appropriate. If the wetland is nearby, monitor the rate of flow at different times such as after heavy rain, as snow melts, or during a dry spell. Compare the results.

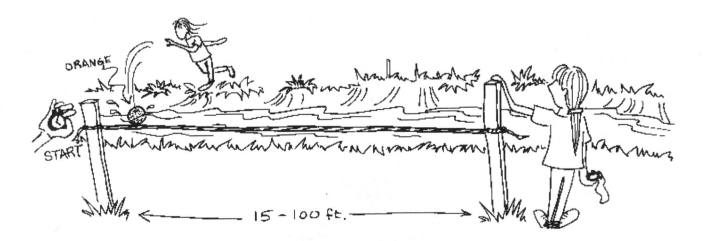

Measuring Excess Nutrients

Background

Phosphorus (P) is an essential nutrient for plant growth and animal metabolism. Plant growth depends on the amount of P available. In many bodies of water, P is present in very low concentrations, so it is a growth-limiting factor.

Nitrogen (N) is another essential nutrient. Plants and animals use N to build proteins. Plants absorb N through their roots and use it to make plant proteins, which are then converted to animal proteins when animals eat the plants. N is usually more available for use than P, because it is found in water in different forms: molecular nitrogen (N_2); ammonia (NH_3), a product of animal wastes and the decay of animal proteins; and nitrate (NO_3^-) and nitrite (NO_2^-) which are formed when specialized bacteria combine ammonia with oxygen.

Although N and P are necessary nutrients, too much of them in the water causes pollution. Algae use up P very quickly. Excess P encourages a vast growth of algae (algal bloom), which makes the water look like pea soup. Algal blooms use up a great deal of dissolved oxygen, causing anoxic conditions. Too much N (ammonia and nitrates) causes similar problems. This excessive nutrient enrichment of water can cause eutrophication (aging of a lake or wetland).

Nutrients enter the water during natural events or human activity. Organic P and N are present in living plant and animal tissues, and become organic matter when the organisms die. The natural weathering of rocks and soil transports minerals and nutrients. Precipitation and snowmelt increase runoff that carries nutrients and other pollutants to waterways. Ground water flow and streams and rivers carry nutrients from place to place. This natural transport of materials helps supply plants and animals with needed nutrients.

However, a variety of human activities can send excess nutrients into an ecosystem. Human and other animal wastes enter waterways through wastewater treatment plants and agricultural runoff. Disturbance of the land and its vegetation adds excess nutrients that are normally held in the soil. Erosion is speeded by these activities, so that soil and its accompanying nutrients end up in the water. And nutrients stored in wetlands are released into waterways when wetlands are drained for development.

Wetlands filter and trap excess nutrients and other pollutants before they can enter waterways. Wetland plants use up many of the excess nutrients that run off the land. Wetlands work to keep things in balance in the water.

Materials

- *Nitrogen and phosphorus level test kit from a chemical supply company such as LaMotte Chemical Products Co. (See Resources for address.)*

Procedure

1. At the wetland, look for signs of eutrophication. Are there a lot of algae in the water and on its surface? What color is the water? If it's very green or brown, it probably has a high nutrient content.

Is there a farm nearby with cow manure or fertilizer in the fields? Are you in a community with lots of dogs? If yes, there is a potential for runoff of animal wastes. Are there construction sites, bare spots on the ground, or other signs of erosion nearby? Are there many paved areas around this area? Runoff from these sites carries nutrients (and toxic substances) to waterways.

2. Test for nutrient levels (nitrogen and phosphorus) using the instructions in the test kit. Remember, some levels of N and P should be there—it is the extra we put in that can be harmful. Levels of N and P differ during growing seasons and in the winter. Why?

3. Test water flowing into and out of the wetland where lots of plants grow. Is there a difference in the two tests? There should be, because plants filter and use up nutrients.

Water Data Analysis Information

Use this chart as a guide as you interpret your water-quality field data. Remember that each aquatic system is different; this chart is only a guide, not a hard and fast rule!

Water Test	What It Measures	Natural Reading	Danger Reading	Source	Remedies
Salinity	amount of dissolved salts	varies— higher in summer and fall, lower in spring	—	• *fresh*: rain and streams • *salt*: ocean water (evaporation can also increase salinity)	—
Dissolved Oxygen	amount of oxygen in the water	7-14 ppm (parts per million)	3-5 = stress 1-2 = poor 0 = anoxic	• wind • waves • running water	• control nutrient content, algae growth • more wind and water movement
pH	acid base of the water	generally 6.5-8.5 (Bogs are naturally acidic, pH can be as low as 4.2)	below 6.5; above 8.5	• acid rain • industrial pollution • chemical spills	• pollution controls
Phosphates and Nitrates	amount of these nutrients in the water	0.0-0.65 ppm 0.0-0.08 ppm	any reading higher than normal	• sewage, industry • detergents • fertilizer, animal wastes	• removal by water treatment • restrictive or banned use
Temperature	average amount of heat in the water	varies	generally above 27°C (81°F) (>24°C for trout streams)	• waste heat • solar heat	• cooling towers, etc. (decreased T also increases DO)
Turbidity	clearness of the water	80-120 cm (0-8 JTU, Jackson Turbidity Units)	increased turbidity	• sediment • excessive algae growth • boat traffic, storms, etc.	• sediment controls • reduced nutrients to reduce algae • boat speed limits

If you will be monitoring water conditions for more than three days, use copies of this sheet and change the day numbers. Compare water data to chart on p. 186.

Water Data

	Day 1: Date_____	Day 2: Date_____	Day 3: Date_____
W pH			
Temperature (T) (in degrees C or F)			
A Salinity (S) (in ppt; or fresh, salty, or brackish)			
Is the water tidal or nontidal?			
T Is it high or low tide?			
Dissolved Oxygen (DO)			
E Turbidity			
R Rate of Flow (give units)			
Nitrogen (N)			
Phosphorus (P)			

Water Data

Work together in small groups and be sure to ask your teacher if you need help.

1. Use a ruler to measure the depth of the water. How deep is the water at the edge near the land?

   _____How deep is it two feet away from the edge?_____

   How deep is it in the middle of the body of water?_____ (guess, if you can't measure there)

2. What color is the water?_____

3. Can you see the bottom?_____

   What is on the bottom?_____

4. Does the water have an odor? What does it smell like?_____

5. Put your hand in the water. Does it feel warm or cold or very cold?_____

6. Is the water still or moving?_____

   If it is moving, is it flowing or is the wind making waves?_____

   If it is flowing, is it moving quickly or slowly?_____

7. What would you call this body of water?_____Describe the land around the edges of the water.

   _____

   What would you call this part of the land?_____

8. Find and list two ways that humans have changed this place:

Nutrients: Nutrition or Nuisance?

[Adapted from an activity conceived by Britt Slattery for Virginia's State Parks . . . Your Backyard Classrooms.]

Grade Level
K-8, parts labeled as appropriate

Subject Areas
Environmental Science

Duration
30-50 minutes for each part

Setting
Classroom and outdoors

Skills
Interpreting

Charting the Course
See "Water We Have Here?" for a procedure to test nitrogen and phosphorus levels in the field.

Vocabulary
phosphorus, nitrogen, nutrients, algal bloom

Summary

Students play innovative games that illustrate the movement of chemicals, nutrients, and energy in a marsh.

Objectives

Students will:

• interpret the benefits of nutrients and the dangers of excess nutrients.

• describe the filtering ability of wetland plants.

Materials

• *bottle of multivitamins*
• *green, yellow, blue, and brown construction paper*
• *markers*
• *scissors*
• *tape*
• *chairs*
• *cassette player or radio*

Making Connections

By studying the flow of nutrients in a wetland, students will be able to discuss water pollution and may become more aware of their own nutritional needs.

Background

All plants and animals need nutrients for the cell activity that sustains life. Phosphorus (P) and nitrogen (N) are essential nutrients for plant growth and metabolism.

Plant growth depends, in part, on the amount of phosphorus available. Phosphate molecules provide vital energy for metabolic processes in plant cells. In many bodies of water, phosphorus is present in very low concentrations, so it becomes a growth-limiting factor.

Nitrogen is found in several forms, so it is often more available than phosphorus. Plants use nitrogen to make plant proteins, which plant-eating animals convert into their own proteins.

Although nutrients are necessary, an overabundance of nitrogen and phosphorus in an aquatic system can cause problems. Algae will use up phosphorus very quickly. Excess phosphorus promotes a vast growth of algae (algal bloom), that makes the water look like pea soup. Algal bloom eventually robs the water of oxygen, and other forms of aquatic life suffocate. Some forms of nitrogen can cause similar problems.

The nitrogen and phosphorus in living plants and animals return to the nutrient cycle when the organisms die and decompose. Such nutrients are often held in the soil, including wetland soil, until they are used by other plants. Excess nutrients can enter water in several other ways. Natural events such as flooding move nutrients along. Human, animal, and industrial wastes contribute to nutrient overload as do activities such as road-building, farming, and draining wetlands for development. When soil erodes and washes away, it carries nutrients along to waterways downstream.

Wetlands often act as buffer zones by temporarily holding floodwaters and filtering materials such as excess nutrients from surface waters. When a wetland is lost, its buffering function is also lost.

Procedure

Warm Up

Sometimes too much of a good thing is bad. Have students think of examples (candy, soda, dessert, staying up too late, even too many carrots, which can make you turn orange). Ask them to think about what might happen if everyone living around a wetland loaded their lawns with fertilizer (which contains phosphorus).

Nitrogen and phosphorus are just two of the nutrients plants and animals need. Some of the others are calcium, magnesium, iron, and zinc. Read the label on a bottle of multivitamins. What kinds of nutrients do the pills contain?

The Activity
Part I: *Musical Nutrients*
(Grades 1-4)

To demonstrate the growth-limiting effects of nutrient deficits, play a special version of musical chairs.

1. **Make a green name tag for each student. Print "algae" on half of the tags and divide the rest between "minnows" and "cattails." Cut out the same number of blue squares and print a large "P" (for phosphorus) on each. Cut out five brown circles and label them "soil"; these are soil particles. Cut out five yellow triangles and label them "organic matter." Attach** tape to each of these tags and set aside.

2. **Discuss the need for phosphorus in wetlands and other bodies of water. Explain how plants and animals get phosphorus from water.** Plants take in phosphorus through their roots. Some algae are free-floating and do not have roots, so they take in phosphorus through their cell walls. Animals take in phosphorus by eating plants or organic matter (decomposed plants and animals).

3. **Have students arrange chairs in two rows, back to back, musical-chairs style. Have them tape one "P" tag (blue) to the seat of each chair. Have each student stick an organism tag (green) to his or her clothing. Have a radio or cassette player ready to play.**

4. **Explain that this nutrient game is like a form of musical chairs. When the music is playing, the organisms must swim in a circle around the chairs; when it stops, they must sit on a chair with available phosphorus ("P") to "take in for growth."** Remind students that plants such as cattails and algae, and animals such as minnows need phosphorus for growth.

5. **Try a round to show how it works. Everyone should be sitting this time.**

6. **Now stick a soil particle (brown circle) to one chair ("P"). Explain that phosphorus tends to stick to soil particles and organic matter. If phosphorus is sticking** to a soil particle, it is unavailable to algae and other organisms. Therefore, no one can sit in that chair when the music stops (this is the same as removing a chair). The student who does not find a chair when the music stops is "out." Continue the game and see what happens.

7. **Stick an organic matter tag (yellow triangle) on another chair. Explain that when plants and animals die, the phosphorus in them can be consumed by minnows who eat decaying organic matter (detritus) on the bottom. Therefore, if a chair has a yellow triangle, only the minnows can still sit there.**

8. **Try a few rounds, adding one or two new soil particle or organic matter tags each time. Ask students what is happening to the aquatic organisms.** (With less phosphorus available, fewer organisms get enough nutrients for growth.)

9. **Change the game to demonstrate what happens when too much phosphorus gets into the water. Tell the class that algae happen to be very good at using up phosphorus before any other living things do. If too much phosphorus gets into the water, algae grow and multiply quickly. Have students who are left in the game remain seated; remove the soil and organic matter tags from some of the empty chairs to "free up" some phosphorus. All algae who are seated may now each choose someone who is "out" to**

return to the game as new algae. **Play one more round, giving algae first choice of the remaining chairs. You should be left with a lot more algae than cattails or minnows.** This much algae would make the water look like pea soup!

As a variation, give students a token each time they successfully find a seat. When they are "out," they must turn in their tokens. For every three tokens turned in, a chair can be added or a "P" can be freed up. This shows how nutrients are added back into the system when plants and animals die.

Part II: *Wetlands—The Nutrient Trap* (Grades 2-8)

An outdoor tag game demonstrates how plants take up nutrients.

1. **Take the class outdoors or to a large indoor play area. Divide the class into two teams, "plants growing in a wetland" (Team 1) and "soil particles with nutrients attached" (Team 2). The soil team should wear nutrient tags (colored tags with "N" for nitrogen or "P" for phosphorus printed on them).**

2. **Explain the rules below and play a few rounds, using student suggestions for modifying the plant spacing to change the results. Count the number of rounds required to complete each game with the modified spacing. Give each student a chance to play both roles.**

Rules of the Game

• The plants form an irregular line at one end of the field. Their outstretched arms should not touch.

• The area behind the plants is designated as the waterway.

• Have the soil particles line up facing the plants and, on signal, make their way to the waterway without being touched by a plant. The soil particles must drag one foot as they run or hop on one foot (so they don't move too quickly).

• The plants may bend, stretch, and stoop, but may not move their feet ("roots") while attempting to tag the soil particles. Soil particles may not go around the end of the plant line.

• When a soil particle is tagged, he or she is trapped by that plant in that exact spot, and must remove the nutrient tag and give it to the plant (plants use up nutrients). The trapped soil particle must then help the plant tag other nutrients.

• Any soil particles that escape to the waterway should go back to the starting line and, on signal, try to "safely" pass through the wetland again. The game continues until all of the soil particles have been trapped.

Part III: *Building With Nutrients* (Grades K-2)

Use this song to "act out" the building of proteins from nutri-

ents. *Note:* The reference to nitrogen and phosphorus building proteins is not complete or accurate, but is used only as an illustration.

1. **Use pieces of colored construction paper (about 5 x 8 inches) as signs for the students to wear (two for each child). On half of the pieces, print a large letter "P" or "N" for phosphorus or nitrogen. Mark the other pieces with the letters of the words *protein* and *energy* (one letter per piece). Spell the words as many times as you can (e.g., if there are 26 students in your class, you will be able to spell each word twice). Have each student wear a "P" or "N" on his chest and one of the letters in the words on his back. (Omit the letters if your students are kindergartners.)**

2. **Have the students stand in two lines facing each other, in correct order to spell the words *protein* and *energy* (be sure the two words are spelled out in each line). Have them begin singing "We All Need Nutrients". When "protein" and "energy" turn around when the song motions indicate for them to do so, facing students will be able to read the words.**

Wrap Up

Have students summarize why phosphorus and nitrogen are needed. Discuss what would happen if there was too much nitrogen or phosphorus in a wetland. Have them ask a wetland specialist about nutrient-overloading in local wetlands, or have them design a poster showing how phosphorus and nitrogen cycle through a wetland system.

After The Nutrient Trap game, discuss the roles played and relate the results of the rounds to what actually happens when it rains or

when water flows through a wetland. Were the plants able to trap more particles in the areas where they grew close together? What happened when there were gaps in the line of plants? Would it have helped if there were more plants? Why are shoreline and wetland plants important to the water they border? Why it is important to plant and maintain plants, even in yards near pavement?

Assessment

Have students:

• describe how organisms use phosphorus and nitrogen.

• draw a poster that shows how phosphorus and nitrogen get into the wetland and then cycle through plants and animals.

• identify ways people can limit the amount of nutrients in runoff.

Extensions

Perform the demonstrations in "Treatment Plants," p. 120, and "Recipe for Trouble," p. 199.

If you are doing a unit on nutrition, discuss the difference between the calories from healthy foods and those empty calories from fats, sweets, and other goodies.

We All Need Nutrients

Sung to the tune of "When Johnny Comes Marching Home"

The water's full of nutrients,
hurrah, hurrah!
The soil's full of nutrients,
hurrah, hurrah!
We need these things to make us strong,
And that is why we sing this song.
And we all need nutrients,
to grow, to grow, to grow!

"Nutrients" dance around and wave their hands.

(Same)

Make muscles with arms.

Stoop low, then "grow" up to stand with hands in air.

Plant roots take up nutrients,
slurp, slurp!
Nitrogen and phosphorus,
slurp, slurp!
They use these things to build proteins,
It makes them grow up tall and green.
And we all need nutrients,
to grow, to grow, to grow!

Cross outstretched arms and clasp a partner's hands, forming a bond between nutrients. (Slurp loudly.)

The "proteins" turn halfway around without letting go, swinging arms over heads.

(Same as last verse)

The animals that eat the plants,
chomp, chomp!
Reuse the nitrogen themselves,
chomp, chomp!
It gives them muscles and energy,
So they can grow up in harmony.
And we all need nutrients,
to grow, to grow, to grow!

Proteins turn back around and let go. Others make eating motions with hands.
All link arms side-by-side.
Now "energys" let go of the others and turn halfway around, then link arms again.

(Same as other verses)

We all use energy to live,
to work, to play.
We all need nutrients every day,
hooray, hooray!
We need these things to make us strong,
And that is why we sing this song.
And we all need nutrients,
to grow, to grow, to grow!

The "energys" wiggle in place.

Shake "scolding" fingers.

Make muscles with arms.

(Same as other verses, but jump up at end.)

Marsh Munchies

[Adapted from "For the Common Good" in Teachers' PET Project, Zero Population Growth, Inc., 1400 Sixteenth St. NW, Washington, D.C. 20036.]

Grade Level
5-8

Subject Areas
Environmental Science, Mathematics

Duration
50 minutes

Setting
A clear floor space in the classroom, gym, or outdoors.

Skills
Gathering, analyzing, and applying information

Charting the Course
Try "Nutrients: Nutrition or Nuisance?" for other games related to nutrient flow in a wetland.

Vocabulary
phosphorus, nitrogen, nutrients, calorie

Summary

Be a muskrat! Play a calorie calculation game.

Objectives

Students will understand the concepts of resource limitation and cooperative conservation.

Materials

• *100 poker chips or 1-inch colored paper squares: 50 red, 25 white, 25 blue (have students help with the cutting)*
• *copies of Marsh Munchies Nutrition Information and Marsh Munchies Game Card (one of each per student)*
• *Marsh Munchies Activity Cards (at least one per student)*
• *a poster showing the values of the chips (optional—may be needed if you go outside)*

Background

A common wetland mammal like the muskrat needs a great deal of phosphorus and nitrogen to stay healthy and active. A muskrat also needs an amazing number of calories daily to build and maintain its lodges, find and eat food, swim and walk, sleep, mate and rear young, watch for predators and flee when necessary, and so on. Muskrats eat cattails and other plants and sometimes supplement their diets with insects and small aquatic animals. During severe food shortages, they have been known to eat each other!

Muskrats use the nutrients they take in for energy and to build proteins and body tissues. The nutrients that build proteins are held together by bonds. Bonds join atoms to other atoms, and the energy required to break these bonds is measured in calories.

You need fuel to live, and that fuel comes from breaking bonds (burning calories). Different activities require different amounts of energy. For instance, you burn more calories playing tag than you do playing video games.

Procedure

Warm Up

What are muskrats? Describe the animals' habits. What do students need to do everyday to maintain *their* lifestyles? Lead a discussion to find out if they know what foods are good for them. Identify food groups and types of nutrients. Have students identify some of the essential nutrients in our foods.

The Activity

1. **Tell students they are going to take on the role of muskrats in a marsh. In nature, muskrats eat plants (e.g., cattails), insects, small animals—and sometimes even each other!** *Note:* Some of the behaviors in this activity do not represent true muskrat activities, but are used to illustrate a point.

2. **Inform the class that it will get to know all of the ingredients in Marsh Munchies, a new kind of cereal for muskrats. (Marsh Munchies are very nutritious, and muskrats love them for breakfast, with hibiscus tea!) Hand out and discuss the Marsh Munchies Nutrition Information from the "package" (card handout). How much phosphorus and nitrogen does a muskrat get from one serving of Marsh Munchies? Discuss the other nutrients listed on the label.**

3. **Have students share what they know about calories. Explain that**

calories indicate the amount of potential fuel in the food—when you eat high-calorie foods, you have more fuel to burn. Discuss what would happen if a person ate too many or too few calories.

4. **Explain that this game will show how much energy a muskrat needs to carry on his daily activities, and, therefore, how much food he needs each day.** *Note:* Caloric amounts used in this activity are not meant to be considered as actual caloric requirements of a muskrat; rather they help students make comparisons in the exercise.

5. **The poker chips represent the different foods available to the muskrat, who must eat enough food to carry out daily activities. Hand out the Marsh Munchies Game Cards and write these figures on the board:**

• A **red chip** is one serving of Marsh Munchies, which contains 10 units of nitrogen (10 percent of the daily requirement), 5 units of phosphorus, and 500 calories.

• A **white chip** is 5 cattail stalks with 6 units of nitrogen, 3 units of phosphorus, and 150 calories per chip.

• A **blue chip** is one serving of wild rice with 4 units of nitrogen, 1 unit of phosphorus, and 100 calories.

6. **For the first round, toss the chips out onto the floor so that they scatter widely. This is the food that can be found in the marsh. Remind students that muskrats do not talk; if they must communicate with each other, it must be through gestures. On the word "Go," all students have 30 seconds to eat (collect chips) as much as they can. Call "Stop" when the time is up. Have each student calculate** the total calories he or she has just gathered and record the figure on the game card.

7. **Now have each student choose an activity card and calculate the total number of calories (energy) needed for the activity. Have them record that number on the game card. Give them time to figure out how many chips they need to have enough energy for the activity. Then have them read their game cards aloud and turn in the appropriate number of chips. If a muskrat has not eaten enough, he or she cannot complete some activities.**

8. **Have the students calculate their surplus or deficit, depending on whether they had any energy left over or did not have enough. Those who had a surplus have stored energy for more activities (if they are lazy muskrats, they may just gain weight). Those who had a deficit may now go out into the marsh and find something else to eat to make up the deficit.**

9. **Ask students why they may not have had the right amount of energy for some of the activities. Explain that they didn't eat enough food or enough of the right kinds of food. Also, they didn't know in advance how many calories they needed, so they ate randomly. Ask why there was not enough food left at the end. Introduce the idea that the food is a limited resource which they must conserve.**

10. **Round 2 (and 3): Collect all chips and activity cards and shuffle the cards. Hand out the cards and ask students to read theirs. Without discussing a better plan for collecting food, toss out half the chips. Add two new rules:**
1) For each chip that is left in the marsh, two more chips of the same color will be added. **2) Muskrats who still need energy may take *only* what they need from the marsh. Remind the class that muskrats do not talk, and play again (two more times if necessary).**

Do the new rules bring about a change in behavior? Were students more conservative or more thoughtful of others this time? They should have taken fewer chips the second time because they realized conservation efforts were rewarded by additional food sources that they could use as needed. Were students able to communicate and work together even though they couldn't talk? Ask students what they learned about conserving resources.

Wrap Up
Discuss the variation among the different rounds. Do students think this game shows real muskrats' habits? How? Do students think they can apply information from this activity to their own lives? Have them write a fable about the day, using muskrats as characters. Encourage them to include a moral.

Assessment
Have students:

• interpret a food label to determine nutrients and calories available.

• calculate calories needed to sustain a certain activity.

• compare intake of calories to calories needed to sustain an activity.

• write a story describing the activities of a muskrat.

Extensions

Have students write short reports about the status of a rare or endangered species (e.g., bog turtle) or a declining ecosystem (e.g., rain forest) with a focus on the causes of their decline. Were they impacted by human activity? Natural catastrophe? Competition for habitat from other plants or animals? Lack of available sustaining resources? What are students' opinions about these outcomes?

Have each student write a report about on a specific aspect of nutritional well-being. Have them choose their topic from the Marsh Munchies Nutrition Information Card or from a multivitamin package label (e.g., carbohydrates, fat, vitamin C, sodium, iron).

Notes:

Marsh Munchies Game Card

	Round 1 #Calories	Round 2 #Calories	Round 3 #Calories
Total Consumed			
Total Needed			
Surplus (+)			
Deficit (-)			

Marsh Munchies Activity Cards

Lodge Maintenance

You are making lodge repairs. To fix up a lodge, you must find cattail stalks and old hibiscus twigs and cut them down with your teeth, an activity that uses 105 calories. Actually making the repairs takes 143 calories per lodge. You have four lodges. How many calories will you use to repair all of the lodges?

Kids!

Now that you have a mate, you will have a family, and you must build a nursery lodge for the young. Building a new lodge requires 105 calories to cut materials with your teeth; 20 trips to the new lodge times 5 yards per trip times 12 calories per yard to swim there; and 315 calories to put the lodge together. Whew! That's a lot of work! How many calories does it take?

Courtship

After three days of courting, you have found a mate! It took a lot to get this critter interested in you; in fact, you spent 534 calories each day bringing gifts and showing off! How many calories did it take to win your mate over?

It's a Miracle!

You and your mate have nine little muskrats. Every day you must feed and bathe each of your young. It takes 150 calories to feed each one, and 57 calories to give each a bath. How many calories do you spend on child care each day?

Swimming

You swim from lodge to lodge making repairs. You have 4 lodges, and there are 125 yards between each lodge (500 yards total). Swimming uses 12 calories per yard. How many calories do you use in all?

Teach Your Children

Your young are weaned. Now you will need to teach them how to get their own food. This takes 670 calories per young muskrat. You have five young! How many calories are needed to teach all of your young?

Watch Out!

You are happily munching away on some Marsh Munchies when you spot the shadow of a hawk flying overhead! You look around frantically for a place to hide (this uses 39 calories), but you've eaten all the plants near you! The only thing left to do is run for the closest creek (this takes 1,576 calories—you're a lousy runner), dive in (217 calories), and hold your breath (341 calories) until the hawk goes away! How much energy did the ordeal take?

Brrrr!

It's winter and you're freezing! You're snuggled in your sleeping lodge with your mate and young cuddled around you. Usually that's enough to keep you warm, but tonight it's colder than usual outside. As you lie there shivering, you use up 431 calories per hour. The sun won't come up for six more hours. How many calories will you shiver away from now until then?

Snack Time!

You're sick of eating cattails and Marsh Munchies! To supplement your diet, you go fishing for crayfish (Southern muskrats call 'em "crawdads"). You figure five crayfish would make a nice snack. As you look for crayfish, you swim back and forth in the creek for a total of 40 yards, at 12 calories per yard. Catching one crayfish uses 26 calories. You catch all five and go home happy. But were they worth it for the energy you expended to catch them?

Suppertime!

You must swim through the marsh to find the choicest cattails to eat. You cover 483 yards to get enough cattails to fill you up. You use 12 calories per yard to swim. How much energy must you expend to get a good supper?

Building a City

You've just moved to a new section of marsh, since you and your buddies ate all of the plants in the old part. You need to build new tunnels ("muskrat streets") so you can swim from place to place. It takes 372 calories to excavate 200 yards of tunnel. You need 2,400 yards of tunnel for this part of the marsh. How many calories will you use?

Spending Energy to Get Energy

Finding food and eating uses energy, too. You use 423 calories to gather and eat your breakfast, 1,521 calories for lunch, and 3,987 calories for dinner. How many calories do you burn in a day just to get fed? (You have to eat a lot more to do anything else!)

Answers:

Lodge Maintenance: (105 x 4) + (143 x 4) = 420 + 572 = 992

Courtship: 3 x 534 = 1,602

Swimming: 500 x 12 = 6,000

Kids!: 105 + (20 x 5 x 12) + 315 = 1,620

It's a Miracle!: (150 x 9) + (57 x 9) = 1,350 + 513 = 1,863

Teach Your Children: 670 x 5 = 3,350

Watch Out!: 39 + 1,576 + 217 + 341 = 2,173

Snack Time!: (12 x 40) + (5 x 26) = 480 + 130 = 610

Building a City: 372 x (2,400 ÷ 200) = 4,464

Brrrr!: 431 x 6 = 2,586

Suppertime!: 483 x 12 = 5,796

Spending Energy to Get Energy: 423 + 1,521 + 3,987 = 5,931

Marsh Munchies
NUTRITION INFORMATION PER 1-OUNCE SERVING

(Servings per package = 15)

CALORIES..500

PROTEIN...3 grams

CARBOHYDRATES...45 grams

    Sugars..21 grams

    Other..24 grams

FAT...12 grams

SODIUM..55 mg

PERCENTAGE OF U.S. RECOMMENDED DAILY ALLOWANCES (U.S. RDA)

PROTEIN....................8	RIBOFLAVIN.................6	PHOSPHORUS.............5
VITAMIN A..................2	NIACIN.........................3	NITROGEN...................10
VITAMIN C....................*	CALCIUM......................6	
THIAMINE....................3	IRON.............................2	

*Contains less than two percent of the U.S. RDA of these nutrients

INGREDIENTS: Cattail flour, hibiscus syrup (natural sweetener), bulrush stalks, iris seeds, wild rice puffs, partially hydrogenated soil oil, sun-dried sea salt, insect parts, crayfish tails, polyscorbic carrageenagobbledy-goop, monosodium gibbledyslop (a preservative), natural and artificial colors

Recipe for Trouble

[Adapted from "What's In the Water?," Living In Water by Valerie Chase, National Aquarium in Baltimore.]

Grade Level
4-12

Subject Areas
Environmental Science, Chemistry, Biology

Duration
Takes place over the course of about one month. Set up about two weeks ahead of experiment.

Setting
Classroom

Skills
Gathering information, drawing conclusions

Charting the Course
Combine this activity with other activities that show how wetlands function to control pollution. (See "Treatment Plants," "Marsh Mystery," or "Nutrients: Nutrition or Nuisance?") This activity will help students visualize the effects of different water pollutants. See "Water We Have Here?" for information on how to test for levels of pollution.

Vocabulary
pollution, acid rain

Summary
What goes into a recipe for trouble?

Conduct a classroom experiment to test the effects of various pollutants on water environments.

Objectives
Students will:

- describe potential effects of pollution on plants and animals.

- classify pollution sources.

Materials
Two weeks before class:
- *5 clear 1-quart or larger containers (plastic soda bottles or canning jars)*
- *water that contains algae from a classroom freshwater aquarium or a pond, or pond water purchased from a biological supply company*
- *plant fertilizer (the dye in most of these will fade when exposed to light)*
- *aged tap water (water that has been allowed to sit for about 48 hours)*
- *good light source (direct sunlight or strong artificial light)*
- *copies of Pollution Sources Information*

For class:
- *plant fertilizer*
- *"pollutants" of students' choice— household products people commonly pour down the drain without thinking (safest to handle might include detergent [not green, due to color masking], motor oil, vinegar)*
- *camera and roll of 12-exposure print film (35 mm or Polaroid is best)*
- *copies of Recipe For Trouble student page*
- *a long pan*
- *motor oil*

Note: If time allows, do each test twice to be scientifically accurate. This will double the number of containers needed.

Making Connections
It is hard to imagine the cumulative effects of seemingly harmless actions. This activity gives students a closer look at causes of local and global pollution.

Background
Read the information given in "Nutrients: Nutrition or Nuisance?" on p. 188 or in the nutrients section of "Water We Have Here?" on p. 184.

Procedure
Warm Up
As a class demonstration, at least two weeks before the experiment begins:

Set up the five bottles or jars. Fill them with aged tap water. Add one teaspoon of plant fertilizer to each jar and stir thoroughly. To improve the quality of the model, use pond water if you can or try adding a bit of soil from the bottom of a pond or gravel from your aquarium tank along with the water. Put the jars near a window where they will get direct light or give them a strong incandescent or fluorescent light. Do not place them in a location that gets very cold.

Explain that you have just set up model water environments for an experiment to be done later. As in all aquatic environments, the plants in these models need nutrients to grow. In this case nutrients are supplied by the fertilizer.

Explain that students will be using these model aquatic environments to test effects of fertilizer and other pollutants that come from homes. Have the class decide which household products to use. Ask students to choose frequently used products that often end up in waterways after going down storm or household drains. Students should bring samples of these selected products from home.

On the day of the experiment:

Hand out the Pollution Sources Information sheet. Tell students this information will help them organize what they already know about water pollution. Explain that some water pollution comes from specific sources such as outfalls (drains, pipes, effluent from industry, etc.). This is called point source pollution. Other kinds of pollution come from many widespread sources and are called nonpoint source pollution. Write these words on the blackboard as column heads and have the students begin to suggest things that pollute the water. Help students connect their suggestions to the specific categories given in the Pollution Sources Information chart.

The Activity

1. Hand out the Recipe for Trouble student page. Explain that the class will be conducting pollutant tests with the models that were set up two weeks ago. Explain that it would not be acceptable to test pollutants by dumping them in a natural environment, so you are using models to avoid damaging the natural world.

2. Take out the jars containing the model environments. The jars should contain growing algae by now. Use three jars for the students' household product samples and add more plant fertilizer to the fourth jar, and use the fifth jar as a control.

Add reasonable amounts of the selected pollutants. For example: two tablespoons of a strong

detergent, enough motor oil to just cover the surface, ¼ to ½ cup of vinegar, one or two teaspoons of plant fertilizer. Ask the students to explain how each pollutant could get into the environment in "real life." Leave the jars in the light as before.

Safety First!

Meat or other animal products of any kind could grow dangerous bacteria. Do not cover jars tightly, as you might grow some undesirable bacteria this way. Regular household items should be fine. As an acid, vinegar can represent acid rain or acid discharges such as the "pickling liquor" from steel production or strip mine acid runoff. Detergent is a common component of human sewage. Motor oil commonly ends up down storm drains. Regardless of what you use, make all your observations without coming into contact with the water, and dispose of the material carefully after the experiment is over.

3. Have students write their predictions about what will happen to each test container. Two or three times each week for several weeks, photograph the jars with labels and a date showing. Have the film developed.

4. **Study the results.**

• A few kinds of pollutants (particularly the fertilizer) favor plant growth and will cause an algal population explosion. This is

not healthy, as it disrupts the balance of organisms. When the algae die and decompose, the oxygen in the water is depleted. Ask the class to name some plants and animals that would be affected by this situation. Note that oysters and clams will suffocate, because they cannot move to a place with more oxygen, and the thick mat of algae will block out sunlight that other aquatic plants need for growth.

• Other pollutants, such as acids, will cause very clear water because they kill everything in it. Needless to say, they are not good for natural systems, either. Ask the class how plants and animals would be affected by this situation.

• If you used oil as a pollutant, that sample may have done better than you expected. Algae that have enough sunlight can produce enough oxygen to keep themselves (and other organisms that live below the oxygen-impervious oil layer) alive.

However, if this were a larger oil spill, the animals that came in contact with the oil would be harmed—ducks and other water birds would be coated with oil and wouldn't be able to fly, fish gills would be clogged, and so on.

To demonstrate the far-reaching dangers of oil spills, fill a long pan with water, drop a few drops of oil onto the surface, and watch the oil spread out. Help it along by blowing on the water, as if it were a windy day or there were a current in the water.

Wrap Up and Action

Discuss results of the experiment with students. Make a list of their conclusions. For example:

1. Human activities can affect water environments in ways that are harmful to natural communities.

2. Healthy aquatic habitats must contain nutrients, but excesses are harmful.

See if students can suggest natural wetland functions that could help lessen the effects of the pollutants tested. Because they take up excess nutrients, wetland plants can filter out many pollutants before they have a chance to enter larger water bodies. In fact, plants actually use some pollutants, while others are stored in plant tissues or in the soil. After a point, however, wetlands may be harmed by these pollutants. Large amounts of some toxic chemicals may begin to kill wetland plants and animals.

Discuss some actions students can take to keep these pollutants from ever reaching the water, or ways to reduce the amount that does enter it.

Assessment

Have students:

- identify ways in which water is polluted.

- describe the effects of oil spills, acid rain, and human wastes on water and wetlands.

- formulate methods to alleviate pollution problems.

- describe how wetlands can be harmed by pollution.

Extensions

Have students devise methods to reverse or improve the water quality in their model polluted systems. Here are two examples:

1. Add baking soda to the acid test to neutralize the acid (this is similar to adding lime or limestone rocks to lakes or streams to neutralize the effects of acid rain).

2. Mop up the oil spill with straw, feathers, or cotton. Can students skim the oil off of their models to let the oxygen through again?

Pollution Sources Information

Kinds of pollution	Point source	Nonpoint source
Disease organisms, sewage	Human waste, household pollutants, treatment plants	Failing septic systems; some problems where people camp or backpack
Human-made and naturally occurring organic compounds	Chemical manufacturing plants and disposal; oil spills	Runoff containing pesticides, herbicides, and fertilizer
Inorganic or mineral compounds; plant nutrients	Mining and manufacturing operations; electric power generation (thermal pollution)	Runoff of lawn and garden fertilizer; runoff from paved areas
Biological wastes that use oxygen in decomposition	Human sewage, animal wastes, agricultural wastes, paper and food processing	Runoff of livestock manure and pet droppings
Sediment	Stormwater carrying eroded soil—from drains or washed directly off land	Erosion from development, fields, bare lawns, and unprotected shorelines
Heated water	Primarily from electrical generating plants; some from manufacturing	
Radioactive material	Mining, manufacturing, and accidental discharge and disposal	Airborne following testing or an accident

Recipe for Trouble

Arrange all the photographs of the test jars in order from the first date to the last. Study the changes you can observe over time in each sample. Write in the pollutant used in each jar and describe the changes.

Jar 1. Tap Water:_____

_____

Jar 2. Fertilizer:_____

_____

Jar 3. _ _ _ _ _ _ _ _ : _____

_____

Jar 4. _ _ _ _ _ _ _ _ :_____

_____

Jar 5. _ _ _ _ _ _ _ _ :_____

_____

Which pollutant had the greatest effect in terms of visual appearance and/or odor?_____

Which pollutant had the least effect?_____

Were you surprised at the results? How did they compare with your predictions?_____

_____

_____

Why did one jar contain only tap water?_____

_____

Water Under Foot

[Adapted from "There Is No Away" in Living Lightly on the Planet by Maura O'Connor, National Audubon Society, 1989. Used with permission of Schlitz Audubon Center, 1111 E. Brown Deer Road, Milwaukee, WI 53217. The Hazard Cards and all references to wetlands were added.]

Grade Level
4-12

Subject Areas
Environmental Science

Duration
1 hour, plus setup time

Setting
Classroom

Skills
Gathering and interpreting information

Charting the Course
Precede this activity with "Soak It Up!" for a look at how wetlands are supplied with water. Try "Do You Dig Wetland Soil?" and "How Thirsty Is The Ground?" later to study wetland soil types and what makes them unique.

Vocabulary
aquifer, percolation, leach, ground-water discharge, ground-water recharge

Summary

Students make a ground-water model and demonstrate its relationship to the land and to wetlands.

Objectives

Students will:

• describe ground water as part of the water cycle.

• visualize how ground water is stored in an aquifer.

• describe the relationship between ground water and wetlands.

• explain how discarded materials leach from land and contaminate ground water.

Materials

• *clear, flat-bottomed container (e.g., glass or plastic aquarium from Delta Education [see Resources])*
• *enough sponges to cover bottom of container*
• *scissors*
• *watering can full of water*
• *5 clear jars*
• *red and blue food coloring*
• *meat baster*
• *2 quarts sand for each demonstration (replace each time)*
• *Hazard Cards*
• *clean, empty containers from consumer products (described on the cards)*
• *paper and pencils*

Prepare the model for the demonstration. Fill the clear container no more than two-thirds full of sand. Place a layer of sponges on top of the sand to represent topsoil. (Soil is not used because it will discolor the water and prevent the results from being clearly visible.) Elevate one end of the container to create a slope. Mix approximately 10 drops of red and blue food coloring (separately) in two jars filled with ¼ cup of water each. These solutions will represent pollutants in step four of the activity.

Making Connections

Often, what is out of sight is out of mind. Students may not think of water once it seeps into the ground. Likewise, they may think only of surface water when they consider water pollution. An investigation of the role of wetlands in replenishing the ground-water supply and reducing pollution helps students appreciate a hidden resource.

Background

Ground water is an important component of the water cycle, especially in terms of its contribution to clean drinking-water supplies. Half of the United States' freshwater supply comes from ground water. Wetlands can help replenish the ground water stored beneath them. Ground water, in turn, helps sustain many wetlands by keeping them saturated.

Ground water is stored underground in sediments or water-bearing rock layers called aquifers. Rainwater percolates down through the topsoil and is stored in pore spaces between soil, sand, gravel, and rock material below. Aquifers can be found just below the surface of the ground (as in many wetlands) or much deeper. In some places, wells must be at least 100 feet deep to reach an aquifer.

When the aquifer beneath a

wetland is at or very near the surface, ground water feeds the wetland from below. During periods of dry weather, ground water also seeps into rivers, lakes, and wetlands and helps maintain their water level. This is called ground-water discharge. Conversely, when the ground-water level is low, any rain and runoff that collects in a wetland will trickle down to the aquifer and replenish it. This is called ground-water recharge.

In some highly populated areas, the demand for water is so great that the water stored underground is used up more quickly than it can naturally be replenished. The recharge and discharge functions of wetlands help prevent this situation. However, much of the wetland acreage in such developed areas has been filled or paved over, and this important benefit is lost.

The health of wetlands affects the quality and quantity of our water supply. Improperly used or disposed substances can leach through soil to contaminate the ground water and, ultimately, our drinking water. In many areas there have been incidences of illness due to contaminated drinking water. When wetlands are degraded because of their association with contaminated ground water (as well as from

substances deposited with runoff), their important cleansing functions can be diminished or lost.

The government has begun to regulate the disposal of toxic substances as well as the construction and operation of landfill dumps. Each of us should also become aware of ways we can avoid contributing pollutants to the environment.

Procedure
Warm Up
Ask students to describe what happens to water after it percolates into the ground. Where might it end up? In many communities, it may end up in someone's water glass! Do students think wetlands are related to ground water? How might wetlands affect ground water. Have students present possible connections.

Present students with the following scenario:

Jessica has just changed the oil in her car. What should she do with the old oil? What would happen if she poured it in her backyard?

Have students express their views about Jessica's action. Tell students that the following demonstration will help them visualize the effects of pollutants leaching into ground water.

The Activity
1. **Have students gather around**

the model to investigate the role of aquifers. Explain that the layer of sponges represents the topsoil, the layer of sand represents an aquifer, and the bottom of the container represents a layer of bedrock. Use the watering can to sprinkle a few cups of "rain" on the model. Note how the "topsoil" becomes saturated, and how the water percolates down into the aquifer. Continue sprinkling until the model is saturated, but not to the point of creating standing water. Explain that ground water is not visible because it is stored between the pore spaces in the sand.**

Note: It takes a few minutes for the water to percolate down into the sand. Do not add water too quickly or, before you know it, the model will contain standing water and you will have to begin again.

2. **Designate an area of sponge near the lower end of the model as a wetland. Discuss how wetlands aid in replenishing ground water and how they are also fed by ground water. Pour some rain directly onto the wetland area and watch how it eventually soaks through to the ground water.** This demonstrates ground-water recharge, the wetland supplying water to the ground-water supply.

3. **Relate the sponges' absorbing action to the way the wetland is fed with water from below. Pick up a sponge and wring it out. Put it back on the saturated sand to soak up more water, then wring it out again.** This is ground-water discharge. Ground water is released or absorbed into the wetland.

4. **At the lower end of the model (near the wetland), use a meat baster to simulate a town well pumping water from the aquifer.**

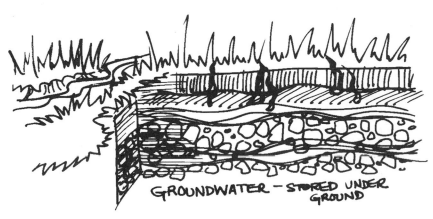

GROUNDWATER — STORED UNDER GROUND

Place some of the pumped water in a clear jar. Some sand will also come up, but it will settle to the bottom of the jar. Ask how the wetland "helps" the well and explain that it does so by replenishing the water supply, especially during dry seasons when other surface areas dry out more quickly.

5. Introduce the idea of pollution from household products. Divide the class into groups and give each group one of the product

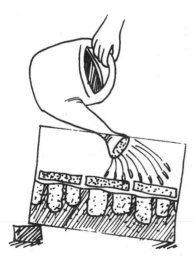

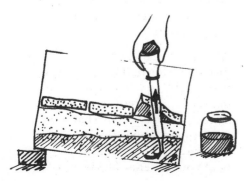

samples and the corresponding Hazard Card. Give them a few minutes to decide how that product was improperly disposed of or poorly used. Remember: Pollutants are often dumped or applied directly onto the land—they do not always leach from landfills!

6. **Develop a scenario for your model, one to which your students can relate. Make up a name for the town or use the name of a town in your area. Include the students as characters: uninformed citizens who pollute. Designate the sponge surface at the elevated end of the model as the town's landfill. Remind the class that the lower end is a wetland that replenishes the town's ground-water supply, and is in turn replenished through ground-water discharge. Ask them to describe some other benefits this wetland gives the town.**

7. **Have students use the meat baster to drop samples of the colored pollutants onto the landfill and other areas designated as yards, parking lots, and so on. Call on a representative of each group to present the group's product to the class: how it has been misused or discarded (one of the choices on the Hazard Cards), and how the product might leach into the ground.** For example, a student might hold up a bottle of cleaning fluid and say, "I bought this triple-strength spot remover which removed the spot so well that it put a hole in my carpet! I then threw it in the trash can, but the lid was loose and the container was not well wrapped, so it leaked at the dump." The student would then drop some colored solution onto the model. Repeat for each group. *[This part adapted from "The Drain Game" in*

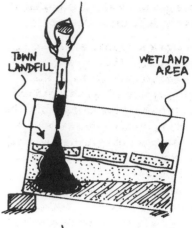

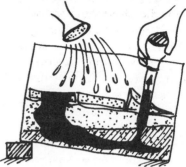

Bay B C's: A Multidisciplinary Approach to Teaching about the Chesapeake Bay *by Britt Slattery, U.S. Fish and Wildlife Service, 1989]*

8. **When all the groups have presented and added their pollutants, simulate rain by sprinkling water over the model's surface. As the food coloring soaks through the sponge layer, suggest that the rain is washing pollutants away. Ask: Where is "away"? Is the pollutant really going away? Then use the baster to pump some water from the town well. What has happened to the ground water?** The pollutants have leached or percolated down through the topsoil into the aquifer.

9. **Keep pumping water out of the well until the well runs dry. Then add more rain and see if the added water is purer when it is pumped from the well. It will still be colored. Make the point that**

once ground water is polluted, it is very difficult to clean it up.

10. **Draw students' attention to the wetland. Has anything happened to it? Some of the pollutants may have spread or run off along the surface into the wetland area, contaminating it. (If this has not occurred, remind the class that it could.)** Toxic substances can kill plants and animals in a wetland, and may destroy the wetland—and its beneficial functions—altogether. Review the idea that ground-water discharge can pollute a wetland. As contaminants accumulate in a wetland, they can spread back into the ground water through ground-water recharge when it rains. Be sure the class understands that this residual effect is not the "fault" of the wetland—thoughtless human activity caused the problem!

Wrap Up and Action

Discuss a few of the other improper disposal choices on the cards. Why are these wrong? What harm will these actions cause? Discuss some ways to prevent this sort of pollution. Use the answers on the backs of the cards for help.

Have students sketch a ground-water system, identifying the role of wetlands in the system.

Can students think of other ways to keep such pollutants out of the water? *Hint:* Wetland plants and soils filter out many pollutants before the pollutants can enter the ground water.

Students can develop a nontoxic/safe disposal brochure to distribute to friends and family.

Assessment

Have students:

- sketch the location and functions of topsoil, an aquifer, and bedrock in a ground-water system.

- describe the function of wetlands in ground-water discharge and recharge.

- discriminate between correct and incorrect disposal of hazardous wastes.

- identify ways to prevent ground-water contamination.

Extensions

- Look in the government listings in the phone book (under "Public Works") for offices of landfills and utilities (sewer collection, wastewater treatment, etc.). Call your state, county, or city office of waste management to arrange a visit to a nearby landfill. If possible, arrange to have someone at the facility talk with the students briefly about how the trash is handled. Is the trash crushed? Can toxic substances leak out of well-wrapped containers? Is leaching a problem? What procedures do they recommend for disposing of potentially harmful products? Are there facilities to handle hazardous waste? Does the city or county offer special collection for hazardous waste?

Before the visit, have the class locate the facility on a topographic map. Locate nearby waterways and wetlands that might be harmed by runoff from the landfill. If you have time and a nearby site is accessible, check out its water when you visit the landfill (you may be able to make arrangements through the landfill staff). Bring a small jar to collect a water sample. Use some of the water-quality tests in this book

or take the sample to a lab for analysis. What have you found out? Are students now more willing to change the products they use and the ways they dispose of them?

- Ask the office of municipal wastewater treatment in your area if any facilities use wetlands to treat wastewater. This method of treatment using natural systems was developed at NASA in the mid-1970s. Today there are more than 100 created marsh and aquatic systems treating municipal sewage in the United States. Have older students research the communities that use constructed marshes to treat their wastewater. Could something similar be done in your community? Hundreds of other constructed marshes are used to treat the highly acidic water that flows from coal mine sites. Is there a mine in your area that the class could visit? Call your state's department of natural resources or environmental management for mine information.

Nature in Your Neighborhood

Make a list of chemicals and other products used in your home. Check the kitchen, bathroom, laundry room, and garage. Read ingredients and warnings listed on the labels. Could any of these products be harmful to the environment? Many companies' labels now include information for the safe use and disposal of the product and container. Is your family using and discarding things carefully?

Ask your family members to discuss which of these products they might do without, or more natural substances they might use instead. If your family shares your concern, participate in the next shopping trip by reading labels to help your parents decide on safer (and often less expensive) products to purchase and use. Were you able to change any of your family's practices? Share your results with the class.

Can you find places in your neighborhood where pollutants are running from their point of use? For example, paved, impermeable surfaces (streets, sidewalks, parking lots, and driveways) collected oil, antifreeze, road salt, etc. When it rains, these substances wash off the hard surfaces and enter and harm wetlands, other bodies of water, and, eventually, ground water. What can you do? Try asking a gas station manager if he or she would be willing to absorb oil spills with sawdust, sand, or cat litter that can be swept up later. At school, work with other students, teachers, and friends to put plants all around the parking lot to help slow and filter the runoff. See "Helping Wetland Habitats" for more ideas.

Notes:

Hazard Cards

The card on the left offers some choices for improper disposal of hazardous products. Don't laugh; some people really do these things without knowing that they cause harm! The card on the right states the correct way to dispose of the product. Cut out cards and paste them back-to-back.

Hazard: House Paint (Oil-based) I wanted to repaint my bedroom, but this color was all wrong, so I: a) dumped it down the drain in the kitchen sink; b) poured it out in the gutter in the street; c) threw the whole can in the trash.	**Correct Disposal** Oil-based paint is toxic and should be sent to a place that collects hazardous waste. Even a small amount of leftover paint can leak out when the can is crushed at a landfill. Pour leftover paint onto newspapers, let it dry, then stuff the papers into the can, seal the lid, and throw in the trash. But why waste leftover paint? Consider giving the leftover to a neighbor who can use it. And next time, buy latex paint; it's safer.
Hazard: Carpet Cleaner This triple-strength rug cleaner removed spots so well that it put holes in my carpet, so I: a) threw the stuff in the trash can; b) used it to clean oil stains off my driveway; c) dumped it on a clump of weeds in my yard (at least it got rid of the weeds).	**Correct Disposal** If this is strong enough to put holes in a carpet, imagine what it could do to the environment! Send it to a hazardous waste site. If thrown in a landfill, it could leak if the lid is loose, the container is not well wrapped, or the container is crushed at the dump. **Never** dump poisons onto the street or anywhere else on the ground—that's one way they end up in our water!
Hazard: Motor Oil When I change the oil in my truck, I: a) park in the woods and let the oil drain out onto the ground (it's easiest that way); b) collect it in a basin and pour it in the gutter; c) bury the old oil in a hole in my backyard.	**Correct Disposal** Motor oil can spread for miles if spilled, especially in water! Many communities or gas stations now have facilities for collecting and recycling used oil (that way, we save oil resources *and* keep the land and water clean). If you accidentally spill oil, absorb the oil with sand, sawdust, or kitty litter, then sweep it up and send it off to a hazardous waste site (never hose off oil spills).
Hazard: Shoe Polish I got tired of an old pair of dress shoes that constantly needed polishing, so I gave them away. I had a whole bottle of shoe polish left, so I: a) poured it into the toilet and flushed it away; b) threw the bottle in the trash; c) painted my mailbox with it (but it washed off).	**Correct Disposal** It's okay to throw this in the trash, *if* the top is closed tightly and the bottle is wrapped in lots of newspaper and sealed in a trash bag. This way, if the bottle is crushed, the polish will not leak right out onto the ground. Never pour this down the drain.
Hazard: Roach Traps The guy who lived next door had filthy living habits that brought roaches into our building and *my* apartment! Since the landlord got an exterminator, I don't need to use traps anymore, so I: a) threw the traps out with the trash in the alley; b) took them right to the city dump; c) threw them at the guy while he moved out!	**Correct Disposal** While roach traps might seem contained, they do hold poison. These should only be disposed of at a hazardous waste collection site, not in the regular trash or with other garbage at the dump. Wrap the containers well before handling.
Hazard: Hair Remover I always cut myself when I shave my legs, so I bought some hair removing lotion. It smelled horrible and burned, so I: a) dumped it out with the bath water; b) put the cap on the bottle and threw it in the trash; c) used it to take the pills off my sweater!	**Correct Disposal** Even though it smells pretty strong, this product, like many personal care products, is safe enough to pour down the drain with plenty of water. It's not safe enough for anyone to swallow, so putting it in the trash is not the best idea. Reading labels on containers will help you decide the safest disposal method for similar items. And it might ruin your sweater!

Runoff Race

[From "Settle Down," in Discover Wetlands.]

Grade Level
2-12

Subject Areas
Earth Science, Geology

Duration
About 20 minutes

Setting
Classroom

Skills
Gathering and interpreting information

Charting the Course
A study of wetland plant types complements this activity; after conducting the "Runoff Race," have students investigate actual wetlands. Check "Tracking Plants and Keeping Track" to help students learn how to collect and study plants. The Nutrient Trap in "Nutrients: Nutrition or Nuisance?" is an active game that demonstrates the filtering concept. Also try "Wetland in a Pan."

Vocabulary
runoff, sediment, suspension, filtration

Summary

How would you define water quality? Do you have the same definition as your friend?

This demonstration offers a hands-on demonstration of wetlands' ability to improve water quality by filtering out sediments.

Objectives

Students will understand how wetlands affect water quality.

Materials

- *quart jar with lid*
- *pebbles, sand, dirt, clay, crushed leaves, etc.*
- *piece of artificial turf (doormat)*
- *2 flat sheets of wood or plastic similar in size to the doormat*
- *2 shallow aluminum pans*
- *2 containers of water (equal amounts)*
- *something to prop up models so they tilt (see diagram on p. 211)*

Making Connections

Water quality is an all-encompassing term, with many facets that are commonly misunderstood. As future citizens, homeowners, and professionals, students should be able to discuss the importance of wetlands and plants in tempering some of our most pressing environmental problems, including water quality.

Background

Waterborne sediments and other wastes from land are a threat to water quality and to the many plants and animals that depend on clean water. Some of these wastes come from human activities, others are of natural origin. They enter waterways through storm and other runoff, groundwater seepage, and direct dumping into water. Once in the water, wastes are carried along to other areas.

We can soften this threat by being very cautious about our land-use practices, particularly our waste disposal methods and our direct applications to the land. Even so, there will always be pollutants that we miss—and we need wetlands to help keep those pollutants at bay!

Pollution by sediments is partially controlled by upland plants, which help keep soil in place and slow runoff. However, since wetlands often lie on the borders between uplands and open waterways, they are the last stopping place for any sediment-laden runoff heading toward open water. Wetland plants slow the flow of water enough to allow the heavier particles to settle out. Smaller particles are trapped in the mesh of leaves, stems, and roots of a densely vegetated wetland. Fine silt particles commonly coat wetland plants and the water flows on without them.

By slowing the flow of water, wetlands are also helpful in flood control. For instance, when a heavy rainstorm increases runoff, the added water may cause waterways to overflow and flood adjacent lands (towns, lawns, farms). Wetlands offer runoff a place to "rest" and soak into the soil, thereby reducing the potential for flooding.

Procedure
Warm Up

Explain that flowing water carries sediments of different sizes. The faster the flow, the larger the sediment particles that can be transported in suspension. As the water slows, the larger particles settle out first. In still water, the finer sediments (clay and silt) will settle to the bottom.

The Activity

Before class begins, prepare the demonstration models, as in the diagram.

1. **In class, mix the different sediments (sand, dirt, etc.) together in the quart jar, filling it one-half to three-fourths full. Top off the jar with water and secure the lid. Have a student shake the jar until the contents are thoroughly mixed and set the jar on a table in front of the class.**

2. **As the class watches the sediments settle, explain that muddy water can be harmful to wildlife.** Ask students to think of reasons this might be so. (Clogs filter feeders such as clams, clogs and abrades fish gills, smothers fish eggs, blocks sunlight and impairs plant growth, "blinds animals" that hunt for food by sight, etc.) Would more sediments settle to the bottom if the water was flowing quickly, or slowly? (Slower flow allows even small particles to settle out.)

3. **Describe how the particles are settling in the jar.** (In layers: largest or heaviest particles settle first; fine or light particles may remain in suspension)

4. **Describe how wetlands and their plants can slow the flow of water by simply being in the way. Use the models to demonstrate. Explain that the model with the doormat is a healthy wetland, filled with plants, and that the model with only a piece of wood is an unhealthy wetland** where the plants have died or been removed. **Ask students to imagine that in each wetland, water enters through a stream, flows through the wetland, and eventually into a lake (the pan).**

5. **Add sediment to the two containers of water. Ask two volunteers to pour water simultaneously onto the high end of each model.** Which wetland produced the fastest water flow? (The bare, unhealthy one) In which wetland would more sediments settle out? (The healthy one with plants) Which one would have cleaner water flowing from it? (Healthy)

Wrap Up and Action

Ask students:

How would digging a ditch through a wetland affect water quality downstream? (It would create a channel where water would flow quickly, without passing through the wetland plants. This would mean that the filtering action of the wetland would be diminished, and water quality downstream would be degraded.)

Why might someone dig a ditch through a wetland or channelize (change the course of) a stream? (There are several reasons, but ditches are usually dug to drain a wetland to make the land more useful for farming or building. Sometimes ditches are dug for mosquito control, as they allow small fish to come up into marshes to eat mosquito larvae. People may channelize a stream to move it out of the way of new housing development or road construction.)

Would these activities have other effects? (May decrease fisheries, drinking-water quality, swimming and other recreational uses, aesthetics, etc.)

Assessment

Ask students to :

- explain how sediments affect water quality.

- demonstrate how wetland plants help prevent sediment runoff.

- identify or draw pictures of situations where alterations to wetlands affect sediment runoff.

Extensions

The Nutrient Trap, an active game that demonstrates the filtering concept, can be found on p. 190.

Wetland in a Pan

[Adapted from the "Wading Into Wetlands" issue of NatureScope, copyright 1992. Questions and some text added. Used with permission of the National Wildlife Federation, Washington, D.C.]

Grade Level
3-12

Subject Areas
Environmental Science, Earth Science

Duration
90 minutes if students make model; 30-40 minutes for demonstration only

Setting
Classroom

Skills
Gathering and analyzing information

Charting the Course
Other activities that explore filtering effects of wetlands include "Water Purifiers," "Runoff Race," "Treatment Plants," "Recipe for Trouble," and "Water Under Foot."

Vocabulary
runoff, flood retention, sedimentation, wetland buffer

Summary
Students make a model that demonstrates the flood-buffering and filtering effects of wetlands.

Objectives
Students will:

- describe interrelationships among precipitation, runoff, and wetlands.

- relate the importance of wetland functions to their own needs and daily lives.

Materials
- *modeling clay*
- *long shallow pan. Tip: A long (13" x 9"), sturdy metal or glass pan with a smooth, flat bottom works well; or perhaps a rolling paint pan.*
- *scraps of indoor-outdoor carpeting, florist's "oasis" foam, (or sponges)*
- *watering can or similar device*
- *cup of soil*
- *jar of muddy water*

To make the model for the demonstrations:
1. Spread a layer of modeling clay in half of the baking pan to represent land. Leave the other half of the pan empty to represent a lake or other body of water such as a river or ocean.
2. Shape the clay so that it gradually slopes down to the water. Smooth the clay along the sides of the pan to seal the edges. You can also form meandering streams in the clay that lead into the body of water.
3. Cut a piece of indoor-outdoor carpeting [or a sponge or florist's foam] to completely fill the space across the pan along the edge of the clay (see diagram). This represents a wetland buffer between dry land and open water. Tip: Make sure the wetland fits

well. The model won't work if there are large spaces under the wetland or between it and the sides of the pan.

Making Connections
Students will be able to discuss practical, everyday issues concerning the beneficial functions of wetlands.

Background
See information given in "Runoff Race" and throughout Procedure, below. (See chapter 3.)

Procedure
Warm up
Review with the students what they have learned about wetlands and their functional values. Show the class pictures of different types of wetlands including freshwater and salt marshes, swamps, and bogs. Have the students think about the animals and plants that might live in each kind of wetland.

The Activity
1. **Present the wetland model and point out its features. Explain that wetlands, like all habitats, are very complicated natural systems. They perform some very important functions such as filtering pollutants, reducing flood damage, and preventing soil erosion. Some wetlands, at times, recharge underground water supplies. Explain that the model will demonstrate some of these functions in a very simplified way.**

Ask: If I make it "rain" on the model, what do you think will happen to the rainwater? (Rain will run downhill and end up in the body of water.)

2. **Fit the piece of carpeting or sponge into the wetland area, slowly sprinkle some "rain" on land, and let the students observe and describe what is happening.** Some of the water is slowed down by the wetland (carpeting). The excess slowly flows into the body of water. Point out, if the students do not, that the wetland absorbed some of the water (pick up the wetland and squeeze some water out to prove it).

3. **Ask: What do you think will happen if the wetland is removed? (The water will not be absorbed; it will flow more quickly into the body of water.) Remove the carpeting and water. Pour the same amount of water on the model at the same spot and rate as before. Have the students note any differences.** The water should fill the body of water much more quickly and may eventually overflow and flood the land. That's because it is no longer buffered by the wetland.

Explain that most wetlands are shallow basins that collect water and slow its rate of flow and also retain water for a time. This slowing process helps reduce flooding and also helps prevent soil erosion.

Ask: If a wetland is destroyed and houses are built there, what might happen to the houses during a severe rainstorm? Why? (They might be flooded because the wetland will not be there to absorb and slow the rush of water from higher ground.) In many areas, wetlands are drained and filled in, and houses and marinas are built right along the water. Without a wetland buffer, these developed areas particularly

along the coast are often subjected to severe flooding and erosion, especially during violent storms.

4. **Pour the water from the last demonstration out of the model and replace the piece of carpeting. Explain that this demonstration will be just like the first, except that soil will cover the clay. Ask: What do you think will happen to the bare soil when it rains?** (The rain should pick up and carry some sediment over the land and into the body of water.)

5. **Spread soil over the clay and make it rain, or pour muddy water from the jar onto the land. Explain that this water represents polluted runoff. Ask the students to compare the water that ends up in the body of water with the water in the jar.** Explain that the soil particles were trapped by the carpeting, making the water in the body of water much clearer. The "uphill" side of the wetland should be coated with trapped sediment.

6. **Remove the carpeting, pour out the water, and try the experi-** ment again. **What happens without the wetland in place? Ask the kids why all the dirt particles end up in the body of water this time.** The thick mat of plant roots in a wetland helps trap silt and some types of pollutants much as the carpet or foam did in the model. Without a wetland, excessive amounts of silt and pollutants can end up in lakes, rivers, and other bodies of water.

Wrap Up and Action
Ask students:

• How might muddy water affect fish? (Makes it harder for them to see and breathe with clogged gills, and could lead to their death.)

• How might other animals and plants be affected by the muddy water? (Settling sediment smothers oysters, plants do not get sunlight needed for growth, birds and other animals who eat fish or plants have less to eat if food sources die or can't be seen in muddy water, etc.)

• How would boats and ships be affected by muddy water? (The mud settles out and eventually

fills channels important for navigation.)

• How might all of this affect you? (Decrease in natural resources and food sources; decline in quality of drinking water; impacts on recreation such as swimming and fishing; change in aesthetics; change in community economy, such as shipping problems that affect jobs and industry, etc.)

• How can we prevent these undesirable effects? (By protecting wetlands and helping to make their benefits known!)

Assessment

Have students:

• describe how wetlands function to reduce flooding and retain sediments.

• analyze what would happen to water, sediments, homes, and wildlife if wetlands were destroyed.

Extensions

Students, individually or as small groups, can make their own, more detailed wetland models using small aluminum foil pans, clay, and florist's foam. Then students can attach plants and animals to the model with toothpicks. They can make a freshwater or salt marsh, freshwater or mangrove swamp, or bog. Provide reference books with pictures of different types of wetlands (see magazines and field guides, p. 326). Students can use an assortment of materials, including natural ones they collect, to decorate their models. Some ideas:

• For cattails, use cotton swabs. Paint sticks green and cotton parts brown, or paint toothpicks green and stick bits of brown clay to the tops.

• Use long pine needles for reeds.

• Shape wetland creatures from clay, or cut them from paper and glue them onto toothpicks.

• Make trees by gluing pieces of green sponge onto twigs. Some dried flower heads also make nice trees; use a small pine cone painted green for an evergreen.

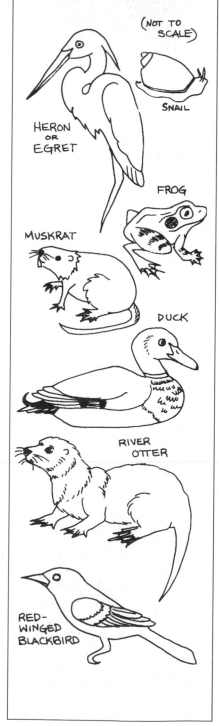

For those who don't wish to draw their own, use these patterns for toothpick animals. Color, then place a second piece of paper behind and cut them out double thickness, then glue the two pieces together with a toothpick stuck between.

(NOT TO SCALE)

HERON OR EGRET

SNAIL

FROG

MUSKRAT

DUCK

RIVER OTTER

RED-WINGED BLACKBIRD

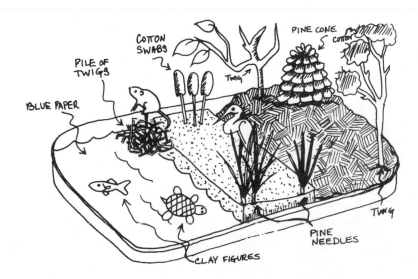

COTTON SWABS

PINE CONE

COTTON

PILE OF TWIGS

TWIG

BLUE PAPER

TWIG

PINE NEEDLES

CLAY FIGURES

Water Purifiers

[Adapted from "Pollution Solution" in Dirty Water: Who Needs It?, National Science and Technology Week '88, Secondary Activity Guide.]

Grade Level
6-12

Subject Areas
Environmental Science, Chemistry

Duration
Divide this activity between two class periods, if needed. The Mechanical Method takes 45 minutes. Nature's Filter takes 20 minutes for the demonstration and 30-40 minutes for the experiment.

Setting
Classroom

Skills
Gathering and analyzing information

Charting the Course
See "A Drop in the Bucket," p. 158, for an understanding of how limited our freshwater supplies are (for Warm Up). Demonstrations modeled in "Runoff Race" and "Treatment Plants" are referenced in this activity. See "Water Under Foot" for an activity that explores how wetlands interact with ground-water supplies. Try also the "Nutrient Trap" game on p. 190.

Vocabulary
water treatment, sedimentation, filtration, flocculation

Summary

Students conduct demonstrations of mechanical and natural methods of filtering impurities from water.

Objectives

Students will:

- describe the process used to treat drinking water.

- identify waste products of water treatment and human and natural resources used.

- compare the efficiency of natural versus mechanical/chemical treatment.

Materials

- *topographic map of your area*

Part I
- *water*
- *25 ml each of gravel, sand, soil, salt*
- *container large enough to hold the above plus one liter of water*
- *1-liter glass beaker*
- *250-ml glass beaker*
- *500-ml glass beaker*
- *alum*
- *glass stirring rod*
- *coffee filter*
- *rubber band or masking tape*
- *bleach*
- *scale or balance that measures grams*
- *copies of the Mechanical Method student page (or an overhead projector)*

Part II
- *25 ml each of gravel, sand, soil, salt*
- *crushed leaves, grass, etc.*
- *old kitchen knife*
- *quart jar with lid*
- *3 clear glass containers*
- *2 long, shallow observation pans—clear or white if possible*
- *piece of sod, cut to fit snugly in one of the pans*

- *books or device to tilt the pan.*

Note: For an alternate to the model requiring materials above, see model described in "Runoff Race," p. 210.

You may want to demonstrate how wetland plants can absorb nutrients and pollutants from water. If so, set up the celery and colored water demonstration a day or two before class. (See "Treatment Plants," p. 120.)

Making Connections

People drink water every day. However, they may not consider all the steps involved in ensuring safe drinking water. An understanding of what is needed to treat and sustain a clean drinking-water supply helps future citizens (voters, landowners, and planners) prepare to make wise decisions about the use of land and water resources.

Background

The average American uses about 200 gallons of water per day! That water is used in the home, at school, at businesses, and in industrial and agricultural activities that supply us with things we need and use. That's a lot of water, and it must be treated before we can drink it. Our wastewater (the part that goes down the drain) must also be treated before it is released back into the environment.

Many impurities—sewage, dissolved minerals, and toxic chemicals—make their way to rivers and lakes. Treatment plants utilize various water-purification methods, including biological treatment, during which microorganisms digest certain impurities.

The water you drink probably contains some chlorine and a variety of salts used to improve the quality of the water. In many communities, fluoride is added to the water to help prevent tooth decay.

Several steps are required to purify water. One step is flocculation, which produces aluminum hydroxide particles called floc. Another step is sedimentation, during which suspended particles in the water settle out. More solids are removed through filtration. The last step, sterilization, uses chemicals to further clean the water.

Water can be filtered and purified naturally to some extent in wetlands. Many wetlands lie in depressions or basins in the land. When runoff collects there, it has a chance to stop and "rest" before it is slowly released to ground water or an adjacent waterway. While the water is being held in the wetland, particles of soil and other pollutants have a chance to settle to the bottom as sediment. The water moves on without this sediment. Over time, the soil particles that collect will build up the wetland. If the wetland is eventually filled in, the plant community there will evolve into another type of habitat through a process called succession.

Procedure

Warm Up

Explain that the fresh water available to us for drinking is only 0.0003 percent of the earth's total water supply. (To illustrate the limitations of the drinking-water supply, see "A Drop in the Bucket.")

Ask students if they would drink wetland water. Is their drinking water connected to water in a wetland? Explain that wetlands

could be connected directly to your town's water source (e.g., a reservoir). If the homes in your town rely on wells, the ground water that the wells draw may be connected to a wetland through the water cycle.

Use a local topographic map to find the water body that supplies your area. Look for connected bodies of water and try to trace them to the wetland you are studying and to other wetlands. You might want to take the class on a visit to the reservoir. The same factors that pollute water in the wetland could potentially pollute this water. The healthier the wetland this water flows through, the cleaner it will be.

Tell students that you will now be exploring two different ways to filter impurities from water: mechanically (using chemicals), and naturally (using a "wetland").

The Activity

Note: For younger students, perform the Mechanical Method as a demonstration. For Nature's Filter, you may substitute the soil filter activity on page 250, if you wish.

Part I: *The Mechanical Method*

1. **Divide the class into lab groups. Give each a prepared sample of "polluted" water. Each sample should contain approximately 25 ml each of sand, gravel, soil, and salt mixed with 1 liter of tap water. Stir to mix. Hand out copies of The Mechanical Method student page (or project it overhead), and have students follow along as you conduct the experiment with their assistance.**

Part II: *Wetlands: Nature's Filter*

1. **Ask the students if they think of natural methods that will purify water more efficiently**

than the mechanical method. Tell students they will participate in demonstrations that show how wetlands filter water. Note that these are only models, and it is impossible to simulate indoors exactly what happens in a natural system. Set up the following demonstrations.

a. Prepare a container of "polluted" water as in Part I, but add crushed leaves, grass, etc. Stir the mixture and immediately pour some into the quart jar to fill it about three-fourths full; cap the jar and set it aside. Divide the rest into two containers.

b. Dig up a piece of sod and place it in one of the pans so it fits snugly. The surface of the sod should be level with the top of the pan so water can run off the surface and out of the pan. Tilt the pan by setting one end on a stack of books. The other end of the pan should rest in another pan or basin to catch the runoff. Use a clear or white pan if possible. Otherwise, have a clear container

nearby (you will pour the runoff into this for observation).

2. **Hold up the jar of polluted water and tell the class what is in it. Ask a student to shake the jar vigorously while you ask the class to predict the order in which the particles will settle when the jar is at rest. Ask the student to stop shaking and place the jar where everyone can see it.** While waiting for all particles to settle, explain that pollutants come from human activities and from the environment itself.

3. **Now ask the class to list the particles in the order in which they settled to the bottom. Write the list on the board.** Why did some particles settle faster than others? (Because they were heavier or more dense, not just because they were larger—large pieces of bark would have floated). Did any *not* settle to the bottom? Why? (Be sure to note that the salt has dissolved into the solution.)

4. **Ask students if there is a way to filter out some particles before they enter the wetland, or a way that wetlands themselves can filter polluted runoff. Present the "pan full of grass" or the "Run-off Race" model. These models represent a lawn or a wetland. Ask what will happen when a sample of polluted water is poured over this ground. (The plants will trap some of the particles, others will run off with the water.) Have a student slowly pour one of the containers of polluted water over the model; give it time to run down the model, then observe the runoff in the collection pan.** If you want to run this experiment again, use the second container of polluted water.

Ask students to explain soil's role

in purifying water. Discuss how particles are trapped as the water soaks into the soil structure.

Point out that although not all of the particles were trapped, it could be that the plants were not close enough together. Wetlands can only do so much, but they do help. If we don't overload them, they produce much cleaner water.

5. **Point out the particles in the runoff. They should be the finer ones. Ask whether these particles will settle out in the wetland, and carefully decant the water off into another clear container to demonstrate that they will.** Do students think the runoff still contains pollutants? Suggest that the salt should still be there. How do students think invisible pollutants such as nutrients and chemicals could be removed from the water in a wetland? Explain and review the Treatment Plants model (p. 120) as an answer. Plants can use waterborne nutrients; toxic substances may be stored in plant tissues. Chemicals and excess nutrients may kill plants. However, when the plants

die for other reasons and decay, they end up back in the wetland (one reason to prevent toxic substances from getting into the wetland in the first place!).

Wrap Up and Action
Remind students that the impurities added to the water sample represented pollutants such as sewage, dissolved minerals, and toxic chemicals. Many steps, including flocculation, sedimentation, filtration, and sterilization were required to purify the water.

Ask the class to name the waste products left after each step of the Mechanical Method (the floc, filter paper, and so on). Compare the end products of both purifying methods. Have students compare strengths and weaknesses of each method. Nature's Filter should have worked better. If not, point out "bugs" in the demonstration that would work more efficiently in nature. Challenge students to devise a method to test for the salt left in the water, without tasting. They might choose to measure mass and compare density to that of a sample of tap water; they may also choose to let the water evaporate and see if anything is left behind.

Other questions for discussion:

• Which method of treatment is more expensive, in terms of natural and human resources?

• Does anyone think that we need both kinds of treatment? Realistically, we will always have to treat drinking water somehow because there will always be some kinds of pollution (we can't stop it all) and because wetlands cannot clean up all of the pollutants people put into the environment.

Discuss the idea of creating wetlands to filter both drinking water and wastewater. Many areas are currently using wetlands to treat wastewater.

Assessment

Have students:

- describe the processes involved in water treatment.

- identify the similarities in natural and mechanical water treatment.

- compare the strengths and weaknesses of the natural and mechanical methods.

Extensions

Have students estimate the money, time, jobs, electricity, and land (to house treatment plants) it takes to clean up all of this water?

What happens to the floc and other wastes after water treatment, or to the solid waste (sludge) left from sewage treatment? Have students find out what their community does with wastes. Can they think of any alternative means of disposal or uses for these wastes?

When studying water at a wetland, try to find places where water is running into and out of the wetland. Collect some water from each spot in clear jars and compare.

Have a watery film fest! Watch movies about the value people place on water. Suggestions:

Chinatown. Jack Nicholson and Faye Dunaway (1974). A Los Angeles private eye stumbles upon a scandal involving greed over the water supply.

The Milagro Beanfield War. Directed by Robert Redford (1988). A humorous culture clash over water supply erupts between bean farmers and developers in a New Mexico town. Farmers band together to protect and preserve their way of life.

Both movies are rated "R," so review for content.

Notes:

The Mechanical Method

1. Fill a 1-liter glass beaker with the well-stirred mixture of "polluted" water. Observe and record the water's color and clarity. Describe the particles and their positions in the solution.

2. Weigh the empty 250-ml beaker; record its weight. Stir the polluted water and immediately pour 250 ml of it into the beaker. Determine and record the mass of this sample (weight of the filled beaker minus the weight of the empty beaker).

3. Divide the sample's weight by its volume to determine the approximate density of the sample (density equals weight in grams divided by the volume in milliliters); record the result. Set this sample aside as a control.

4. Add approximately 0.5 g alum to the polluted water that remains in the original one-liter beaker. Stir with a glass stirring rod for three to five minutes. Aluminum hydroxide particles will develop. This step demonstrates flocculation

5. Allow the water to settle for 10-15 minutes. Observe and record the water's color and clarity. Describe the position of the particles in the solution. This step demonstrates sedimentation.

6. Insert the coffee filter into the 500-ml beaker and secure it with a rubber band or masking tape. Allow room for 250 ml of water between the bottom of the filter and the bottom of the beaker.

7. Carefully pour approximately 250 ml of the polluted water through the filter, leaving the particles behind in the 1-liter beaker (this is called "decanting" the liquid). Be careful not to stir up the particles as you pour. Observe and record the filtered water and compare it to the density of the 250-ml control that was set aside earlier.

8. Determine and record the density of the 250 ml of filtered water and compare it to the density of the 250-ml control that was set aside earlier.

9. Add one drop of household bleach to the filtered sample and stir the solution. Observe the final sample and compare its appearance to the control. This step demonstrates sterilization. Save all samples and materials for reference in the next part of the activity.

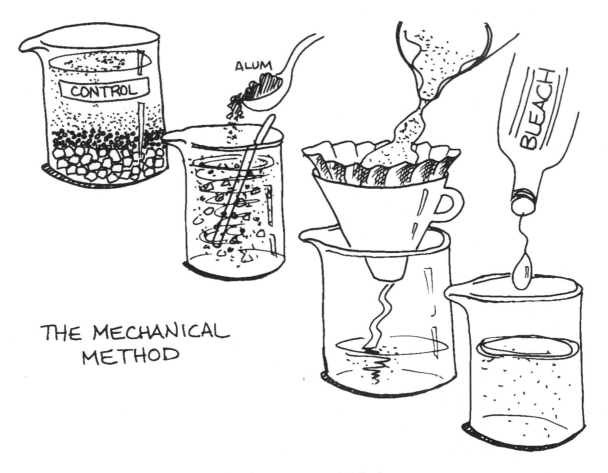

THE MECHANICAL METHOD

Over Hill and Dale

[The watershed model is adapted from River Times, Math and Science Center, 2401 Hartman Street, Richmond, VA 23223]

Grade Level
3-4, with guidance; 5-12

Subject Areas
Geography, Environmental Science

Duration
Classroom, 1 hour; outdoors, at least 1 hour, depending on course chosen to walk and map

Setting
Classroom and outdoors

Skills
Gathering, organizing, analyzing, and applying information

Charting the Course
To study the quality of water that students map in this exercise, you may want to combine this activity with "Water We Have Here?" which presents techniques for measuring physical and chemical characteristics of water. "Helping Wetland Habitats" provides a series of stewardship activities students can undertake at local wetlands.

Vocabulary
topographic map, watershed

Summary

Students follow a waterway and map their course, noting sites that affect water quality along the way.

Objectives

Students will:

- interpret a topographic map of their area.

- recognize human-influenced features and activities that affect water quality.

Materials

To make a watershed:
- *shallow baking pans*
- *small cups or blocks*
- *aluminum foil*
- *dark-colored powdered fruit drink mix*
- *cups or watering cans*
- *water*
- *topographic or city maps (or National Wetland Inventory maps—see pp. 54, 329 for more information)*
  Obtain topographic maps of your area from the National Cartographic Information Center, U.S. Geological Survey, 507 National Center, Reston, VA 22092. Ask for free index maps and order forms. Or, use city or county street map books sold in book and office supply stores, gas stations, and convenience stores. Many local libraries carry these. Photocopy the pages needed, but be sure all features show on the copy. Cover your maps with contact paper so students can mark local features on them with erasable markers.
- *clear contact paper*
- *colored marking tools (erasable markers or grease pencils)*

For each field trip group:
- *large sheet of paper*

- *premade key symbols and tape, or markers*
- *photocopy of topographic map*
- *first-aid kit*
- *emergency phone number and quarters*
- *chaperon*

Making Connections

Students learn about human activities that pollute as they follow a watercourse. Identifying sources of pollution close to home is the first step in preventing harmful practices.

Background

Water in wetlands is connected to the landscape around it. All of the land that feeds water into aquifers, lakes, and streams between ridges (topographic high points) is called a watershed. Harmful human activities in the watershed ultimately affect the water, particularly through runoff. Wetlands filter out and absorb many pollutants from runoff as it travels across the land. These pollutants include soil (sediments), fertilizer, chemicals, trash, gasoline, and oil. Our survival depends upon a clean water supply, and the protection of wetlands is vital to sustaining good water quality.

Many features affect water quality. These include:

Construction sites

- soil erosion and control measures
- habitat destruction

Factories

- effluent (discharge)
- air pollution

Parking lots, streets, driveways

- paved surfaces (impermeable surfaces)

- runoff of sediment-laden rainwater and pollutants
- illegal dumping

Storm drains

- pollutants disposed of in drains (Drains or grates in streets collect rainwater so the streets don't flood. Storm drains lead directly to the nearest body of water.)

Lawns and farms

- runoff of pet and livestock wastes
- livestock standing in streams (adds wastes directly; trampling increases streambank erosion)
- soil erosion from bare spots or tilled fields
- improper application of fertilizers, pesticides, and other lawn and crop care products (leads to runoff)

A topographic map, or "topo" (TOE-poe), is a very useful tool to have on hand when exploring a watershed. It shows the relief (shape and elevation) of the land, as well as waterways and human-made features such as roads, buildings, bridges, and mines. Brown contour lines show the elevation of ridges, hills, and other bumps and dips. Each contour line on a topo map represents an elevation in number of feet above sea level. Topo maps indicate some wetlands as well. They are marked by symbols like these:

National Wetland Inventory maps are a new resource similar to topographic maps, but they focus on local wetlands.

Procedure

Warm Up

Introduce the watershed concept. Note that gravity causes precipitation to run downhill and eventu-

ally into waterways, the heart of a watershed. In fact, most waterways and wetlands lie downhill from the land around them.

Because wetlands receive water after it flows overland, how do students think activities on land affect the water quality of wetlands?

The Activity
Part I

Make a watershed: Divide the class into groups and give each group the following directions and materials.

- Tape or secure small cups or blocks in one end of a shallow baking pan; prop this end up on a book.

- Tear off a piece of aluminum foil the size of the pan. Crinkle the foil. Cover the blocks with the foil and make a basin in the foil at the other end of the pan. In this model watershed, the high end represents mountains, while the creases in the foil are streams and rivers that are bordered by wetlands. The basin is a large body of water (a lake or bay) that the rivers flow into.

- Pour "rain" over the watershed, using cups or watering cans, and watch where it runs. Sprinkle some drink mix ("pollutants")

on various locations around the watershed. Imagine how the land might be used in each location (e.g., farms, mining, malls, etc.). Make it rain again and watch what happens. Ask students what kinds of pollutants the drink mix might represent.

Part II

1. **Explain that students will be making their own maps of a watershed near school.**

2. **To help them understand what kinds of features to put on their maps, have students study the laminated topographic or city maps, marking significant features.** Have them locate and mark the school and the closest body of water. See if students can trace an entire watercourse from its source (beginning) to its destination (pond, lake, bay, ocean). The body of water does not have to be natural (constructed ponds and lakes are usually made by blocking, or impounding, a stream or river until it overflows). Have students mark particular areas of interest: industrial areas; malls, shopping centers, commercial areas; airports; wastewater treatment plants; roads and highways; urban, suburban, and rural zones; natural areas and parks; wetlands

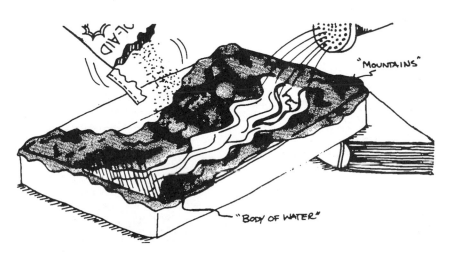

(especially); etc. You may choose to have students complete the Topo Maps student page.

3. **Have the students plan an outdoor mapping trip. Ask where they will begin. Suggest starting at the wetland site used for other studies in this guide. Plot the course.** Is there private property involved? If students will not be able to go around this property, secure permission to cross beforehand. Have students decide how far they should go. (It should be a walking trip, so there may not be time to go too far.) Estimate the distance and assume it may take the group an hour to go about two miles. To cover more territory in a short amount of time, enlist some adult chaperones. For younger students, choose one small area (a mile or less) to map. Have them practice by making a map of the classroom first.

Note: Some prior research on local laws concerning discharge may be required. If you want to visit a factory with your class, it is strongly recommended that you make arrangements with the facility ahead of time. Many are sensitive to scrutiny or have safety regulations governing visits. Students do not need to get close to a facility to note that it has a potential impact on the water.

4. **Review these safety guidelines for the trip:**

• Use the buddy system, even with older students, and require groups to stay with chaperons at all times.

• Follow the water from land only (stay out of the waterway).

• Obey No Trespassing signs and respect all properties.

• Be sure each group has a copy of the map and a first-aid kit, just

in case. Designate an emergency contact at the school.

5. **Divide the class into groups and assign a small section of the course to each group. Have each group make a simple draft map of their section of the course that includes only streets, the waterway, and a few pertinent boundary marks. The rest of the features will be filled in as students go along. Make up a key of symbols to mark features of interest and landmarks, or use the Sample Map Key on p. 224. Have groups carry premade symbols and tape (or markers) to mark feature locations.** Features would include those noted on the topo maps as well as anything else found along the way, such as stream blockages or large items dumped in the waterway. When you design your symbols, include one for natural-looking wetlands with lots of plants (vegetated wetlands) and one for wetlands that are obviously disturbed (plants are torn up or dead, etc.).

6. **Have chaperoned student groups follow their portions of the course, noting activities in the local watershed that contribute pollutants to the water. During the trip, stop to observe areas and mark the map.** If you have been unable to secure chaperones, conduct the field research as a class.

There may be places where students think they have lost the waterway. In many areas the path of the water may have been routed through artificial structures, and the waterway may even be hidden by human-made features or underground culverts. For example, if a road built over a stream has a pipe or culvert below to allow the stream to continue unobstructed, you will need to cross the road and maybe even

some distance beyond to pick up the waterway again. In this case, have students proceed in the same general direction the water was flowing when last seen until they find water again. Refer to the topo map for help.

7. **Map the wetlands encountered. Assume that any land that borders the water is wetland unless it is paved or a steep slope up to a road, etc. Students will have to make judgment calls.** One type of constructed wetland students may see is a stormwater management pond. This is a basin created to catch water running from a highway or development site. In the basin, soil and some pollutants settle to the bottom instead of continuing on with the runoff. These ponds are often planted with wetland plants that help filter the water.

8. **When the map is complete, return to the classroom. If the class worked in groups, have groups share their information and connect their maps.**

Wrap Up and Action

What did students learn from their walk? Perhaps they saw that many everyday activities have an impact on our water supply.

Was the water they saw fairly clean, severely polluted, or somewhere in between? How could they tell? What are some specific ways to improve the quality of this water?

Now that some problems have been identified, have the class choose one problem they feel they can change for the better. Use the action guide (chapter 6) and the restoration guide listed in the resource section to plan a course of action. Involve the students in actions that make a difference!

Assessment

Have students:

- make a model of how water travels in a watershed.

- identify the path of a watershed on a topographic or city map.

- construct a map of local water resources.

- describe how people can affect the quality and movement of water.

Extensions

If students find a healthy-looking, vegetated wetland in their travels, have them observe or collect samples of water running into and out of it and compare samples. Does the water seem cleaner after traveling through the wetland? If the difference is not visible, students may need to perform a few water tests for pH, turbidity, etc. (See "Water We Have Here?" p. 174.)

K-2 Option

Take the class out to the schoolyard. Find the spot that has the highest elevation (it may be only slightly higher). Ask students to imagine they are tiny raindrops falling on this spot. Have them slowly walk the path they think the drops would take as gravity pulled them along. They should stop anywhere they think the raindrop would stop. Some may not move at all, since they were absorbed into the ground. Others may stop at a puddle or depression or at the very bottom of a slope or hill. Still others may roll around a stone or other raised spot in the path. If there is a body of water nearby, some may trickle all the way there. Afterwards, ask: What changed the path you took? What sorts of things might shape the path of a body of a watercourse such as a stream?

Notes:

Topo Maps

Study a real topographic map. Look at the symbols shown in the key and try to locate as many of these features as you can. Then answer the questions on this sheet.

1. Name the area shown on the map.

   _____

2. How many schools are there?_____

3. What is the highest elevation on this map?_____

4. What do the green areas stand for?

   _____

5. Name a road that crosses a pipeline.

   _____

6. Name three bodies of water.

   _____

7. If you canoed the longest river on the map, how far would you paddle?_____

8. Name the waterway(s) bordering the largest wetland on the map.

   _____

9. What is the elevation of this wetland?_____

10. There may be wetlands that are not shown on the map. Where do you think they would be located. Why?

    _____

    _____

Sample Map Key

For younger students, photocopy these or other symbols; have students cut them out and tape to their maps where appropriate.

 Houses

 School

 Stores

 Industry

 Construction

 Wetland (vegetated)

 Wetland (disturbed)

 Dump site (illegal)

 Landfill

 Parking lot

 Marina

• • • • • Waterway

═══════ Highway

─────── Paved street

─ ─ ─ ─ Dirt or gravel road

Section

Going Down Under (soil)

Activities that explore the role of soils in a wetland environment, including filtration, percolation, and decomposition. Soil formation and characteristics are also studied.

Nature's Recyclers

Grade Level
K-6

Subject Areas
Life Science, Ecology, Biology, Earth Science

Duration
30 minutes indoors; 30 minutes outdoors

Setting
Classroom and outdoors

Skills
Gathering, organizing, and interpreting information

Charting the Course
This activity can be preceded by "Marsh Market," for a study of food webs. Follow this activity with "Do You Dig Wetland Soil?" which provides an in-depth look at the wetland soils produced by nature's recyclers!

Vocabulary
decomposition, humus, organic material, detritus

Summary
Centipedes, earthworms, and copepods, oh my!

Students investigate the connections between soil and a decomposing log or leaf litter.

Objectives
Students will:

• describe the process of decomposition.

• explain the role of decomposers in soil formation.

• analyze a variety of interactions that occur in nature and at home.

Materials
• *a few flashlights*
• *humus, decomposed acorns, or moldy bread*
• *field guides to insects, spiders, reptiles, amphibians, etc.*

For each student or small group of students:
• *hand lenses*
• *bug boxes or clear jars with small air holes punched in the lids*
• *index cards*
• *small cup and spoon*
• *pencils*
• *copy of the student page (grades K-2, p. 229; grades 3-6, p. 230)*
• *clipboard or thick cardboard with the paper taped to it*
• *extra paper (optional)*

Making Connections
Students may have sifted through leaf litter and noticed a variety of insects and worms. They may not, however, appreciate the importance of these critters to healthy soil. The study of soil formation leads to an understanding of related natural processes as well as relationships between organisms in an ecosystem.

Background
Soil is the loose material on Earth's surface in which plants can grow. The top layer of soil, topsoil, is a dark color in some areas because it contains humus. Humus is formed when decomposers break down organic material (the remains of living organisms such as plants and animals). Because it is rich in nutrients and well-aerated (contains lots of spaces filled with oxygen), humus provides some of the things plants need for growth. It is a very important part of the food web. Without it, we would not have many of the foods we eat.

There are several different types of decomposers. Fungi (mushrooms and bread molds) cannot make their own food, as plants do, so they must absorb their nutrients from either dead or living organisms. Bacteria are microscopic, single-celled organisms that also absorb their nutrients from other organisms. Tiny sow bugs, like some insects and other animals, digest organic matter and deposit the decomposed material as a waste product. Earthworms also contribute to the soil in this manner, and their movement through the ground helps aerate the soil. Cows contribute to the recycling process in a similar way. Their digestive tracts contain decomposers (bacteria) that turn ingested grasses and grains into a nutrient-rich waste product (manure).

Decomposers (or detritivores) consume organic matter, digest it, and leave behind (excrete) other forms of nutrients. During digestion and excretion, detritus is changed both physically (in size) and chemically (in molecular structure). The decomposition process releases nutrients such as phosphorus and nitrogen, which can then be used again by plants for growth. This form of natural recycling—discarded (and dead) materials made into different forms that can be reused—is a slow, continual process. It takes nature 250 to 2,000 years to produce one inch of topsoil!

A fallen log or layer of leaf litter can be used to study nature's recyclers at work. Observe material that is lying on or just under the soil layer—this is the most decomposed. A great deal of activity centers around these areas.

Wood-eating insects such as termites and some beetles feed on logs, softening the wood; their tunnels provide access for other creatures. Some insects lay their eggs in decaying wood or leaf litter, and when the larvae hatch, they feed on the dead plant material. These tiny creatures attract hungry birds and other insect-eaters. Look for small holes tapped into the wood by a woodpecker.

Many creatures use fallen logs for home sites or hiding places. Moisture trapped under logs is favored by animals such as salamanders, who must be moist to breathe through their skin. Logs often have a narrow tunnel used by a chipmunk, or even a larger hole that was home to a woodpecker, wood duck, raccoon, or flying squirrel. These "cavity nesters" find that standing dead trees and fallen logs are softer and therefore easier to burrow through for nesting. In some cases, animal activities may have caused the death of these trees in the first place.

Procedure

Warm Up

Note: Before the lesson, look for a place on or very near the schoolyard that has at least one fallen, rotting log. If you cannot find logs, parts of this activity can be done with leaf litter or a pile of leaves that has been around for a good while. As a last resort, a woodpile in someone's yard will do.

Introduce the concept of decomposition to your students before going outside. Bring in some humus and some partly decomposed acorns for the class to poke through and look at with hand lenses. You may want to bring to class some moldy bread or rotten vegetables that have been in your kitchen too long. Discuss what is happening to these items.

Ask students what would happen if we allowed this process to continue? Explain that the food would continue to be broken down. If we left it long enough, we would not be able to recognize the vegetable or bread.

How long do students think it would take for these food items to become unrecognizable? It would take a long time. Perhaps students could conduct a controlled experiment in the classroom, to find out how long.

Keep these things for a few more days and let the process continue; have students periodically check them for changes. Explain that decomposition adds nutrients to the soil. Introduce the word humus. Discuss why plants need soil. Help students identify minerals and other nutrients plants need. By checking a vitamin or cereal package, students can see we use some of these nutrients as well.

The Activity

1. **Prepare the class for a short trip outdoors. Review rules and safety precautions given below. Stress that you are going outside only to observe, and that everything should look the same when you leave as it did when you arrived (removing trash is okay). Explain that the class will be observing the many interactions that contribute to decomposition.**

Guidelines for Outdoor Manners and Safety

• Do not stick bare hands into dark holes, since they may contain sharp objects or biting insects. Instead, use flashlights to look into holes.

• Do not break logs apart. Leave nature to its own course. If there has not been enough opportunity to see inside a log by the end of the

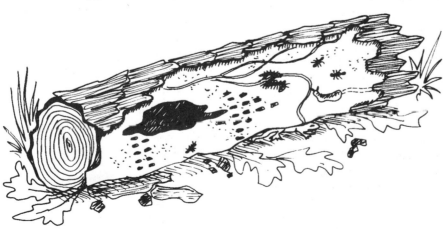

lesson, the teacher may break open one portion for all to observe.

• Respect living organisms and their homes. Try to disturb them as little as possible. If you would like to observe a lively critter more closely, gently scoop it into a bug box or jar with an index card. Keep it only long enough to study and share it with others. Release or replace all living things after observing.

• Be sure to "put the roof back on the house" (roll logs back into the exact position in which they were found).

• Do not pick live plants. Hitting tree trunks or picking off bark harms trees (bark is the outer skin that protects trees). It is okay to collect a few fallen leaves, twigs, and other discarded objects, if you wish.

2. **Outside, divide the class into small groups; hand out supplies. Explain the use of the equipment and let students practice a bit with each item.** The cup and spoon are for collecting a small soil sample.

3. **Give each group a copy of the appropriate student page and a clipboard. Choose a "recorder" for each group. Review the instructions and questions on the page and have individual students or groups fill in the answers.**

Wrap Up
Either in the field or back in the classroom, review the student pages and discuss findings.

Note: Some books refer to fungi (mushrooms, bread molds, shelf fungus) as plants, though fungi are now classified in their own kingdom. To avoid confusing younger students, fungi are

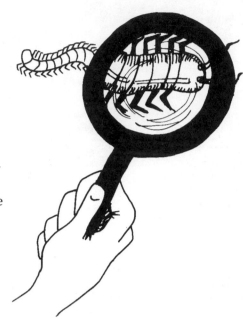

referred to as plants in this activity. Please make the distinction with more advanced students.

Assessment
Have students:

• outline the process of decomposition.

• identify animals that aid in the process of decomposition.

• write a story (from the perspective of an insect or earthworm) describing the process of decomposition, and why it is important.

• envision what the ground would look like without detritivores.

Extensions
Make and use a desktop composting bin, as described in "A Rottin' Experiment," p. 245.

Nature's Recyclers: What's in a Log?

These are some of the things that help make a log decay. How many can you find? Finish the name below each picture, then write answers to questions on the lines.

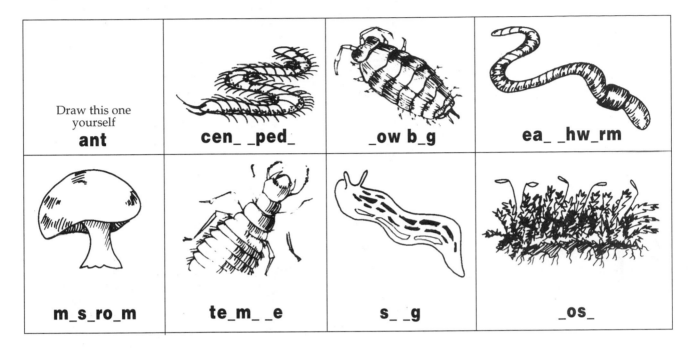

Draw this one yourself **ant**	**cen_ _ped_**	**_ow b_g**	**ea_ _hw_rm**
m_s_ro_m	**te_m_ _e**	**s_ _g**	**_os_**

1. How many creatures can you find on the log?_____

   How many plants do you see on the log?_____

2. What colors are most of the things on or under the log?_____

   Do you see any bright colors?_____

3. What is happening to the log?_____

4. Look at the soil under the log. Use a magnifying glass. What is the soil made of? _____

_____

5. Now feel the soil under the log. Describe how it feels._____

_____

Nature's Recyclers: A Log's Log

1. Approach the log quietly and observe it before touching it.

   a. Describe what you see (creatures, what they are doing, etc.)._____
   _____

   b. Are there parts that could be easily broken apart? (But do not break them apart!) Why would they be easily broken?_____
   _____

   c. Are there other plants growing on the log? Describe or name them. Look for mushrooms, shelf-shaped fungi, lichens, mosses, algae, ferns, and other plants._____
   _____
   _____

   d. Can you tell how these plants are changing the log? Look for roots growing through the wood._____
   _____

2. Now you may touch the log. Carefully roll it back, just enough to see under it.

   a. Draw and label three decomposers that you see. Field guides will help you identify them.

   b. How are these animals changing the log?_____

   c. Can you find insect holes, tunnels, or other signs that creatures have been moving through the log? Describe them._____
   _____

   d. Describe any evidence (signs) that creatures have made their home in this log (leaf litter in a cavity, animal droppings, a nest or nesting material, etc.)._____
   _____

3. Dig up a small sample of soil underneath or next to the log and study its contents. Describe the soil._____
   _____

4. What role does the log play in this natural community?_____
   _____

When you are through, make sure the log is in exactly the same place as it was when you found it, and nothing else has been disturbed. Release all living things that you caught to study.

Do You Dig Wetland Soil?

[Soil texture flow chart adapted from Steve Thein, 1979. Source unknown.]

Grade Level
K-12, as indicated

Subject Areas
Earth Science

Duration
Part I, 30-40 minutes;
Part II, 60 minutes

Setting
Classroom and wetland

Skills
Gathering, organizing, analyzing, and interpreting information

Charting the Course
Once students have studied soil types and identification procedures, they can investigate the permeability of various soils in "How Thirsty Is the Ground?"

Vocabulary
hydric soil, anaerobic, organic, mineral

Summary

How is wetland soil like a box of crayons?

Students make and use a wetland soils color chart, then dig a hole in a wetland area to study the physical characteristics of the soil.

Objectives

Students will:

• describe physical differences between wetland and upland soils.

• use keys to recognize wetland soils.

Materials

Part I:
• *Crayola® Crayons, 64-color boxes*
• *scissors*
• *paste*
• *posterboard or manila folders*
• *copies of the Color Me Wet! student pages (grades 4-12, p. 237; grades K-3, p. 236).*

Part II:
• *clay cat litter premixed with water to make a paste (see "How Thirsty Is the Ground?" p. 239)*
• *spade or narrow shovel*
• *yard (meter) stick*
• *pencils*
• *hand lenses*
• *copies of the Soils Data Chart, p. 235.*
• *copies of Key to Soil Texture by Feel (for older students), p. 238.*

Making Connections

Students may have dug holes in the ground and noticed variations in soil coloration, but they may not know what causes these colors, or how soil colors are important for keying out soil type. In this activity, students will learn to recognize common wetland soil types and begin to locate wetlands in their communities.

Background

There are many different types of soils, as well as sophisticated classification systems to categorize them. Most soil types are well-drained, nonwetland varieties. Because of the prolonged presence of water, wetland soils are physically different from nonwetland (often called upland) soils.

Wetland (hydric) soils are saturated, flooded, or "ponded" long enough during the growing season to develop anaerobic conditions in upper layers. That is, wetland soil is at times so saturated with water that it cannot hold much, if any, oxygen. The prolonged presence of water, and the resultant lack of oxygen, causes chemical reactions that eventually affect the color of the soil.

The study of a soil sample's color can determine if it is hydric soil even if the sample is not wet at the time of the investigation. By "reading" color characteristics, a soil scientist can tell how long or how frequently an area has been wet. You and your students can learn to recognize some wetland soils in this manner, too.

There are two major types of wetland soils: organic and mineral. Organic wetland soils are those that contain a noticeable amount (more than ten percent) of partially decomposed plants within at least 1.5 feet (0.46 meters) of the ground's surface. In waterlogged spots, organic materials accumulate. The lack of oxygen results in a decrease in bacterial decomposition, and plants do not decompose as they do in aerated situations. Wet organic soils look like black muck or black to dark brown peat.

Soils that contain little or no organic material are classified as mineral soils. Mineral soils usually consist of a wide range of materials such as sand, silt, and clay. Mineral wetland soils can be gleyed (pronounced "glade") or mottled. Gleyed soils are usually formed when the soils are saturated all of the time (and thus anaerobic). These soils are usually neutral gray, greenish, or bluish gray.

Mottled soils are formed in areas that have wet (anaerobic) conditions, followed by periods of dry (aerobic) conditions. These conditions alternate continuously, possibly seasonally. The basic (matrix) soil color often includes concentrated splotches of brown, orange, red, or yellow. When the soil is very wet, minerals such as iron and manganese collect in spaces in the soil. When air moves into the soil during dry periods, these mineral concentrations oxidize. The iron rusts, leaving a permanent indicator of this process. Oxidized iron concentrations are various shades of red, orange, and yellow, while manganese mottles are black.

When you dig a hole to study wetland soil, you may find horizontal banding of colored materials in the soil profile. The soil types you find will depend on the area studied; you may want to contact your county Natural Resources Conservation Service office for expert help in identifying soil types. Wetland scientists use sophisticated tools such as the Munsell Soil Color Charts to identify wetland soils. Each color

chip in the Munsell book represents a combination of hue (color), value (lightness or darkness), and chroma (purity) that reflects the degree of wetness in the soil. The color chart developed in Part I of this activity is a simplified version of the Munsell book.

Keep in mind that the soils on many properties have been altered by human activities. Tilling for agriculture, filling for development, and stripping for mining are a few examples of activities that change soils. Try to find a relatively undisturbed site, if possible. If you are looking at soil in a city, a suburban housing community, or near farmland, you may have to dig deeper to find undisturbed soils, including the original hydric soil. (Remember to ask for permission to dig, and be sure you fill up holes when you're done.)

Part I of this book contains other information on soils (p. 12) and helpful hints about finding wetland study sites (see chapter 6).

Procedure
Warm Up
Do students have a garden or flower box at home? Have they ever noticed the color of soil? Explain that chemical reactions in water-bearing soils cause color changes, and that soil color can therefore be used as an indicator of the frequency and duration of wetness. You might have your more advanced students study these reactions. Younger students should understand that the presence of water causes chemical changes that make wetland soils look different from other soils.

The Activity
Part I: *Make Your Own Soil Color Chart*

Hand out copies of the appropriate color chart student page for your grade level and review the directions. Explain that this is a very simplified version of the Munsell book. Have students color the chart using the Crayola® Crayon color names given. (It is important to use the indicated colors in order to identify the soils correctly.) Have students complete the other steps to prepare the charts. They will use them for Part II.

Part II: *Dig In!*

1. Before going outside, show students the premixed cat litter. Have each student feel the mixture's texture. Give each student a copy of the Soils Data Chart student page.

2. At the wetland, use the spade to dig a hole about two feet deep to find and study wetland soils. *Note:* If you do not find indications of wetland soils, try another spot.

3. Avoiding the topmost layer of surface material, pick at the inside surfaces of the hole with the end of a yardstick to reveal the true structure of the soil. Remove golfball-sized pieces of soil from a side of the hole at the indicated depths (see data chart). Ask students to examine both the outside and the inside of these samples (break the soil balls into two or three pieces).

4. Have students record soil characteristics and observations in the Soils Data Chart, using the color chart from Part I and the word lists that accompanies the data chart. Older students can use the Key to Soil Texture by Feel on p. 238 to identify soil types.

Wrap Up and Action
After the data charts have been

completed, use the Dig In! questions below for group discussion.

DIG IN!

1. *What soil characteristics did you observe?* Share data and observations from students' completed charts. Wetland soils may have any of the characteristics listed below. If you were able to dig down to wetland soil, the students' charts should in one way or another match these descriptions.

• some shade of dark brown or black (see color chart)

• feels like sticky clay and is some shade of gray, green, or darker color (see color chart)

• made up of peat or organic material, sand and/or other minerals, clay, silt, loam, or some combination of these materials in layers or mixtures

• when squeezed, sticks together or oozes out of fingers in a ribbonlike strand

• broken surfaces of the samples reveal mottles or splotches of color throughout the sample in some shade of red, orange, or yellow (see color chart)

• shades of red or orange "rusty" soil surrounding roots and root channels (the oxygen that wetland plants send to their roots often "leaks" out, oxidizing the iron in the soil)

• no earthworms in very wet, saturated soil (they would drown or suffocate!)

• sulfur gas from anaerobic activity; smells like rotten eggs

2. *How did soil at the bottom of the hole differ from soil near the surface in color and texture?* This depends on the type of wetland you were in and the level of the water table in your sample area. You may

have observed layering of soils similar to the diagram shown here. Most wetland soils have a dark layer of (aerobic) organic soil at the top, where oxygen is exchanged with the atmosphere, and (anaerobic) mineral or organic soils below.

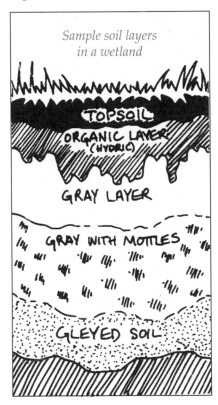

Sample soil layers in a wetland

3. *Can you find evidence around your sample area that shows where the soil particles came from?* Most organic topsoil is the result of the breakdown of fallen leaves and dead plants, as described in "Nature's Recyclers." Organic wetland soil is the accumulation of organic material that has not decayed because of the anaerobic soil condition. Mineral soils are formed over time from weathering of rocks. Wetland soils on the banks of streams and rivers may have been formed through the gradual deposition of soil particles that were carried in (and eroded) by water.

4. *Can you tell where the water and soils in this area are coming from? What watershed drains to this spot?* Have the students look at factors that bring water into the area, since it is the degree of wetness and how it affects the condition of the soil that we are most interested in here. Look at topographic features of the area and weather conditions. For example, if the wetland lies in a depression at the bottom of a slope, runoff from the slope will end up in the wetland, eventually seeping into the soil to make or keep it wet.

5. *Did you find anything that was not natural (i.e., human-made) in the soil? How do you think it got there?* In many cases, human products (e.g., litter, chemical pollutants) enter a wetland just as deposited soil and other natural materials do—with the inflow of water. These materials are introduced to the environment at some point, whether intentionally or unintentionally. Discuss these possibilities with the class. Have students speculate on the source of any human-made materials they have found.

6. *Compare wetland soil to soil you have observed at home and around school. How do the soils differ, and what makes them different?* The primary difference is that wetland soil is wet or saturated for an extended period, and upland soil is not saturated. The colors of the two soils are different because chemical reactions that occur in anaerobic (saturated) soils differ from those that occur in aerobic soils. The differences that students may observe in wetland and upland soils depend on the areas sampled—there are many possibilities. Organic soils are wetland soils, if the overall matrix of the soil throughout the hole is organic.

Assessment

Have students:

- observe soil samples and record their observations.

- classify soil types through color analysis.

- identify environmental and human-made factors that influence soil conditions.

Extensions

If you find clay or sticky soil while outside, have students make small wetland sculptures to take home!

Invite an extension agent or soil scientist to visit the class to discuss the results of the field work. Ask this visitor to share aspects of his or her career with students.

Nature in Your Neighborhood: Be a Wetland Watchdog!

Are there wetlands in your neighborhood that need protecting? Find a stream or other body of water—or even a puddle that stays wet for a week or more. Dig a small hole in the ground and use your color chart to see if it may be a wetland. How are people using the land in and around this spot? Check areas where the ground has been plowed to build a road, house, or other building. If the soil is gray or very dark, it could be a wetland. Ask officials if the construction there is legal. Devise a neighborhood plan to make the area even better. You might clean up the area, or plant wetland plants to prevent erosion and attract more wildlife. See chapter 6 for more ideas.

Notes:

Soils Data Chart

Record the words or phrases that apply to each soil sample in the chart below.

Texture/moisture: Rub the soil between your fingers. Choose words that describe how it feels.

- *dry, moist, wet, very wet,* or *drippy*
- *falls apart, sticks together, sticky* (sticks to fingers)
- *feels like clay* (easily molded into shapes)
- *slippery, oozes* (extrudes between fingers when you squeeze it)

Soil particles: Draw the size and shape of the particles. What is the sample made of?

- *sand* (feels gritty)
- *minerals* (tiny bits of rock)
- *clay* (like the cat litter sample)
- *silt* (like flour or powder; slippery when wet)
- *pebbles*
- *organic matter* (bits of leaves, twigs, bark, etc.)

Color: Use color chart

Other features or creatures: What does the soil smell like? List or describe any rocks, dead plants, or other nonliving materials in the soil. List or describe any living things such as worms, roots, or insects. Do you see any roots with "rusty" red or orange soil around them?

Depth From Soil Surface	Texture/ Moisture (describe how it feels)	Soil Particles (describe or identify them)	Color # (use color chart)	Other Features or Creatures
2 inches (5 cm)				
4 inches (10 cm)				
6 inches (15 cm)				
12 inches (30 cm)				
18 inches (45 cm)				

Color Me Wet!

1. Use Crayola® Crayons (a box of 64) to color in the squares on the chart below. It is very important to use the right colors!

2. Fold the rectangle in half and cut out the dark circle.

3. Use your chart when studying soil. Your chart is similar to the complicated color charts wetland scientists use to identify wetland soils.

Hold the chart in one hand and hold a sample of soil behind the hole with your other hand. Try to match the color of the soil to one of the squares. If it nearly matches a box above the diagonal line, it may be wetland soil.

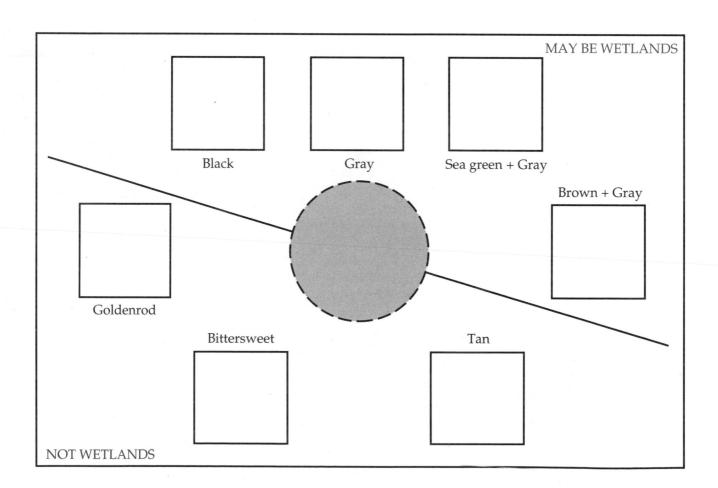

Color Me Wet!

Use Crayola® Crayons to color in the squares on the chart below. It is very important to use the right colors! Press firmly when coloring, unless the name says "light." Cut out the whole chart and paste it to a piece of posterboard or half of a manila folder. Carefully cut out the black circles, through all thicknesses.

Use this color chart when studying soil in the field. Wetland scientists use similar but much more complicated color charts to identify wetland soils. Hold the chart in one hand; in the other hand hold a sample of soil behind the chart, so that it is visible through one of the holes. Your soil sample may contain bits of rock, organic material, and mineral concentrations. You must key out only the dominant soil color and ignore all other materials. Move the sample around until you find one or two colors that nearly match or approximate the dominant color.

Numbers 1, 5, 6, 9, 10, 13, 14, 15, 16, and sometimes 2 are probably wetland soils; the others are probably not wetland soils. Any soil with a basic (matrix) color that is a shade of dark brown, black, or gray may be a wetland soil. You will probably see other colors and materials within the matrix soil color. These colorful streaks may be the result of certain minerals. They appear as shades of red, orange, and yellow (associated with iron in the soil), or black (associated with manganese, not to be confused with dark organic material). These areas are good indicators of seasonal wetlands and other wetlands that are not always wet. Do not use these color mottles to key out the soil, but recognize that they are an additional indicator of wetland conditions.

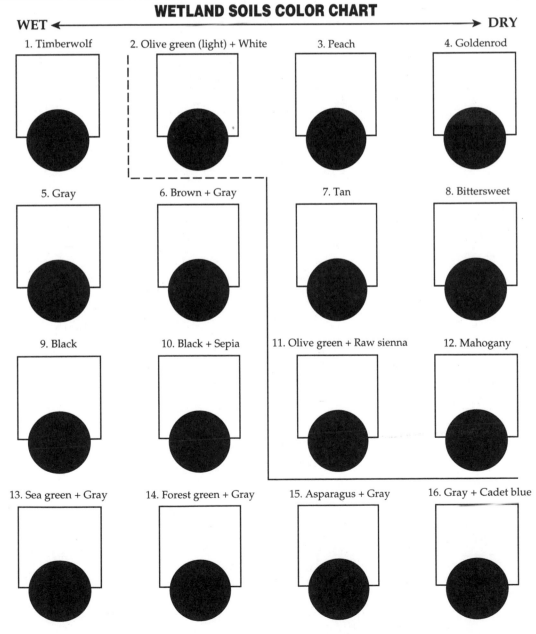

WETLAND SOILS COLOR CHART

WET ←——————————————————————————————→ DRY

1. Timberwolf   2. Olive green (light) + White   3. Peach   4. Goldenrod

5. Gray   6. Brown + Gray   7. Tan   8. Bittersweet

9. Black   10. Black + Sepia   11. Olive green + Raw sienna   12. Mahogany

13. Sea green + Gray   14. Forest green + Gray   15. Asparagus + Gray   16. Gray + Cadet blue

Key to Soil Texture by Feel

Begin at the place marked "Start" and follow the flow chart by answering the questions, until you identify the soil sample.

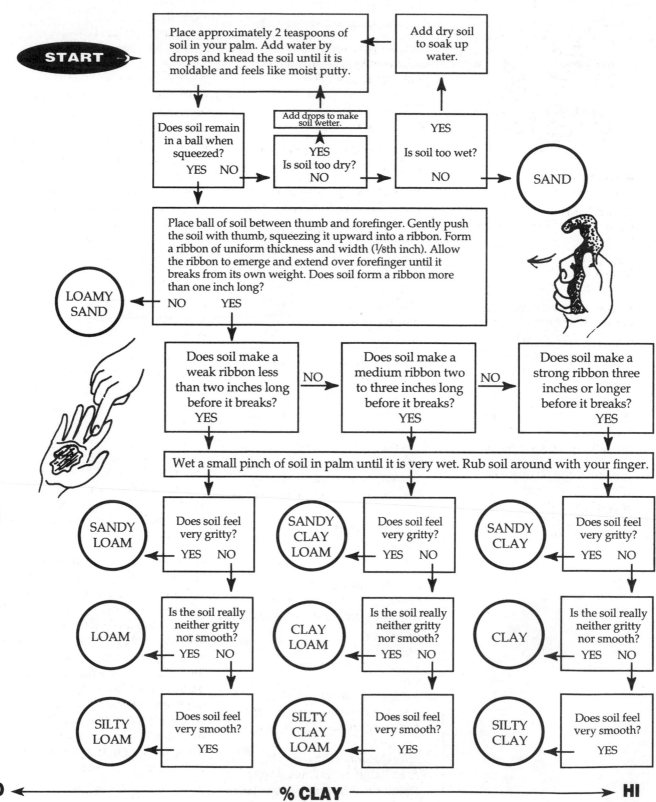

START

Place approximately 2 teaspoons of soil in your palm. Add water by drops and knead the soil until it is moldable and feels like moist putty.

Add dry soil to soak up water.

Does soil remain in a ball when squeezed? YES   NO

Add drops to make soil wetter.

YES Is soil too dry? NO

YES Is soil too wet? NO

SAND

Place ball of soil between thumb and forefinger. Gently push the soil with thumb, squeezing it upward into a ribbon. Form a ribbon of uniform thickness and width (1/8th inch). Allow the ribbon to emerge and extend over forefinger until it breaks from its own weight. Does soil form a ribbon more than one inch long? NO   YES

LOAMY SAND

Does soil make a weak ribbon less than two inches long before it breaks? YES

NO

Does soil make a medium ribbon two to three inches long before it breaks? YES

NO

Does soil make a strong ribbon three inches or longer before it breaks? YES

Wet a small pinch of soil in palm until it is very wet. Rub soil around with your finger.

HI

% SAND

LO

SANDY LOAM — Does soil feel very gritty? YES   NO

SANDY CLAY LOAM — Does soil feel very gritty? YES   NO

SANDY CLAY — Does soil feel very gritty? YES   NO

LOAM — Is the soil really neither gritty nor smooth? YES   NO

CLAY LOAM — Is the soil really neither gritty nor smooth? YES   NO

CLAY — Is the soil really neither gritty nor smooth? YES   NO

SILTY LOAM — Does soil feel very smooth? YES

SILTY CLAY LOAM — Does soil feel very smooth? YES

SILTY CLAY — Does soil feel very smooth? YES

LO ←——— % CLAY ———→ HI

How Thirsty Is the Ground?

Grade Level
3-12

Subject Area
Earth Science, Environmental Science

Duration
30 minutes in class;
60 minutes outdoors

Setting
Classroom and outside

Skills
Gathering, organizing, analyzing, interpreting information

Charting the Course
"Do You Dig Wetland Soil?" provides an excellent background for this activity. "Nature's Filter" examines how wetland soils filter out impurities.

Vocabulary
permeability, infiltration, percolation, porosity

Summary
How does the ground drink?

Students perform percolation tests on different types of soil and compare results.

Objectives
Students will:

- predict and test permeability of different types of soil.

- relate makeup of the soil and use of the area to permeability.

- analyze this information to explain how some wetlands are formed.

- consider oxygen levels of wetland soils versus well-drained soils.

Materials
- *small bag of plain clay cat litter; blender (Blend the litter to a fine powder. You will need about 2 cups, but make enough to do this experiment twice, in case of error.*
- *1 cup of fine soil*
- *sand (from garden shop)*
- *3 same-size, clear, tall drinking glasses, or wide-mouth pint mason jars*
- *measuring cups*
- *3 paper cups*
- *mixing bowl*

For each small group:
- *6 clear, plastic 16-ounce soda or drinking water containers with caps*
- *funnel*
- *jug of water*
- *watch with second hand*
- *ruler*
- *waterproof marker*
- *3 equal-size tin cans (coffee cans or large vegetable cans work well)*
- *can opener*
- *several sturdy sticks*
- *How Thirsty Is the Ground? and Percolation Rate Chart student pages*

- *clipboard*
- *pencil*
- *calculator (optional)*
- *scales; oven (optional)*

Making Connections
Most students have observed water seeping into the ground. They may have noticed that water seeps, or percolates, into some soils faster than others. A percolation test is a routine step in the process of developing property, and an understanding of soil permeability is important. Soil permeability is a key factor in the formation of wetlands.

Background
Review the information on wetland soils in "Do You Dig Wetland Soil?"

Soils are comprised of many materials including organic matter, pieces of rock, and mineral deposits. Two of the most common components of soil are sand and clay. The mixture, by percentage, of these materials usually determines the porosity of a given soil, because the size and shape of soil particles determine the amount of space that air and water can move through.

Water typically percolates (moves down through the soil) faster in soils that are mostly sand than in soils that are mostly clay. Sand particles are fairly large and irregularly shaped, so there are lots of large pore spaces between them for water to trickle through. Clay particles are finer and lie closer together, so there are smaller spaces for water to move through. In addition, wet clay particles realign, filling in the pore spaces even more.

Simple percolation tests can assess the permeability of soil. The tests determine if the ground is already saturated with water or if the soil will allow water to infiltrate (penetrate the surface) and percolate. Permeability is the rate at which water percolates through the soil. In general, the slower the percolation rate, the less permeable the ground. Soil that drains quickly is usually not wetland soil, although sandy soils near the water table are sometimes an exception.

Wetlands usually form in areas where the soil is saturated for long periods of time, or where the soil is impermeable or poorly drained. For example, saturated clay soils often dry to form an impermeable layer called hardpan. This hardpan causes additional water to remain "perched" near or on the ground's surface, and can lead to the development of a wetland. Similarly, a high water table (one near the surface of the ground) can saturate subsoils enough to slow or stop surface-water percolation, a situation that favors wetland formation.

The pore spaces in soil near the surface of the ground and several feet above the water table are usually occupied by air and some moisture. When water from precipitation or runoff percolates into the soil, air is forced out. Water occupies the pore spaces previously filled by air. This creates an anaerobic condition in the soil, at least until the water percolates through the soil and air moves back into the pore spaces. The longer the precipitation or runoff continues, the longer the period of low-oxygen conditions.

Well-drained soils (e.g., soils well above the ground-water table, or porous soils) usually experience only short periods of low-oxygen conditions (several minutes to a few days). On the other hand, wetland soils, which are usually near the water table or not very porous, often experience long periods of low-oxygen conditions (a few days to several weeks). Anaerobic conditions produce physical, chemical, and biological reactions that ultimately lead to related changes in wetland soil, plants, and animals.

Procedure
Warm Up
Show students a cup of sand and a cup of fine soil. Ask students which one would allow water to percolate faster. Ask them to explain their answers.

The Activity
Part I

1. **Conduct the following demonstration to compare the percolation rates of some "homemade" soil compositions. Mix the ground litter well with the sand in these volumes:**

Sample one: ¾ cup sand + ¼ cup clay

Sample two: ½ cup sand + ½ cup clay

Sample three: ¼ cup sand + ¾ cup clay

2. **Place the mixtures in separate glasses or jars. Do not pack the mixtures down, but jiggle the containers to settle the "soil".**

3. **Pour ½ cup of water into each of the paper cups. Have students pour the water into the glasses of soil at exactly the same time. They should watch for bubbling during the percolation. Explain that the water forces oxygen out of the soil, creating the anaerobic condition that makes wetlands unique. Note how long it takes for all of the water to percolate down into the mixtures. (It should take about 5 minutes to see which sample percolates fastest; another 5 minutes or so for all of the water to percolate.) Discuss reasons why sample one percolates fastest and sample three percolates slowest.**

Water percolation through the various sand/clay mixtures.

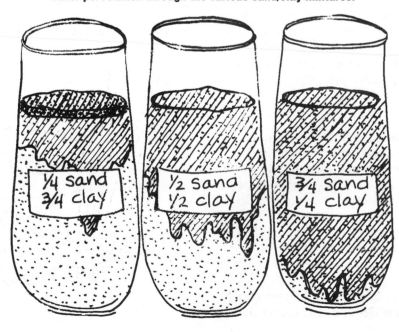

¼ sand
¾ clay

½ sand
½ clay

¾ sand
¼ clay

4. **Have students describe the appearance of sample two and sample three after a few minutes.** Did anything surprising happen in that time? The water may have seemed to stop percolating, and a thin layer of solid clay may have formed at the top, blocking the water.

5. **Explain what happens to clay as water passes through it.** The wet clay at the top of samples two and three made it harder for the water to pass through. In fact, the clay became almost impermeable. Even after all of the water soaked into the soil, it may have travelled only part of the way down the glass (the soil in sample one could be wet all the way to the "bedrock" at the bottom of the glass). This is a common occurrence in clay soils that become saturated; the impermeable clay layer, or hardpan, causes water to remain standing on the surface, eventually creating a wetland.

6. **Ask students which soil is most typical of wetlands.** In both level areas and depressions, soils that allow very slow or no percolation are more likely to support wetland formation. Everything else being equal, clay soils, or significantly compacted soils, will form wetlands more readily. Regardless of soil makeup, shale or bedrock just below the ground's surface can act like clay, retaining water to form wetlands.

7. **Just for fun, pour another ¼ cup of water on each of the samples to duplicate rain's effect on saturated wetlands. What happens?**
Note: Each sand/clay mixture may be dried out and used again a few weeks later.

Part II

Note: Read through How Thirsty Is the Ground? student pages before class begins.

1. **Measure a depth of exactly 2 inches (5 cm) in one of the tin cans and pour water to that level. Funnel that water into one of the plastic bottles and mark the water level on the bottle. This is the premeasured 2 inches of water for the outdoor percolation test. Repeat this procedure, filling and marking all six water bottles in this fashion. Now, remove the bottoms from all tin cans.**

2. **At or near a wetland site, divide the class into small groups. Choose students in each group to be "pourer," "timer," and "recorder" (or, you may choose to do this as a class, if the group is small).**

3. **Give each group a copy of the student pages. Review the instructions and procedures, and explain each column in the chart on the data sheet as well as the calculations. (For grades 3-4, use a stopwatch to time the percolation, then compare times for each site; omit the chart and calculations.) Test the permeability of the ground in six different level areas:**

a) ground that is bare and compacted (a path or play area);

b) a grassy area that gets little use;

c) a forest area where there is leaf litter (brush the litter away), or near shrubs in a landscaped area;

d) a muddy spot (wetland edge);

e) a paved area; and

f) sandy ground, if available, or a sandbox or small pile of purchased sand.

4. **Divide the test sites between the groups so that two groups together will have a complete set of results to share at the end of the testing. Each group will need a watch, a ruler, and three cans and should be performing two or three trials at each of the three sites. Have students practice the coordination of timing and pouring, if needed. Be sure students perform the tests on level ground, since slopes are usually well-drained. Using both student pages, conduct the tests.**

5. **When students have completed the percolation tests at each compacted site, have them pour some water directly onto the ground and ask them to describe what happens.** If a gully begins to form as the soil washes away, note that this demonstrates

erosion. Students will not be able to get a can into the paved surface, and the water will wash right off. This is a simple demonstration of runoff.

6. **After each percolation test, have students dig under the cans with sticks to investigate the substrate. What do they see?**

Wrap Up

Have the students compare their test results. More advanced students should graph their results. Percolation rate should be expressed as inches (or centimeters) per minute or hour. The sandy area will likely percolate the fastest, followed by forest/garden area, the grassy area, the muddy area, and the compacted area. The paved area will not allow water to permeate at all.

Note: Though you are extrapolating the percolation rates to X number of inches per hour, and the percolation rate may be dozens or even hundreds of inches per hour, explain that the soils would not be able to maintain this rate for an entire hour.

Assessment

Have students:

- compare the permeability of different soil types and predict the permeability of soil based on soil type.

- describe soil types commonly found in wetlands.

Extensions

Advanced students may calculate the volume (V) of water needed to fill the can to two inches. Use the formula for the volume of a cylinder: $V = \pi r^2 h$, where $\pi = 3.14$, "r" is the radius of the container, and "h" is the height of the water in the container.

To compare the amount of water present in various soil samples, collect soil from several areas (such as the six areas listed in the student page). Record the "wet weight" of each sample immediately after it is dug out of the ground. Dry samples thoroughly (possibly bake at low heat); weigh again (dry weight). All weight loss is due to water loss through evaporation. Calculate the amount of water that evaporated (wet weight minus dry weight equals water weight); 1 gram (.035 oz.) equals 1 milliliter (.061 cubic inches). Calculate the percentage of weight that was due to water (weight loss divided by wet weight).

Nature in Your Neighborhood

Test the soil around your neighborhood. Are there spots that are more permeable than others? Why? Find a heavily traveled path or play area. Watch the ground during a rainstorm. What happens to the rain when it hits the ground there? What happens to the soil?

Many communities have covered walking trails and playgrounds with mulch (chopped wood). Since mulch is a permeable material, rainwater is less likely to run off of ground's surface to flood nearby streets and waterways. Mulch also helps keep the soil from washing away.

Is there a place in your neighborhood that needs mulch? Work with your classmates, teachers, parents, and local officials to improve these areas—they will look better, and you will be helping to clean up your environment!

How Thirsty Is the Ground?
Measuring Percolation Rate of Different Soil Types

1. Before you begin, look over the accompanying chart so that you are aware of all of the data you must gather. As a group, predict how quickly you think the same amount of water will percolate into the soil at each site. Which site will allow the fastest percolation? Which will be slowest? Will any sites be impermeable? Why?

   Record your predictions in the left margin of the chart with the fastest labeled "1", and so forth.

   Perform the test at what you think will be the slowest site first. At each site, repeat the test in two different spots with the same type of ground. To save time, run the trials at the same time.

2. At your first site, choose a flat, level spot. Clear away leaves, etc. Twist a can into the soil to sink it in the soil up to 2 inches (5 cm). (If the ground is hard, do not bend the can. Just sink it as far as you can or hold it firmly down on the surface.)

3. The timer should get ready. Begin timing as the pourer pours the water from the plastic bottle into the can. Record this premeasured water level (two inches) in the chart column marked **Beginning Water Level**. Record the **Start Time** in your chart (for example, "twelve-o-three and six seconds" is written as 12:03:06).

4. When all of the water has disappeared, stop timing and record the **Finish Time**. Record the **Ending Water Level** as "0." If the water in the can has not drained within 10 minutes, stop timing and measure the remaining water in the can using the ruler. Record **Ending Water Level** with a **Finish Time** of 10 minutes.

5. Record the **Number of Inches or Centimeters Drained** (subtract **Beginning Water Level** from **Ending Water Level**). Where did the water go? Be specific.

6. Now move to the next site. Change jobs (timer, etc.). Perform your trials, using the same procedure as at the first site. Pour the same amount of water into the can. Continue to the net test site. Make sure that all data gathered have been entered in your chart.

7. After doing all tests, complete your chart by performing these calculations.

   • Total Percolation Time (in minutes) equals Finish Time minus Start Time (in minutes). Round to the nearest quarter minute.

   • Average Percolation Time equals total percolation time from all trials divided by number of trials.

   • Average Percolation Rate may be calculated as follows:

   Number of Inches or Centimeters drained per minute = $\dfrac{\text{\# inches or cm drained}}{\text{Average Perc. Time, in minutes}}$ Convert seconds to minutes: $\dfrac{\text{\# inches or cm}}{\text{sec.}} \times \dfrac{60 \text{ sec.}}{\text{min.}} = \dfrac{\text{inches or cm}}{\text{min.}}$

   If the **Average Percolation Time** was more than one minute, you may want to convert minutes to hours:

   $\dfrac{\text{\# inches or cm}}{\text{min.}} \times \dfrac{60 \text{ min.}}{\text{hour}} = \dfrac{\text{in. or cm}}{\text{hour}}$ An example: 2 in./15 sec. X 60 sec./min. = 8 in./min.

   8 in./min. X 60 min./hour = 480 in./hour

8. On the right side of the page, number the sites according to the actual percolation rate, with fastest shown as "#1," and so forth.

   Now, answer these questions:

   a.) How do your predictions compare with your results?_____
   Do you think that your results are accurate? Why or why not? (Think about the condition of the ground.)_____
   _____
   Were you able to calculate the percolation rate for the bare or paved areas?_____
   The water may have run out quickly, but what can you say about infiltration and the percolation rate?_____
   _____
   b.) Which area represents a wetland?_____
   Even though it was already saturated, did some of the water still penetrate into the ground? _____
   Wetlands act like sponges. Even when saturated, they can take in more water if some is released first._____
   c.) At the compacted site, what happened to the ground around the can?_____

   What do you think would happen on the compacted ground when it rains?_____
   Compare this to what you predict would happen in the garden or sandy area._____
   _____

How Thirsty Is the Ground?

Measuring Percolation Rate

Important: At each site, do the test at least twice (three times is best) to be certain that your data is accurate (see column labeled "Trial #").

Site	Trial #	Beginning Water Level	Ending Water Level	# of Inches or Centimeters Drained	Start Time	Finish Time	Total Perc. Time (in min. or sec.)	Average Perc. Time (in min. or sec.)	Average Percolation Rate inches (cm)/min.	Average Percolation Rate inches (cm)/hour
Bare and compacted	1									
	2									
	3									
Grassy, not used	1									
	2									
	3									
Forest or garden	1									
	2									
	3									
Muddy (wetland)	1									
	2									
	3									
Paved	1									
	2									
	3									
Sandy	1									
	2									
	3									
Example		2 in.	0 in.	2 in.	2:20:00	2:20:15	15 sec.	(average of trials)	8 in./min.	(480 in./hr.)

A Rottin' Experiment

[Composter design courtesy of Bottle Biology Project, University of Wisconsin-Madison, 1630 Linden Dr., Madison, WI 53706; 608-263-5645. Funded by the National Science Foundation.]

Grade Level
2-12

Subject Areas
Biology, Ecology, Environmental Science

Duration
A few weeks

Setting
Classroom

Skills
Gathering, organizing, analyzing, interpreting, and applying information

Charting the Course
"Nature's Recyclers" provides good preactivity background information on decomposition. An experiment in "People of the Bog" highlights the relationship between decomposition and anaerobic soil conditions. "Wetland Weirdos" takes a look at plants' adaptations to anaerobic conditions. (See parts of chapters 2 and 4 for more information.)

Vocabulary
decomposition, anaerobic, compost

Summary

How is soil affected when it is saturated with water?

Your class will construct compost bins that contain different levels of oxygen and water to observe the effects on the decay of organic matter and the growth of plants.

Objectives

Students will:

• understand how soil saturation affects the processes of decomposition and plant growth.

• describe conditions that promote decomposition.

Materials

• *slices of bread*
• *small plastic bags*
• *clear drinking glass or glass jar*
• *a small amount of sand*
• *9 plastic 2-liter beverage bottles*
• *marker*
• *knife or razor blade*
• *scissors*
• *hot water, or candle with matches*
• *pliers*
• *sewing needles*
• *clear tape*
• *netting or mesh fabric*
• *rubber bands*
• *shredded newspaper*
• *measuring cup*
• *food and lawn scraps*
• *bucket and shovel or shredded mulch from a garden shop*
• *2 small potted plants*
• *watering can full of water*

Making Connections

Composting, recycling, and waste disposal have become prominent conservation issues. Students are probably aware of these topics, but unaware of the processes of decomposition and composting in wetland conditions. Is the smell of a wetland familiar to them? How or when? The exercise of simulating and observing conditions that make wetlands unique not only demonstrates the process of decomposition, but also the importance of reducing the waste load in landfills.

Background

The process of decomposition requires oxygen. The organic topsoil found near a log is formed by decomposition that took place above the surface of the soil, where oxygen is readily available. Organic wetland soil is not formed by decomposition, but by the accumulation of organic material. In anaerobic wetland conditions, organic material does not break down, or does so very slowly. In northern peat bogs, the anaerobic and very acidic peat actually preserves buried plant and animal matter. *National Geographic* magazine has published articles on this subject, including one about the perfectly preserved body of an ancient man found in a peat bog—he still even had his hair!

Wetland soil below the first few inches is anaerobic because it is saturated with water all or part of the time. Oxygen is not available to plants or decomposers because the pore spaces in the soil are taken up by water molecules, leaving little or no room for oxygen molecules. Oxygen diffuses more readily across air than across water, so there is little chance of plants extracting oxygen from the water.

Plants that are not adapted to saturated soil conditions will die when the soil below them is flooded, just as houseplants die when they are overwatered. In a pond created by a beaver dam, or at a river with banks constantly inundated by water, trees and other plants soon die from flooded conditions.

Wetland plants, on the other hand, have adapted to life in anaerobic, saturated soils. These plants are able to transport oxygen from their leaves, through their stems, and down to their roots. Many wetland plants also have shallow, spreading roots which can take some oxygen from the more aerobic surface soil.

Procedure

Warm Up

Ask students if they compost their garbage at home. If any do, ask them to describe what happens to the food items in the compost pile.

Discuss factors that make the food decay and decompose. Explain that microscopic bacteria and fungi are two types of decomposers that turn dead plants and animals into compost.

Show students a fresh piece of bread in a plastic bag, and one that is moldy, also stored in a plastic bag. Explain that one was kept in the refrigerator, and one was stored on top of it. Which one do they think was stored in the fridge? Why?

Next ask students to think of conditions that allow mold to grow. List these conditions on the board. Make sure the list includes dampness, presence of oxygen, and heat. Heat made the unrefrigerated bread "sweat" inside the plastic bag. Because the atmosphere inside the bag was both warm and moist, the bread molded quickly. Inside the refrigerator, the temperature was cold enough to keep mold and bacteria at bay.

Explain that moisture, air, light, temperature, bacteria and fungi sources, and the nature of the decomposing material are all important variables in the composting process. Soft food items will decompose faster than twigs and bark. The compost must be warm and moist for the decomposing bacteria to survive. Composting materials produce their own heat, and the added warmth in the compost bin furthers the process of decomposition.

Explain that the class will set up an experiment to see which conditions are the best for composting organic matter. Part of this experiment will illustrate conditions in wetland soil.

The Activity
Part I

1. **Divide the class into three groups and have each group make one of three composter bins (the control, the "wetland," or the aerobic environment) as follows:** For each composter, remove the labels from three bottles, and the black plastic bases from two of the bottles. Cut the

bottles as illustrated. Cover the mouth of the bottle that hangs upside down with mesh, securing it tightly with a rubber band. Assemble the bins. For ventilation, poke air holes into the plastic with a needle heated with a candle flame or very hot water. (Hold the needles with pliers during the heating process.) As shown in the diagram, cut four ½-inch-square (1 cm²) holes with a knife or razor blade; tape mesh over the holes. Do this for each composter.

2. **Have students refer to the list they made in the Warm Up. What things on the list promote decomposition? Which are characteristic of a wetland?**

3. **Describe wetland conditions. Do students think saturated soil conditions will speed up or hinder decomposition? If water fills up all the spaces between soil particles, what can't get in?** To illustrate this, fill the glass or jar half full of sand and pour water to the top. What do students see bubbling out of the sand? Air bubbles! Explain that saturated soil does not allow room for air (oxygen).

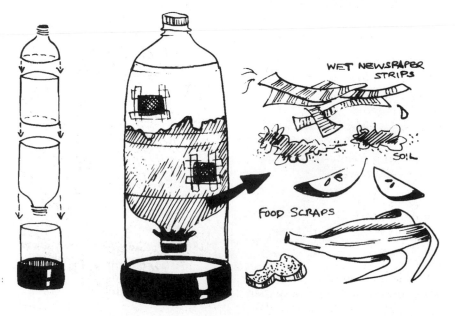

4. Ask students how they could set up an experiment to test whether saturated soil decomposes differently than wet soil that has room for oxygen. What if they put one bottle with wet materials in a sunny spot and kept another bottle with wet soil in a closet, but shook it once in a while to disperse oxygen? If the first bottle got moldy and the second didn't, could they be sure it was only saturated conditions that caused the mold to grow? Since you are studying wetlands, you are interested in the effects of soil saturation. The effects of light and temperature, therefore, are not the most important factors to test at this time. This means that temperature and the amount of light should be kept constant (the same for all three test bins). Organic materials decompose in the presence of light. Therefore, the composters should be kept in the light. You know from the bread discussion that decomposing organisms favor warmer temperatures. You should, then, keep the composters in a warm place (the classroom is probably warm enough; the windowsill may prove a bit warmer if sunlight hits there). The experimental variables, then, are the amounts of *moisture* and *oxygen*.

5. Ask students how they could add oxygen to saturated soil. Explain that as water flows over rapids, it gets oxygenated as it is churned up (the air mixes with water). Inform them that shaking and mixing actions add air (oxygen) to water.

6. Give each group equal amounts of shredded newspaper. Have them do the following:

• *Constants*

Sprinkle the same amount of water on each pile of newspaper to wet it well, then put each pile into one of the composters. Dig up a bucket of soil or use purchased shredded mulch. Measure two cups of soil or mulch for each composter. Add the soil to the composters and shake well to mix.

Collect garbage such as pieces of apple, bits of bread, chips, candy-coated nuts, grass clippings, leaves, twigs, etc. Students can make contributions from their lunches. Do not use any meat or bones. Make sure each composter gets exactly the same types and quantities of each of these organic materials. Push each item down into the soil mixture and press it against the plastic for observation. On the outside of each composter, attach small labels next to each item so that identification will be easier when composting progresses. Mark the date on each composter.

• *Variables*

Composter #1, The control: Sprinkle the compost regularly with just enough water to keep it moist at all times.

Composter #2, The "wetland": Saturate the compost with enough water to fill all spaces between particles. Keep the compost completely saturated at all times.

Composter #3, Oxygen added: Add the same amount of water as in the second composter, but shake vigorously each day to mix in oxygen.

7. Have students predict which composter will work the fastest. Why? Formulate hypotheses (example: too much water, and consequently not enough oxygen, will slow the composting process). Record the predictions and hypotheses for later reference.

8. Set the composters aside. The amount of time it takes for any visible decay will be different for each material. In general, it will take at least a week or two. You should be able to see changes through the plastic. Have students check the composters every day or every other day until changes are visible. Record these changes. Once the process has visibly begun, check every day until the items are no longer recognizable. More advanced students can assign a numerical value to each stage of decay, based on a scale of 0 to 10:

0 = no change
1 = first sign of mold or change
↓
10 = complete decay

Have students graph their data using a different color for each composter. Put the days on the horizontal axis of the graph, and the 0-10 scale on the vertical axis.

Part II

1. At the time that the composters are set up, present the two potted plants as the second part of the

experiment. Is soil condition important to plant growth? Why? (Plants take oxygen and nutrients in through their roots, which grow down through the soil.) Predict what will happen when one of the plants is given too much water.

2. **Water one of the plants every other day, or just enough to keep the soil moist. Keep the soil of the other plant completely saturated by giving it a lot of water every day. Record what happens to both plants.**

3. **Discuss why plants die when overwatered. Explain that roots cannot get oxygen when the spaces in the soil are filled with water.**

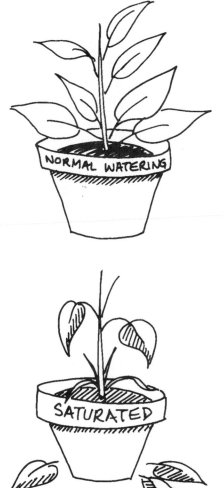

4. **Tell students that certain plants have adapted to survive in saturated wetland soils. Have them suggest how.** Through special adaptations these plants transport oxygen from their leaves to their roots.

Wrap Up

Have students summarize the results of the composting experiment. Under which conditions did the compost decompose the slowest? Why? (The saturated composter had little or no oxygen—it was anaerobic and decomposition was therefore very slow. The oxygen in the control and aerated composters promoted faster decomposition.)

Discuss the factors that "shake up" or mix soil in nature. (Earthworms, sow bugs, moles, and lots of other critters do! These organisms do not live in saturated wetland soil, because they can't breathe in such wet conditions.)

The saturated composter exemplified slow decomposition in saturated wetland soil. If organic material decomposes so slowly in a wetland, what happens over time as more and more material (leaf litter, etc.) falls to the ground or washes into the wetland? (The organic material accumulates, forming a thick layer of slowly-decaying organic soil or peat. In a salt marsh, for example, the accumulation of organic matter helps build up and expand the marsh, creating more habitat for animals, more surface area for food production, and so on.)

Assessment

Have students:

• describe conditions that promote decomposition.

• assemble an experiment that compares decomposition in saturated and aerated soils.

• explain why a regular houseplant may not survive in wetland soils.

Extensions

Two *National Geographic* articles, "Mysteries of the Bog" and "Life-like Man Preserved 2,000 Years in Peat" may be of interest to your students (see Resources, below).

If you have a beaver pond in your area, take your students to see it. The sight of standing dead trees is quite dramatic.

Use the composters again to compare the rate of breakdown of human-made items to natural materials. Use small pieces of paper products, plastic, aluminum soda can rings, cloth, rubber bands, etc. Do these materials decompose at all, even with oxygen?

Have students apply what they've learned to conditions in a landfill dump. We have shown that saturation in a wetland causes anaerobic conditions in the soil. A landfill can also become anaerobic. It is difficult for oxygen to permeate through an enormous amount of compacted garbage. Without oxygen, the organic materials will not decompose. What happens when the trash and garbage in our landfills does not break down? (It piles up until we have to find yet another place to put it.) Can students suggest some ways to solve this problem? (We can all be more careful about what we throw away. We can recycle and reuse nonbiodegradable products and compost garbage for reuse as garden fertilizer. The class can begin by monitoring trash disposal in your classroom. How much paper, plastic, and food wastes are students throwing away? How can they cut down on these quantities? (Try using both sides of paper and sending it to a recycling center instead of to the landfill. Seal lunch items in reusable containers rather than in disposable products.) Can students think of more ways to reduce trash?

Nature in Your Neighborhood

Can you make soil? Compost kitchen and yard wastes at home! Make a small indoor composter like the one in this activity, or make a larger one for your yard.

With the help of an adult, remove the bottom from an old metal or plastic garbage can. Find a permanent spot for it in your yard. Put damp grass clippings, leaves, shredded newspaper, and soil in the bottom to start the process. Then add food scraps and other organic garbage. Remember, no meat, bones, or other animal products. Leave the lid off or cut lots of quarter-sized holes in the lid so the pile can get oxygen. Use a big stick or a shovel to stir your compost once a week or so to aerate it. With frequent aeration, your compost will have little odor. As the materials decompose, you will see that new soil is forming in the bottom of the compost bin!

Help your neighbors make their own composters, or ask them to contribute to yours! This will help cut down on the amount of garbage you send to the landfill. After a few months, you can use the rich soil you have created to plant a beautiful garden for all to enjoy!

Resources

Levanthes, Louise. March 1987. "Mysteries of the Bog." *National Geographic*.

Glob, P. V. March 1954. Life-like Man Preserved 2,000 Years In Peat. *National Geographic*.

Notes:

Nature's Filter

[Adapted from "Soil Filtration" in ECO: A Handbook of Classroom Ideas to Motivate the Teaching of Elementary Ecology by Charles Hamilton, Educational Service, Inc., 1974. Available from Educational Service, Inc., P.O. Box 219, Stevensville, MI 49127.]

Grade Level
K-3 as a demonstration, 4-12 as a team or individual project

Subject Areas
Earth Science

Duration
40-50 minutes, plus preparation (may be assigned as homework)

Setting
Classroom, with potential for outdoor soil collection as a class

Skills
Gathering and analyzing information

Charting the Course
"How Thirsty Is the Ground?" provides an excellent review of soil permeability. "Wetland in a Pan," "Treatment Plants," and "Water Purifiers" ask students to examine other ways wetlands clean water through filtering actions.

Vocabulary
filter, pollution, sediments, percolation

Summary

Students test the filtering ability of several types of soil.

Objectives

Students will describe the ability of wetland soils to filter pollutants from water.

Materials

- a coffee filter
- clear plastic cup
- bags or other containers for collecting soil
- half-gallon samples of several soil types (e.g., sand, clay, gravel, loam, humus from a forest or garden)
- a nail
- large funnel
- 5 aluminum pans
- scissors
- water
- 5 1-gallon plastic bottles (punch many small holes in the bottom of each plastic bottle with a nail; cut off the top of each; see diagram, p. 251)
- 5 clear glass containers

Making Connections

Wetlands are vital to water quality, since they filter out pollutants in several ways. Students who understand this will better appreciate the value of maintaining and protecting wetlands.

Background

As water passes through soil, suspended particles are filtered out. The makeup of the soil determines how well it will act as a filter. For instance, a sieve with large holes will trap only particles that are larger than the holes. A coffee filter which has very tiny pore spaces will filter out very fine particles. Likewise, finer-textured soil with small pore spaces will trap more sizes of "pollutants" than course-textured, loosely packed soil. If flowing water is slowed, as it is in wetlands, it is more likely to penetrate the surface of the ground and percolate down through the soil. The slower the percolation, the greater the filtration.

The percolation rate of wetland soil is usually fairly slow, one reason the area is a wetland. Water stays near the ground's surface longer. (See "How Thirsty Is the Ground?" p. 239.) As polluted runoff slowly percolates through wetland soil, many particles are trapped within the soil or chemically bound to the minerals in the soil. These pollutants are therefore stored in the soil, even if temporarily, and cleaner water flows on to the body of water beyond the wetland.

Procedure

Warm Up

Show students a clear plastic cup filled with muddied, sandy water. Ask if they would drink this water. Ask how they would remove the sediments from the water. Show them a coffee filter as a hint.

The Activity

1. **Take the class on a short field trip to collect soil samples, or assign the collection as homework (as appropriate to age level). Collect sand, clay, gravel, loam, and humus.** (Loam is a mixture of sand, silt, and clay; humus, made of decomposed plants and animals, is the rich, organic soil in the top few inches of a forest floor or garden.)

2. **Fill each plastic bottle half-full**

of one type of soil. Ask students what will happen when water is poured into the soil samples. What quality of water will drain from the bottles? Hold each bottle over an empty aluminum pan and pour water on the soil. Collect the drainage in the aluminum tray and use the funnel to transfer drainage from each sample to the five glass containers. Compare the clarity of the five samples.

Ask students to describe natural situations where this would occur. Explain that rain can wash loose soil off construction sites, bare spots in lawns, plowed farmland, etc. This process of erosion eventually washes soil into waterways. Adding sediments to waterways clouds the water, choking fish and other animals and blocking sunlight that plants need for growth. Erosion also makes our drinking water harder to clean up and can eventually fill in waterways.

Ask students how we can clean up the muddy water that is washing off the land. (We can reduce the amount of loose soil by limiting construction or exercising greater care in our building, agricultural, and gardening practices.)

3. Pour drainage samples back into their respective soil samples and observe what happens. Repeat several times (record the number of times). If there is still muddy water left from other samples, see if it clears up when poured through the best filter. Does the water eventually become clear? Which soil filtered the water best? Ask students to discuss why some soil samples filtered better than others. The class may decide that samples with fine, loosely-packed particles or

tangled roots are better filters than coarse, loosely packed samples.

Wrap Up

Have students summarize what they've learned about the various soil types' filtering ability. Note that filtering can occur in any place where there is time for water to penetrate and percolate into the soil. When runoff is allowed to rest in one place, as in a wetlands, pollutants will gradually pass through the soil filter. Wetlands are often the last stop for runoff before it enters waterways. Since pollutants carried in runoff are trapped by wetland plants and soil, cleaner water flows on to the waterway.

Have students list other ways that wetlands clean water (plants help filter out silt and other pollutants; wetlands offer a place for sediment particles to settle).

Assessment

Have students:

• describe the characteristics of soils that retain pollutants best.

• explain why wetlands are good for pollution control.

Extensions

Study wetlands near your school and determine how they might be contributing to pollution control.

Section

Wetlands and People
(culture and issues)

*Activities that focus on the
interactions between humans
and wetlands. Contemporary
social and political issues are
considered, along with
historic and cultural topics.*

Hear Ye! Hear Ye!

Grade Level
3-4 with assistance;
5-12

Subject Areas
Language Arts, English,
Social Studies

Duration
One hour

Setting
Classroom

Skills
Gathering and applying
information

Charting the Course
Try "Hydropoly!" or
"Regulation Rummy" for
other approaches to understanding wetland regula-
tions.

Vocabulary
public hearing

Summary
Hear Ye! Hear Ye! Who has a say about what your community does with wetlands? You do!

Students conduct a mock public hearing to make a group decision on an important project.

Objectives
Students will:

• describe the process of a public hearing.

• analyze some effects of a development on an adjacent wetland.

• weigh factors in a proposed building project and decide whether or not to proceed.

Materials
• *copy of the script for each student*
• *an enlarged copy of the project proposal sketches*
• *any desired props or costumes*

Making Connections
Though the legal process for regulating wetlands accommo-dates public participation, many citizens are unaware of the importance of their role in envi-ronmental decision-making. This introduction to the goings-on at a public hearing may encourage students to attend and participate in this part of the democratic process at some time in their lives. Students will learn that every voice makes a difference.

Background
When someone wants to build on or alter wetland areas, he or she must first apply to both the state and the federal governments for a permit to do the work. Represen-tatives of government agencies will visit the proposed project site, determine where the wetland boundaries lie, and assess the ecological functions and social and wildlife values of the wet-land.

Before each agency makes its final decision on whether or not to issue a permit, the project will go out on public notice. Public notices may be posted in the local newspaper and will be sent to individuals who have placed their names on a mailing list (see chapter 6). If any individual requests it, a hearing will be held to discuss all relevant issues surrounding the project.

At the hearing, involved agencies are represented and their testimo-nies presented. Citizens may sign up to testify or give their views on the project as well. Citizens' statements really matter and will become part of the public record! Points brought out during the hearing will be used by the agencies in decision-making.

Procedure
Warm Up
Give the class a brief background on public hearings. The play in this activity depicts a public hearing on a proposed building project in a wetland. Although the case is fictional, the process of the hearing and the nature of the testimonies are realistic.

Decisions are normally not made at the hearings, but at the end of this hypothetical scenario, stu-dents will discuss the issues and reach a group decision on the project's fate. Although the names of state agencies and their permit requirements differ from state to state, but the ones depicted here are fairly representative.

to make their own recommendations, and there are certainly no right or wrong answers to this activity. However, the goal is to come up with a building plan that does the most good for the greatest number of people *and* the environment—a compromise plan to meet everyone's objectives as fully as possible.

1. *Whenever possible, avoid building in the wetland itself.* For example, move the building and parking lot back from the stream area (see diagram). This would make the walk from the building to the parking lot longer, but it would also save most of the wetland area, protect the stream, and give residents a nice view of wildlife. The building may also need to be a bit smaller. This entire plan would cost less.

2. *Follow agency recommendations to reduce the effects of runoff and erosion.* Install and maintain silt fences during construction; install infiltration trenches to cool and

The Activity

1. **Review the proposal, then assign the roles in the play. Students who do not play a part will represent the hearing audience and take the lead in the final decision-making process as a "hearing committee."**

2. **Have the class perform the hearing as described on the student pages.**

Wrap Up and Action

After the performance, give students time to discuss the case as a group or in small groups, or lead a class discussion. Have students present decisions to the class, including revisions to the proposed project (see Suggested Solutions, below).

Have students attend an actual public hearing. How does it compare to the one they enacted in the classroom?

Suggested Solutions:

Here are some suggested revisions and solutions that will make the project more environmentally sensitive and reduce impacts to the wetland. Most are brought forth in the play, but review them as the final discussion and decision-making process proceeds. Students should be encouraged

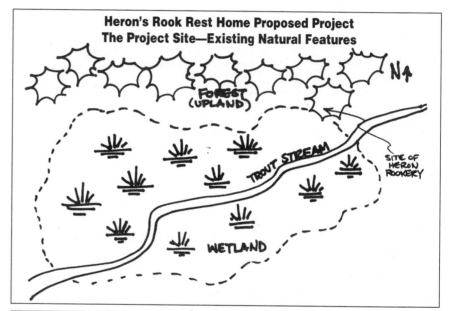

**Heron's Rook Rest Home Proposed Project
The Project Site—Existing Natural Features**

FOREST (UPLAND)

TROUT STREAM

SITE OF HERON ROOKERY

WETLAND

N↑

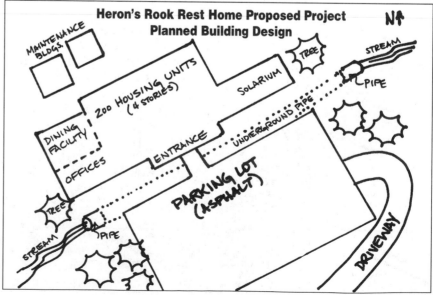

**Heron's Rook Rest Home Proposed Project
Planned Building Design**

N↑

MAINTENANCE BLDGS.

200 HOUSING UNITS (4 STORIES)

SOLARIUM

TREE

STREAM

PIPE

DINING FACILITY

OFFICES

ENTRANCE

UNDERGROUND PIPE

PARKING LOT (ASPHALT)

TREE

STREAM

PIPE

DRIVEWAY

filter runoff before it enters the stream; landscape the area to blend it into the surrounding environment and help filter and slow runoff; to reduce runoff in the parking lot, use gravel or oyster shells instead of pavement (crushed gravel surfaces can be made wheelchair-accessible).

3. *After the building has been completed, develop an interpretive trail around the wetland for community use.* This would allow citizens continued access for fishing, birdwatching, etc. Involve residents of the facility in on-site wetland education programs for area youngsters.

4. *Make the long walk from the parking lot to the building pleasant and educational (see #1).* Landscape it to make it attractive, and build a bridge and boardwalk over the stream and wetland. Install a sign or two along the way to point out natural features such as wildlife habitat.

Assessment

Have students:

• perform character roles in a mock public hearing.

• decide on a solution to an environmental issue based on the proceedings of a public hearing.

• critique the process of the mock public hearing.

Extensions

Place your class on a public notice mailing list by writing to your local U.S. Army Corps of Engineers district office. Look in the government listings (blue pages) of the phone book under "United States Government, Department: Army, Corps of Engineers." You may need to check the book for the nearest large city to find a district office. You must specify the watershed (the area surrounding a particular body of water) in which you are interested.

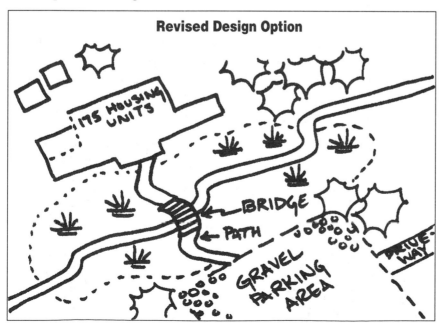

Revised Design Option

stormwater management pond is called for. This would be a basin that collects runoff and allows sediment to settle to the bottom. The sediment would be trapped in the basin, while the cleaner water would flow out through a pipe near the pond's surface.

Ms. Cleanwater: Yes, that's true, but remember that in this case we're talking about a trout stream. Water sitting in a shallow pond like that would heat up quickly. Then we'd have more problems for the fish. A better idea would be to install infiltration trenches. These are basically boxes that are built into the ground. They allow the runoff to filter down into the ground before it gets into the stream. This actually cools the water off and filters out the sediment and pollutants. If the area around the trenches is planted with vegetation to add more filtering ability, then the problem would be well taken care of.

H.O.: Thank you. We should move on now. There are two more federal agencies here tonight.

Mr. Waters: I'm Phil Waters from the Army Corps of Engineers *[clears his throat loudly]*. The Corps is actually the deciding factor, here, for the federal government. We will be issuing or denying the permit under the Clean Water Act. We have not made our decision, as yet, but are taking all of these issues into account, including comments from the public. We will balance the public benefits against the natural resource losses and try to arrive at a fair decision. That's all I have to say for now.

H.O.: And finally, Ms. Powers...

Ms. Powers: Good evening. I am Vee Toh Powers from the U.S. Environmental Protection

Agency, or EPA. For those of you who are not familiar with our role in this process, I will explain. EPA relies on the reports from the Fish and Wildlife Service and National Marine Fisheries for information about the project's impacts on natural resources. We have the ability to override the Corp's decision on the application, and I feel that we would not allow the Corps to issue the permit as it stands. I recommend that the applicant pay careful attention to the recommendations made here tonight. The rest home would be a valuable asset to the community, if the project is managed well with respect to the environment.

H.O.: Thank you, all agency representatives. Now I would like to open the floor to those members of the public who have signed up to speak. May we have the first speaker?

Mr. Gotbucks: I am Ron Gotbucks, the applicant. I felt I should make my presence known. I think everyone knows where I stand on this project. I have a lot of money at stake here. The project was designed this way because I felt that it would remove the hazards posed by the wetland—you know, mosquitoes, bad odor, and so on. But if you all think the marsh has some value, I'm willing to listen to suggestions to improve the project. I have to, or I won't get my permit.

[The crowd chuckles.]

Mr. Nailenhammer: Harry Nailenhammer, here. I'm the builder, hired by Mr. Gotbucks. I need to know what I'm supposed to be responsible for in this project. These safeguards you're talking about could cost a lot of money and time. I need to keep costs down for my client. I already counted on putting up silt fences

to catch the eroding soil—that's common practice for my people. I need to know where it's okay to cut down trees and where I can and can't drive my equipment.

Mr. and Mrs. Sellers: We're the current owners of the property in question. We've agreed to sell the land to Mr. Gotbucks. We were going to give the property to our daughter, but she was transferred to another state for her work. We can't afford to pay taxes on the land, and we need the money from the sale for our retirement. If Mr. Gotbucks doesn't get his permits, he won't buy the land, and we'll be stuck!

Ms. Socialcause: I'm Louise Socialcause and I work for the state's Bureau of Economic Development. Frankly, I think we can't afford not to have this rest home built! The housing situation for the elderly in this area is poor. With this new facility, we'll have a better draw for more types of people to the area, which also means more consumers and a better economy. And think of all the visitors who will come here to see their loved ones and spend some money while they're here! It's something we've needed for a long time.

Mrs. Nimby: I'm Helen Nimby. I live in the adjoining community. I have two small children. The traffic in our area is bad enough as it is. Bringing more people to the area will worsen the situation. I moved here to give my kids a nice, quiet lifestyle. Now I'm worried about them getting hit by a car! And I know how long these construction projects take. We'll have noisy tractors and such disturbing us for months! What do I say to this project? Not in MY backyard!

Mrs. Hugger: Hello, everyone.

I'm Bun E. Hugger. I represent the We Protect Nature and Wildlife Society. We at WeePNoW are very disturbed at the prospect of destroying such valuable wildlife habitat. The home should be built in another location, and the area sold as reserve land. Keep it protected, for the wildlife. Wetlands are critical to maintaining clean air and water. Our children need a healthy environment! I say, stop the project altogether!

Mr. Nicerman: I'm Arthur Nicerman. This little girl here with me is my granddaughter, Sally-Jane. She's nine.

[Sally-Jane waves, beaming at her grandfather proudly.]

Every Sunday Sally-Jane and I go to the marsh there and go fishing and birdwatching. It's a nice, quiet place to spend some quality time with the little one—you should all go there some time! Well, I understand that everybody's got their reasons for wanting to use the land more profitably, but isn't there some way that they can do that and still keep a nice place for me and Sally and the critters? Maybe they could build around the marsh. That's all I wanted to say.

Mr. Pierpont Pospistle:

[He moves very slowly and takes a while to reach the front of the room.]

My name is Pierpont Pospistle. I'm 82 years old. My hearing is lousy and my eyesight is going. They don't let me drive anymore. I've been living with my son and his family but we can't stand each other anymore, not in the same house, anyway. I've already got my place in line for one of those apartments in Heron's Rook. That would give me back some feeling of independence. I like the project just as it is. I don't need to be

walking a long way from the parking lot to the building. It'd make me not want to go places when my son comes to visit and take me out. Other than that, just build the danged place so I have somewhere to live!

Ms. Planwell: I am Marcia Planwell. I'm here this evening as an interested citizen, but I am employed as a wetland and environmental consultant. I'd like to make a few comments. First, Mr. Pospistle. There is a solarium (a sun room) planned for the east wing of Heron's Rook. Would you be happy looking out at a parking lot? Wouldn't you rather have a view of a natural area? If the building is set back as the gentleman from DNR suggested, this could be incorporated into the plan. Mr. Gotbucks, if you want to save money on construction, do not choose to fill in the wetland! This is very expensive, and the ground will not be very stable over the long term. It could sink! If you make the building a bit smaller, say 175 units instead of 200, you would harm a bit less wetland area. You might not make as much money on the housing, but it's a small price to pay. Certainly, the best alternative would be to put the building somewhere else completely, but a compromise on all sides is not impossible.

H.O.: Since Ms. Planwell was the last speaker, I will remind everyone that all testimony presented here is now part of the public record and will be used in deciding this case. After the permitting deadline, the public may contact the agencies to find out about the outcome of the case. I thank you all for coming. The hearing is adjourned.

THE END

Hydropoly

Grade Level
4-12

Subject Areas
Environmental Science,
Government

Duration
1 hour or more

Setting
Classroom

Skills
Application and evaluation

Charting the Course
Precede or follow this activity
with "Wetland Tradeoffs" for
another approach to decision
making and the exploration
of wetland values.

Vocabulary
wetlands management

Summary
*A game of wetlands management and
"eco-nomics"!*

Students play a board game to
hone their decision-making skills.

Objectives
Students will:

• infer and discuss land-use
practices that affect wetlands.

• make decisions and recognize
personal priorities with regard
to wetlands.

• describe some of the economic
factors that often drive land use.

Materials
• *copies of the game board (one per
small group of students*
• *1 set of the Decision Cards per
game board*
• *1 die (not a pair) per game board*
• *tape*
• *scissors*
• *6 different-colored playing pieces
per game board (construction paper
squares or pieces from another
game).*

Prepare the game board(s) by
photocopying pp. 262 and 263.
Trim the left edge of p. 263 and
tape the two pages together to
form a continuous game board.
You may wish to attach the board
to a piece of tagboard and/or
laminate it to make it more
durable. Students may want to
color the board before it is
laminated. Copy and cut out the
cards (you may want to laminate
these, too), and place them
facedown on the boards. The
game can be played by two to
six individual players or teams.
Prepare enough game boards and
playing pieces to suit your class.

Making Connections
We are required to make choices
every day (e.g., deciding what to
wear, what to eat, how much time
to allow for homework, etc.).
Some decisions require advanced
cognitive skills such as conse-
quential and critical thinking.
Through the various choices
posed in this game, students are
asked to consider both economic
and environmental well-being in
making decisions. This is good
practice for real life situations
they may encounter.

Background
What is it that drives people to
make certain decisions throughout life? Usually, personal interests play a major role. Money
(economics) can often be the
biggest factor. Decisions are also
based upon personal values such
as concern for the environment.

When it comes to land-use issues,
the health of the environment is
one of the most important aspects
to consider. Individual monetary
gain and the stability of the
regional economy often override
consideration for the environment, particularly for wetlands.
The two considerations should
not be mutually exclusive, but
should carry relatively equal
weight. We could call this "eco-
nomics"—the healthy marriage
of **ECO**logical concerns and
eco**NOMIC** growth.

Procedure
Warm Up
Ask students to describe decisions
they have made recently. What do
they like and dislike about
making decisions? What helps
them make a wise choice? Have
them list important consider-

ations. Have any of them made a wrong decision recently (or ever)? How can wrong decisions be a good experience? (We can learn from our mistakes.)

The Activity

1. **Divide the class into groups to play the game. The game may be played by two to six players or two to six teams of players. Discuss eco-nomics before you begin to play.**

2. **Review the rules with students:**

Rules and How to Play

• Each player (or team) selects a game piece and places it on the space marked Start. Each player rolls the die and the player rolling the highest number goes first; play proceeds in a clockwise direction.

• The first player rolls the die and moves his or her playing piece the number of spaces indicated on the die. Move in the direction indicated by the arrows on the board. When a player lands on a blank space, his turn is over and play advances to the next player. When a player lands on a space marked Roll Again she may do so and move along the board as before. If a player lands on Lose A Turn, the turn is over and he must skip his next turn.

• Decision Cards: When a player lands on a Decision Card space, she must randomly select one of the cards (cards should be face-down). An opponent reads the top portion of the card aloud. (Do not read out the Consequences.) The player has a maximum of two minutes to make a decision. If playing in teams, team members may discuss the decision quietly. When a player announces his or her decision, the person holding the card reads the Consequences,

which tell how many spaces the player has earned or lost for the decision. The player must follow the instructions given on the card and return the card to the pile. The player's turn continues until landing on a blank space or Losing A Turn. Play then moves to the next player or team.

• Players may only reach THE WINNER space by an *exact* roll of the die. If a player is four spaces away, for example, and rolls a five, he may not move and must forfeit his turn; if he rolls a three he must move three spaces, but must then roll a one to win.

Note: The consequences specified on each Decision Card reward students for choosing to protect wetlands. If you wish other values to be considered, have the class or a team of students determine a new set of consequences and substitute them on the Decision Cards before the game begins. See "Wetland Tradeoffs" (p. 285) for some decision-making ideas.

3. **When students understand the rules, Hydropolize! You may choose to have students play "blind" first, then discuss eco-nomics after the game. Play several games.**

Wrap Up and Action

After the games have ended, discuss the results. Who won, and why did the winner reach the end more quickly than others? What did players think about while making decisions? Students can revise or confirm the considerations they made in Warm Up.

Discuss why it is important to consider wetlands in scenarios like those presented in the game. Have students research community actions regarding wetland management. Do they think wise decisions were made?

Assessment

Have students:

• demonstrate their understanding of good wetlands management by choosing consequences that allow them to move ahead on the game board.

• identify considerations that are important when making decisions.

Extensions

Students can write a series of decision cards that apply to the management of a wetland in their town.

Hydropoly!

The Game of Wetlands Management and Eco-nomics

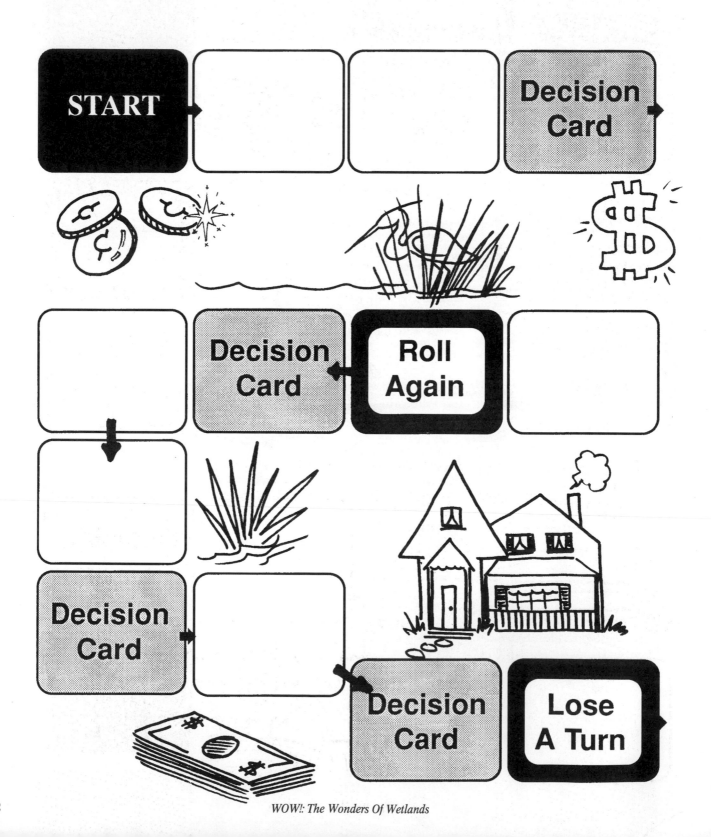

People of the Bog

[Adapted from Project WET Curriculum and Activity Guide, 1995. Used with permission of The Watercourse and the Western Regional Environmental Education Council.]

Grade Level
6-12

Subject Areas
Earth Science, History, Life Sciences

Duration
A semester or school year for artifact observation

Setting
Classroom

Skills
Gathering, analyzing, and interpreting information

Charting the Course
Students can learn more about wetlands decomposition in "A Rottin' Experiment" and wetland cultural values in "What a Boat!"

Vocabulary
bog, decomposition, aerobic, anaerobic

Summary

Feeling bogged down? You're in good company—except they're 3,000 years old!

Students construct a classroom bog and a mini-composter to observe the rate of decomposition in anaerobic (little or no oxygen present) and aerobic (oxygen available) environments.

Objectives

Students will:

- describe characteristics of bog environments.

- explain the conditions of bogs that allow for the preservation of artifacts from the past.

- compare the rates of decomposition of articles in aerobic and anaerobic environments.

Materials

(Encourage students to contribute materials.)
- *20-gallon (76 liter) glass tank (aquarium/terrarium) (As an alternative, students can make individual bogs in plastic soda bottles.)*
- *small water container (cut-off cottage cheese container or fruit juice bottle)*
- *watering can*
- *clear plastic soda bottle (mini-composter)*
- *5 pounds (2.2 kg) gravel*
- *1 pound (0.45 kg) perlite (purchase at garden center)*
- *3.5 pounds (1.6 kg) activated charcoal*
- *10 pounds (4.5 kg) dry peat moss (purchase at garden center)*
- *3 pounds (1.4 kg) sphagnum moss*
- *several plants (a carnivorous plant or two, like a Venus fly trap, and several water-tolerant plants, like ferns or violets)*
- *potting soil*
- *several snails (optional)*
- *items to represent artifacts*
- *3 3-inch (7.5 cm) long nails*
- *3 thin pieces of wood (popsicle sticks will work)*
- *6-8 pieces of fruit (pear, banana, apple)*
- *other things students want to test*
- *distilled/dechlorinated water (To dechlorinate water, place a 5-gallon (19 liter) bucket of water in a closet. Within one day the chlorine should evaporate out of solution. Chemicals from pet stores can also be obtained to remove chlorine from the water.)*

Making Connections

A student's experience with bogs may be limited to images from horror movies. By constructing an artificial bog in a classroom, students become acquainted with the complicated balance of environmental circumstances that must combine to create and maintain this unique environment.

Background

Bogs (sometimes called peatlands) are wetland environments created over thousands of years. Vast sections of northern Europe and northern North America qualify as peatlands, along with many alpine and tropical settings where environmental conditions favor the accumulation of organic material (dead plant and animal litter).

Bog formation requires a location with standing or slow-moving water (where the water inflow exceeds outflow or where the ground water table is at the surface). Certain plants, such as sphagnum moss, grow well in these still or stagnant waters. As these plants live and die, their by-products increase the acidity of the soil and water. Other plants, such as cranberries, Labrador tea, pitcher plants, and Venus fly traps are also adapted to live in these acidic conditions. For example, the pitcher plant and Venus fly trap are carnivores; they compensate for living in these nutrient-poor soils by trapping and digesting insects.

In bogs, the supply of dead organic material exceeds the rate of decomposition, so that layers accumulate through time. Waterlogged conditions inhibit the level and distribution of oxygen (resulting in anaerobic conditions), which, in turn, inhibits bacterial action and other processes of decay. Cool environments (in alpine or northern latitudes) further reduce bacterial activity. As organic material (mostly dead plants) builds up, it is compressed into peat by its own weight.

Variation in bog types depends on the level of acid in the water, available nutrients, and the extent of saturation. A bog in Florida is quite different from a bog in northern Ireland because the plant types and climates are so different.

In northern Europe peatlands have, for centuries, been mined for fuel. Strips of peat are cut away, allowed to dry, and then burned to heat houses and to fire factory furnaces. Peat miners have made many startling discoveries as they dig through the organic layers. The same lack of oxygen that retards the decay of plant material also slows the decomposition of archaeological artifacts and even human bodies, so that it sometimes takes thousands of years.

Imagine the peat farmer suddenly face-to-face with a human who perished 3,000 years ago, a body that looks fresh enough to have died only weeks earlier! Clothing, pieces of rope, undigested food in the stomachs of ancient people, and building materials have all been found preserved in a state of freshness.

Hundreds of bodies scattered throughout northern Europe have added substantially to our understanding of our ancestors. Sites such as Little Springs, Florida, and Monte Verde, in the Andes Mountains of South America, have brought into focus new parts of the picture of human existence—parts that could never have been reconstructed without the ability of bogs to preserve material.

Procedure
Warm Up
Ask students what they know about building and maintaining a compost pile. Why is it necessary to "stir" a compost pile weekly? Help them to understand that stirring helps introduce the oxygen needed by microorganisms for decomposition. What would happen to a compost pile if it were not stirred? This would promote anaerobic conditions, inhibiting the growth of decomposers. If any students have ever been to a bog, ask them to describe it.

Readings about archaeological finds (see resource books) might heighten students' curiosity. Make sure students understand that not all bogs have people or things buried in them.

The Activity
1. **Discuss the process of and conditions for bog formation as outlined in the background material.**

2. **Tell students that artifacts are remarkably well preserved in bogs because of anaerobic conditions, and that such evidence has contributed significantly to the study of our ancient ancestors.**

3. **Provide students with the Bog-Making Activity Sheet. Have them work in groups or as a class to prepare the bog and to bury the artifacts. For comparison, set up a mini-composter bottle. This** consists of a plastic soda bottle with the top cut off and holes cut in the bottom for drainage. Fill the bottle with soil and add similar artifacts. Water periodically to keep the soil damp, but not soggy, and stir the mini-composter once every week or two—being careful to position artifacts so they can always be clearly seen through the plastic. Place in a well-ventilated area; it may be odorous.

4. **Have students predict what will happen to the artifacts. Discuss the conditions of each container. Which is anaerobic? Note that the soil in the bog is saturated. (All spaces between sand particles are filled with water.) Ask students what they think usually fills these spaces.** If necessary, to demonstrate the presence of air (oxygen), fill a clear container half full with dry sand. Add water until the water line is even with the top of the container. As water displaces the air between sand particles, air bubbles will rise to the surface.

5. **At regular intervals throughout a semester or school year, have students rotate responsibility for observing and documenting the decomposition of the different artifacts in each container. For each artifact at each level in the bog, they should describe any changes or note that**

no obvious change has occurred.
Do not remove artifacts from the bog; observe them through the glass.

6. **Have students research bog ecology.** What lives in bogs? Of what value are bogs? Why are bogs unique ecosystems? What kinds of adaptations do plants living in a bog have to make? Why do they need these adaptations? How are bogs different from other types of wetlands? Students should relate findings to what is occurring in their bog model.

Wrap Up and Action

Instruct students to write a report summarizing their observations and conclusions about their bog and mini-composter. Can students confirm that "Artifacts are remarkably well preserved in bogs"? Ask them to describe the characteristics of a bog (relate to their own model bog) and include reasons why bogs are important ecosystems that should be managed and preserved. Encourage students to determine if bogs exist in their state or region. What is the condition of a local bog? If possible, arrange a field trip to a bog. Students can write articles for their local paper to inform others in their community about the importance of bogs.

Assessment

Have students:

- compare conditions in the bog and the mini-composter.

- record and interpret their observations of the bog and mini-composter.

- provide reasons why bogs are unique environments and should be managed and protected.

- relate items in the model of a bog to characteristics of a real bog.

Extensions

Students can research several archaeological sites that have been found in wetland bogs. Encourage discussion of these sites and the mysteries presented by the artifacts found there. Students can write "site reports" focusing on a particular area, and then make presentations to the rest of the class.

Bury other artifacts in the classroom bog and observe the rates of decomposition.

If a local bog is near the school, organize a field trip to compare the real thing with the classroom variety.

Resources

Coles, B., and J. Coles. 1989. *People of the Wetlands.* New York, N.Y.: Thames and Hudson.

Glob, P. V. 1965. *The Bog People.* Ithaca, N.Y.: Cornell University Press.

Hanif, Muhammad. 1990. "The Vanishing Bog." *Science and Children* (April): 25–26.

Williams, M., ed. 1990. *Wetlands: A Threatened Landscape.* Cambridge, Mass.: Basil Blackwell.

Bog-Making Activity Sheet

1. To create the permeable lower layer of an artificial bog, first spread the perlite to an even depth on the bottom. Add 1-2 inches (2-5 cm) of gravel above that, followed by an even layer of the activated charcoal. These materials facilitate the processes of drainage and evaporation that occur in a natural bog.

2. Before adding the next layer, place several artifacts against the glass on top of the charcoal. A piece of wood, a nail, several pieces of fruit, and one cube of meat should be adequate.

3. Place 1-3 inches (2-7 cm) of peat moss above the charcoal. Compress this layer of peat with a block of wood or pack with your hands.

4. Arrange more artifacts on top of the compressed peat, so they can be seen through the tank glass.

5. Loosely pack sphagnum moss and the remaining peat moss, creating some topography, with a gentle slope toward a marked depression. Place a final layer of artifacts on the surface of the loose peat moss.

6. In the depressed section of your "landscape" bury the small water container, so that it is slightly below the surface of the bog. This simulates a small bog pond and helps add humidity to the tank.

7. Plant the carnivorous plants in the peat at the low end of the tank (with the dirt intact) and the water-tolerant varieties towards the high end (gently remove dirt and separate the roots). Pack soil around the plant bases. Aquarium may be covered with plastic wrap or sheet of glass.

8. Water the bog evenly with distilled or dechlorinated water (chlorine may harm the plants). Water the bog often enough to maintain a high level of humidity. Condensation droplets should appear on the tank glass. Place the tank near an outside window or alternate daily periods of light and darkness, so that photosynthesis occurs.

9. Every two weeks, feed insects to the carnivorous plants. (Don't overfeed.)
CAUTION: When this activity concludes, do not release plants or animals into the wild unless they are species native to your area. If you are unsure what to do, consult the department of natural resources in your state for advice.

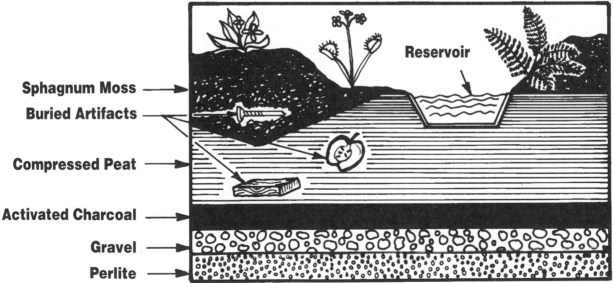

Illustration by Laurie "gigette" Gould

Bog construction adapted from "The Vanishing Bog," by Muhammad Hanif, NSTA Publications, copyright 1990 from Science and Children *27 (7):25-26, National Science Teachers Association, 1840 Wilson Boulevard, Arlington, VA 22201-3000.*

Regulation Rummy

Grade Level
9-12

Subject Areas
History, Government

Duration
1 hour

Setting
Classroom

Skills
Organizing and analyzing

Charting the Course
Try "Hydropoly!" or "Wetland Tradeoffs" for a look at values that come into play when alternatives (development in wetlands versus wetlands protection) are considered.

Vocabulary
regulation, law, effluent

Summary
What are the rules?

Students play a card game designed to increase awareness of the multitude of federal wetlands regulations.

Objectives
Students will:

• identify how wetland regulations apply to certain activities.

• analyze the complexity of wetland regulations, enforcement, and jurisdiction.

Materials
• *packs of 3 x 5-inch index cards to make deck(s) of Regulation Rummy playing cards. Deck includes regulation cards, clue cards (which describe each regulation), scenario cards (project or activity description), and violation cards. Make several decks if the size of your class requires it. See Instructions for Making Regulation Rummy Cards, p. 275*
• *copies of the Regulation Rummy Scenario Answer Sheet*
• *copies of the Regulation Review student pages*
• *reference materials*

Making Connections
Regulations and laws: as a topic, some people would respond, "Boring!" But as a fact of life, laws and regulations are essential for maintaining order for the good of society and the environment. An understanding of the laws helps us live responsibly and make informed decisions.

Background
Regulations are a part of our everyday lives. Think of speed limits, drinking and voting age limits, and deadlines for submitting annual tax returns. As you might expect, a multitude of regulations have been formulated to guide wetland management decisions.

Although the Constitution never mentions water, a series of complex federal laws govern how water is regulated and supplied, and set up programs to pass some responsibilities to the states. Federal water policy has generated a network of inland waterways, dams, reservoirs, water treatment systems, scenic rivers, fish hatcheries, municipal supply systems, irrigated lands, and hydroelectric operations.

Simply stated, United States water policy can be viewed as having had a five-phase evolution:

1. Early regulation of harbors, waterways, and fisheries, with an emphasis on settlement and development (navigation, flood control, and irrigation);

2. Promotion of a conservation ethic, for benefit of future generations (1900 to 1920s);

3. Major large-scale construction of multipurpose reservoirs (1930s and 1940s);

4. Nationwide river basin planning (1950s and 1960s); and

5. Environmental protection and education (1970s to present).

Water resources have been vastly improved in recent years. Although the United States is a big consumer of water, compared to other nations, overall water use in this country has declined since 1980. Point-source water pollution has also declined, and an incredible infrastructure of fundamental, well-thought-out legislation enacted during the last 20 years is in place to effectively guide our water future.

Still, problems exist. Water pollution from runoff (nonpoint sources) still has not been effectively restrained, and the level of toxins in local ground-water supplies has become a national sore spot. Add global warming, acid rain, and drought to the picture, and our national water policy is put to the test.

Because wetlands are vital components of watersheds, regulations have been developed to protect them from continued alteration, destruction, and degradation. While perceived by some to be an invasion of personal property rights, wetland regulations are designed to maintain the quality of surface waters, protect the health and safety of citizens, monitor wetland development and mitigation, protect valuable ecological functions, and manage development for the good of all people. These regulations, administered by a variety of federal and state agencies, underscore the importance of planning in projects that may involve wetlands.

The Regulation Review student pages summarize some of these regulations. This list is not complete; many others not reviewed here may apply, especially state laws. You will find more background information in chapter 5.

As you investigate national wetlands policy, recognize that there is no single specific national wetlands management law. Instead, a series of laws govern separate pieces of the big picture, and responsibility is spread over several agencies—the Environmental Protection Agency, the U.S. Army Corps of Engineers, the

U.S. Fish and Wildlife Service, the Natural Resources Conservation Service, and others. Also, the unique nature of wetlands brings them under both water-quality and land-use constraints.

Procedure

Warm Up
Discuss laws and regulations affecting us. What would it be like without them?

The Activity
1. **Hand out the Regulation Review student pages. Review the regulations in enough detail to give students a thorough understanding of each. (It is important that students remember the key provisions of each regulation.) Ask students why these regulations were written. Can they identify regulations that have local impact or significance?**

2. **Break the class into small groups of three to five. Give each group a deck of the Regulation Rummy cards and an answer sheet. Explain the rules of the game:**

• The deck consists of regulation, clue, scenario, and violation cards. One student serves as the scorekeeper/dealer, and refers to a copy of the Answer Sheet throughout the game. All others are dealt the regulation cards (the entire deck). The dealer makes separate stacks of the clue, scenario, and violation cards.

• The starting player draws a scenario card from the stack. If the player can match a regulation that would apply to the given scenario, the pair is laid down in front of the other players and the player draws another scenario card. ("No Regulation" cards match scenarios that do not require regulation.) Several regulations may apply to a given scenario; however, only one regulation applicable to that scenario is needed to make a match. This continues until 1) the player can no longer match scenarios to regulations or 2) three matches have been made.

Illustration by Susan Ferber

• If a player would like a clue to help match scenarios to a regulation, he or she can draw from the clue card stack. If the clue card does not help, the player may keep it for help later. If this is done, he or she cannot pick a scenario card until the next round.

• If a player lays down an incorrect match, and the mismatch is identified by other members of the group, the player must draw a violation card. The scorekeeper checks to be sure the match is incorrect. The incorrect match must be identified before the next player takes his or her turn. If a player declares a match incorrect when, in fact, it is correct, he or she receives a violation card.

• Each scenario/regulation match is worth ten points, and each violation card is worth minus ten points. At the end of the game, the scorekeeper should point out any incorrect matches that may have been overlooked.

• The student with the most points wins.

Note: There may be other nonwetland-related regulations that apply to each scenario. These are not discussed as part of this activity.

3. **Before students play the game, read the following scenario as an example of the types of regulations that might apply to a real-life situation. Then, play the game.**

A city wants to use federal funds to construct an airport within the coastal zone management area. This would affect a tidal wetland. The following regulations would apply: Rivers and Harbors Act, Clean Water Act, Coastal Zone Management Act, NEPA, Executive Orders 11988 and 11990, and other federal, state, and local regulations not discussed. If a wildlife study found a bald eagle nest on the property, the Endangered Species Act would also apply.

Wrap Up and Action
Have scorekeepers report scores. If the game was difficult to play, discuss why. Discuss the intricacies of the laws.

Have each group research the history of an existing law. Why was it written? Who was involved at the time, and why? In some communities, students may be able to interview older folks who were involved to get their perceptions of what was done and how things have changed over the years. Have students write their own wetland laws. How would they differ from current laws?

Assessment
Have students:

• match regulations to actions pertaining to wetlands.

• analyze proposed matches of scenarios and regulations to determine if they are correct.

• summarize reasons for initiating regulations for wetlands management.

Extensions
Students can get a clearer picture of wetlands laws by contacting federal and state wetland management or regulatory agencies to discuss the regulations that apply in your state. These agencies might include the Environmental Protection Agency, U.S. Fish and Wildlife Service, Army Corps of Engineers, Natural Resources Conservation Service, and state and local departments of natural resources, game and fish, water resources, environmental quality, health, or conservation. Ask students to write a short report that summarizes their findings.

Resources
Black, Peter. 1987. *Conservation of Water and Related Land Resources.* Totowa: Rowman and Littlefield.

Congressional Quarterly. 1991. "How a Bill Becomes Law" in *Guide to Current American Government*, Fall edition.

Findley, Roger W., and Daniel A. Farber. 1988. *Environmental Law in a Nutshell.* St. Paul: West Publishing Company.

Getches, David H. 1990. *Water Law in a Nutshell.* St. Paul: West Publishing Company.

High Country News. 1987. *Western Water Made Simple.* Covelo: Island Press.

Kusler, Jon A., Corbin Harwood, and Richard Newton. 1983. *Our National Wetland Heritage: A Protection Guidebook.* Washington, D.C.: Environmental Law Institute.

Rogers, Peter. 1993. *America's Water: Federal Roles and Responsibilities.* A Twentieth Century Fund Book.

Salvesen, David. 1991. *Wetlands: Mitigating and Regulating Development Impacts.* Washington, D.C.: Urban Land institute.

Silverberg, Steven, and Mark Dennison. 1993. *Wetlands and Coastal Zone Regulation and Compliance.* New York: Wiley Law Publications.

Strand, Margaret. 1993. *Wetlands Deskbook.* Washington, D.C.: Environmental Law Institute.

World Wildlife Fund. 1992. *Statewide Wetlands Strategies: A Guide to Protecting and Managing the Resource.* Washington, D.C.: Island Press.

Regulation Review

There are many fascinating aspects to each of the laws listed below. You may want to study the details further (ask your teacher for some resources). This list includes only the basic facts you will need to play Regulation Rummy.

1. **Clean Water Act (CWA), Sections 401 and 402.** This act began as the Federal Water Pollution Control Act and was amended in 1972 to become the Clean Water Act. It was passed in response to the deterioration of surface waters in the United States. It set up a national system of federal-state cooperation to regulate pollution, and is administered by the Environmental Protection Agency and state agencies.

Section 401 of the Act requires that states review and certify any federal permit or license that may result in pollution discharges into surface waters and wetlands under state jurisdiction. This means federal permits such as those for filling wetlands, licensing hydropower plants, or discharging pollution into water may be vetoed by a state if the federal action is not consistent with state water-quality requirements. This is called Water Quality Certification.

Section 402 of the Act established a permit system known as the National Pollutant Elimination Discharge System (NPDES). These permits are required for any discharge of pollutants from a point source (such as a pipe, well, or ditch) into navigable waters.

The Environmental Protection Agency, or an approved state program, is authorized to issue these permits to industrial, municipal, or other point source discharges.

2. **Clean Water Act, Section 404.** This section governs the dredging and filling of wetlands. It requires permits from the U.S. Army Corps of Engineers for any discharge of dredged-and-fill materials into waters (including wetlands) of the United States. Dam, bridge, road, and many other construction-related discharges are regulated; normal farming, forestry, and ranching discharges are exempt.

3. **National Environmental Policy Act (NEPA).** NEPA imposes environmental responsibilities on all agencies of the federal government. Specifically, it requires that federal agencies prepare environmental impact statements (EIS) on major federal actions that significantly affect the quality of the environment. These actions include construction projects, permits, and licenses that are issued by the federal government. The preparation of an EIS is a costly and lengthy process that requires thorough review and comment by the public and various agencies. The Environmental Protection Agency is required to review and comment on all environmental impact statements.

4. **Executive Order 11990 (Protection of Wetlands).** Issued by President Jimmy Carter in 1977, this executive order requires federal agencies to take action to minimize the destruction, loss, or degradation of wetlands and to preserve and enhance the natural and beneficial values of wetlands on *federal* lands.

5. **Rivers and Harbors Act.** Enacted way back in 1899, this act establishes the U.S. Army Corps of Engineers' authority to prohibit discharge of solids or construction into tidal and navigable, and adjacent, waters. (Navigable streams are considered to be any blue line stream on a U.S. Geological Survey map, or usually anything with a flow greater than 3 cubic feet per second.) When the Corps was given jurisdiction over Section 404 of the Clean Water Act (which regulates dredging and filling in wetlands), the Rivers and Harbors Act was not repealed; it is still used as an additional remedy against polluters, such as those who spill oil or other hazardous materials.

6. **Food Securities Act of 1985 ("Swampbuster" provisions).** Normal agricultural and silvicultural (forest-related practices) dredged-and-fill discharges were exempted from the Clean Water Act Section 404 permit requirements. Furthermore, federal subsidies to farmers actually encouraged the draining of wetlands for agricultural projects. To alleviate this problem, the Food Securities Act of 1985 denied federal subsidies for conversion of wetlands to agricultural uses after December, 1985. Through provisions of the Act, the Natural Resources Conservation Service now helps farmers identify wetlands on their farms.

Regulation Review (continued)

7. Executive Order 11988 (Floodplain Protection). Issued by President Jimmy Carter in 1977, this executive order establishes a policy for protection of floodplains that requires agencies to avoid activities in floodplains whenever possible. Federal floodplain policy now calls for the protection of the natural and beneficial functions of floodplains (including wetlands), in addition to protecting public safety and property. The National Flood Insurance Program, administered by the Federal Emergency Management Agency, offers communities advantageous insurance rates if they exceed minimum federal standards for open-space preservation on floodplains.

8. Coastal Zone Management Act. Passed in 1972, this Act requires that coastal states set up coastal zoning regulations. The federal government was concerned that coastal areas would become degraded due to increased population and resultant water quality issues. For federal approval, state CZM plans must demonstrate that they provide standards for the protection of coastal resources, including coastal and non-coastal tidal wetlands. CZM programs, therefore, require state or local approval for any alteration of a wetland. The program is administered by the Department of Commerce, Office of Coastal Zone Management.

9. Endangered Species Act. Under this act, states, local governments, and private groups of citizens are all entitled to enforce protection of wetlands (and other areas) that offer unique habitat for endangered and threatened species. The U.S. Fish and Wildlife Service administers the provisions that pertain to inland species, and the National Marine Fisheries Service administers the marine species provisions.

10. Fish and Wildlife Coordination Act. Administered by the U.S. Fish and Wildlife Service, this act requires that federal agencies give wildlife conservation "equal consideration . . . with other features of water-resource development programs." Therefore, all water-related federal projects (such as the construction of dams) must be reviewed by the U.S. Fish and Wildlife Service and or the National Marine Fisheries Service, as well as by the state agency in charge of wildlife management. These agencies review the project's potential impact on fish and wildlife. If impact is significant, reviewing agencies can modify or deny permits.

Instructions for Making Regulation Rummy Cards

Mark a large pack of 3 x 5-inch index cards as follows (*Note:* Use a laser printer or photocopier to save time.):

1.

Scenario Cards: Write the word **Scenario** in bold letters on the back of 32 cards. Write a different scenario, from the list below, on the front of each card.

Building a boat ramp on the bank of a river.

Building a U.S. Environmental Protection Agency office adjacent to a wetland.

Use federal funds to build a state highway adjacent to a wetland.

Removal of woody vegetation in a wetland on land that is enrolled in a federal farm program.

Draining wetlands on land that is enrolled in a federal farm program.

Constructing private houses on a tidal wetland.

Building a non-federally funded bridge over a river.

Building a post office on a floodplain.

Constructing an oil platform in a coastal wetland.

Building houses adjacent to wetlands in coastal zone.

Discharging sewage treatment effluent into a wetland.

Discharging heated water from a power plant into tidally-influenced channels that flow through a wetland.

Using federal funds to build a fishing pier next to a least tern and piping plover (endangered/threatened species) nesting site.

Constructing a private home in a freshwater wetland.

Building a motel in a tidal wetland adjacent to a bald eagle nesting tree.

Using federal funds to build a public airport with no wetlands impact in a coastal management zone.

Creating a pond with an impoundment (dam) in a wetland.

Building a private dam on a stream that supports a population of snail darters (an endangered species).

Filling a private created wetland.

Building a fish pond in a wetland.

Filling wetlands with debris.

Building an island in a wetland.

Without using federal funds, building highways through wetlands.

Draining a wetland for agricultural use.

Planting a grain crop.

Pumping irrigation water out of wetlands, with return water not re-entering wetlands.

Mowing cattail vegetation in wetlands.

Creating a pond with an impoundment (dam) in a nonwetland.

Grazing cattle in a wetland.

Creating a wetland from an upland.

Spraying herbicide on a crop.

Filling in a gravel pit immediately after mining activities cease.

2.

Regulation Cards: Write the word **Regulation** in bold letters on the back of 54 cards. Write a different regulation from the list below on the front of the number of cards indicated in parentheses.

Rivers and Harbor Act, Sections 9 and 10 (4)

Coastal Zone Management Act (4)

Sections 401 and 402 of the Clean Water Act (5)

National Environmental Policy Act (4)

Clean Water Act, Section 404 (12)

Endangered Species Act (3)

Executive Order 11988 (Floodplain Protection) (3)

Food Securities Act of 1985, "Swampbuster" provisions (5)

Executive Order 11990: (Protection of Wetlands) (2)

Fish and Wildlife Coordination Act (3)

No Regulation (9)

3.

Clue Cards: Write the word **Clue** in bold letters on the back of 30 cards. Put a different clue from the list below on the front of each. Be sure to include the name of the regulation and the clue itself. Make three cards for each clue and shuffle.

Rivers and Harbor Act, Sections 9 and 10:

Don't dump solids or construct anything into navigable waters and adjacent wetlands, or you'll be in trouble!

Clean Water Act, Sections 401 and 402:

Could this activity degrade the water quality of the state? You must get a Water Quality Certification (Section 401); if it will discharge non-solid pollutants from a point source (such as a pipe, well, or ditch) into navigable waters, better get a CWA Section 402 discharge permit.

Coastal Zone Management Act:

Are you out of compliance with the state coastal zoning regulations? Better get approval!

National Environmental Policy Act:

Start writing that environmental impact statement if the project is a major federal action significantly affecting the quality of the environment.

Clean Water Act, Section 404:

Simply said, if you're dredging or filling in wetlands, get a Clean Water Act, Section 404 permit from the U.S. Army Corps of Engineers.

Endangered Species Act:

Are you muddling up unique habitat for endangered and threatened species? You'd better visit the U.S. Fish and Wildlife Service or National Marine Fisheries Service.

Executive Order 11988 (Flood-plain Protection):

Protect those floodplains! A federal project constructed on floodplains must get special review.

Food Securities Act of 1985 ("Swampbuster" provisions):

Converting a wetland to a farm field? Go see the Natural Resource Conservation Service!

Executive Order 11990: (Protection of Wetlands):

Federal agencies are required to take action to minimize the destruction, loss, or degradation of wetlands and to preserve and enhance the natural and beneficial values of wetlands on federal lands.

Fish and Wildlife Coordination Act:

If you are requesting a permit to impact wetlands, the U.S. Fish and Wildlife Service or the National Marine Fisheries Service, as well as the state agency in charge of wildlife management must review your application.

4.

Violation Cards: Mark the back of 34 index cards with the word **Violation**.

Regulation Rummy Scenario Answer Sheet

• Building a boat ramp. *Rivers and Harbors Act; CWA, Section 404; CWA, Section 401*

• Building a U.S. Environmental Protection Agency office adjacent to a wetland. *National Environmental Policy Act; Executive Order 11990; Executive Order 11988; Endangered Species Act; Fish and Wildlife Coordination Act*

• Using federal funds to build a state highway adjacent to a wetland. *National Environmental Policy Act; Executive Order 11990; Executive Order 11988; Endangered Species Act; Fish and Wildlife Coordination Act*

• Removal of woody vegetation in a wetland on land that is enrolled in a federal farm program land. *Food Securities Act ("Swampbuster")*

• Draining wetlands on land that is enrolled in a federal farm program. *Food Securities Act ("Swampbuster")*

• Constructing private houses on a tidal wetland. *Section 404 (key); Section 401; Coastal Zone Management Act; Rivers and Harbor Act; Fish and Wildlife Coordination Act*

• Building a non-federally funded bridge over a river. *River and Harbor Act; Section 404; Fish and Wildlife Coordination Act*

• Building a post office in a floodplain. *Executive Order 11988 (Floodplain Protection); National Environmental Policy Act; Fish and Wildlife Coordination Act*

• Constructing an oil platform in a coastal wetland. *Coastal Zone Management Act; Rivers and Harbors Act; Clean Water Act, Section 401; Clean Water Act, Section 404; Fish and Wildlife Coordination Act*

• Building houses adjacent to wetlands in coastal zone. *Coastal Zone Management Act*

• Discharging of sewage treatment effluent onto a wetland. *Clean Water Act, Section 401; Section 402; Clean Water Act, Section 404; Rivers and Harbors Act if wetland tidal or adjacent to navigable waters*

• Discharging heated water from a power plant into tidally-influenced channels that flow through a wetland. *Clean Water Act, Section 401; Clean Water Act, Section 402*

• Using federal funds to build a fishing pier next to a least tern and piping plover nesting site. *Rivers and Harbors Act; Endangered Species Act; Executive Order 11988; Executive Order 11990 (Floodplain Protection); Section 401, Section 404; Rivers and Harbors Act*

• Constructing a private home in an isolated freshwater wetland. *Fish and Wildlife Coordination Act; Clean Water Act, Section 404; Clean Water Act, Section 401*

• Building a motel in a tidal wetland adjacent to a bald eagle nest tree. *Endangered Species Act; Clean Water Act, Section 401; Clean Water Act, Section 404; Rivers and Harbors Act; Fish and Wildlife Coordination Act*

• Using federal funds to build a public airport with no impact to wetlands in a coastal management zone. *Clean Water Act, Section 401; National Environmental Policy Act; Executive Order 11988; Coastal Zone Management Act; Fish and Wildlife Coordination Act*

• Creating a pond with an impoundment (dam) in a wetland. *Clean Water Act, Section 401; Clean Water Act, Section 404*

• Building a private dam on a stream that supports a population of snail darters. *Clean Water Act, Section 401, Clean Water Act, Section 404; Endangered Species Act; Fish and Wildlife Coordination Act; Rivers and Harbors Act*

• Filling a private created wetland. *Clean Water Act, Section 401; Clean Water Act, Section 404*

• Building a fish pond in a wetland. *Clean Water Act, Section 401; Clean Water Act, Section 404; Fish and Wildlife Coordination Act*

• Filling wetlands with debris. *Clean Water Act, Section 401; Clean Water Act, Section 404; Fish and Wildlife Coordination Act*

• Building an island in a wetland. *Clean Water Act, Section 401; Clean Water Act, Section 404; Fish and Wildlife Coordination Act*

• Without using federal funds, building highways through wetlands. *Clean Water Act, Section 401; Clean Water Act, Section 404; Fish and Wildlife Coordination Act*

• Draining a wetland for agricultural use. *Food Securities Act ("Swampbuster")*

• Planting a grain crop. *No regulation*

• Pumping irrigation water out of wetlands, with return water not re-entering wetlands. *No regulation*

• Mowing cattail vegetation in wetlands. *No regulation*

• Creating a pond with an impoundment (dam) in a nonwetland area. *No regulation*

• Grazing cattle in a wetland. *No regulation*

• Creating a wetland from an upland. *No regulation*

• Spraying herbicide on a crop. *No regulation*

• Filling in a gravel pit immediately after mining activities cease. *No regulation*

What a Boat!

Grade Level
1-5

Subject Areas
Social Studies, Art

Duration
1 hour

Setting
Classroom

Skills
Organizing and analyzing information

Charting the Course
"People of the Bog" and "Chrysti the Wordsmith on Wetlands" also touch on cultural values of wetlands.

Vocabulary
buoyancy, aerenchyma

Summary
Up a creek without a boat!

Students learn to appreciate wetlands' values to indigenous cultures as they build miniature boats with wetland plant materials.

Objectives
Students will:

• demonstrate how wetland plants could be used to build boats.

• increase their understanding of the value of wetland plants.

Materials
• *glass container filled with water*
• *cattails (Typha sp.), rushes (Scirpus and Juncus sp.), reeds (Phragmites sp.), or other buoyant plant material (a bundle 4 to 6 inches in diameter will be sufficient for a class of 35 students). Note: Where appropriate, make sure you have permission to collect these plants.*
• *several pairs of scissors*
• *string, or plant fiber substitute such as milkweed*
• *enough water to float the boats*
• *pans, trays, or other receptacles deep enough to float the boats*
• *small rocks or pebbles, smooth if possible*
• *markers and other art materials*
• *slides or pictures of boats and household items made from wetland materials*
• *books on wetlands and reed boat expeditions*

Making Connections
Students may not realize that wetlands were and are a critical source of food, protection, and building supplies for indigenous cultures. By creating a simple boat with raw wetland materials, students expand their appreciation of these materials.

Background
Sections of chapters 1 and 3 discuss information on baskets, boats, rice, wildfowl, fish, shelters, bedding, fuel (peat), caribou, timber, cranberries, clothing, furs, hay, housing structures, and other necessities that come from wetlands!

Throughout human history, incredible boats have been constructed from simple raw materials. In fact, the design of most modern boats can be linked to four ancient boat designs: the raft, the animal skin boat, the bark boat, and the dugout. Traditional wetland rafts were watertight and made from plant materials with structural adaptations to the wetland conditions that made them naturally buoyant.

Cattails, bulrushes, and reeds all have adaptations for survival in wetland environments. These emergent plants often have long stems with channels called aerenchyma that transport oxygen to the roots. These channels are often surrounded by water-conducting vessels that are closely bound by stem-supporting fibers. Emergents' strong and buoyant oxygen-conducting system makes them ideal boat-building material.

Procedure
Warm Up
Ask students what wetlands are. Do they know of any wetlands near the school or their homes? Have them list some of the plants commonly found there. What animals need these plants? Make sure humans are included in this

list of animals. How could humans use wetland plants? How about for making a boat?

Ask what type of material could be used to make a boat. Show students the bulrushes, cattails and/or reeds. Ask them if they could make a boat from these plants that they could float on if they had enough plant material. Drop a piece of bulrush or cattail into a glass container filled with water. What happens?

The Activity

1. **Hand out string, pebbles, scissors, and markers. Give each student eight to ten 12-inch (30 cm) pieces of plant material.**

2. **Ask them to build miniature boats of their own design with these materials. They may decorate their boats if they wish.** They may want to use ideas from various craft books.

3. **Once completed, have students put pebbles inside their boats and gently lower the boats into the pans of water. Do the boats float? Students may want to write a story about how this boat or its life-size counterpart could actually have been used in the past to transport materials or explore the countryside.**

Wrap Up and Action

As a group, comment on the structure and design of the boats. Have students summarize what worked and what didn't. If they were to write a manual on boat construction, what would they include? Show slides or pictures of boats (e.g., the *Kon Tiki*) and household items made from wetland materials.

Students can create a display of their boats and relate them to actual boats used in ancient or contemporary wetland cultures.

Have the class produce an illustrated fact sheet on wetlands, wetland plants, and local wetland cultures.

Assessment

Have students:

- describe everyday items that are made from wetland materials.

- design and build a boat with rushes, cattails, or reeds.

- determine the best design and construction techniques for boats made of wetland materials.

- set up a display that relates model boats to facts about wetlands and wetland cultures.

Extensions

Research wetlands in Ireland, New Guinea, Japan, the Alaskan tundra, the Tigris and Euphrates area, or other parts of the world. Write a short report or make an oral presentation on the importance of wetlands plants and animals in native cultures.

Invite a resource person (e.g., local tribal member, extension agent, biologist) to visit the class and make a presentation on the value of wetlands plants and animals.

Read sections of *The Ra Expeditions* or *Kon Tiki* to the class. These books describe Thor Heyerdahl's trans-Pacific and trans-Atlantic expeditions in boats made of *Papyrus* reeds.

Resources

Coles, Bryony, and John Coles. 1989. *People of the Wetlands: Bogs, Bodies, and Lake Dwellers*. New York: Thames & Hudson.

Glob, P.V. 1965. *The Bog People: Iron-Age Man Preserved*. New York: Cornell University Press.

Greenhill, Basil. 1976. *Archaeology of the Boat*. Middletown: Wesleyan University Press.

Heyerdahl, Thor. 1950. *Kon Tiki*. Chicago: Rand McNally.

_____. 1971. *The Ra Expeditions*. New York: Doubleday & Company.

Wheat, Margaret M. 1967. *Survival Arts of the Primitive Paiutes*. Reno: University of Nevada Press.

Williams, Michael, editor. 1990. *Wetlands: A Threatened Landscape*. London: Basil Blackwell.

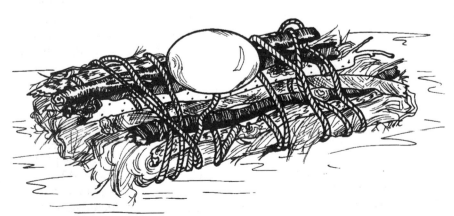

Chrysti the Wordsmith on Wetlands

Grade Level
7-12

Subject Areas
Social Studies, Geography, English

Duration
1 hour; longer for research (Part II)

Setting
Classroom and library

Skills
Analyzing, organizing, and presenting information

Charting the Course
"Introducing Wetlands" is handy for establishing a basic understanding of wetland environments. "People of the Bog," "What A Boat!" and "Wetland Tradeoffs" also deal with wetlands and human culture.

Vocabulary
derivation, root, etymology

Summary

Ever wonder where some of those wild wetland names came from?

Play a word game and research the etymology (word origins) of wetland names.

Objectives

Students will:

• recognize some of the many names for wetlands.

• appreciate the derivation of words and the evolution of language.

• use research skills to discover word derivations.

Materials

• *copies of the Word List student page (one per student)*
• *pencil and paper for each group*
• *copy of the Answer Sheet (for teacher)*
• *research books from the library (see Resources)*
• *local area map*

Making Connections

Language is a tool we all use as we interact, discuss ideas, name objects, and get through the daily tasks of living. However, we hardly ever stop to think where individual words, terms, and phrases came from, or how they have changed through time. By studying wetland names, students gain an appreciation for the dynamic way language evolves, and for its power to reflect culture.

Background

Just as plants and animals develop adaptations in response to specific habitat conditions, language also evolves as time passes and circumstances change. Most words can be traced back to their "roots." Many English words stem from Latin roots, although English is actually a Germanic rather than a Romance (Latin-based) language. In many cases, place names can be traced to some characteristic of the landscape (Grand Canyon), to a significant event that took place there (Dead Horse Pass), or to a singular or common resident of the region (Rattlesnake Gulch).

Names and other words commonly indicate the impact of former cultures. Many North American words can be traced back to Native American languages or to the European homelands of early settlers.

We can learn a great deal about a region's culture, history, and character by reconstructing the development of its language. Wetlands are extraordinary for the great number of names they go by in different cultures and parts of the world. Some of these ("swamp," for instance) are widely known, but others are obscure and colloquial. It's fascinating to travel the pathways language has taken to its present form. A study of the many strange names for wetlands is an ideal way to begin. (See chapters 1 and 2 for more wetlands and culture information.)

Procedure

Warm Up

Using the preceding information, discuss the fact that language is in a constant state of evolution. Ask students whether they know the origin of their first or last names. Are their names related to geography or culture (e.g., nationality of parents or grandparents)? Last names often relate to a kind of work or profession (e.g., Miller), or indicate a relationship to a relative (e.g., John-son). Suggest that the many wetland terms are a fascinating way to focus on the study of language.

The Activity

Part I

1. **Split the class into groups of three or four and hand out copies of the Word List student page to each student.**

2. **Tell the class that the list of words includes ten names for wetlands, but that these names** are hidden among words that may or may not be familiar. The student's job is to identify as many of the ten wetland names as possible. They will be scored accordingly. Give the groups time (10-15 minutes) to discuss their selections quietly among themselves. One student in each group will act as the spokesperson and scorekeeper. At the end of the time period, each group should have marked their ten wetland names. (If groups finish early, they can try their hand at writing definitions for the words they have chosen.)

3. **Ask each spokesperson to report his or her group's selections. No changes allowed once time has been called!**

4. **Read off the correct wetland names (in boldface on the Answer Sheet) along with their correct definitions. For fun, read the definitions of the other words as well.**

5. **Each group should score itself as follows:**

correct selection = +2 points

incorrect selection = -1 point

Part II

1. **After the word game, discuss the fact that these wetland names all came from somewhere (were derived) and have evolved to their present state. Read the selection below to the class so students gain an appreciation for the rich history behind one wetland name.**

Playa

Wetlands can occur where you least expect them. In the desert regions of Texas, Arizona, New Mexico, California, and Nevada, you can find an unusual type of wetland called a playa. Playas are shallow basins in the flat, sandy soil of the desert. During the rainy season, playa beds fill with water. In that brief period of time, playas are an important source of water for desert plants and animals. When the dry season returns to the desert, the water evaporates or seeps into the sand, and the playa becomes a dry hollow until the next heavy rain.

Playa is a Spanish word which means "beach." The Spanish-speaking people of the southwestern United States named these desert wetlands playas because they contain a lot of sand, just like an ocean beach.

There are playas in other parts of the world. Each country has its own name for this type of wetland. In Saudi Arabia, a playa is called Sabkha. In Iran, it's a kavir. In South Africa, people call these areas pans because they resemble shallow cooking pans.

2. **Tell students they will be conducting their own research on**

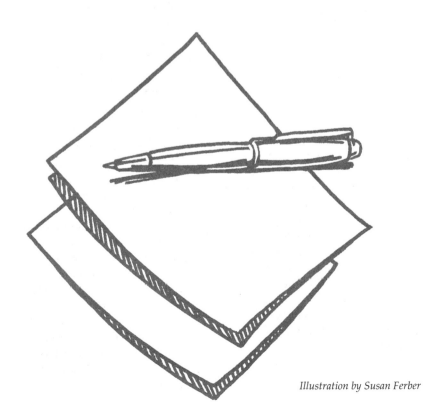

Illustration by Susan Ferber

the etymology of other wetland names. Give them the following pointers to help them get started:

• Ask your school or public librarian to show you the reference section of the library and several etymological guides (see Resources, below).

• Start by looking in a dictionary that includes etymological information (root languages, etc.).

• An encyclopedia is often a useful resource for general background information, which may include word origins.

• Use as many of the books listed below as you can to compile more information.

3. **Have teams of students research the derivations and histories of several wetland names and make short reports of their findings to the class (or submit written reports).**

Wrap Up

Have students summarize the factors that contribute to a place name's development (root language, physical characteristic, geography, significant event, etc.). See if they can identify local place names that illustrate these influences. Study a local map for ideas. Is a local wetland known by some unique name? Have students found other wetland names in their research? Ask if they can guess where some of the other wetland names came from.

Assessment

Have students:

• identify wetland names.

• research and report on the evolution of wetland names.

Extensions

Find more wetland terms from around the world and research their derivations and backgrounds.

Resources

Adams, Ramon. *Western Words*. Norman: University of Oklahoma Press.

Ayto, John. *Dictionary of Word Origins*. New York: Arcade Publishing.

Barnhart, Robert K., editor. *The Barnhart Dictionary of Etymology*. H. W. Wilson Company.

Hendrickson, Robert. *The Henry Holt Encyclopedia of Word and Phrase Origins*. New York: Henry Holt & Company.

The Oxford English Dictionary. Oxford: Clarendon Press.

Shipley, Joseph T. *Dictionary of Word Origins*. New York: Philosophical Library, Inc.

Stewart, George R. *American Place Names*. Oxford: Oxford University Press.

Word List

moray

plat

bog

hoyden

whey

pocosin

bursa

carr

cravat

moire

fen

playa

pompadour

espadrille

pothole

dashiki

swamp

cygnet

umiak

muskeg

slough

sconce

bower

ague

mire

• In terms of property values, wetlands are seen as both nuisance and amenity. They are a nuisance to some because protective regulations hinder development timelines, but are valuable to others because they add the benefits of open space and wildlife habitat to adjacent property.

• Many people value wetlands primarily for their aesthetic beauty. Regardless of these benefits, controversies arise when people who directly benefit from a wetland are not the people who pay for its protection. And it is true that some people benefit more directly than others. For example, a person who likes to fish in a wetland may value it more than another person who does not enjoy fishing.

Wetlands affect the economy, and the distribution of benefits and costs affects people's opinions about wetlands. Some would prefer to convert wetlands to more highly valued uses (a land practice more financially beneficial to them), while others would prefer to protect wetlands for their ecological contributions.

Procedure
Warm Up
Ask students what they think about wetlands. Why do they think they are important? Why would people want to build in or near a wetland? Why would other people want to protect wetlands? List wetland functions and the benefits and disadvantages of those functions on the board.

The Activity
1. **Distribute among the students the reference materials you have found in local newspapers or national magazines and newsletters. As you discuss the controversies surrounding wetlands, encourage students to think in terms of problems rather than issues (issues divide us, problems are something we can solve).** A newspaper might feature a headline such as: "Developer Seeks Permit to Fill Wetlands For Subdivision." But what is the problem? A problem-solving approach will ask, "How can water quality be protected if this subdivision is approved?" or "Are there alternative plans for protecting the wetland?" or "Can we assure jobs and housing and still protect the environment in this case?"

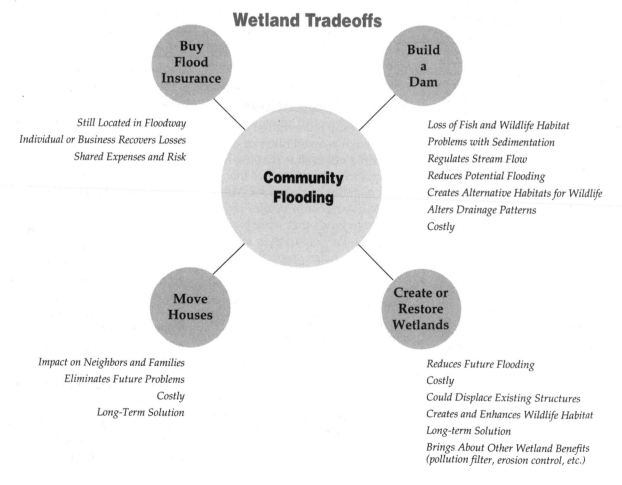

Wetland Tradeoffs

Buy Flood Insurance
- *Still Located in Floodway*
- *Individual or Business Recovers Losses*
- *Shared Expenses and Risk*

Build a Dam
- *Loss of Fish and Wildlife Habitat*
- *Problems with Sedimentation*
- *Regulates Stream Flow*
- *Reduces Potential Flooding*
- *Creates Alternative Habitats for Wildlife*
- *Alters Drainage Patterns*
- *Costly*

Community Flooding

Move Houses
- *Impact on Neighbors and Families*
- *Eliminates Future Problems*
- *Costly*
- *Long-Term Solution*

Create or Restore Wetlands
- *Reduces Future Flooding*
- *Costly*
- *Could Displace Existing Structures*
- *Creates and Enhances Wildlife Habitat*
- *Long-term Solution*
- *Brings About Other Wetland Benefits (pollution filter, erosion control, etc.)*

2. **Focus the discussion on a particular wetland controversy. Have students describe the cause of the problem, determining if it was a natural occurrence, human-made, or a combination of the two.**

3. **Identify the major players in the controversy. Will others be affected by the outcome of this dispute? Compare the values and needs each of the people or groups bring to the negotiating process.**

4. **Write a brief description of the problem in the center of the board. Circle the description.**

5. **Brainstorm potential alternative solutions to the problem. Write proposed solutions on the board surrounding the problem description. Circle each solution.**

6. **Have students evaluate each solution; list pros and cons under each solution. Encourage discussion about the economic and environmental factors in the controversy. List the consequences of each proposed alternative solution. Invite students to research the questions that arise in the discussion; add information they discover to the lists.** Students can consider values, cost, time, resources, ecological balance, jobs, wildlife habitat, wilderness, historic perspectives, and other variables when evaluating the solutions. Could a proposed solution benefit some people while making the situation worse for others? Could a proposed solution actually create more problems in the long run?

7. **Have students rank the solutions and explain their reasons for the preferred order. Does the** ranking reflect student's personal values? Did they arrive at a viable solution? Did it involve some negotiation or compromise?

Wrap Up and Action

Have interested students attend and participate in a local public hearing on a land-use action. Encourage them to state their opinions.

Have students research the consequences of a proposed solution and write advocacy statements for the polar views of these consequences.

Assessment

Have students:

- list beneficial wetland functions.

- describe potential alternatives to wetland protection and wetland destruction.

Extensions

Organize class debates on a variety of wetland issues and problems. Scenarios might include:

- the filling and development of one of the last wetlands in a county;

- filling and developing a wetland that is surrounded by many acres of other wetlands;

- creating a wetland nature preserve in an area pressured by an expanding population's need for economic development.

Have the class do a public opinion survey on the importance of wetlands. Present findings in a newsletter produced by the students.

Have fun with role-playing. Create a wetlands management scenario and ask students to take on the roles of a real estate developer, a farmer, a homeowner, a canoeist, an ecologist, an agency regulator, and others. What alternative solutions came up during the role-play? (See "Hear Ye! Hear Ye!" p. 253.)

Have students research the attempts that have been made to assign dollar values to each wetland function. Perhaps their research will introduce them to cost-benefit analysis. Discuss the pros and cons of this approach to wetlands valuation.

Have students read newspaper accounts of a wetland controversy and analyze which arguments are based on myths and which on facts.

Resources

Caduto, M. 1985. *A Guide on Environmental Values Education.* UNESCO-UNEP international Environmental Education Program, Environmental Education Series 13. Paris: UNESCO.

Coughlan, B., and C. Amor. 1990. *Group Decision Making Techniques for Natural Resource Management Applications,* Resource Publication 185. Washington, D.C.: U.S. Department of the Interior, Fish and Wildlife Service.

Council on Agricultural and Science Technology. 1994. *Wetland Policy Issues.* Ames, Iowa.

Decision Making: The Chesapeake Bay. 1985. An Interdisciplinary Environmental Education Curriculum Unit, 2d ed. College Park: Maryland University, Sea Grant Program.

House, Verne W., and Ardis A. Young. 1988. *Education for Public Decisions.* Working With Our Publics, Module Six. Cooperative Extension and Community College Education, North Carolina State University.

Polesetsky, Matthew, editor. 1991. *Global Resource: Opposing Viewpoints.* San Diego: Greenhaven Press, Inc.

Scodari, Paul F. 1990. *Wetlands Protection: The Role of Economics.* Washington, D.C.: Environmental Law Institute.

Helping Wetland Habitats

Grade Level
K-12

Subject Areas
Biology, Social Studies,
Trades and Industry (Shop)

Duration
Variable

Setting
Classroom and outdoors

Skills
Organizing, applying, and
presenting information

Charting the Course
"Introducing Wetlands"
provides a foundation for
students' identification of
and appreciation for wet-
lands. "Wetland Weirdos,"
"Wet 'n' Wild," "Whose
Clues?" "Tracking Plants and
Keeping Track," and several
other activities provide
lessons on wetland wildlife
habitat. Explore wetland
topics like functions, soils,
and social history with other
WOW! activities.

Vocabulary
enhance, restore, create

Summary
How can people help wetlands?

Students who have acquired an
understanding of wetland functions and benefits and an appreciation of wetland environments
may want to help improve
(enhance) a wetland site. The
following projects will provide
some direction.

Objectives
Students will:

• research wetlands to identify
needs for enhancement.

• build appropriate structures to
enhance wetland habitat for
plants and animals.

• participate in projects to improve wetlands.

Materials
*Materials will depend on project(s)
conducted.*

Making Connections
Students may be familiar with
wetlands and the benefits they
provide to people and wildlife
(see chapter 3). They may be
aware that some wetlands are
threatened and need to be protected. This series of enhancement
activities pinpoints specific steps
that can be taken to make a
wetland a better home for plants
and animals and to restore
damaged wetland features.

Background
Wetlands are home to many
species: fish, insects and their
relatives, reptiles, amphibians,
birds, and mammals (see chapter
4). Animals look for food and
water, good shelter or hiding
places, and plenty of space. These

elements make up their habitat.
The most productive wetland
habitats have a large number and
variety of plants that provide food
and shelter for different animals.
Also, the greater the plant density
in a wetland, the better filter it is
for pollutants.

Sometimes various natural phe-
nomena or other human uses of
wetlands change or damage them,
compromising their value as
habitat. People can help plants and
animals by creating, enhancing, or
restoring habitat features. Enhancement measures can also add
to wetland benefits such as water
quality improvement and flood
abatement. Create means to build
or make something where it wasn't
before. Enhance means to make
something greater or more desirable, to increase its value. Restore
means to put something back into
its original or less damaged form
(see chapters 5 and 6).

Kinds of Projects to Do:

First, have students answer this
question: What is our goal?

• We want to attract wildlife
(birds, dragonflies, butterflies,
other insects, frogs, salamanders,
etc.).

• We want to improve habitat for
wildlife (provide animals with a
better place to live).

• We want to make a damaged
wetland in our community
healthier.

• We want to help solve or reduce
water pollution problems in our
community.

• Other: (write your own)_____
_____
_____

In the spring, place t
a sunny window. Th
develop first, but yo
them because they'i
soil. A month or tw
will appear. If the r
start to turn yellow
fertilizer (spray the
Miracle-Gro® or ar

When the plant
centimeters (2 i
will begin to g
move them to
containers wil
holes in the bc
in a pan that c
inch of water.

When the see
centimeters (
plant them a
a wetland.

Hibiscus: Wl
drops off, it
pod that tur
brown and
hard like
wood. In
October or
November
pod will o
slightly, ar
you can se
brown se
inside. So
the seeds

Projects Will Have Greater Success if You:

• enlist the help of local wetland resource experts.

• obtain adult help for the harder details of the project and ask friends and neighbors to lend a hand.

• follow planting guidelines given in this guide; place native plants only in the proper type and depth of water.

• always get permission from property owners before starting any project, and check on local, state, and federal environmental laws whenever you plan a project that alters the land or water.

Procedure

Warm Up

Ask students to share their knowledge and feelings about wetlands. See if they can identify some local wetlands. What do they know about them? Discuss the wildlife they may have seen there. Are these places important to them? Valuable to the region?

The Activity

1. **Students who are concerned about the health of local wetlands can conduct an enhancement project or create a wetland. Use the following guidelines to focus the search for a site.**

Locating a Project Site

Start by looking around your community. It will be easiest to complete a project and see your success if the location is near your homes or school.

• Look for wetlands on the school grounds, in a nearby park, or elsewhere in your community. The edges of a pond (including a farm's irrigation pond), lake, or slow-flowing stream might be improved by the addition of

wetland plants. (See p. 329 for wetland map sources.)

• Construction projects (roads, buildings, etc.) often include human-made sediment control or stormwater management ponds that filter and control runoff from the site. These may be good spots to plant wetland plants, if the areas stay wet long enough. Check with the builder, landowner, or state highway department for permission and assistance.

• When it rains, is there lots of water running off your school (or any other) parking lot? Consider planting wetland plants just downhill of the pavement in a wet spot to help filter pollutants and sediment in the runoff. You might have to dig out a depression to hold water in the planted area.

• If you can't find any of the above, you might want to build a small pond in the schoolyard (see Appendix, p. 317). This will make a nice place for everyone to learn about wetlands.

2. **Organize a field trip to several sites and help the students determine the best place to conduct a project.**

3. **Use the following checklist to assess a site's need for enhancement.**

Clues to Enhancement Needs

Every site is different, so it's hard to predict needs in advance. You should visit each potential site and consider the following:

• Take a close look at the plants growing there. How many kinds do you see? If the site is a freshwater wetland with only one or two kinds of plants, it might help to add a few more to the plant community.

• Have you seen any animals or signs of animals in the area? If there are few signs of life, it may mean that the water quality is poor or that the habitat doesn't provide enough food or cover. The addition of wetland plants, nesting boxes, and feeders may help. Plant things that animals like.

• Are there bare areas of ground? Planting there will help hold the soil.

• Is the water cloudy and brown or green? Additional plants could help remove excess sediment and nutrients.

4. **Review the range of projects on the following pages students could participate in and help them select an appropriate project or projects.**

5. **Help students plan and conduct the project.**

Wrap Up and Action

Summarize steps students took to complete the project(s). What do they think they did well? What would they do differently next time? What recommendations would they make to someone taking on a similar project?

Encourage the students to publicize their enhancement measures. They could contact the media or write a class editorial for the paper.

Discuss the long-term maintenance and follow-up needs of their project site(s).

Assessment

Have students:

• identify potential sites for wetland enhancement projects.

• participate in projects aimed at improving wetland habitat.

- develop a plan for
  wetland enhancem

- evaluate the outc
  project.

- maintain and mo

Extensions

Wetland enhancem
can expand almos
both in scope and
graphic area that
dress. Communit
can add an impor
to future projects
skills and energie
dents. Monitorin
for maintenance
projects, and gen
is an important
enhancement, re
creation efforts.
be encouraged

Resources

POW!: The Plan
Karen L. Rippl
Garbisch, PhD
mental Concer
MD.

Other specific
with the activ

Wetland F
Projects
Grow a W

Materials

small plastic
cartons, jars
with lids, bak
screening, pc

Homegrow
beautify a
enhance w
Be certain
can grow i
(fresh, bra
project site
pp. 298-30
appropria
and choos

When the seedlings are about 5 centimeters (2 inches) tall, move them to larger pots. When they are about 10 centimeters (4 inches) tall, plant them in a wetland, above the water's edge. These seedlings will eventually grow into shrubs.

Solve a Problem: Plant a Wetland

Many water pollution problems can be solved, or at least lessened, by increasing the number and quality of wetlands! Since plants' roots help hold soil in place, strategic plantings will reduce erosion in sparsely vegetated areas. Soil that erodes from other areas can be trapped by wetland plants, before it has a chance to cloud the water. Plants also help remove excess nutrients (nitrogen and phosphorus) from the water. And don't forget that animals need healthy habitats with a nice variety of plants for food and hiding places. Increasing the number and/or variety of plants in a wetland improves its value as wildlife habitat. And your "gardening" will make the area look prettier, so people will want to take better care of the wetland in the future!

Planting Tips:

- Planting a wetland plant is basically the same as planting any other type of plant. You can plant at any time the ground is not frozen. Pick a spot that provides the essentials for growth: appropriate sunlight, soil, and water. For wetland plants, the type and depth of water is very important; follow the guidelines for each plant on pp. 299-302. Once you've chosen a site with the proper conditions, plan where each plant will go, and decide how many plants you'll need (spacing suggestions given will allow

plants to fill the area within one year). Then all you have to do for each plant is dig a hole big enough to hold the roots, set the plant in the hole, and tamp the soil down around it.

- Plant herbaceous emergent plants when they are tall enough to stick up above the water in the wetland. Plant tree and shrub seedlings when they are about a year old, if possible. *Note:* In wetlands that are only sometimes wet (e.g., wet during the rainy season), plant tree seedlings during drier periods, since the seedlings may not be able to tolerate flooding at first.

- Plants to be placed in brackish or salt areas must be acclimated to the salinity of the water. If you are buying plants from a nursery, be sure to tell the staff what the water salinity will be so they can acclimate the plants correctly.

- Buy plants only from a nursery that is within your general geographic region (northeast, southwest, etc.). If you live in Maine, for example, and buy plants from a Florida nursery, the plants may not grow well in your area, even though they are a species that you see around you. Some plants develop regional adaptations, and are called ecotypes. Choose the nursery closest to you from the list provided on p. 303.

- Plants are sold in various forms. Ask for seedling "plugs" or plants in peat pots, as these will survive best. Buy older trees in containers.

- Plant the plants as soon as you receive them from the nursery. If you can't plant them right away, keep them well watered and in the shade until planting time.

- Ask the nursery about fertilizer requirements. If you're planting in

an established wetland, one application at the time of planting should be enough. Slow-release formulas in pellet or tablet form are recommended.

- You may collect plants from other wetlands, but it is not recommended. If you choose to collect wild plants, take very few from a wetland similar to the one you'll plant in; disturb the area as little as possible. Collect plants in a checkerboard pattern, leaving plants in the 4 ½ square meter (5 square feet) surrounding each spot from which one was taken. Be sure any holes left are filled with soil, not water. The surrounding plants should eventually spread to fill the empty spaces.

- If you are interested in planting trees, shrubs, and other herbaceous species, or if the planting information provided here doesn't apply to your area, consult local wetland experts or nurseries.

Plant a Salt Marsh or Shoreline

Salt marshes and shoreline areas are very important habitats. They are a link between land and water. They are often the last stopping place for rainwater runoff that is flowing toward the water supply. These areas provide nursery and feeding areas for fish, shrimp, crabs, other aquatic animals, and many kinds of birds.

What good is a salt marsh or shoreline wetland without plants? Plants help filter nutrients and pollutants, and they slow the flow of runoff so waterways don't overflow as readily. Plants provide hiding places and food sources for animals. The roots of plants help hold soil in place, so the shore doesn't wash into the water. And plants make an area look more attractive to us!

So if you know of a bay shoreline, salty tidal creek, or salt marsh that seems rather bare and unhealthy-looking, get some helpers together and plant more wetland plants!

Instructions

1. Check the times of high and low tide for your project site for the day(s) you want to work.

2. Go to a nearby, healthier wetland area and study the plants growing there; obtain biological benchmark data (see below).

3. Plan which plants to install in the project area. Draw a diagram to show where the plants will go. Contact a nursery and order the plants (plan for them to arrive on or just before the planting day).

4. Have a planting day! Bring friends! Plan to work at low tide.

5. Come back and check on the project after a few days, then from time to time, to see how it is doing. You may want to replace plants that don't survive. Properly spaced, plants should cover the marsh area in about a year.

Obtaining Biological Benchmark Data

Materials

a few yard or meter sticks or a folding carpenter's ruler; large ball of twine; 5 stakes, painted brightly or with colored ribbon attached; hammer to drive the stakes; clipboard, paper, pencil; at least one partner; field guide to plants; camera (optional)

Wetlands in one region of the country will differ from wetlands in other regions. The best way to decide what to plant in any wetland is to study a similar, fairly healthy one nearby. Wetland plants grow in specific zones or groupings at specific elevations (height of the ground relative to the water level in the wetland). The elevations at which these plants grow are called biological benchmarks.

Part I

1. Find a fairly healthy-looking wetland (salt marsh) within about two miles of the project site, on the same waterway. Use a field guide and the drawings on pp. 299-302 to find these plants: saltmeadow hay (Latin name is *Spartina patens*), groundsel tree (*Baccharis halimifolia*), and cordgrass (*Spartina alterniflora*). For planting projects on the west coast, substitute west coast cordgrass (*Spartina foliosa*) for *Spartina alterniflora* and Pacific

A wetland with few plants: The area is flooded by the tide twice each day, and the lack of plants is allowing the soil to wash away from the shore. Few animals frequent the area.

Before

A wetland with numerous plants: The plants' roots are holding the soil, so the shore is no longer eroding. The water nearby looks cleaner. Native (naturally occurring) plants have filled in the area. The wetland looks lush and healthy, and lots of animals are using it.

After

Wetlands often occur in a depression or basin in the land, with edges that slope up to the elevation of the surrounding ground:

Sometimes this basin is shaped like a bowl. If the bowl is deep, the wetland is usually found on the sloping edges of the bowl— e.g., the edges of a pond.

Sometimes the basin is just the low area at the base of a land slope. The slope can be steep or gradual. The lowest end of the slope is under water, and is then called the bottom of the waterway. Wetland plants are often found growing along the slope that forms the waterway's shoreline. If the water is salty, the wetland is called a salt marsh.

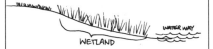

If the basin is very shallow, the wetland probably occurs throughout the basin.

Sedge (*Carex opunta*) for *Spartina patens*. If you are looking in a field guide, use the Latin name to be sure you find the correct plant (common names vary).

2. Find the location closest to the water (farthest down the slope of the land) where the saltmeadow hay or the groundsel tree is growing and place a stake there. This should also be about as far from the water as the cordgrass grows (cordgrass should be growing from here down toward the water). Walk along the shore, parallel to the water line, and mark two or three other spots. The line created by connecting these points is the Mean High Water (MHW) line. This line marks the elevation (the height on the slope of the land) to which the average high tide reaches. This is your reference point, to be used to measure the elevations of the plant zones. For this exercise, we will say that the elevation of MHW is 0 (zero). Anything below the line is a negative elevation; anything above the line is a

positive elevation. (see diagram)

3. Now find the highest place where the saltmeadow hay is growing and mark the spot with a stake. Measure the elevation difference between this spot and the MHW line, as in the diagram; record the distance as a positive number of feet or inches (or meters or centimeters).

Find the lowest place the cordgrass grows to and mark the spot. Measure the distance between this spot and the MHW line, as in the diagram; record the distance as a negative number of feet or inches (meters or centimeters).

Mark and measure the elevations of any other types of plants you see in these or other zones. Make sketches or take pictures to help you remember what the area was like. When you have gathered your data, remove all stakes and save them for Part II.

Part II

Transfer the data collected in Part I to your project's site. Here's how:

1. Obtain a copy of this year's tide tables from the library or from the U.S. Department of Commerce, National Oceanic and Atmospheric Administration (NOAA), Distribution Branch, 6501 Lafayette Avenue, Riverdale, MD 20737; 1-301-436-6990.

Find the daily tidal predictions for the city or town closest to your project site (listed alphabetically). Find the tide chart for the month you will be working at the site; place a bookmark at that page.

Look up the name of the city in the Index to Stations and find the number assigned to the city. Look at the Tidal Difference Table near the back of the book. Find the mean tidal range for your city, which will be listed by the city's assigned number (see example, at the top of the next page).

Go back to the tide chart you have marked. Look at the high tide listings for that month and find a few dates when the high tide will be the same as the mean tidal range in the tidal table. Write these dates down. You will need to go to the project site on one of these days to do your planning, but you should only go when there is no strong wind or storm to alter the tide. Plan to go on the earliest date; if the weather is bad, you will have other days to choose from.

2. When you go to the project site, bring the biological benchmark data you gathered at the other wetland. Arrive at least 30 minutes before the scheduled high tide. Sit and wait for the tide to reach its peak, then place a few stakes along the high tide line. This is the MHW line. Now

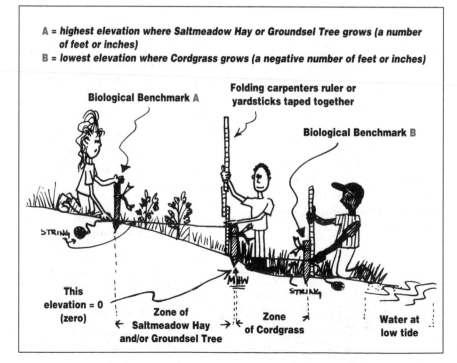

A = **highest elevation where Saltmeadow Hay or Groundsel Tree grows (a number of feet or inches)**

B = **lowest elevation where Cordgrass grows (a negative number of feet or inches)**

Biological Benchmark A

Folding carpenters ruler or yardsticks taped together

Biological Benchmark B

STRING

This elevation = 0 (zero)

MHW

STRING

← **Zone of Saltmeadow Hay and/or Groundsel Tree** →

Zone of Cordgrass

Water at low tide

NO.	PLACE	POSITION		DIFFERENCES				RANGES		Mean Tide Level
				Time		Height				
		Lat.	Long.	High Water	Low Water	High Water	Low Water	Mean	Spring	
		° ′	° ′	h. m.	h. m.	ft	ft	ft	ft	ft
2115	Fort Carroll......................	39 13	76 31	-0 01	+0 01	0.0	0.0	1.1	1.3	0.6
2117	BALTIMORE, Fort McHenry.............	39 16	76 35	Daily predictions				1.1	1.3	0.6
2119	Fells Point, Baltimore Harbor.......	39 17	76 35	+0 05	+0 06	+0.1	0.0	1.2	1.3	0.6
2121	Middle Branch, Baltimore Harbor.....	39 16	76 38	+0 22	+0 18	-0.1	0.0	1.0	1.2	0.5

TABLE 2. — TIDAL DIFFERENCES AND OTHER CONSTANTS

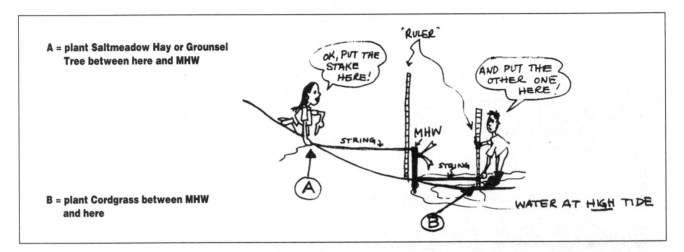

A = plant Saltmeadow Hay or Grounsel Tree between here and MHW

B = plant Cordgrass between MHW and here

measure and mark the same elevations at this site as you recorded at the first site. The areas marked will be planted with the same kinds of plants as those in the first wetland. Keep in mind that if the slope of the land here is very different from the slope at the first site, then the elevations may occur farther from or closer to the MHW line.

Part III

Sketch a planting design based on the biological benchmark data collected and transferred in Parts I and II. Save all of your notes and data. Use the design as a guide when ordering plants from a nursery, and when installing plants on the planting day.

Remember:

• Plan ahead so that you will be planting at low tide.

• Plant saltmeadow hay, cordgrass, soft rush, or common three-square in rows that run

parallel to the shore or water line. Space plants in a checkerboard pattern (see diagram). This will help prevent the formation of gullies between vertical rows of plants.

Enhance or Create a Pond

Although ponds themselves are not necessarily considered wetlands, the shallow edges and the area surrounding the water can be wetlands. The pond system as a whole provides habitat for numerous species of wetland and aquatic animals such as fish, birds, dragonflies and other insects, frogs, salamanders, and turtles. Even a few mammals may visit the pond looking for food and water.

If there is a pond in your community, you may want to consider enhancing or enlarging the surrounding area of wetland plants. This will improve or add habitat and can help improve the quality of the water. Don't forget about working with human-made ponds on farms (used for irrigation or other purposes) and near recently completed construction sites such as roads, buildings, or parking lots (these ponds help filter runoff from the site).

Maybe you'd like to create new habitat for birds, dragonflies, frogs, and other wildlife by building a small pond or a small, shallow marsh! The school grounds might be a good spot for this living classroom; an area

NO: Gullies may form between vertical rows of plants.

YES: Shoreline is more stabilized

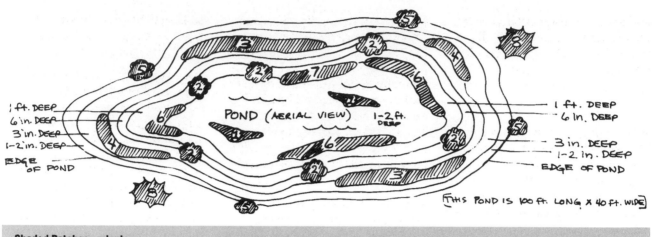

I ft. DEEP
6 in. DEEP
3 in. DEEP
1-2 in. DEEP
EDGE OF POND

POND (AERIAL VIEW)   1-2 ft. DEEP

I ft. DEEP
6 in. DEEP
3 in. DEEP
1-2 in. DEEP
EDGE OF POND

[THIS POND IS 100 ft. LONG x 40 ft. WIDE]

Shaded Patches = plants

1 = Sago Pond Weed	3 = Blue Flag (Iris)	5 = Hibiscus	7 = Cattail
2 = Buttonbush	4 = Sweet Flag	6 = Pickerel Weed	8 = Black Willow

where everyone can watch nature in their own back yard. Of course, you'll need permission from landowners or school administrators for this or any other project.

Enhancing an Existing Pond:

Ponds are not all alike; each one has a different water depth and side slope. The quality and quantity of the water in the pond can be affected by the land around it, and how that land is used. There is no set formula for vegetating (adding plants to) a pond. To decide what to plant, observe the plants that are already growing and the condition of the water. How deep is the water in different spots? You may decide to simply add more of the species that are there already, to fill in bare spots or improve the look of the pond. The goal is not to make an arboretum, but to add a few strategic plantings of species that naturally grow together.

Choose a pond that has some outflow, such as a stream or culvert (large pipe), since an enclosed pond could overfill and drown your plants. Also, choose a pond with a bottom that is muddy (silt or clay soil) instead of sandy,

since a sandy-bottomed pond could drain away.

As you begin to plan your project, obtain biological benchmark data if you can (see p. 293; omit tide references if inappropriate). Measure and record water depths for each zone of plants; measure elevation differences in relation to the water level of the pond instead of MHW. Compare the biological benchmark data you obtained to the recommended water depths for specific species on pp. 298-302. You may find that the plants at the pond are growing outside their predicted range. This is a sign that the water level changes with different seasons. If there are few or no plants already growing at the pond, you should study the pond over a long period of time, particularly during the dry summer months, to get information on seasonal changes in water level. If you know that the water will be shallower during part of the year, adjust your planting design so the plants won't die for lack of water.

Sketch your project before you begin planting; mark planting locations for each type of plant. The sketch will communicate your design to those

helping with the planting.

You needn't limit your plant choices to the species that are already growing in the pond. Pages 299-302 provide a nice variety of alternatives. Be sure to read the water type and depth information ("Where it grows . . ."). If you follow those guidelines, your planting should be successful. Underwater plants such as sago pond weed, widgeon grass, and wild celery should be planted in water that is clear, not muddy. Remember that wild plants are sensitive to too much or too little water, just like house plants. If your first attempt at planting is unsuccessful, don't be discouraged! It may just have been a dry year, so try again! Next time, include drought-tolerant plants like switchgrass, three-square, sweet flag, buttonbush, rice cutgrass, or cattail.

Building a Small Pond or Marsh:

If you'd like to create a living learning center in your yard or schoolyard, you can build a small, shallow pond or marsh where there wasn't one before! First, get permission from the property owner and check local ordinances and state environmental laws to make sure it is okay to install a pond. Then make a few planning decisions.

Where will you put your pond or marsh?

A low-lying spot is probably the best, since it is likely to catch water from higher areas. Choose a spot that is out of the way of human and pet traffic—wild animals prefer areas that are relatively undisturbed. But don't go too far away from a water source such as a hose—it takes a lot of water to fill even a small pond! Also, choose a spot that will not be shaded most of the day by trees or buildings. Many pond plants require full sun for at least five hours each day.

Will the ground hold water or will the water drain right down?

If the soil has lots of clay in it or the ground usually stays wet for several days in the spring or after a rain, the pond may hold water. To be more certain, dig a hole about 60 centimeters (2 feet) deep and 30 centimeters (1 foot) wide and fill it with water. If the water stays in the hole for several days, your pond will probably hold water. If water seems to drain right down through the ground, you'll need to line the pond with something waterproof. For best results, obtain the assistance of your local soil conservation district (see U.S. Government listings in the phone book—look up "Agriculture, Department of").

What size and shape will your pond or marsh be?

• For a wider variety of animals (not just fish), makes shallow pond with gently sloping edges. This will provide areas for amphibians, invertebrates, and birds to use.

• Think small if your resources (money, time, and helpers) are limited. At least 4.5 square meters (50 square feet) is a good size (an 8 foot by 6 foot rectangle, or an 8-foot diameter circle). The pond doesn't have to be a regular shape. In fact, curves, dips, points, and coves provide more shoreline area and better hiding places for animals.

• The pond should be at least 45 centimeters (18 inches) to 60 centimeters (2 feet) deep. Even at that depth, the whole pond will probably fill in with spreading plants within a year or so—which is okay, because then it will be a marsh that animals will value as much or even more than the pond. If you really want to have fish in the pond, make it much larger and deeper (5 to 7 feet deep). The water in a small, shallow pond will get too hot in summer to keep fish alive.

What kinds of animals will the pond attract?

With a good variety of plants and habitat areas, the pond may attract insects (dragonflies, damselflies, other aquatic insects), crayfish and microscopic crustacea, frogs, toads, salamanders, turtles, water or marsh birds (kingfishers, wading birds, ducks, geese), songbirds (red-winged blackbirds, many others), and even mammals such as raccoons. If you want to get a head start and supply the beginnings of the food web, add a few animals that you've collected from a similar body of water. Collect dragonfly nymphs and other aquatic insects, snails, crayfish, frogs, or small fish (large pond only) such as minnows and sunfish.

Plants are important! Choose a variety of freshwater plants. Plant small patches of each kind of plant, since many will spread or multiply within the year.

Note: When the project is complete, no more than half of the pond's surface should be covered with plant material (sunlight should be able to reach aquatic animals and underwater plants). If you create a marsh instead of a pond, the area can be fairly covered by plants. If your pond has a liner, you will have to keep the plants in pots (use topsoil, not potting soil) and just sit the pots in the water; otherwise, the plants' roots will puncture the liner and the pond will drain. (For a sample planting design, see p. 296. A small pond will have fewer plants.)

Instructions

1. Study a model pond or design your own using the plants on pp. 299-302. Draw your plans and make notes. Order the liner, plants, and other supplies.

2. Gather lots of friends with shovels, rakes, and tape measures. Review your design and plans. Lay out the lines of the pond with string and small stakes.

3. Clear all grass and weeds from the ground within the pond limits. Dig out the pond basin, then rake any loosened soil on the sides and bottom of the pond until it is fairly even.

4. Seal the pond by inserting a liner, if necessary, and fill the pond with water. Liners cost money, but they may be the only way to successfully build your pond. You have a few choices:

• Clay-lined pond: Cover and seal the bed of the pond basin with a layer of bentonite clay, which is available from building supply companies.

• Easier, cheaper solution: Purchase flexible, stretchable, 20- to 32-mil PVC liner from a garden center, or look in the back of a gardening magazine for suppliers. Measure the dimensions of the pond and calculate the size you'll need.

Width = width of pond + (three x depth)

Length = length of pond + (three x depth)

You'll also need rocks or other weights to hold the edges of the liner in place while you s-l-o-w-l-y fill it with water. The weight of the water will stretch the liner into place. You can hide the over-lapped edges with potted plants, stones, etc.

• Some garden and building supply stores sell plastic or fiberglass preformed ponds. If you use one of these, dig out a basin to fit the pond mold, set the mold in level, and fill the spaces around it with soil. Vegetate with potted plants.

5. Let the water age for a week, then arrange your potted plants or plant some in soil.

Wetland Planting Guide

The following four pages show illustrations and descriptions of plants you can use to create or improve wetlands, or to plant fringe wetlands to filter and slow runoff. Most of these plants require direct sunlight to thrive. Certainly many other plants will grow in wetlands, but these species are available at most wetland nurseries (see list on p. 303). The plants are more likely to survive if you plant them as described. You can design your own project. Contact local wetland resource specialists for information on appropriate wetland plants for your area.

Note: Most of the plants shown are for the eastern United States.

Key for this guide:

• fresh water = 0-0.5 parts per thousand (ppt)

• brackish water = .5-30 ppt

• saltwater = 30-35 ppt

• MHW = the average high tide elevation

• MLW = the average low tide elevation

• IZ = intertidal zone, the area between MHW and MLW

• on center = space plants the specified distance apart on all sides; they'll spread and fill in spaces in about a year. Trees and shrubs do not spread. Plant shrubs 2 to 3 meters (6 to 8 feet) on center, trees 3 to 5 meters (10 to 15 feet) on center (branches will fill in space in 5 to 10 years).

• sometimes wet = wetlands that are sometimes dry, but wet during rainy seasons

Wetland Planting Guide

(See legend, p. 298.)

Soft Rush

(*Juncus effusus*)

Where it grows...
• tidal fresh water, upper part of IZ to above MHW
• in nontidal fresh water that is up to 15 centimeters (6 inches) deep

How to plant it...
• 15 centimeters (6 inches) on center

Wildlife value:
• food, cover, nesting for wood ducks, and other waterfowl

Switchgrass

(*Panicum virgatum*)

Where it grows...
• in tidal salt, brackish, and fresh water, above MHW (and drier)
• nontidal fresh water areas that are sometimes wet; tolerates dry

How to plant it...
• 15 centimeters (6 inches) from center

Wildlife value:
• food for waterfowl, upland game birds, some songbirds, muskrats, rabbits, deer

Saltmeadow Hay

(*Spartina patens*)

Where it grows...
• in tidal salt and brackish water, above MHW
• characteristic of the high marsh

How to plant it...
• 30 centimeters (1 foot) on center
• full sun, no shade

Wildlife value:
• food for geese, black ducks, sparrows, rails

Groundsel Tree

(*Baccharis halimifolia*)

Where it grows...
• in tidal salt, brackish, and fresh water, above MHW; nontidal areas that are sometimes wet

How to plant it...
• shrub; plant 2 to 3 meters (6 to 8 feet) on center
• full sun, no shade

Wildlife value:
• cover, nesting, breeding grounds for songbirds, waterfowl, shorebirds

Wax Myrtle

(*Myrica cerifera*)

Where it grows...
• in tidal, brackish, and fresh water, above MHW (and drier)
• nontidal areas that are regularly wetted or have saturated soil

How to plant it...
• shrub; plant 2 to 3 meters (6 to 8 feet) on center
• north of VA, use Bayberry (*Myrica pensylvanica*) instead

Wildlife value:
• food for songbirds

Common Three-Square

(*Scirpus pungens*)

Where it grows...
• in tidal brackish and fresh water, upper half of IZ
• nontidal fresh water up to 15 centimeters (6 inches) deep and wetlands that are only sometimes wet; tolerates dryness

How to plant it...
• 60 centimeters (2 feet) on center

Wildlife value:
• food, cover for most waterfowl, shorebirds, muskrats, fish

Smooth Cordgrass

(*Spartina alterniflora*)

Where it grows...
• tidal salt water, upper half of IZ
• characteristic of low marsh

How to plant it...
• 60 centimeters (2 feet) on center
• full sun, no shade

Wildlife value:
• food for black ducks, geese, rails, sparrows, muskrats

Sago Pond Weed

(*Potamogeton pectinatus*)

Where it grows...
• tidal brackish and fresh water, below MLW (under water)
• nontidal fresh water that is 60 centimeters (2 feet) deep or deeper

How to plant it...
• 60 centimeters (2 feet) on center, *in clear water only*

Wildlife value:
• important food source for waterfowl, shelter for fish, amphibians, reptiles, invertebrates, mammals

Red Mangrove

(*Rhizophora mangle*)

Where it grows...
• in tidal salt water *at* MWH
• coastal Florida and the tropics

How to plant it...
• tree; plant as many as needed, 3 to 5 meters (10-15 feet) on center
• in U.S., Florida only

Wildlife value:
• food and habitat for many wading birds, fish, invertebrates

Buttonbush

(*Cephalanthus occidentalis*)

Where it grows...
• tidal fresh water, upper half of IZ to above MHW
• nontidal fresh water up to one meter (3 feet) deep and areas that are sometimes wet; tolerates dry periods

How to plant it..
• shrub; plant 2 to 3 meters (6 to 8 feet) on center
• can tolerate full shade

Wildlife value:
• food for waterfowl, rails, red-winged blackbirds, hummingbirds

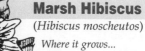

Marsh Hibiscus

(*Hibiscus moscheutos*)

Where it grows...
• tidal brackish and fresh water, upper part of IZ to above MHW
• nontidal fresh water up to 8 centimeters (3 inches) deep and areas that are sometimes wet

How to plant it...
• shrub; plant 2 to 3 meters (6 to 8 feet) on center
• full sun, no shade

Wildlife value:
• food for hummingbirds

Widgeon Grass

(*Ruppia maritima*)

Where it grows...
• tidal fresh, brackish, and salt water, below MLW (under water)
• nontidal fresh water 60 centimeters (2 feet) or deeper

How to plant it..
• 60 centimeters (2 feet) on center, *in clear water only*

Wildlife value:
• food for waterfowl, marsh birds, shorebirds; shelter, nursery for fish and invertebrates

Sweet Flag

(*Acorus calamus*)

Where it grows...
• tidal brackish and fresh water, above MHW
• nontidal fresh water up to 15 centimeters (6 inches) deep and areas regularly wetted; tolerates dry periods

How to plant it...
• 30 centimeters (1 foot) on center
• tolerates partial shade

Wildlife value:
• food, cover for waterfowl, muskrats

Blue Flag (Iris)

(*Iris versicolor*)

Where it grows...
• nontidal fresh water up to 15 centimeters (6 inches) deep, and areas regularly wetted

How to plant it...
• 15 centimeters (6 inches) on center
• full sun (won't flower in shade)

Wildlife value:
• food for muskrats, marsh birds

Rice Cutgrass
(*Leersia oryzoides*)

Where it grows...
• tidal fresh water, upper part of IZ
• nontidal fresh water up to 8 centimeters (3 inches) deep and areas that are sometimes wet; tolerates dry periods

How to plant it...
• 30 centimeters (1 foot) on center

Wildlife value:
• harbors food-source animals for waterfowl, rails, herons and other birds, fish, reptiles, etc.

Spatterdock
(*Nuphar lutea*)

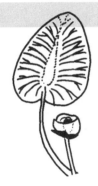

Where it grows...
• tidal fresh water, below MLW
• nontidal fresh water 30 centimeters to 1 meter (1 to 3 feet) deep and areas regularly wetted

How to plant it...
• 1 meter (3 feet) on center (leaves are big)

Wildlife value:
• food for waterfowl, beavers, porcupines, deer, muskrats, fish; also shade, shelter for fish, etc.

Arrow Arum
(*Peltandra virginica*)

Where it grows...
• tidal fresh water, upper half IZ
• nontidal fresh water up to 30 centimeters (1 foot) deep and areas regularly wetted

How to plant it...
• 60 centimeters (2 feet) on center (leaves are big)
• tolerates partial shade

Wildlife value:
• food for wood ducks, rails, other birds, muskrats

Swamp Rose
(*Rosa palustris*)

Where it grows...
• tidal fresh water, in drier areas above MHW
• nontidal fresh water areas that are regularly wetted

How to plant it...
• shrub; plant 2 to 3 meters (6 to 8 feet) on center

Wildlife value:
• food for upland game birds, food and cover for songbirds

Duckweed
(*Lemna minor*)

Where it grows...
• floats on the surface of fresh water (not rooted to bottom)

How to plant it...
• just place in on water's surface
• often carried in by ducks, etc.

Wildlife value:
• food for waterfowl, coots, rails, and beavers

Cinnamon Fern
(*Osmunda cinnamomea*)

Where it grows...
• nontidal fresh water areas that are always or sometimes wet or have saturated soils

How to plant it...
• 1 meter (3 feet) on center (fronds are big)
• can tolerate full shade

Wildlife value:
• food for upland game birds, deer

Pickerel Weed
(*Pontederia cordata*)

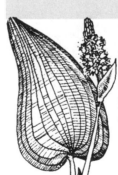

Where it grows...
• tidal fresh water, upper half of IZ
• nontidal fresh water up to 30 centimeters (1 foot) deep and areas regularly wetted

How to plant it...
• 60 centimeters (2 feet) on center (leaves are big)
• tolerates full shade

Wildlife value:
• food for some waterfowl

Duck Potato
(*Sagittaria latifolia*)

Where it grows...
• tidal fresh water, middle of IZ
• nontidal fresh water up to 60 centimeters (2 feet) deep and areas regularly wetted

How to plant it...
• 60 centimeters (2 feet) on center
• tolerates partial shade

Wildlife value:
• food for many waterfowl, rails, muskrats, beavers

Cattail

(Typha latifolia or angustifolia)

Where it grows...
• *angustifolia* in tidal brackish water, upper part of IZ
• both species in tidal fresh water, upper part of IZ; nontidal fresh water up to 30 centimeters (1 foot) deep and areas that are sometimes wet; tolerates dryness

How to plant it...
• 60 centimeters (2 feet) on center, spreads rapidly

Wildlife value:
• food: waterfowl, muskrats, beavers
• nesting: waterfowl, marsh wrens, red-winged blackbirds, young fish

Lizard Tail

(Saururus cernuus)

Where it grows...
• nontidal fresh water up to 30 centimeters (1 foot) deep and areas regularly wetted

How to plant it...
• 60 centimeters (2 feet) on center
• tolerates partial shade

Wildlife value:
• food for wood ducks

Wild Celery

(Vallisneria americana)

Where it grows...
• tidal fresh water, below MLW (under water)
• nontidal fresh water 60 centimeters (2 feet) deep or deeper

How to plant it...
• 60 centimeters (2 feet) on center, *in clear water only*

Wildlife value:
• important food source for waterfowl; habitat, shade; harbors food for fish, invertebrates

Wild Rice

(Zizania aquatica)

Where it grows...
• tidal fresh water, middle of IZ
• nontidal fresh water up to one meter (three feet) deep and areas regularly wetted

How to plant it...
• an annual plant (dies back each year, new plants grow from the seed dropped); plant as needed to fill space desired

Wildlife value:
• food: waterfowl, rails, muskrats;
• nesting: marsh wrens

Wetland Nurseries

Plant-A-Plug Systems, Inc.
P.O. Box 1953
Pine Bluff, AR 71613
501-536-4768

Freshwater Farms
5851 Myrtle Ave.
Eureka, CA 95503-9510
800-200-8969

Las Pilitas Nursery
Las Pilitas Road
Santa Margarita, CA 93453
805-438-5992

Tree of Life Wholesale Nursery
P.O. Box 635
San Juan Capistrano, CA 92693
714-728-0685

Aquatic & Wetlands Nurseries
2045 Broadway, Suite 100
Boulder, CO 80302
303-442-5770
Arizona nursery also; same phone #

Florida Natives Nursery, Inc.
16018 Milam Drive
Odessa, FL 33556
813-920-9509

Horticultural Systems
P.O. Box 70
Golf Course Road
Parrish, FL 34219
941-776-1760

Plants for Tomorrow Inc.
16361 Norris Road
Loxahatchee, FL 33470
407-790-1422

Eco-Gardens
P.O. Box 1227
Decatur, GA 30031
404-294-6468

The Natural Garden
38 West 443 Highway 64
St. Charles, IL 60175
708-584-0150

Prairie Grass Unlimited, Inc.
P.O. Box 59
Burlington, IA 52601
319-754-8839

Environmental Concern Inc.
P.O. Box P
St. Michaels, MD 21663
410-745-9620

Bigelow Nurseries
P.O. Box 718
Northborough, MA 01532
508-845-2143

Grass Roots Nursery
24765 Bell Road
New Boston, MI 48164
313-654-2405

Prairie Moon Nursery
Box 163, RR 3
Winona, MN 55987
507-452-1362

Gilberg Perennial Farms
2906 Ossenfort Road
Glencoe, MO 63038
314-458-2033

Bitteroot Native Growers
445 Quast Lane
Corvallis, MT 59828
406-961-4991

Stock Seed Farms, Inc.
28008 Mill Road
Murdock, NE 68407
402-867-3771

L.A. Brochu & Son Nurseries, Inc.
121 Commercial Street
Concord, NH 03301
603-224-4350

Pinelands Nursery
323 Island Road
Columbus, NJ 08022
609-291-9486

Southern Tier Consulting, Inc.
P.O. Box 30
West Clarksville, NY 14786
716-968-3120

Gardens of the Blue Ridge
P.O. Box 10
Pineola, NC 28662
704-733-2417

Cherryhill Aquatics
2627 North County Line Road
Sunberry, OH 43074
614-965-2798

William Ticker, Inc.
7125 Tanglewood Drive
Independence, OH 44131
216-524-3491

Balance Restoration Nursery
27995 Chambers Mill Road
Lorane, OR 97451
503-942-5530

Ernst Crownvetch Farms
R.D. 5, Box 900
Meadville, PA 16335
814-425-7276

Octoraro Wetland Nurseries
P.O. Box 24
Oxford, PA 19363
610-932-3762

Doremus Wholesale Nursery
Route 2 Box 750
Warren, TX 77664
409-547-3536

Lilypons Water Gardens
839 FM 1489, P.O. Box 188
Brookshire, TX 77423-2188
713-391-0076
301-874-5503 - Lilypons Youth Prgm.

Frosty Hollow Nursery
Box 53
Langley, WA 98260
360-221-2332

J & J Tranzplant Aquatic Nursery Inc.
Box 227-WJ
Wild Rose, WI 54984-0227
414-622-3552

Kester's Wild Game Food Nurseries
P.O. Box 516
Omro, WI 54963
414-685-2929

Of course, there are many more nurseries that sell native wetland plants than those listed here. Contact local nurseries and agencies to locate other plant sources.

Bird and Wildlife Enhancement

Wetlands are excellent places for many animals to raise young, since there is plenty of water, food, and protective cover (plants). Sometimes you can help birds by building nesting boxes or platforms to suit certain species, and installing them in a nearby wetland.

If you want to start with a simpler project to attract nesting birds, here are some things you can do:

• Supply building materials for nests. Pile sticks and other natural materials out in the open, in or near the wetland. Don't be surprised if animals other than birds use the pile for nesting or hiding.

• Encourage wetland managers and landowners to leave dead trees standing. These make great homes for woodpeckers, wood ducks, and other cavity nesters.

• Erect roosting structures such as natural-looking posts and poles, a wire line (posts connected by a length of wire), or a fencerow. These are good perching and resting spots for birds. As an added bonus birds will leave droppings which often contain seeds—eventually leading to an interesting new crop of plants!

Osprey Nesting Platform

Ospreys, sometimes called "fish hawks" or "fish eagles" because they eat mostly fish, are usually found around lakes, rivers, and coasts. They like to nest above water in tall dead trees. When trees are not available, ospreys will nest on the highest structure they can find, such as a power line pole (which can be very dangerous for the birds) or a buoy or channel marker. Nesting platforms like the one below will offer ospreys safer places to build their nests and raise young. Put one in a marsh near where you live!

Materials and Instructions

Construct mounting posts and support structures with three meter (16-foot-long) four-by-fours of seasoned oak or white cedar. The mounting posts should be buried at least 1 meter (3 feet) into the soil and braced by four

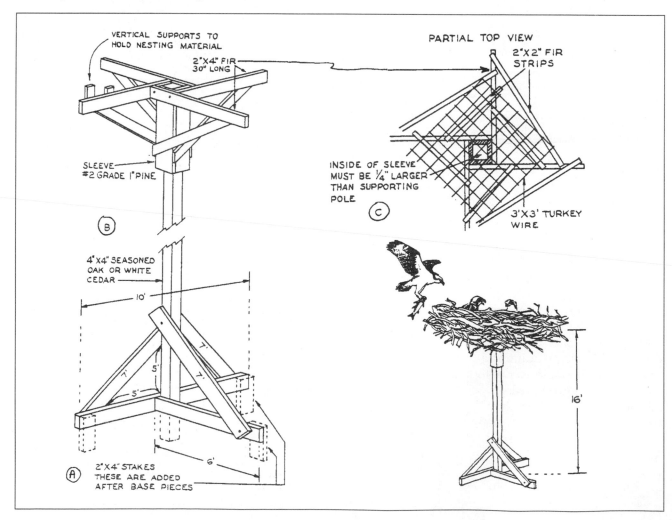

2-meter (6-foot) strut braces. The braces should be predrilled and nailed together with galvanized nails.

The platform is constructed around a pine sheath that slips over the top of the mounting pole. Four 2-inch x 4-inch, 30-inch-long fir struts form a foundation for eight 1-inch x 2-inch fir strips that support a 3-foot x 3-foot piece of turkey wire tacked to the struts.

Artificial nesting platforms similar to the one described here have been successfully used by ospreys, bald and golden eagles, red-tailed and ferruginous hawks, great horned owls, and ravens. Nesting platforms in sunny, arid habitats should have a wooden protective canopy the size of the nest platform to provide partial shade.

[Instructions and illustrations from a design by Peter Ames and Paul Spitzer of Old Lyme, CT. Reprinted with permission of Charles Scribner's Sons, an imprint of Macmillan Publishing Company, from *The Audubon Society Guide to Attracting Birds*, Stephen W. Kress. 1985. Illustrations by Anne Senechal Faust.]

Nesting Platform for Ducks or Geese

Canada geese, mallards, black ducks, and many other kinds of waterfowl prefer to nest on small islands, where they can keep an alert watch for predators. Beaver and muskrat houses also serve as nesting sites. Artificial nest sites can be fashioned by building a floating 2-meter x 2-meter (6-foot x 6-foot) wooden raft over a Styrofoam core. The raft should be anchored to the bottom using bleach bottles filled with sand or instant concrete mix. Fill the raft with straw and paint the Styrofoam a dark brown color to

help it blend with the environment. Position the raft near emergent vegetation at the edge of the pond or lake so young birds can find food and shelter.

A goose or duck nesting platform for use in marsh habitats can be constructed on 7-foot-long steel posts set into the marsh soil. The platform consists of a 2-inch x 4-inch frame that supports 1-inch x 8-inch planks. A truck tire wired to the platform and filled with straw makes an excellent goose nest site.

[Instructions and plans reprinted with permission of Charles Scribner's Sons, an imprint of Macmillan Publishing Company, from *The Audubon Society Guide to Attracting Birds*, Stephen W. Kress. 1985. Designs redrawn in Kress publication from J. Yoakum, et al., "Habitat Improvement Techniques" *Wildlife Management Techniques Manual*, 4th ed., Stanford D. Schemnitz, editor, 1980. The Wildlife Society, Bethesda, MD. Illustrations by Anne Senechal Faust.]

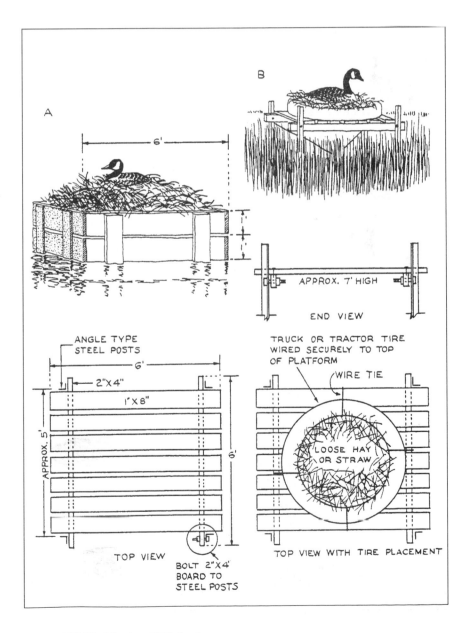

Wood Duck Nest Bucket

Wood ducks are a bit different from most other ducks because they nest in cavities above the water, usually in trees. When the young are ready to fledge (venture away from the nest), they drop out of the cavity and land in the water. Plop!

Wood duck nest boxes can be made of wood and attached to a tree or a post set in the wetland soil. A simpler nesting structure can be made from a 5-gallon plastic bucket (the kind that holds caulking, joint compound, vegetable oil, pickles, etc.). These buckets are fairly easy to come by—look for empty ones at building sites and restaurants.

Materials and Instructions

Thoroughly clean out the bucket. Cut a 3-inch-high by 4-inch-wide entrance hole in the side of the bucket, 2.5 inches from the top. Drill six $\frac{1}{4}$-inch diameter drain holes in the bottom. Remove the handle. Use a wood rasp or coarse sandpaper to rough up the inside of the bucket beneath the entrance hole. The young ducks will use the roughed up area to climb out of the box.

Drill mounting holes ($\frac{1}{4}$-inch diameter) in the bottom. Attach a threaded metal flange to the bottom of the bucket and mount the bucket on the top of a threaded metal pipe. An alternate approach is to drill two mounting holes in the back of the bucket and bolt two buckets back-to-back on a single pole.

Metal poles should be a minimum of $\frac{3}{4}$-inch in diameter. If the structure will be placed in the open marsh, a 2-inch metal pipe or 4-inch x 4-inch wooden post is recommended. If the pole will be in the water constantly, you may use 4-inch PVC pipe (raccoons cannot climb wet PVC pipe).

Important! Equip the mounting poles with a predator guard or baffle to keep young ducks from becoming food for raccoons,

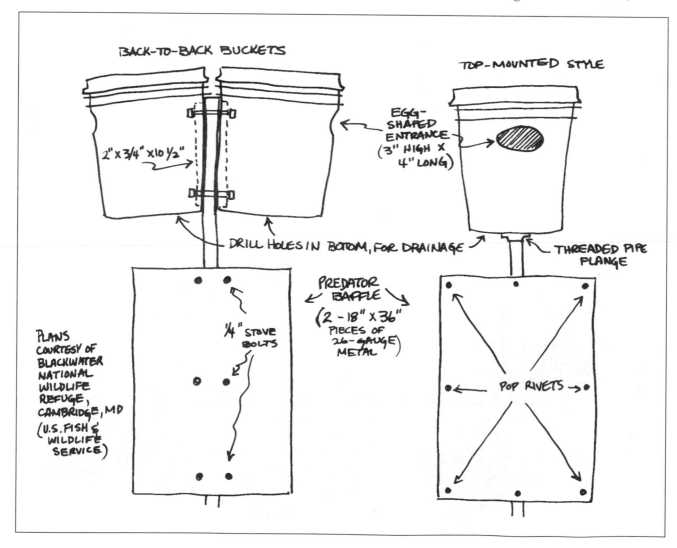

BACK-TO-BACK BUCKETS

TOP-MOUNTED STYLE

EGG-SHAPED ENTRANCE (3" HIGH X 4" LONG)

2" x 3/4" x 10 1/2"

DRILL HOLES IN BOTTOM, FOR DRAINAGE

THREADED PIPE FLANGE

PLANS COURTESY OF BLACKWATER NATIONAL WILDLIFE REFUGE, CAMBRIDGE, MD (U.S. FISH & WILDLIFE SERVICE)

1/4" STOVE BOLTS

PREDATOR BAFFLE (2 - 18" X 36" PIECES OF 26-GAUGE METAL)

POP RIVETS

snakes, etc. (If bucket was mounted on PVC pipe, no extra guard is needed.) A "sandwich" predator guard is easy: bolt two 18-inch by 36-inch pieces of 26-gauge metal around the post.

Paint the finished bucket(s) with a durable outdoor paint. Black, gray, or brown are colors that seem natural in wetland surroundings. Place 8 to 12 centimeters (3 to 4 inches) of wood shavings, wood chips, or sawdust in the bucket as a base for the nest. Place the lid(s) on firmly.

Place the nest structure(s) in or near shallow, calm bodies of water, out in the open where they can easily be found. It is best that the area have overhanging trees, brush, or emergent vegetation along the shore to provide cover for the fledglings. Be sure that predators cannot reach the bucket from the trees above. The bucket should be 2 meters (5 to 6 feet) above the surface of the water.

Clean and repair boxes each summer.

Build a Wildlife Observation Blind

As you approach a wetland or other natural area, you might get a fleeting glimpse of a heron, duck, or other animal just as it hurries out of sight. If you'd like to create a place to watch wildlife, try this idea for an observation blind. You'll be hidden from view, and the animals will have a chance to go about their business undisturbed (as long as you remain fairly still and quiet). It's a great way to learn about animal behavior.

Materials

- 3 4-inch x 4-inch x 11-foot pressure-treated wood fence posts*
- either: 46 boards that measure 2 inches x 4 inches x 8 feet (pressure-treated wood*)
  or: 23 boards that measure 2 inches x 4 inches x 16 feet (pressure-treated wood*)
- 5 pounds of eight-penny galvanized nails*
- hammers*
- post-hole digger*
- tape measure or string and yardstick*
- rocks, tree stumps, logs, or sturdy wooden crates for seats
- at least one adult, for help and supervision
* available from a building supply store; or perhaps a neighbor may have some to donate.

Instructions

1. Find a spot at the edge of a wetland that is naturally somewhat screened by shrubs, trees, or other plants. The ground at the spot will have to be fairly level. Pick a spot that will allow you to view wide areas of water and vegetation.

2. Mark the spot where the first post will be placed. Using a long tape measure or string as a guide, mark spots for the other two posts along a straight line (hammer a stick into the ground to mark each spot).

3. Dig 1-meter (3-foot) deep post holes at the places you marked. Set the posts in the holes and have someone hold each post level (perpendicular to the ground). Fill in the hole around the post, tamping the soil down firmly as you fill the hole (a long tool handle will help pack the soil down).

Get Involved!

Grade Level
K-12

Subject Areas
Social Studies, Political Science, Music

Duration
Variable

Setting
Classroom and community

Skills
Gathering, analyzing, and presenting information

Charting the Course
Start with "Introducing Wetlands" "Wetland Metaphors," "Hear Ye! Hear Ye!" "Wetland Tradeoffs," or "Hydropoly!" to get students to understand the complexities of wetland environments and the issues that surround them.

Vocabulary
hearing, conservation, brochure, legislation

Summary
Are wetlands republican, democrat, or independent?

Wetlands are everyone's concern. Students learn how to involve themselves in the grassroots process of wetland stewardship.

Objectives
Students will:

- describe citizens' roles in the democratic process.

- become aware of basic conservation measures.

- participate in community service activities focused on wetland stewardship.

Materials
Materials will depend on activity selected.

Making Connections
All citizens, regardless of their age, are continuously affected by social and political actions. Some young people may already be involved in some kind of social or political activity (school elections, 4-H or scouting groups, etc.), while others may be only slightly aware of their role as citizens. These activities focus on wetland awareness and ways to transform that awareness into responsible environmental actions.

Background
There are many things citizens can do to help keep the environment clean and healthy, and to help wetlands in particular. We live in a democracy, "by the people, for the people." Our opinions matter, but we have to make our voices heard and our actions felt in order to have any impact.

Students can help wetlands, and the overall environment, by teaching others. Wetlands are a fascinating topic with interesting features that will grab people's attention.

Students can do a great deal to further a cause, whether it's water conservation, habitat improvement, or community involvement in a local issue. Their example of concerned and involved citizenship will show others how to live by their own convictions and, one person at a time, how to make a difference.

Procedure
Warm Up
Ask students to discuss their perceptions of the political process. Tell them that every group decision (what to have for dinner, what game to play, how to get from one place to another) is, in some way, a demonstration of small-scale politics. The debate, discussion, lobbying, and informal voting that they use in everyday decisions can also be useful in community and national political action. Encourage students to think of school policies (dress code, lunchroom discipline, etc.) that affect them. How were these policies established? If students wanted to bring about a change or review, how would they proceed? Students may not know it, but they are involved in politics all the time.

Wetland stewardship is often in the spotlight of the political process, and students can participate more significantly than they may suspect. Brainstorm to see if the class can identify a local controversy that has had some impact on wetlands (e.g., housing developments, highway construction, wildlife sanctuaries, etc.).

The Activity
Consider your local issues, the age and abilities of your students, and select one or more of the following activities.

Wrap Up and Action
Ask students to summarize the specific actions they have taken to affect the outcome of a political issue. Ask them to describe some of the ways the political process touches their everyday existence.

Suggest that they follow up on their efforts by keeping abreast of news and networking with other groups involved with the issue(s).

Have students discuss their impact on the issue(s) and list the results of their actions.

Assessment
Have students:

• take steps to promote a cause of their own choosing (e.g., wetland stewardship, town planning, environmental awareness).

• evaluate the results of their activities.

Extensions
The political process affects us all throughout our lives. Encourage students to be aware of the issues that have an impact on them, and to participate in the political actions that determine these issues' outcome.

Set up committees of students to follow several local issues and make periodic reports to the class.

Resources
"National Wetlands Newsletter. " Bimonthly. Environmental Law Institute, 1616 P Street NW, Suite 200, Washington, D.C. 20036.

Wetland Policy Issues. 1994. Council for Agricultural Science and Technology, 4420 West Lincoln Way, Ames, IA 50014-3447.

Statewide Wetlands Strategies: A Guide to Protecting and Managing the Resource. 1992. World Wildlife Fund. Island Press, Washington, D.C. and Covelo, CA.

Wetland Journal. Environmental Concern Inc., P.O. Box P, St. Michaels, MD 21663

Wetlands Hotline; 1-800-832-7828

Be a Good Citizen: Get Involved
First, Get the Facts

If you want something done about the way wetlands in your community are being treated, you'll have to be well-informed. Before you begin, do your homework. Here's what you need to know:

• Why are these wetlands important or valuable to people? To wildlife?

• What (or who) is threatening the wetlands?

• Are wetlands protected? Know the law.

• Who's in charge of protecting wetlands in your state and community?

• What are your rights as a citizen?

Here are some places to find answers:

• Library

• Newspaper and magazines

• Biology or environmental sciences department of a nearby college

• The rest of this guide (your teacher will have it)

• Phone book (government listings—blue pages)

VOTE!

Okay, maybe you're not old enough to vote yet, but there are things you can do to prepare for that time. Keep up with news from the paper, radio, and TV. Who are your state and local politicians, and what are their views on the environment? Do you agree with their views? Have they acted in a way that represents your views? Do they seem to listen to the people? Are they doing what they promised when elected? When election time comes around, study candidates' positions and discuss these issues with your parents. Encourage parents and older friends to be informed voters and to keep

wetlands and the environment in mind when pulling those levers!

Participate in Local Government

Keep abreast of the environmental issues in your area. Are wetlands getting the attention they deserve? Where are the wetlands in your district located, and what does the planning and zoning office have in store for them? If you feel that these offices are planning too much development near a fragile wetland, say so! Schedules of public hearings can be found in your newspaper or by calling an office of the U.S. Army Corps of Engineers. Watch for notices of public hearings on development projects that may affect wetlands in your community.

Power in Numbers

Gather your neighbors and inform them of the problem. Those who feel the same way you do can help you write a petition stating your views. Get as many signatures as you can, then take the petition to the hearing and present your case!

Practice General Conservation at Home and School

Be a good example and encourage others to conserve, too!

• Save water, paper, energy, gas, and other natural resources.

• Take short showers.

• Use both sides of writing paper before you recycle it.

• Turn the faucet off while doing dishes (fill sink instead), and while brushing your teeth.

• Carpool, ride the bus or your bike, or walk.

• Keep heat or air conditioning turned down and dress appropriately instead.

• Turn off lights.

• Let nature water your lawn.

• Reduce, reuse, and recycle paper products, aluminum, glass, and plastics. This helps keep litter down and reduces overload on landfills.

• Dispose of trash and toxic wastes properly so they don't become pollutants.

• Take good care of your lawn or school grounds to reduce runoff and soil erosion.

• Respect all parts of the environment—help clean up whenever and wherever you can!

Write, Write, Write!

The people who make changes happen need to hear from YOU! Decide on a specific concern, think up a possible solution, and write to the people who have the power to address it. Your parents, teachers, or a librarian can help you identify your delegates in Congress (representatives and senators) and the state legislature. You may also want to write to someone on your county council, the mayor of your city or town, your state's governor, or other appropriate government officials. Keep up with the news about

legislation. If you strongly agree or disagree with a proposed bill, let your legislator know your feelings before the bill comes up for a vote.

If you can, write to someone who is known for listening to what people have to say. Sometimes it's best to write to an official who is already on the "side" of the environment, but you might also try to change the opinion of someone who seems to be working in the other direction.

No matter what the issue, or who you write to, follow these simple rules:

• Do your homework (see "First, Get the Facts," above). Be certain that you understand the issue and can discuss it clearly.

• Make a list of what you want to say before you start to write.

• Use language that shows you are courteous and respectful of the person to whom you are writing. Thank him or her for taking the time to read your letter.

• Explain the problem and your feelings about it, but keep your letter short (one page). Be specific. For example, "I am concerned that the shopping mall planned in my community will destroy valuable wetlands nearby." Or, "I am writing to show my support for bill number ___, which states," and say why you support it.

• If you have a reasonable solution in mind, state it. Ask the official to let you know what he or she feels can be done about the

problem. Be sure your address appears on the letter, in case the envelope is lost.

• Have someone check your grammar and spelling. Write the final letter on clean paper in your best handwriting, or type it.

• If you do not get a response in a few weeks, write a second letter, briefly restating what your first letter said. If this doesn't work, don't give up! Try another representative.

How the U.S. Government Works

Legislation (bills) become law in Congress, which is made up of the Senate and the House of Representatives. Each state is represented by two senators and a number of representatives (the number depends on the size of the state's population). Senators are elected every six years, representatives every two years.

• A senator or representative introduces a bill into Congress. Each bill is given an identifying prefix ("H.R." in the House, "S." in the Senate) along with a number. A bill may also have a name or title.

• The bill is then sent to an appropriate committee and its subcommittee(s) for consideration. If no one is interested in the bill, it dies. If there is enough support, the subcommittee(s) will hold hearings to review the bill and gather information. Various people may give testimony at the hearings. These may include an expert on the subject, someone from a government agency, or a concerned citizen like YOU!

• Next, the legislators hold meetings to change or amend the bill as suggested by the subcommittee(s). If you choose to send a letter about the bill to a subcommittee or committee, this is the best point at which to do so, because the bill will next proceed to the full committee for final revisions and consideration. The committee may recommend that the bill be passed; otherwise, the bill will die.

• If the committee approves the bill, it goes to the floor, which means that it becomes open for debate by all members of the House or Senate. Action on the bill is scheduled by the speaker of

the house or the senate majority leader.

• After all amendments have been accepted or rejected, the bill comes up for a vote on the floor. (If similar bills have been passed by the House and Senate, a conference committee will be formed to work out differences between the two versions. The combined bill will then go back to the floor for a final vote.)

• If the legislation is passed, it is sent to the president, who will either sign the bill into law or veto it. Congress may still make the bill a law, even if the president vetoes it, by overriding the veto by a two-thirds majority vote in both chambers of Congress.

Public Awareness and Education
Advertise!

Start a campaign in your school or neighborhood to let people know about wetlands and why they are valuable. Think of a catchy slogan or a phrase that's easy to remember. Make colorful posters and put an ad in your school or community newspaper or newsletter. These ads should tell people how they can help conserve and protect wetlands.

Make a wetlands brochure to distribute in your community. First, decide what you want to say and who you'll be addressing. Your brochure should point out the facts, the problem or issue, and what can be done about it. Language should be clear, brief, and positive. Appeal to the readers' interests and ask for their help in specific, concrete ways. Suggestions should be simple, making it easy for them to help out. Decide how you want to distribute the brochures. Will you hand them out or put them in

HOUSE	Bill introduced
	Subcommittee or full committee hearings/amendments
	Debates and passes bill
	Conference committee reaches compromise
	House and Senate approve conference committee bill
	President signs into law
SENATE	Bill introduced
	Subcommittee or full committee hearings/amendments
	Debates and passes bill

mailboxes or on windshields? Make enough copies to go around.

Give out buttons that show your cause. Use the slogan from your posters and show a wetland scene or animal. Here's a neat idea for making inexpensive buttons:

• Collect lots of used paper— dittoes from school or writing, office, or computer paper. Tear the paper into strips and soak it overnight in a bucket of water. Ask an adult to donate an old blender that you can use to grind up the wet paper (add more water as you grind). Pour the paper mush into a shallow pan, then scoop it onto a piece of screen (you can get screening at a hardware store). Even the mush out to a thin layer and place another piece of screen on top. Press the "screen sandwich" between two old towels and use a rolling pin to squeeze the water out. Carefully tip the new re-cycled paper onto a clean surface to dry. After it dries, cut the paper into shapes, paint on your design, and glue a safety pin or lapel pin on the back of each label!

Be a Role Model for Younger Kids

Help younger kids learn about wetlands and responsibility. Work with your younger brothers and sisters, with schoolmates, or at a community center. Take kids fishing, crabbing, bird-watching, or hiking and use the time to teach them about the importance of wetlands and respect for nature. Make a presentation about wetlands, such as a puppet show or play, or sing songs about nature with the kids. Volunteer to help with local schools' outdoor lessons or field trips for younger students.

Newsy Notes

Keep up with news about local issues that affect wetlands. Inform others and help them interpret news reports by writing a letter to the editor of your local paper. Remember that not all news is reported without bias. If you disagree with the viewpoint of an article, make it known! You'll alert others to your concerns and may drum up new supporters.

Volunteer

Feeling a bit uneasy about working on your own at first? Why not start by joining others who have experience? There are plenty of citizens' groups and conservation organizations that would love your help. It's a great way to learn and build up your confidence! Your school or local library may have the names and addresses of groups in your area. A number of national organizations, including the Izaak Walton League of America, the Sierra Club, the National Association of Conservation Districts, the National Audubon Society, The Nature Conservancy, and the Wilderness Society, have local chapters. There may be a group right in your own community!

Get the Community Involved

Hold a clean up day in your community and/or at a neighboring wetland site. Organize a committee to help you plan the day. Advertise the clean up well in advance and let people know what to bring (old clothes, boots or old tie shoes, heavy gloves, rakes, wheelbarrows, etc.). Try to get a local business to donate a dumpster for the day (if you think there'll be that much trash), or ask everyone to bring trash bags.

Combine the cleanup with something fun and educational, such as a picnic, fishing, canoeing or rafting trip, wetland theme dance, or nature presentation after the work is done. It will make the project more rewarding and give everyone time for fun with old and new friends. Circulate press releases about the entire event to broaden public awareness.

Start a neighborhood recycling program to help keep litter down and reduce the need for landfill space (wetlands are sometimes lost to landfill development). If a program already exists, encourage more people to recycle, or offer to take their materials to the collection center for them. Call your town's office of public works for information.

If you're planning a project to enhance or restore a local wetland, you might need money for supplies. Hold a fundraiser, such as a bake sale, dance-a-thon, or sport played for hourly pledges. Use your imagination! You may need to work through your school, a community group, or neighborhood association to make the collection of money legal.

Combine some or all of the ideas above into one big festival to stir up interest and concern about local wetlands. Be sure to have a few educational displays (made by you and your friends!) on hand to inform the public about the wetlands in their community.

Conduct a survey or assessment of the health of a wetland area in your neighborhood and show the results to the members of the community. Work together to develop an action plan to fix damage or reduce pollution problems. Decide on a plan that the majority can agree to, and make it simple to follow and stick to.

Develop an interpretive trail around a wetland in your neighborhood. Of course, you'll need permission from the property owner (even if it belongs to the town). Clear or construct mulched (not paved!) trails that are clearly marked with posts, signs, and/or

rest stops (use benches, large logs, or rocks for seats and use metal signs on secure metal posts to discourage theft or vandalism). Discourage the use of shortcuts by planting shrubs, trees, or flowers across old paths. Position stopping points where people can spot wildlife, take in views of the wetland, or appreciate interesting plants. Encourage educational groups to use the trail. Draw up an educational trail guide to further people's appreciation of the area; put copies in an enclosed metal or wooden box or kiosk at the start of the trail. Enlist as many neighbors and friends as you can to help. Those who help will appreciate the results the most!

A Wetland Pledge

I pledge to do my share to keep wetlands in our neighborhood clean and healthy by letting my concern for wetlands and the environment shape how I:

Act: I pledge to my utmost to recycle and dispose of all trash

properly, conserve energy, save water, use efficient transportation, and adopt a lifestyle in harmony with the environment.

Behave as a Citizen: I pledge to consider wetlands when making decisions on land use at home and throughout the community. I will participate in local issues and decision-making as a representative of wetland conservation. I will help elect officials who have the best interest of wetlands management in mind.

Learn: I pledge to keep myself well informed about wetland issues so that I may understand complex issues and help shape decisions about the future of our community and world.

The Wetland wRAP

Music provides a great means for expressing one's self. If you want a fun way to spread the message that it's cool to conserve and protect wetlands, try using this "wRAP"! Use your own beat, and practice with friends and classmates. Then you can sing it to others, for instance a group of younger kids or for a gathering of parents. Why not make a recording or video of your wRAP? (You can use your own name instead of Oscar's)

Yo! I'm Oscar. I'm an otter and I'm really hip.

I've come to rap with you—I've got a serious tip:

Ya' know, lately this place seems to be in a mess!

That's one big problem that we should address.

We've gotta keep the air clean, keep our water clear—

Do ya' wanna know how? Well, gimme your ear!

Wetlands are an answer to some of this trouble,

So listen to me, and on the double!

These are lands that are wet—with water, ya' know—

Those mucky mushy places where awesome plants grow!

These are homes to fish, birds, mammals (like me!)

And the really neat thing is they keep the water free

Of the glop and slop that washes off our land—

Are you listening, friend? Do you understand?

It's the wetland wRAP!

There's lots to do!

We can wRAP up this mess,

Yes! Me and you!

Yeah, wetlands are cool, they're something to enjoy,

But people don't know, and they're working to destroy

These lands that we need, from coast to coast!

So I've got a solution (though I don't like to boast)—

We've gotta work together! This is your world and mine.

There are things we can do to keep it workin' fine.

So get off your chair and stand up and shout!

Yo! This is what livin' is all about!

We've gotta clean up our act, keep trash in its place!

And those critters I mentioned need lots of space,

So don't wreck their homes—build yours on drier ground!

Keep those plants in wetlands, cause this is what we've found:

They trap silt, debris, chemicals, and stuff

Without wetlands, drinking water would really be rough!

So get out and about and keep wetlands protected

If you do, you'll be one who's really respected!

It's the wetland wRAP!

There's lots to do!

We can wRAP up this mess,

Yes! Me and you!

The solution to pollution is in our hands,

What we all need to do is understand

That what's ours today, will be our children's tomorrow;

We need to take good care of what we borrow!

So tell all your friends, tell the neighborhood, too!

Keepin' it clean is up to me and you!

Ya' know, YOU have the power to turn it around,

So start today, right in your own town!

wRAP up this mess! Yo! wRAP up this mess! Yeah! wRAP up this mess! (clap) wRAP. . .

Appendix

Planning and Developing a Schoolyard Wetland Habitat

by Mark L. Kraus, Ph.D.

Director of Education
Environmental Concern Inc.

A planned (restored, enhanced, or created) schoolyard wetland can be an exciting addition to the school's curriculum and a focal point for environmental programs. In addition, the wetland can become a tangible source of pride for the students, teachers, and volunteers involved.

Local government offices and some private organizations can be very helpful. The Natural Resources Conservation Service (NRCS) of the U.S. Department of Agriculture can provide information on soil types and drainage patterns for the site. State and federal environmental resource agencies (e.g., U.S. Fish and Wildlife Service, state departments of natural resources or environmental conservation) are frequently happy to lend their expertise.

Site Selection

Site selection is the first critical step in the project. Not every location will provide a site supported by natural hydrologic input (e.g., rainfall, runoff, ground water), regardless of how the wetland is designed. Locations need to be evaluated with respect to their suitability for supporting the wetland. In general, low spots in the topography are best. Under many circumstances, stormwater retention areas can be used as well. After a site has been chosen as having potential, further

studies will be needed.

Hydrology

It is crucial that sufficient water to sustain the planned wetland be available during the seasonal drought period (generally July through September in most of North America). Therefore, understanding the site's hydrology is important. Planned wetlands in tidal areas generally require less intensive study than do freshwater, nontidal wetlands, since water supplies for tidal systems are assured. Even so, studies should include gathering information on tidal amplitudes, recording the elevations where adjacent wetland plants are growing, and cataloging the types of vegetation that are growing on adjacent tidal wetlands.

Studies of potential nontidal sites can be much more extensive. You cannot assume that just because you dig a hole, it will fill with water. There are four basic ways by which water can be supplied to a nontidal wetland. These are: adjacent lake or pond water, rain and surface runoff, ground water, and water diverted from rivers and perennial streams. Frequently, a combination of these will be best.

It is relatively easy to construct a wetland beside a lake or pond. As in a tidal system, a fairly dependable water supply is present. The key is to ensure that land elevations are such that the created wetland community will have water during appropriate periods. Some survey work to establish the proper elevations and field study to establish the appropriate types of vegetation will be needed prior to design. With this type of water

supply, the smaller the water body, the greater the risk of losing the wetland during periods of prolonged drought. Water level studies may be needed prior to final design and construction.

Of the freshwater sources, rainwater runoff (from building roofs, parking lots, sports fields) is the easiest to calculate, but most difficult to guarantee. To verify that the planned wetland site will have sufficient water, the drainage area will have to be calculated, and average rainfall data obtained. Generally, the NRCS will assist you with this.

Prolonged drought could cause the failure of a wetland that relies solely on runoff. Therefore, a back-up supply is recommended. Access to a water spigot or fire hydrant, or even a source of gray water (runoff from watering sports fields or wash water, for instance), is desirable.

A stormwater retention basin (storm pond) is another source of surface water runoff. If your school grounds contain such a basin, you can plant in and around it to create a wetland. Generally, the design of the basin will have included hydrologic calculations. The plans for the basin, along with the hydrologic calculations, should be available at the school office or through the school system's engineering department.

In some situations, ground water may be an adequate water source. Although ground water may be available, it cannot be assumed that there is enough water to support a wetland just because water-saturated soils are found below the ground's surface.

hearing. An investigatory session for listening to arguments or testimony; opportunity to be heard, to present one's side of a case.

hemoglobin. A component of the red blood corpuscles essential to the process of respiration.

herbaceous. Green and leaflike in appearance or texture. Not woody.

herbarium. A collection of dried plant specimens usually mounted and systematically arranged for reference.

herbivore. An organism that feeds chiefly on plants.

hibernate. To pass the winter in a dormant or torpid state.

humus. A brown or black material resulting from partial decomposition of plant or animal matter and forming the organic portion of soil.

hydric soil. Soil characterized by, and showing the effects of, the presence of water.

hydrologic cycle. The circulation of water from the sea, through the atmosphere, to the land, and then back to the sea by overland and subterranean routes, or directly back into the atmosphere by evaporation and transpiration.

hydrology. The study of the behavior of water in the atmosphere, on the earth's surface, and underground.

hydroperiod. The seasonal and cyclical pattern of water in a wetland.

hydrophytic plant. A plant characterized by its adaptations to a water-saturated environment.

impervious. Incapable of being penetrated (e.g., impervious to water).

indicator species. An organism whose prominent presence in an environment serves as a marker for that particular ecosystem.

infiltration. The migration of water through soil.

insectivore. A plant or animal that depends on insects for food.

invasive plant. A plant that moves in and takes over an ecosystem to the detriment of other species (often the result of environmental manipulation).

inventory. A scientific survey of natural resources (plants, animals, etc.).

ion exchange. A reversible chemical reaction between a soluble solid (e.g., a salt) and a solution (e.g., water) during which ions may be interchanged.

lacustrine. Having to do with lakes.

lagoon. A shallow body of water, often separated from a sea by sandbars or reefs.

larvae. The earliest developmental stage of various animals that undergo metamorphosis, differing markedly in form and appearance from the adult.

law. A rule of action or conduct established by authority, society, or custom.

leach. To subject to the action of percolating liquid (as water) in order to separate the soluble components.

legislation. A law or group of laws proposed or enacted by a legislature.

lenticel. One of the corky pores or narrow lines on the surface of stems of woody plants that allow the interchange of gases between the interior tissue and the surrounding air.

levee. A raised embankment that prevents river overflow.

mangrove. Tropical evergreen trees and shrubs that have stilt like roots and stems, and often form dense thickets along tidal shores.

marsh. A wetland characterized by soft, wet, low-lying land, marked by herbaceous vegetation.

mastodon. Several varieties of large, extinct mammals resembling the elephant.

metabolism. The complex of physical and chemical processes occurring within a living cell or organism that are necessary for the maintenance of life.

mineral soil. A soil characterized by its predominately inorganic makeup.

mire. A wetland of wet, soggy, muddy ground; sometimes called a bog.

mitigation. The policy of constructing or creating wetlands to replace those lost to development.

moor. A wetland in high, poorly drained country; also called peatland.

morphological. Referring to form and structure, as in plants and animals.

muck. Dark, fertile soil containing a high percentage of organic material.

muskeg. A swamp or bog formed by the accumulation of sphagnum moss, leaves, and decayed matter, resembling peat.

nitrate. A salt of nitric acid; a common water pollutant.

nitrite. Formed from the combination of nitrogen, ammonia, and oxygen. A common pollutant.

nitrogen. A colorless, tasteless, odorless gaseous element that occurs as a constituent of all living tissues.

noxious plant. A harmful plant species.

nutrients. Element or compound needed for the reproduction, survival, or growth of plants or animals

omnivore. An organism that eats both animal and vegetable foods.

organic. Derived from living organisms.

osmoconformers. Organisms which mimic the external osmotic pressures of their environment with their internal osmotic balance.

osmosis. Diffusion of fluid through a semipermeable membrane until there is an equal concentration of fluid on both sides of the membrane.

oxidized rhizosphere. A zone around a plant root system in hydric soils that shows staining from oxidation ("rust" stains).

paleocamel. Prehistoric species of camel.

palustrine. Having to do with small, nontidal wetlands (wetlands with ocean-derived salts below .5 parts per thousand) dominated by trees, shrubs, persistent emergents, or emergent mosses and lichens.

parasitism. The behavior or mode of existence of an organism that grows, feeds, and lives on or in another organism to whose survival it contributes nothing.

peat. Partially carbonized vegetable matter (mosses) found in bogs and peatlands; can be used as fuel and fertilizer.

percolation. The process of filtering or trickling through a porous substance.

periderm. The outer tissue of woody roots and stems.

permafrost. Permanently frozen subsoil.

permeability. The ability of fluids (water) to pass through the pores or interstices of soil.

pH. A measure of the relative acidity of a solution based on a scale of 1-14 where pH 1 is the most acidic, pH 7 is neutral, and pH 14 the most basic.

phloem. Vascular tissue in a plant through which food is distributed.

phosphate. Salt of phosphoric acid, often found in pesticides.

phosphorus. A nonmetallic chemical element; an important plant nutrient.

photosynthesis. The process by which green plants and some other organisms synthesize carbohydrates from carbon dioxide and water using light as an energy source, usually releasing oxygen as a byproduct.

phytoplankton. Minute, free-floating aquatic plants.

plant identification. The process of distinguishing among different plant species through a formal classification method.

playa. A nearly level area at the bottom of an undrained desert basin, sometimes temporarily covered with water; some playas qualify as wetlands.

pocosin. A swamp in an upland coastal region (chiefly the southern Atlantic United States).

pollutant. A substance that contaminates an environment, especially human-made wastes.

porosity. The ratio of the volume of all the pores in a material to the volume of the whole. Also, the state of being porous.

prairie pothole. Lacustrine and palustrine wetlands found in rolling grassland, especially in central North America.

predation. The capture of prey as a means of maintaining life.

predator. One that captures prey as a means to sustaining life.

prey. An animal taken by a predator as food.

producer. A photosynthetic green plant or chemosynthetic bacterium that constitutes the first nutritional level in a food chain.

productivity. Rate of production of organic mass by the utilization of solar energy by organisms (mostly plants).

protist. Unicellular organisms of the former kingdom *Protista*, which now belongs to the kingdom Protoctista; includes protozoans, slime molds, and certain algae.

public hearing. A session open to the public at which testimony, comments, and questions are taken from interested citizens.

quadrat. An approximately square or cubical area, space or body.

radiocarbon dating. The determination of the approximate age of an ancient object by the amount of carbon 14 it contains.

recharge. The addition of water to rivers or to aquifers by natural infiltration, that tends to raise the water table.

regulation. A principle, rule or law for controlling behavior.

restoration. The process of bringing back to existence, or reestablishing, the original condition of a degraded environment.

riverine. Associated with rivers, streams, and their floodplains.

root system. The underground portion of a plant that provides support; draws minerals, oxygen, and water from the surrounding soil; and sometimes stores food.

runoff. An overflow of rainfall that cannot be absorbed by soil and vegetation.

salinity. The degree of saltiness, usually referring to water.

salt water. A solution of water and dissolved salt.

saturation. Soil that is soaked to capacity with water.

scat. An animal fecal dropping.

sedge. A variety of grasslike plants of the family *Cyperaceae*, having solid stems and leaves in three vertical rows.

sediment. The matter that settles to the bottom of a liquid; material deposited by water, wind or glaciers.

sedimentation. The action or process of forming or depositing sediment.

sign. Something that indicates the presence of something else (e.g., animal tracks).

siltation. The process of becoming filled with silt.

silviculture. The care and cultivation of forest trees.

slough. A backwater wetland, usually associated with bays and inlets.

soil horizon. A layer of soil parallel to the surface and differing from adjacent layers in physical, chemical, and biological properties.

soil permeability. The rate at which liquid (usually water) can pass through a soil.

species. A category of taxonomic classification, consisting of related organisms capable of interbreeding.

sphagnum moss. Pale or ashy mosses which decompose to form peat.

spiracular gill. A respiratory opening found in some species of insects, spiders, and fish.

stomate. One of the minute pores in the epidermis of a leaf or stem through which gases and water vapor pass.

submergent. A wetland plant that has adapted to grow under water.

subsistence. A means of existence that is barely sufficient to maintain life.

surface water. Water on or above the surface of the land, including lakes, rivers, streams, ponds, flood water and run off.

suspension. State where solid particles are mixed with but undissolved in a fluid.

sustainable. Capable of continuing for the foreseeable future, as in a level of timber harvest.

swamp. A saturated lowland or seasonally flooded bottomland characterized by trees or woody vegetation.

symbiosis. A relationship of mutual benefit between two or more organisms of different species.

temporary wetland. An environment which only periodically exhibits the characteristics of a wetland (e.g., vernal pool).

terrestrial. Of the land or living on land.

tidal flat. An unvegetated mud flat alternatively covered and exposed by tidal action.

topographic map. A map which marks the variations in elevation across a given landscape.

torpor. The dormant state of a hibernating or aestivating animal; also, a state of inactivity.

toxin. A metabolic product of a living organism that is poisonous to other organisms, or any substance damaging to living things.

tradeoff. A giving up of one thing in return for another; exchange.

transect. Marked line along which scientific sampling or surveying is undertaken.

transition zone. The intervening area between distinct environments.

tundra. A treeless area between the icecap and the tree line of Arctic regions, having a permanently frozen subsoil and supporting low-growing vegetation.

turbid. Having sediment or foreign particles in suspension or stirred up, creating a muddy look.

turbidity. Thickness or opaqueness made by the stirring up of sediment.

uplands. Land which is neither a wetland nor covered with water.

vacuole. A small cavity in cell cytoplasm, bound by a single membrane and containing water, food, or metabolic waste.

value(s). A wetland function perceived as beneficial to humans (e.g., water quality improvement, flood control).

vascular plant. Any plant in which the phloem transports sugar and the xylem transports water and salts.

vascular tissue. The supportive and conductive tissue in plants, made up of xylem and phloem.

vernal pool. Temporary freshwater pond that exists in the spring.

watershed. The entire land area that contributes surface runoff to a given drainage system.

water table. The upper limit of the portion of the ground wholly saturated with water.

water treatment. Systematic purification of water for human consumption.

wetland. A landform characterized by the presence of water, hydric soils, and hydrophytic vegetation. Often a wetlands form the transition zones between upland and deep-water environments.

wetlander. A person who lives in proximity to wetlands and whose culture is linked to them.

wetlands management. The maintenance or modification of wetlands to achieve desired functions.

wet meadow. Grassland with waterlogged soil near the surface but without standing water for most of the year.

xylem. The vascular (woody) tissue of a plant through which water flows.

Resources

Curriculum Guides

• *Acid Rain Teacher's Guide*, National Wildlife Federation, 1400 Sixteenth Street NW, Washington, D.C. 20036.

• *Aquatic Project WILD*, Western Regional Environmental Education Council, 5430 Grosvenor Lane, Bethesda, MD 20814; 1-301-493-5447.

• *Bay B C's: A Multidisciplinary Approach to Teaching about the Chesapeake Bay*, Britt Eckhardt Slattery. U.S. Fish and Wildlife Service, Chesapeake Bay Estuary Program, 177 Admiral Cochrane Drive, Annapolis, MD 21401. For K-3.

• *The Changing Chesapeake*, Valerie Chase. National Aquarium in Baltimore, Pier 3, 501 East Pratt Street, Baltimore, MD 21202. For grades 4-6 (companion to Aquatic Project WILD, above).

• *Discover Wetlands*, Publications Office, Washington State Department of Ecology, Mail Stop PV-11, Olympia, WA 98504-8711.

• *Field Manual for Water Quality Monitoring*, Mark Mitchell and William Stapp, 2050 Delaware Avenue, Ann Arbor, MI 48103.

• *Hanging on to the Wetlands*, Irwin Slesnick and David Newton. Western Washington University and the Environmental Protection Agency, Bellingham, WA 98225.

• *Living in Water*, Valerie Chase. National Aquarium in Baltimore, Pier 3, 501 East Pratt Street, Baltimore, MD 21202. For grades 4-6.

• *Living Lightly on the Planet* (grades 7-9 and 10-12); *Living Lightly in the City* (grades K-3; 4-6),

Maura O'Connor. Schlitz Audubon Center, 1111 East Brown Deer Road, Milwaukee, WI 53217.

• *NatureScope: Wading into Wetlands*, National Wildlife Federation, 1400 Sixteenth Street NW, Washington, D.C. 20036-2266.

• *OBIS (Outdoor Biology Instructional Strategies) Pond Guide*, available from Delta Education, 1-800-442-5444.

• *Project Estuary* and *Sound Ideas*, Gail Jones. North Carolina National Estuarine Research Reserve, NC Division of Coastal Management, P.O. Box 27687, Raleigh, NC 27611-7687.

• *The Project WET Curriculum & Activity Guide*, Project WET and the Western Regional Environmental Education Council, 201 Culbertson Hall, Montana State University, Bozeman, MT 59717-0057.

• *River Times*, Mathematics and Science Center, 2401 Hartman Street, Richmond, VA 23223 (specific to Virginia).

• *A Study Guide to New England's Freshwater Wetlands*, Laura Vincent, Frank Mitchell, and Ronald Miller. New Hampshire Department of Fish and Game.

• *Virginia's State Parks...Your Backyard Classrooms*, Department of Conservation and Recreation, Division of State Parks, 203 Governor Street, Suite 306, Richmond, VA 23219.

• *Wetlands and Wildlife: Alaska Wildlife Curriculum*, Alaska Department of Fish and Game, Anchorage.

• *WETNET: An Environmental Curriculum Dealing with Wetlands*, Adirondack Teacher Center, Adirondack Park, NY.

• *A World in Our Backyard: A Wetlands Education and Stewardship Program*, New England Interstate Water Pollution Commission. Guide and videocassette available from Environmental Media Center, P.O. Box 1016, Chapel Hill, NC 27514; 1-800-ENV-EDUC.

Books

This is not a full bibliographic listing—check your local library to find more.

For younger students:

• *Between Cattails*, Terry Tempest Williams

• *Clovis Crawfish and His Friends* (and others in the series), Mary Alice Fontenot. Also available on audiocassettes (two tales with songs per tape), Pelican Publishing, 1-800-843-1724.

• *Explore a Spooky Swamp*, Wendy W. Cortesi

• *The First Book of Swamps and Marshes*, Frances Smith

• *Liza Lou and the Yeller Belly Swamp*, Mercer Mayer

• *Of Men and Marshes*, Albert Hochbaum

• *The South Carolina Lizard Man*, Nancy Rhyne

• *Swamp Spring*, Carol and Donald Carrick

• *A Wetland Walk*, Sheri Amsel

• *Year on Muskrat Marsh*, Berniece Freschet

For adults and more advanced students:

• *The Bog People: Iron-Age Man Preserved*, P. V. Glob. Ballantine Books, 201 East 50th Street, New York, NY 10022.

• *Chesapeake*, James Michener

• *The Hound of the Baskervilles*, Sir Arthur Conan Doyle

• *Huckleberry Finn*, Mark Twain

• *Life and Death of a Salt Marsh*, John and Mildred Teal

• *The Life of the Marsh*, William Niering

• *One Day at Teton Marsh*, Sally Carrighar

• *Plantworks*, Karen Shanberg and Stan Tekiela. A field guide, cookbook, and activity guide all in one. Adventure Publications, Inc., P.O. Box 269, Cambridge, MN 55008; 1-800-678-7006.

• *River of Grass* [Florida Everglades], Marjorie Stoneman Douglass

• *National Geographic* articles:

- March 1954, "Life-like Man Preserved 2,000 Years in Peat," by P. V. Glob

- March 1987 (vol. 171, no. 3), "Mysteries of the Bog," by Louise E. Levathes

- July 1990 (vol. 178, no. 1), "South Florida Water: Paying the Price," by Nicole Duplaix

- October 1992 (vol. 182, no. 4), "Our Disappearing Wetlands," by John G. Mitchell

- June 1993 (vol. 183, no. 6), "Chesapeake Bay: Hanging in the Balance," by Tom Horton

- April 1994 (vol. 185, no. 4), "The Everglades: Dying for Help," by Alan Mairson

Films and Videos

For younger students:

• *Fabulous Wetlands*. Starring "Bill Nye, the Science Guy" (all ages; seven minutes plus other short subjects). Washington State Department of Ecology, Wetlands Section, Mail Stop PV-11, Olympia, WA 98504.

• *It's Happenin' Today on the Chesapeake Bay* [watershed/pollution]. *Fun!* Features Billy "B." Brennan songs. Available from Echo Hill Outdoor School, 13655 Blooming Neck Road, Worton, MD 21678.

• *The Marsh Community*. Encyclopedia Britannica Educational Corporation, 425 North Michigan Avenue, Chicago, IL 60611.

• *Ring of Bright Water*. A man and his pet sea otter, 107 minutes. WGBH Educational Foundation, Box 64428, St. Paul, MN 55164-0428 (*Signals* catalog, item #19522, 1-800-669-9696.

• *Rocky Mountain Beaver Pond*. National Geographic, 1145 17th Street NW, Washington, D.C. 20036-4688; 1-800-447-0647 (catalog item #51332).

For older students:

• *Coastal Growth: A Delicate Balance*. Virginia Institute of Marine Science, Gloucester Point, VA 23062.

• *Conserving America: Wetlands*. National Wildlife Federation, 1400 16th Street NW, Washington, D.C. 20036-2266.

• *A Swamp Ecosystem*. National Geographic Society, Educational Services, Dept. 88, Washington, D.C. 20036.

• *Wetlands*. Cooperative Extension Forestry and Wildlife Office, 103 Nutting Hall, University of Maine, Orono, ME 04469.

• *Why Wetlands?* Federation of Ontario Naturalists, 355 Lesmill Road, Don Mills, Ontario M3B 2W8, Canada.

Movies

• *The African Queen* (classic, no rating)

• *The Creature From the Black Lagoon*

• *Crocodile Dundee* (PG-13)

• Bayou/swamp scenes: *No Mercy* (R)

• Rain forest scenes (yes, they're wetlands, too): *The Mission* (PG), *Gorillas in the Mist* (PG-13)

• *The Swamp Thing* (PG or R)

Field Guides, Handbooks, and Texts

This is a basic list. Many more advanced books on wetlands and wetland plants can be found in a large library or university bookstore.

• *Adopting a Wetland: A Northwest Guide*, Steve Yates. 1989. The Adopt-A-Stream Foundation and Snohomish County Planning and Community Development.

• *At Home with Wetlands: A Landowner's Guide*, Joy Michaud. 1990. Washington State Department of Ecology, Olympia.

• *Chesapeake Bay: Nature of the Estuary*, Christopher P. White. 1989. Tidewater Publishing, Centreville, MD 21617.

• *Coastal Wetland Plants of the Northeastern United States*, Ralph W. Tiner, Jr. 1987. University of Massachusetts Press, Amherst, MA.

• *A Field Guide to Animal Tracks*, Olaus J. Murie. 1954. Houghton Mifflin Company, Boston, MA.

Education, 51 Ardelt Avenue, Box 68, Kitchener, Ontario, N2G 3X5, Canada.

Planting Supplies

• Nurseries. See list, p. 303.

• Pond supplies and information. The Pond Society, P.O. Box 449, Acworth, GA 30101.

Assistance—Agencies

Wetland regulations and the agencies that handle them are different in every state. The federal and state agencies responsible for wetlands management will likely have printed material and staff to assist you with questions about wetlands, environmental laws, and where to find wetlands in your area. Since this guide is intended for a national audience, it is impractical to list every agency here. You'll have to do some research on your own— try the library and the phone book U.S. Government and State Government listings. Look for the agencies named below or ones that sound similar.

Federal Agencies:

• U.S. Army Corps of Engineers

• U.S. Environmental Protection Agency

• National Marine Fisheries Service, a division of the National Oceanic and Atmospheric Administration (NOAA)

• U.S. Fish and Wildlife Service (Department of the Interior)

• U.S. Natural Resources Conservation Service (Department of Agriculture)

State Agencies:

• Department of Natural Resources or of Environmental Management

• Department of the Environment or of Environmental Quality

• Water Control Board or other agency that handles water-quality issues

• Others handling natural resource issues

Other Resources

• Marsh Master: A Wetlands Game for ages 8 and up. Available through Great Blue Productions, Box 194, Pittsford, VT 05763, 802-483-6437.

• EnviroScape Wetlands Model. Available (February 1996) through EnviroScape, 1000 Connecticut Avenue, NW, Suite 802, Washington, D.C. 20036, 202-833-3380.

Notes:

Correlation of WOW! Activities with National Science Education Standards

Standards based education began with the publication of the National Science Education Standards developed by the National Research Council. The content standards show what science concepts are essential for students to understand our world as we currently know it, allowing educators to focus efforts on the basics before moving on to other topics.

Administrators have seized this idea of prioritizing what is taught, requiring educators to use either the National Science Education Standards, or a state or local version of the standards. This national focus on standards based education has placed an additional administrative burden on our wetland educators. To ease this situation all *WOW!* activities have been correlated with the national standards. *WOW!* activities have also been correlated with some state standards. It is hoped that the activities will in time be correlated with all relevant state standards as *WOW!* facilitator training is conducted within each state. (Visit www.wetland.org/education.htm for current information on state correlations or contact the Education Department of Environmental Concern Inc. at 410-745-9620.)

The correlations are separated into three groups according to grade levels. Grades K-4 begin on the next page. Grades 5-8 correlations begin on page 136 and correlations for grades 9-12 begin on page 140. The correlations read across facing pages with the activities listed in the first column. Filled circles (l) indicate that without use of extensions the activity satisfies a majority of that content standard. Open circles (m) indicate that the activity partially satisfies that content standard. Activities not intended for the specified grade level will not have any circles.

A more complete description of the National Science Education Standards is available for sale from the National Academy Press, 2101 Constitution Avenue, NW, Box 285, Washington, DC 20055. Call 800-624-6242 or visit www.nas.edu.

CORRELATION OF *WOW!* ACTIVITIES WITH NATIONAL SCIENCE EDUCATION STANDARDS

Grades K-4

Page	Activity	Grade	UNIFYING CONCEPTS & PROCESSES					SCIENCE AS INQUIRY		PHYSICAL SCIENCE			LIFE SCIENCE		
			Systems, order, & organization	Evidence, models, & explanation	Change, constancy, & measurement	Evolution & equilibrium	Form & function	Abilities to do scientific inquiry	Understanding about scientific inquiry	Properties of objects & materials	Position & motion of objects	Light, heat, electricity, & magnetism	Characteristics of organisms	Life cycles of organisms	Organisms & environments
71	Introducing Wetlands	K-12	●	○	○		○	○	○	○			○		○
78	Let the Cattail Out of the Bag!	K-6	●	○			○	●	○	○			○		○
80	Wetlands in the Classroom!	K-8	●	●		○	●	○	○				●		○
85	Wetland Metaphors	1-12	●	○			●	○	○				●		○
87	Wetland Habitats	6-12													
94	Wetland Weirdos	4-12	●	●			●	●	●				●	○	●
99	Wet'n'Wild	K-12	●				○	●	●				●	○	○
104	Whose Clues?	K-12		●			○	○	●				●.		●
109	Marsh Market	2-8	●	○			○	○	○				●	○	●
112	The Wetland Gourmet	K-12					○	○	○				●	○	○
116	Marsh Mystery	5-12													
120	Treatment Plants	2-12	○	●	○		●	●	●				●		●
123	This Plant Key Is All Wet!	3-12	●				○	○	○				●		
129	Wetland Wheel	4-12	○				○	○	○				○		○
138	Tracking Plants and Keeping Track	5-12													
143	Run for the Border	5-12													
147	Wetland Address (extension)	5-10	○				○	○	○				○		○
152	Life in the Fast Lane	3-8	●	●	●			●	●	●		○	●	○	●
158	A Drop in the Bucket (extension)	6-8	○	●	○			○	○						
162	Soak it Up!	3-9	○	●	○			●	○		○				
165	Salt Marsh Players	3-6	●	●	○		●	○	○		○		●	○	●
174	Water We Have Here?	2-12	●	●	●			●	●	●		○			○

CORRELATION OF *WOW!* ACTIVITIES WITH NATIONAL SCIENCE EDUCATION STANDARDS

Grades K-4

Page	Activity	Grade	Properties of earth materials	Objects in the sky	Changes in earth and sky	Abilities of technological design	Understanding science & technology	Distinguish natural & human objects	Personal health	Characteristics & changes in pop.	Types of resources	Changes in environments	Science & tech. in local challenges	Science as a human endeavor
71	Introducing Wetlands	K-12	○								○	○		
78	Let the Cattail Out of the Bag!	K-6	○								○			
80	Wetlands in the Classroom!	K-8	○			○					○	○		
85	Wetland Metaphors	1-12	○								○	○		
87	Wetland Habitats	6-12												
94	Wetland Weirdos	4-12										○		
99	Wet'n'Wild	K-12				○	○				○			
104	Whose Clues?	K-12									○	○		
109	Marsh Market	2-8						○	○	○	●	●	○	
112	The Wetland Gourmet	K-12							○	○	●			
116	Marsh Mystery	5-12												
120	Treatment Plants	2-12					○				○	○	○	
123	This Plant Key Is All Wet!	3-12												
129	Wetland Wheel	4-12									○			
138	Tracking Plants and Keeping Track	5-12												
143	Run for the Border	5-12												
147	Wetland Address (extension)	5-10												
152	Life in the Fast Lane	3-8	○								○	●		
158	A Drop in the Bucket (extension)	6-8	○							○	●			
162	Soak it Up!	3-9	○								○			
165	Salt Marsh Players	3-6		●	○						●	○		
174	Water We Have Here?	2-12	○			○	○				○	○	○	

CORRELATION OF *WOW!* ACTIVITIES WITH NATIONAL SCIENCE EDUCATION STANDARDS

Grades K-4

Page	Activity	Grade	Systems, order, & organization	Evidence, models, & explanation	Change, constancy, & measurement	Evolution & equilibrium	Form & function	Abilities to do scientific inquiry	Understanding about scientific inquiry	Properties of objects & materials	Position & motion of objects	Light, heat, electricity, & magnetism	Characteristics of organisms	Life cycles of organisms	Organisms & environments
			UNIFYING CONCEPTS & PROCESSES					SCIENCE AS INQUIRY		PHYSICAL SCIENCE			LIFE SCIENCE		
188	Nutrients: Nutrition or Nuisance?	K-8	●	●	○		○	○	○	○			○		○
192	Marsh Munchies	5-8													
199	Recipe for Trouble	4-12	●	●	○			●	●	○			○		●
204	Water Under Foot	4-12	●	●			○	○	○	○					
210	Runoff Race	2-12	○	●			○	●	●	○	○				○
212	Wetland in a Pan	3-12	●	●	○		○	●	○	○	○		○		●
215	Water Purifiers	6-12													
220	Over Hill and Dale	3-12	●	●				○	○	○	○				
226	Nature's Recyclers	K-6	○	○	○	●	○	●	●	●			●	○	●
231	Do You Dig Wetland Soil?	K-12	●	●	○	●	●	●	●	●					
239	How Thirsty is the Ground?	3-12	●	●	●		●	●	●	●	○				
245	A Rottin' Experiment	2-12	○	●	○			●	●				●		●
250	Nature's Filter	K-12	○	●	○			●	●	●	○				
253	Hear Ye! Hear Ye!	3-12	●	●	◐		○	○	○						○
260	Hydropoly!	4-12	○	○				○	○						○
266	People of the Bog	6-12													
270	Regulation Rummy	9-12													
278	What a Boat!	1-5		○			○	○	○	●	○		○		
280	Chrysti the Wordsmith on Wetlands	7-12													
285	Wetland Tradeoffs	9-12													
288	Helping Wetland Habitats	K-12	●		○		○	○	○	○			○	●	●
310	Get Involved!	K-12		○				●	○						○

CORRELATION OF *WOW!* ACTIVITIES WITH NATIONAL SCIENCE EDUCATION STANDARDS

Grades K-4

Page	Activity	Grade	Properties of earth materials	Objects in the sky	Changes in earth and sky	Abilities of technological design	Understanding science & technology	Distinguish natural & human objects	Personal health	Characteristics & changes in pop.	Types of resources	Changes in environments	Science & tech. in local challenges	Science as a human endeavor
188	Nutrients: Nutrition or Nuisance?	K-8	○								●	●	●	
192	Marsh Munchies	5-8												
199	Recipe for Trouble	4-12	○				○			○	○	●	○	
204	Water Under Foot	4-12	○				○	○			●	●	○	
210	Runoff Race	2-12	●								○	●	○	
212	Wetland in a Pan	3-12	●								○	●	○	
215	Water Purifiers	6-12												
220	Over Hill and Dale	3-12							○			●	○	
226	Nature's Recyclers	K-6	●						○		●	●		
231	Do You Dig Wetland Soil?	K-12	●				○				○	●		
239	How Thirsty is the Ground?	3-12	●				○				○		○	
245	A Rottin' Experiment	2-12	●			○	○	○			○		○	
250	Nature's Filter	K-12	●				○				○	●	○	
253	Hear Ye! Hear Ye!	3-12	○			○	○	○		●	●	●	○	○
260	Hydropoly!	4-12					○			○	○	●	○	
266	People of the Bog	6-12												
270	Regulation Rummy	9-12												
278	What a Boat!	1-5				●	○	○			●		○	●
280	Christi the Wordsmith on Wetlands	7-12												
285	Wetland Tradeoffs	9-12												
288	Helping Wetland Habitats	K-12	●			●	○	○		○	○	●	○	
310	Get Involved!	K-12				○	○	○		○	●	●	○	

CORRELATION OF *WOW!* ACTIVITIES WITH NATIONAL SCIENCE EDUCATION STANDARDS

Grades 5-8

Page	Activity	Grade	Systems, order, & organization	Evidence, models, & explanation	Change, constancy, & measurement	Evolution & equilibrium	Form & function	Abilities to do scientific inquiry	Understanding about scientific inquiry	Properties & changes of properties	Motions & forces	Transfer of energy	Structure & function in living systems	Reproduction & heredity	Regulation & behavior	Populations & ecosystems	Diversity & adaptations of organisms
71	Introducing Wetlands	K-12	●	○	○		○								○	○	○
78	Let the Cattail Out of the Bag!	K-6	●	○			○									○	○
80	Wetlands in the Classroom!	K-8	●	●		○	●	○	○				○			○	○
85	Wetland Metaphors	1-12	●	○			●						○			○	
87	Wetland Habitats	6-12	●				○									○	○
94	Wetland Weirdos	4-12	●	●			●	○	○				○	○	●	○	○
99	Wet'n'Wild	K-12	●	●			○	○	○				○			○	○
104	Whose Clues?	K-12		●			○	○	○				○			○	○
109	Marsh Market	2-8	●	○			○						○			●	○
112	The Wetland Gourmet	K-12					○		○				○				
116	Marsh Mystery	5-12	●	●	●			○	○				○			●	○
120	Treatment Plants	2-12	○	●	○		●	○	○				○		○		
123	This Plant Key Is All Wet!	3-12	●				○									○	○
129	Wetland Wheel	4-12	○				○									○	○
138	Tracking Plants and Keeping Track	5-12	●	○	●			○	○							○	○
143	Run for the Border	5-12	●	●	●		○	○	○						●	○	○
147	Wetland Address	5-10	○				●						○		○	○	○
152	Life in the Fast Lane	3-8	●	●	●			●	○						●	●	○
158	A Drop in the Bucket	6-8	○	●	○												
162	Soak it Up!	3-9	○	●	○			○	○				○				
165	Salt Marsh Players	3-6	●	●	○		●						○	○	●	●	○
174	Water We Have Here?	2-12	●	●	●		●	○	○								

CORRELATION OF *WOW!* ACTIVITIES WITH NATIONAL SCIENCE EDUCATION STANDARDS

Grades 5-8

Page	Activity	Grade	Structure of the earth system	Earth's history	Earth in the solar system	Abilities of technological design	Understanding science & technology	Personal health	Populations, resources, environments	Natural hazards	Risks & benefits	Science & technology in society	Science as a human endeavor	Nature of science	History of science
			EARTH & SPACE SCIENCE			**SCIENCE & TECHNOLOGY**		**SCIENCE IN PERSONAL & SOCIAL PERSPECTIVES**				**HISTORY & NATURE OF SCIENCE**		
71	Introducing Wetlands	K-12	O												
78	Let the Cattail Out of the Bag!	K-6													
80	Wetlands in the Classroom!	K-8	O			O	O								
85	Wetland Metaphors	1-12	O									O			
87	Wetland Habitats	6-12	O												
94	Wetland Weirdos	4-12											O		
99	Wet'n'Wild	K-12				O	O					O	O	O	
104	Whose Clues?	K-12											O	O	
109	Marsh Market	2-8					O	O	O	O		O	O		
112	The Wetland Gourmet	K-12							O	O					O
116	Marsh Mystery	5-12	O				O		O	O	O	O	O	O	
120	Treatment Plants	2-12					O			O		O	O	O	
123	This Plant Key Is All Wet!	3-12											O		
129	Wetland Wheel	4-12				O							O		
138	Tracking Plants and Keeping Track	5-12				O	O					O	O	O	
143	Run for the Border	5-12	O				O			O		O	O	O	
147	Wetland Address	5-10													
152	Life in the Fast Lane	3-8							O				O	O	
158	A Drop in the Bucket	6-8	O						O						
162	Soak it Up!	3-9	O												
165	Salt Marsh Players	3-6	O		O										
174	Water We Have Here?	2-12	O			O	O	O	O	O		O	O	O	

CORRELATION OF *WOW!* ACTIVITIES WITH NATIONAL SCIENCE EDUCATION STANDARDS

Grades 5-8

Page & Activity	Grade	Systems, order, & organization	Evidence, models, & explanation	Change, constancy, & measurement	Evolution & equilibrium	Form & function	Abilities to do scientific inquiry	Understanding about scientific inquiry	Properties & changes of properties	Motions & forces	Transfer of energy	Structure & function in living systems	Reproduction & heredity	Regulation & behavior	Populations & ecosystems	Diversity & adaptations of organisms
		UNIFYING CONCEPTS & PROCESSES					SCIENCE AS INQUIRY		PHYSICAL SCIENCE			LIFE SCIENCE				
188 Nutrients: Nutrition or Nuisance?	K-8	●	●	○		○								○	○	
192 Marsh Munchies	5-8	○	●											●	○	○
199 Recipe for Trouble	4-12	●	●	○			●	○	○						○	
204 Water Under Foot	4-12	●	●			○		○				○				
210 Runoff Race	2-12	○	●			○	○	○	○			○				
212 Wetland in a Pan	3-12	●	●	○		○	○	○				○		○	○	
215 Water Purifiers	6-12	○	●	○			○	○	○			○				
220 Over Hill and Dale	3-12	●	●				○	○								
226 Nature's Recyclers	K-6	○	○	○	●	○	○	○	○			○	○	○	○	○
231 Do You Dig Wetland Soil?	K-12	●	●	○	●	●	○	○	○							
239 How Thirsty is the Ground?	3-12	●	●	●		●	●	○	○							
245 A Rottin' Experiment	2-12	○	●	○			●	○	○			○		●	○	
250 Nature's Filter	K-12	○	●	○		●	○	○	○			○				
253 Hear Ye! Hear Ye!	3-12	●	●	○		○						○				
260 Hydropoly!	4-12	○	○									○				
266 People of the Bog	6-12	○	●	●	●		○	○	○							
270 Regulation Rummy	9-12															
278 What a Boat!	1-5		○			○						○				
280 Chrysti the Wordsmith on Wetlands	7-12															
285 Wetland Tradeoffs	9-12															
288 Helping Wetland Habitats	K-12	●		○		○						○			○	○
310 Get Involved!	K-12		○													

CORRELATION OF *WOW!* ACTIVITIES WITH NATIONAL SCIENCE EDUCATION STANDARDS

Grades 5-8

Page	Activity	Grade	EARTH & SPACE SCIENCE			SCIENCE & TECHNOLOGY		SCIENCE IN PERSONAL & SOCIAL PERSPECTIVES					HISTORY & NATURE OF SCIENCE		
			Structure of the earth system	Earth's history	Earth in the solar system	Abilities of technological design	Understanding science & technology	Personal health	Populations, resources, environments	Natural hazards	Risks & benefits	Science & technology in society	Science as a human endeavor	Nature of science	History of science
188	Nutrients: Nutrition or Nuisance?	K-8	○						○				○	○	
192	Marsh Munchies	5-8						○	○						
199	Recipe for Trouble	4-12					○	○	○	○	○	○	○	○	
204	Water Under Foot	4-12	○				○	○	○	○	○	○			
210	Runoff Race	2-12	○						○	○		○	○	○	
212	Wetland in a Pan	3-12	○			○		○	○	○	○	○	○	○	
215	Water Purifiers	6-12	○			○	○	○			○	○	○	○	
220	Over Hill and Dale	3-12	○			○	○	○	○	○		○	○	○	
226	Nature's Recyclers	K-6	○						○	○			○	○	
231	Do You Dig Wetland Soil?	K-12	○										○	○	
239	How Thirsty is the Ground?	3-12	○			○							○	○	
245	A Rottin' Experiment	2-12	○			○	○		○				○	○	
250	Nature's Filter	K-12	○					○	○				○	○	
253	Hear Ye! Hear Ye!	3-12				●	●		○	○	○	○	○	○	
260	Hydropoly!	4-12					○		○	○	○	○			
266	People of the Bog	6-12	○	○									○	○	○
270	Regulation Rummy	9-12													
278	What a Boat!	1-5				●	●					○	○	○	○
280	Christi the Wordsmith on Wetlands	7-12													○
285	Wetland Tradeoffs	9-12													
288	Helping Wetland Habitats	K-12	○			●	●		●	●	○	○	○	○	
310	Get Involved!	K-12					○		○	○		○	○	○	

CORRELATION OF *WOW!* ACTIVITIES WITH NATIONAL SCIENCE EDUCATION STANDARDS

Grades 9-12

Page	Activity	Grade	Systems, order, & organization	Evidence, models, & explanation	Change, constancy, & measurement	Evolution & equilibrium	Form & function	Abilities to do scientific inquiry	Understandings about scientific inquiry	Structure of atoms	Structure & properties of matter	Chemical reactions	Motions & forces	Conservation of energy	Interactions of energy & matter	The cell	Molecular basis of heredity	Biological evolution	Interdependence of organisms	Matter, energy, & organization	Behavior of organisms
71	Introducing Wetlands	K-12	●	○	○		○	○	○										○		○
78	Let the Cattail Out of the Bag!	K-6																			
80	Wetlands in the Classroom!	K-8																			
85	Wetland Metaphors	1-12	●	○			●	○	○										○	○	○
87	Wetland Habitats	6-12	●				○	○	○											○	○
94	Wetland Weirdos	4-12	●	●			●	○	●										○	○	○
99	Wet'n'Wild	K-12	●				○	○	○										○		●
104	Whose Clues?	K-12		●			○	○	○										○	○	●
109	Marsh Market	2-8																			
112	The Wetland Gourmet	K-12					○		○										○		
116	Marsh Mystery	5-12	●	●	●			●	●										●	●	
120	Treatment Plants	2-12	○	●	○		●	○	○										●	○	
123	This Plant Key Is All Wet!	3-12	●				○	○	○												
129	Wetland Wheel	4-12	○				○	○	○												
138	Tracking Plants and Keeping Track	5-12	●	●	●			○	○										○		
143	Run for the Border	5-12	●	●	○		○	○	○										●	○	○
147	Wetland Address	5-10	○				●	○	○											○	○
152	Life in the Fast Lane	3-8																			
158	A Drop in the Bucket	6-8																			
162	Soak it Up!	3-9	○	●	○			○	○												
165	Salt Marsh Players	3-6																			
174	Water We Have Here?	2-12	●	●	●			○	●	○	○			○							

CORRELATION OF *WOW!* ACTIVITIES WITH NATIONAL SCIENCE EDUCATION STANDARDS

Grades 9-12

Page	Activity	Grade	Energy in the earth system	Geochemical cycles	Origin & evolution of the earth system	Origin & evolution of the universe	Abilities of technological design	Understanding science & technology	Personal & community health	Population growth	Natural resources	Environmental quality	Natural & human-induced hazards	Science & technology challenges	Science as a human endeavor	Nature of scientific knowledge	Historical perspectives
71	Introducing Wetlands	K-12		○							○	○			○	○	○
78	Let the Cattail Out of the Bag!	K-6															
80	Wetlands in the Classroom!	K-8															
85	Wetland Metaphors	1-12	○								○	○			○		
87	Wetland Habitats	6-12															
94	Wetland Weirdos	4-12													○	○	
99	Wet'n'Wild	K-12													○	○	
104	Whose Clues?	K-12													○	○	
109	Marsh Market	2-8															
112	The Wetland Gourmet	K-12									●						
116	Marsh Mystery	5-12	○				○	○	○		●	●	●	●	○	○	○
120	Treatment Plants	2-12	○					○			●	●	●	●	○	○	
123	This Plant Key Is All Wet!	3-12													○		
129	Wetland Wheel	4-12					○								○		
138	Tracking Plants and Keeping Track	5-12									○	○		○	○	○	
143	Run for the Border	5-12									○	●	●	●	○	○	○
147	Wetland Address	5-10															○
152	Life in the Fast Lane	3-8															
158	A Drop in the Bucket	6-8															
162	Soak it Up!	3-9									○	○	○	○	○	○	
165	Salt Marsh Players	3-6															
174	Water We Have Here?	2-12		○			○	○	○	○	○	●	●	●	○	○	

CORRELATION OF *WOW!* ACTIVITIES WITH NATIONAL SCIENCE EDUCATION STANDARDS

Grades 9-12

Page	Activity	Grade	Systems, order, & organization	Evidence, models, & explanation	Change, constancy, & measurement	Evolution & equilibrium	Form & function	Abilities to do scientific inquiry	Understandings about scientific inquiry	Structure of atoms	Structure & properties of matter	Chemical reactions	Motions & forces	Conservation of energy	Interactions of energy & matter	The cell	Molecular basis of heredity	Biological evolution	Interdependence of organisms	Matter, energy, & organization	Behavior of organisms
188	Nutrients: Nutrition or Nuisance?	K-8																			
192	Marsh Munchies	5-8																			
199	Recipe for Trouble	4-12	●	●	○			●	●		○	○							●	○	○
204	Water Under Foot	4-12	●	●			○	○	○										○		
210	Runoff Race	2-12	○	●				○	○	○									○		
212	Wetland in a Pan	3-12	●	●	○		○	●	○										○	○	●
215	Water Purifiers	6-12	○	●	○			○	○		○	○									
220	Over Hill and Dale	3-12	●	●				○	○												
226	Nature's Recyclers	K-6																			
231	Do You Dig Wetland Soil?	K-12	●	●	○	●	●	○	○		○	○									
239	How Thirsty is the Ground?	3-12	●	●	●		●	●	●	○											
245	A Rottin' Experiment	2-12	○	●	●			●	●		○	○							○	○	
250	Nature's Filter	K-12	○	●	○		●	●	○		○										
253	Hear Ye! Hear Ye!	3-12	●	●	○		○	○	○										○		
260	Hydropoly!	4-12	○	○					○										○		
266	People of the Bog	6-12	○	●	●	●		●	○				○						○		○
270	Regulation Rummy	9-12							○										○		
278	What a Boat!	1-5																			
280	Chrysti the Wordsmith on Wetlands	7-12						○													
285	Wetland Tradeoffs	9-12		○				○	○										○		
288	Helping Wetland Habitats	K-12	●		○		○	○	○										○	○	○
310	Get Involved!	K-12		○				○	○										○		

CORRELATION OF *WOW!* ACTIVITIES WITH NATIONAL SCIENCE EDUCATION STANDARDS

Grades 9-12

Page	Activity	Grade	Energy in the earth system	Geochemical cycles	Origin & evolution of earth system	Origin & evolution of universe	Abilities of technological design	Understanding science & technology	Personal & community health	Population growth	Natural resources	Environmental quality	Natural & human-induced hazards	Science & technology challenges	Science as a human endeavor	Nature of scientific knowledge	Historical perspectives
188	Nutrients: Nutrition or Nuisance?	K-8															
192	Marsh Munchies	5-8															
199	Recipe for Trouble	4-12	○				○	○	○	○	○	●	●	●	○	○	
204	Water Under Foot	4-12	●					○	○		●	●	●	●	○	○	
210	Runoff Race	2-12						○			○	○	●	○	○	○	
212	Wetland in a Pan	3-12						○	○		●	●	●	●	○	○	
215	Water Purifiers	6-12	●				○	○	○	○	●	●	●	○	○	○	
220	Over Hill and Dale	3-12	○					○	○	○		●	●	●	○	○	
226	Nature's Recyclers	K-6															
231	Do You Dig Wetland Soil?	K-12	○					○			○	○			○	○	
239	How Thirsty is the Ground?	3-12	○				○	○			○				○	○	
245	A Rottin' Experiment	2-12	○				○	○			○	○	○	○	○	○	
250	Nature's Filter	K-12	○					○			●	●	●	○	○	○	
253	Hear Ye! Hear Ye!	3-12					○	○	○		○	○	○	●	○	○	
260	Hydropoly!	4-12					○	○	○	○	●	●	●	●	○		
266	People of the Bog	6-12	○								○				○	○	
270	Regulation Rummy	9-12							○	○	●	●	○	●	○	○	○
278	What a Boat!	1-5															
280	Christi the Wordsmith on Wetlands	7-12															○
285	Wetland Tradeoffs	9-12					○	○	○	○	○	●	●	●	○	○	○
288	Helping Wetland Habitats	K-12					●	○			○	●		●	○	○	
310	Get Involved!	K-12					●	○	○		○	●	●	●	○		

Activities by Subject Area

Page	Activity	Grade Level	Environmental Science/Ecology	Life Science/Biology/Botany	Earth Science/Geology	Physical Science/Chemistry	Mathematics	Social Studies/History/Geography	Political Science/Government	Economics	Language Arts/English	Fine Arts/Art/Music	Home Economics	Trade & Industry/Shop
71	Introducing Wetlands	K-12		♦	♦		♦	♦				♦		
78	Let the Cattail Out of the Bag!	K-6		♦	♦	♦								
80	Wetlands in the Classroom!	K-8		♦								♦		
85	Wetland Metaphors	1-12	♦		♦									
87	Wetland Habitats	6-12	♦	♦										
94	Wetland Weirdos	4-12	♦	♦										
99	Wet'n'Wild	K-12	♦	♦								♦		
104	Whose Clues?	K-12	♦	♦										
109	Marsh Market	2-8	♦	♦										
112	The Wetland Gourmet	K-12						♦					♦	
116	Marsh Mystery	5-12	♦						♦					
120	Treatment Plants	2-12	♦	♦										
123	This Plant Key Is All Wet!	3-12	♦	♦										
129	Wetland Wheel	4-12	♦	♦								♦		
138	Tracking Plants and Keeping Track	5-12	♦	♦										
143	Run for the Border	5-12	♦	♦										
147	Wetland Address	5-10	♦	♦				♦			♦			
152	Life in the Fast Lane	3-8	♦	♦										
158	A Drop in the Bucket	6-8	♦				♦	♦						
162	Soak it Up!	3-9			♦			♦						
165	Salt Marsh Players	3-6	♦								♦	♦		
174	Water We Have Here?	2-12	♦			♦								

Page	Activity	Grade Level	Environmental Science/Ecology	Life Science/Biology/Botany	Earth Science/Geology	Physical Science/Chemistry	Mathematics	Social Studies/History/Geography	Political Science/Government	Economics	Language Arts/English	Fine Arts/Art/Music	Home Economics	Trades & Industry/Shop
188	Nutrients: Nutrition or Nuisance?	K-8	♦											
192	Marsh Munchies	5-8	♦				♦							
199	Recipe for Trouble	4-12	♦	♦		♦								
204	Water Under Foot	4-12	♦											
210	Runoff Race	2-12			♦									
212	Wetland in a Pan	3-12	♦		♦									
215	Water Purifiers	6-12	♦			♦								
220	Over Hill and Dale	3-12	♦					♦						
226	Nature's Recyclers	K-6	♦	♦	♦									
231	Do You Dig Wetland Soil?	K-12			♦									
239	How Thirsty is the Ground?	3-12	♦		♦									
245	A Rottin' Experiment	2-12	♦	♦										
250	Nature's Filter	K-12			♦									
253	Hear Ye! Hear Ye!	3-12						♦			♦			
260	Hydropoly!	4-12	♦						♦					
266	People of the Bog	6-12		♦	♦			♦						
270	Regulation Rummy	9-12						♦	♦					
278	What a Boat!	1-5						♦				♦		
280	Chrysti the Wordsmith on Wetlands	7-12						♦			♦			
285	Wetland Tradeoffs	9-12	♦					♦	♦	♦				
288	Helping Wetland Habitats	K-12		♦				♦						♦
310	Get Involved!	K-12						♦	♦			♦		

Activity and Topic Index